The British Industrial Revolution in Global Perspective

ROBERT C. ALLEN
University of Oxford

CAMBRIDGE
UNIVERSITY PRESS

CAMBRIDGE
UNIVERSITY PRESS

University Printing House, Cambridge CB2 8BS, United Kingdom

Published in the United States of America by Cambridge University Press, New York

Cambridge University Press is part of the University of Cambridge.

It furthers the University's mission by disseminating knowledge in the pursuit of education, learning and research at the highest international levels of excellence.

www.cambridge.org
Information on this title: www.cambridge.org/9780521687850

First published 2009
7th printing 2013

Printed in the United Kingdom by Clays, St Ives plc

A catalogue record for this publication is available from the British Library

ISBN 978-0-521-86827-3 Hardback
ISBN 978-0-521-68785-0 Paperback

The British Industrial Revolution in Global Perspective

Why did the Industrial Revolution take place in eighteenth-century Britain and not elsewhere in Europe or Asia? In this convincing new account Robert Allen argues that the British Industrial Revolution was a successful response to the global economy of the seventeenth and eighteenth centuries. He shows that in Britain wages were high and capital and energy cheap in comparison to other countries in Europe and Asia. As a result the breakthrough technologies of the Industrial Revolution – the steam engine, the cotton mill, and the substitution of coal for wood in metal production – were uniquely profitable to invent and use in Britain. The high wage economy of pre-industrial Britain also fostered industrial development since more people could afford schooling and apprenticeships. It was only when British engineers made these new technologies more cost-effective during the nineteenth century that the Industrial Revolution would spread around the world.

Robert C. Allen is Professor of Economic History at Oxford University and a fellow of Nuffield College. His books include *Enclosure and the Yeoman: The Agricultural Development of the South Midlands, 1450–1850* (1992), and *Farm to Factory: A Re-interpretation of the Soviet Industrial Revolution* (2003), both of which won the Ranki Prize of the Economic History Association.

NEW APPROACHES TO ECONOMIC AND SOCIAL HISTORY

Edited for the Economic History Society by

NIGEL GOOSE, *University of Hertfordshire*
LARRY NEAL, *University of Illinois, Urbana-Champaign*

New Approaches to Economic and Social History is an important new textbook series published in association with the Economic History Society. It provides concise but authoritative surveys of major themes and issues in world economic and social history from the post-Roman recovery to the present day. Books in the series are by recognised authorities operating at the cutting edge of their field with an ability to write clearly and succinctly. The series consists principally of single-author works – academically rigorous and groundbreaking – which offer comprehensive, analytical guides at a length and level accessible to advanced school students and undergraduate historians and economists.

Contents

Plates

Figures

Tables

Acknowledgments

This book is the outcome of a research programme that began in the 1980s aiming to computerize the price histories of European cities– and eventually the whole world. This programme grew out of another project with Dick Unger to develop a database of grain prices, and I have benefited enormously from working with him. I am grateful to the Social Sciences and Humanities Research Council of Canada and the US National Science Foundation for funding this research through individual grants and via networks – the Western Network on Education and Training, the Team for Advanced Research on Education, Globalization, Education, and Technology, and the Global Price and Income History Group. Time to write the book was provided by a British Academy Thank-Offering to Britain Fellowship and supplemented by the Oxford Department of Economics. I would like to thank Stuart Murray, Cherie Metcalfe, Ian Keay, Alex Whalley, Victoria Bateman, Cathy Douglas, Tommy Murphy and Roman Studer for research assistance.

My wife Dianne Frank drew the pictures of the pottery kilns, and my son Matthew helped translate the French quotations. I thank them for that and also for their support and tolerance during the intense periods of writing.

I have discussed this research with many people and learned much from them, among them Ken Sokoloff, Daron Acemoglu, Joel Mokyr, Alessandro Nuvolari, David Hendry, Paul David, Peter Temin, Jeff Williamson, Peter Lindert, Jane Humphries, Debin Ma, Jean-Pascal Bassino, Christine Moll-Murata and Jan Luiten van Zanden. I am particularly grateful to Knick Harley, Stan Engerman, Jean-Laurent Rosenthal, Patrick O'Brien, Jo Innes, Nigel Goose, Peter Temin and Joel Mokyr, who read the manuscript and provided me with feedback. Joel Mokyr generously made available a copy of his book *The Enlightened Economy* in manuscript. All of my references are to that text.

My professional development has been shaped by the advice, support and example of two outstanding scholars – Gideon Rosenbluth and

Patrick O'Brien. From them I learned the crafts of the economist and the economic historian. Without the experience of talking and working with them, this book would not have been possible. I thank them for their guidance, their encouragement and their friendship. I am pleased to dedicate this book to Gideon and Patrick.

1 *The Industrial Revolution and the pre-industrial economy*

> The *general* rule is infallible, that, when by *increase of money, expensive habits of life, and taxes*, the price of labour comes to be advanced in a manufacturing and commercial country, more than in those of its commercial competitors, then that expensive nation will lose its commerce, and go to decay, if it doth not counterbalance the high price of labour, by the seasonable aid of mechanical inventions . . . *Nottingham, Leicester, Birmingham, Sheffield*, &c. must long ago have given up all hopes of foreign commerce, if they had not been constantly counteracting the advancing price of manual labour, by adopting every ingenious improvement the human mind could invent.
>
> T. Bentley, *Letters on the Utility . . . of . . . Machines to Shorten Labour*, 1780

This book is about a historical problem: why did the Industrial Revolution happen in Britain, in the eighteenth century? Theories of economic development emphasize technological change as the immediate cause of growth, and that was surely the case for industrializing Britain. The steam engine, the cotton spinning machinery, and the manufacture of iron with coal and coke deserve their renown, for invention on this scale was unprecedented, and it inaugurated an era of industrial expansion and further technological innovation that changed the world. Other features of the Industrial Revolution (rapid urbanization, capital accumulation, increases in agricultural productivity, the growth of income) were consequences of the improvements in technology. Explaining the technological breakthroughs of the eighteenth century is, therefore, the key to explaining the Industrial Revolution, and it is the first objective of this book.

My explanation proceeds in two stages. Part I of this book analyzes the expansion of the early modern (i.e. 1500–1750) economy and shows that it generated a unique structure of wages and prices in eighteenth-century Britain: Wages were remarkably high, and energy was remarkably cheap. In Part II, I show that the steam engine, the water frame, the spinning jenny and the coke blast furnace increased the use of coal and capital relative to labour. They were adopted in Britain because labour was expensive and coal was cheap, and they were not used elsewhere because wages were low and energy dear. Invention was governed by the same considerations, for why go to the expense of developing a new machine if it was not going to be used? The Industrial Revolution, in short, was invented in Britain in the eighteenth century because it paid to invent it there, while it would not have been profitable in other times and places. The prices that governed these profitability considerations were the result of Britain's success in the global economy after 1500, so the Industrial Revolution can be seen as the sequel to that first phase of globalization.

This book is also about the end of the Industrial Revolution. That is usually dated to 1830 or 1850 when new industries – first the railroad and the steamship and then novel manufactures like Bessemer steel – appeared on the scene. I also date the end of the Industrial Revolution to the second third of the nineteenth century, but for a different reason that is the culmination of its origins. The cotton mill and the coke blast furnace were invented in Britain because they saved inputs that were scarce in Britain and increased the use of inputs that were abundant and cheap. For that reason, these techniques were not immediately adopted on the continent or anywhere else in the world. Landes (1969) characterized the period up to 1850 as one of 'continental emulation' because the French, Germans and Belgians were only beginning to use British techniques and pre-industrial practices remained dominant. The 'closing of the gap' only occurred between 1850 and 1873, when modern technology displaced traditional methods, and European industry could compete on an equal footing with British. The slow adoption of British technology on the continent had less to do with war, institutions and culture than with the economics of the new technology, which was not profitable to adopt outside Britain.

This situation did not persist, however – thanks to British efforts. British engineers studied the steam engine and the blast furnace and improved them in order to lower costs. Inputs were saved indiscriminately, including those that were cheap in Britain and expensive elsewhere. The coal consumed per horsepower-hour by a steam engine, for instance, dropped from 45 pounds to 2 pounds. This made it profitable to use steam engines anywhere – even where coal was dear. Britain's success in the early Industrial Revolution was based on inventing technology that was tailored to its circumstances and useless elsewhere. By the middle of the nineteenth century, the genius of British engineering had improved the technologies, thereby eliminating the competitive advantage they had given Britain. The cotton mill, the steam engine and the coke blast furnace were now globally appropriate technologies, and their use quickly spread outside Britain. Global diffusion marked the end of the Industrial Revolution, and it was determined by the life-story of technology. This theme will be developed in the second part of this book. In the first part, we begin with the origins of the Industrial Revolution.

Explaining the Industrial Revolution

The explanation offered here differs from most others. Indeed, explaining the Industrial Revolution has been a long-standing problem in social science and has generated all manner of theories (Hartwell 1967, Jones 1981, Blaut 1993, Goldstone 2002, Bruland 2004). Most approaches fall under the headings of social structure, constitution and property rights, science, and culture.

Social structure

Marxist theories of economic development stress the importance of social structure. Society evolved through stages defined by their property and labour relations: primitive communism (i.e. hunting and gathering), slavery (as in ancient Greece and Rome), serfdom (medieval Europe) and capitalism. Capitalism was the key to growth, for capitalism is characterized by free markets and by a landless proletariat. Markets are necessary to guide economic activity, and the bulk of the population must lose its medieval property rights so that it is willing to move to the cities and for agricultural productivity to grow.

Marx wrote a century and a half ago, and, since then, historians have discovered much about the medieval world including many modern features. Studies of grain prices show that markets were widespread and as efficient as they were in the eighteenth century (Persson 1999, Bateman 2007). The economy of cities and towns was vibrant and commercial (Britnell 1993). Even agriculture no longer appears to have slumbered under a blanket of tradition. Instead, cropping patterns were responsive to environmental and commercial opportunities, and productivity was much higher than once believed (Campbell 2000). An extreme formulation of this upbeat reassessment of the middle ages is Clark (2007), who claims that medieval institutions were almost perfect for economic development.

One can reach an optimistic conclusion about medieval institutions only by glossing over their most characteristic forms – e.g. serfdom (Brenner 1976). For most of the middle ages, a majority of the English were serfs and held land in villeinage (servile tenure). While the free population could defend its ownership of land in the royal common law courts, the serfs could only litigate in the thousands of manorial courts presided over by their lords. They had no recourse to royal courts if the lords violated their rights. They could also not secure public protection for their persons against violence by their lords. They were subject to a variety of assessments that reduced economic incentives. Why improve the quality of your livestock when the lord could take the best beast when the holding was inherited? Land could not be conveyed without arbitrary fines being levied on the transaction. These controls produced a markedly more egalitarian distribution of land-holding than obtained among freehold property not controlled by the lords. Labour mobility was inhibited, since a serf could not leave the estate without permission and that was not lightly given since a distant serf could disappear. Lords could impose arbitrary assessments on their peasants. Tallage is a case in point. Initially, it was an assessment levied for a special purpose – to ransom the lord, for instance, if he were captured on crusade. Tallage was such a convenient and elastic revenue source, however, that it became routine (Allen 1992, pp. 58–66). It is hard to believe that these arrangements did not check the growth of the medieval economy or that the response to the possibilities of globalization after 1492 would have been weaker, had half of the population remained serfs. The emergence of capitalist institutions was a necessary, if not a sufficient, condition for modern economic growth.

Constitution and property rights

While Marxists are concerned with the decline of serfdom and the rise of capitalism, liberals are vexed by despotism and favour 'minimal government' – parliamentary checks on the executive, the security of property rights, the flexibility of the legal system. According to the liberal view, the Industrial Revolution can be traced back to the Glorious Revolution of 1688 that consolidated parliamentary ascendancy, limited royal prerogatives and secured private property. Supposedly, these legal changes created a favourable climate for investment that made the Industrial Revolution possible (North and Weingast 1989, De Long and Schleifer 1993, LaPorta *et al.* 1998, Acemoglu, Johnson and Robinson 2005, Greif 2006, Menard and Shirley 2005).

This interpretation, however, has some weaknesses. Studies of banking and interest rates fail to detect any structural break after 1688, so the improved investment climate was not manifest in anything financial (Clark 1996, Epstein 2000, Quinn 2001, Goldstone 2003). Property rights were at least as secure in France – possibly also in China for that matter – as in England (Bogart 2005a, Bogart 2005b, Hoffman, Postel-Vinay and Rosenthal 2000, Pomeranz 2000). Indeed, one could argue that France suffered because property was too secure: profitable irrigation projects were not undertaken in Provence because France had no counterpart to the private acts of the British parliament that overrode property owners opposed to the enclosure of their land or the construction of canals or turnpikes across it (Rosenthal 1990, Innes 1992, 1998, Hoppit, Innes and Styles 1994). These projects were only undertaken after the French Revolution destroyed local liberties and concentrated power in the national assembly. The English had got there first, however, for the Glorious Revolution meant that 'despotic power was only available intermittently before 1688, but was always available thereafter' (Hoppit 1996, p. 126). Finally, taxes were higher in Britain than across the Channel (Mathias and O'Brien 1976, 1978, Hoffman and Norberg 1994, Bonney 1999). In any event, it was a long stretch from the excise tax on beer or the cost of foreclosing on a defaulting mortgagor (not actually a cheap process in eighteenth-century England) to Watt's invention of the separate condenser. An explanation of the technological breakthroughs has to be more focused on technology than is usual in constitutional discussions. And, what the study of steam engines and spinning jennies shows is that it would not have been profitable to invent the Industrial Revolution in France no matter how good were French institutions. It was the prices that were wrong in France.

The Scientific Revolution

The Industrial Revolution was preceded by the Scientific Revolution of the seventeenth century. It started in Italy with Galileo and ended in England with Newton – a parallel to the reversal in economic leadership that occurred at the same time. Did modern science precipitate modern industry?

This is a favourite theme of university presidents and vice chancellors, and, indeed, has been argued by proponents of scientific research since the seventeenth century (Inkster 1991). In 1671, Robert Boyle claimed that 'Inventions of ingenious heads doe, when once grown into request, set many Mechanical hands a worke, and supply Tradesmen with new meanes of getting a liveleyhood or even inriching themselves'. 'Naturalists' could benefit the economy by inventing new products (e.g. the pendulum clock) and by solving production problems (e.g. the invention of Turkey red dye by Cornelius Drebbel). What particularly excited Boyle, however, were the possibilities of inventing 'engines' to mechanize production. 'When we see that Timber is sawd by Windmills and Files cut by slight Instruments; and even Silk-stockings woven by an Engine . . . we may be tempted to ask, what handy work it is, that Mechanicall contrivances may not enable men to performe by Engines.' Boyle thought that there were more possibilities here 'than either Shopmen or Book men seem to have imagined' and experimental scientists would discover them (Boyle 1671, Essay 4, pp. 10, 20).

Was Boyle right? The impact of scientific discovery on technology was explored thoroughly in the 1960s – and dismissed by most historians (Musson and Robinson 1969, Landes 1969, pp. 113–14, 323, Mathias 1972, Hall 1974). However, there is a good case that these historians went too far, and that scientific discoveries underpinned important technology in the Industrial Revolution. The reason that Hall, for instance, could find no link between scientific discovery and new technology was because he only analyzed the period 1760–1830. In the case of Watt, Hall concluded – correctly – that the theory of latent heat contributed nothing important to the invention of the separate condenser. The trouble with this argument is that the scientific discoveries that mattered for the Industrial Revolution were made before 1700 and not after 1760.

The most important scientific discoveries related to atmospheric pressure, namely, the findings that the atmosphere had weight and that steam could be condensed to form a vacuum (Landes 1969, p. 104, Cohen 2004). How these ideas were discovered is a great story that involved many of the leading figures of seventeenth-century science – Galileo, Toricelli, Otto von Guericke, Robert Boyle, Robert Hooke, Christiaan Huygens and Denis Papin – and we will discuss it in Chapter 7. The culmination of these inquiries was Thomas Savery's steam pump invented in 1698 and Thomas Newcomen's steam engine of 1712. It was the technological wonder of the age, and one of the first examples of industrial technology derived from science.

The discoveries of seventeenth-century physics were necessary conditions for the invention of the steam engine, but they were not sufficient. Much of the science was done on the continent, but the steam engine was invented in Britain. Why? Turning the scientific knowledge into working technology was an expensive proposition, and it was a worthwhile investment only in Britain where the large coal industry created a high demand for drainage and an unlimited supply of virtually free fuel. Without Britain's unusual wage and price structure, the R&D would not have been profitable, and Newton would have done as little for the English economy as Galileo did for the Italian.

Superior rationality?

The rise of the West has also been explained by cultural evolution. This has many dimensions, two of which run back to Max Weber. His first argument is that modern people are characterized by their superior rationality. In one of his most famous works, *The Protestant Ethic and the Spirit of Capitalism* (1904–5), he advanced the theory that the Reformation led to modern Western rationality. It caused the great divergence between the West and the Rest.

Historians have not been kind to *The Protestant Ethic*. Its empirical support was limited to a transitory correlation between Protestantism and high incomes – a correlation which did not obtain in the sixteenth century and which does not obtain today. Weber overstated the differences between Calvinism and contemporaneous strands of Catholic theology (Tawney 1938, Trevor-Roper 1967, Blaut 1993, Lehmann and Roth 1995).

Economists have also been unenthusiastic about Weber's views on rationality. His ideas had a major impact on development policy in the 1950s and 1960s since they indicated that agricultural productivity was low in less developed countries because peasant farmers were 'irrational' (Rogers 1962, McClelland 1961, Hagen 1962). Widespread irrationality was rejected by most agricultural economists beginning with Schultz (1964). Tests of the rationality of peasant cultivators considered their response to changes in agricultural prices and their willingness to adopt new techniques. The results of these studies indicate that small-scale farmers in developing countries are as 'rational' as their counterparts in advanced countries (Berry and Cline 1979, Booth and Sundrum 1985, Mellor and Mudahar 1992).

Economic historians have pursued parallel questions for medieval and early modern cultivators. Once serfdom was ended and peasants acquired *de facto* title to land, the open fields, that were supposed to have embodied the traditionalism of medieval England, became the basis of an agricultural revolution. Peasant farmers in England pushed up their productivity in the same way as their counterparts in developing countries (Allen 1992). These findings have called into question the view that the non-Western or pre-modern economy was held back by irrationality.

Science as culture

In work published after his death, Weber (1927) advanced a second argument about cultural change and economic development, namely, that a scientific attitude had to replace superstition for technological progress to occur. Weber believed that pre-modern people attributed events in the natural world to the interventions of supernatural beings – deities, spirits or fairies. Control over the natural world, therefore, required the manipulation of the spiritual world. Sometimes, this was accomplished through sacrifices, prayers, or the priestly interventions of temples and churches; sometimes, it was accomplished by witches, wizards and shaman. While there was usually some recognition of empirical regularities or 'laws of nature' that proceeded independently of spiritual actors, the latter were so important in influencing human life that they dominated thinking. This orientation stood in the way of the empirical, scientific outlook necessary for technological and social progress.

The creation of modern society, therefore, required what Max Weber called 'the disenchantment of the world'. Once the world was seen as a material realm unaffected by the spiritual, the attention of people could focus on discovering its empirical regularities and natural laws. Technological development could then proceed rapidly. Weber thought that this process began earlier in the West than elsewhere and explained the rise of the West.

The question is: why did the West give up superstition? Historians of science like Jacob (1997, pp. 1, 2, 6–7) propose that the Scientific Revolution transformed popular culture.[1] 'A new scientific understanding of nature preceded mechanized industry and, most important, assisted in its development.' There was widespread interest in science in the late seventeenth and eighteenth centuries, and exposure to science changed human nature. 'The most important cultural meaning to be extracted from the Scientific Revolution . . . lay in the creation first in Britain by 1750 of a new person.' This person was 'generally but not exclusively a male entrepreneur who approached the productive process mechanically'. He saw it 'as something to be mastered by machines, or on a more abstract level to be conceptualized in terms of weight, motion, and the principles of force and inertia. Work and workers could also be seen in these terms.' The effect of this new way of thinking was the mechanization of production. Manufacturing was done 'by using machines in place of labour'. This new culture was adopted more enthusiastically in Britain than on the continent with the result that 'industrial development occurred first in Britain for reasons that had to do with science and culture, not simply or exclusively with raw materials, capital development, cheap labor, or technological innovation'. Rather, Britain's lead over France was due to 'the marked differences in the scientific cultures found in Britain in comparison to France or the Netherlands' (Jacob 1997, p. 105). The French were supposedly theoretical, while the British were practical.

This contrast between British and French engineering is deeply problematic. It is not clear that there was much difference in inventiveness between eighteenth-century Britain and France (Hilaire-Pérez 2000). There are certainly many examples of the French inventing. Mokyr (2009) highlights 'chemical knowledge, paper, and high-end textiles'. Why do we think the British had a more pragmatic engineering culture than the French? Because it was Brits who first smelted iron with coke, invented the steam engine, and discovered how to spin with machines.

[1] Other works of cultural interpretation include Stewart (1992), Levere and Turner (2002) and Jacob and Stewart (2004).

In Part II of this book, I will show that these differences in behaviour were due to differences between the countries in the profitability of doing R&D. If that argument is accepted, then cultural explanations become superfluous. Indeed, they are circular.

Mokyr (2002, 2009) has advanced an influential variant of the cultural argument in which the Enlightenment connected the Scientific Revolution to the Industrial. He coined the term 'Industrial Enlightenment' to describe the essential features. The Industrial Enlightenment emphasized the application of the scientific and experimental methods to the study of technology, the belief in an orderly universe governed by natural laws that could be apprehended by the scientific method, and the expectation that the scientific study of the natural world and technology would improve human life. The Industrial Enlightenment explains 'why the Industrial Revolution took place in western Europe (although not why it took place in Britain and not in France or the Netherlands)' (Mokyr 2002, p. 29). Mokyr highlights two factors that made the Industrial Revolution British. First, the Industrial Enlightenment was more fully realized in Britain than on the continent. Communication between *savants* and *fabricants* was easier and more fruitful. Any such difference in behaviour, of course, could also be explained by the higher rate of return to inventing in Britain. Secondly, Britain was more abundantly supplied with skilled mechanical artisans than France, so it was easier for engineers to realize their inventions. In part, this is a claim about human capital, and the British were, indeed, well endowed in the eighteenth century, although perhaps not more so than people across the Channel. In part, this is also a claim that artisans were adopting the Newtonian worldview.

Cultural explanations of the Industrial Revolution contend that the scientific worldview percolated down the social scale and influenced the second and third tiers of inventors, who were critical in elaborating the breakthrough technologies and applying them across a broad range of activities. Jacob (1997, p. 132) thought that even factory operatives had to become Newtonians. 'Relatively sophisticated mechanical knowledge had to be a part of one's mental world before such mechanical devices could be invented and, more to the point, effectively exploited. If you were a worker having to work in relation to a machine, understanding it meant coming closer to understanding how your employer might view all of nature, yourself included.' These people were not members of elite bodies like the Royal Society, nor did they have any contact with the leading scientists of the day. Jacob and Mokyr suggest that top-level science seeped down to the hoi polloi through provincial 'scientific societies, academies, Masonic lodges, coffee house lectures' and similar venues.

The cultural interpretation of the Scientific Revolution receives equivocal support from historians of popular culture. Culture in the eighteenth century was very different from medieval culture. There were 'two gradual but important changes in popular attitudes' between 1500 and 1800. 'They may be summed up in two clumsy but useful abstractions: secularisation and politicisation' (Burke 2006, pp. 257–8). Most people became more concerned with creating a better life in this world than with the possibilities in a spiritual sequel. 'Wealth and status' were pursued 'as a sign of salvation or even in place of salvation'. This was, of course, Weber's view. It is also disputable in view of the religious enthusiasm of much of the population and the success of preachers like John Wesley in attracting a large following. Why, in any event, did people become more worldly? Was it the result of elite science trickling down to the masses? The most that Sharpe (2007, p. 330) could claim about the impact of Newton on English society was: 'Popular scepticism about magic, and popular receptiveness to Newtonian science, are problems which are in urgent need of further research.' In other words – case not proven!

Culture and the economy: cause or effect?

We are on firmer ground with three other aspects of cultural evolution that also happened to have roots in the economic changes of the time. These developments included the spread of literacy and numeracy, the emergence of consumerism as a motive for work, and the postponement or deferral of marriages when it was economically inconvenient. The full ramifications of these were, of course, not fully realized before the Industrial Revolution. Nevertheless, these cultural shifts were big steps in the emergence of modern men and women. The new culture and the economy evolved together, each supporting the other.

The growth of literacy led to profound changes in knowledge and outlook, and the spread of reading was related to economic developments in several ways. Cities, rural industry and commerce required skills that agriculture had not demanded. As a result, literacy rates in medieval Europe were much higher in cities than in the countryside, so literacy rose with urbanization. Commercial prosperity also made it easier for people to pay for education and knowledge. Beyond that, the invention of printing sharply reduced the price of books, leading to much more reading for both useful knowledge and pleasure (van Zanden 2004a, 2004b, Reis 2005). In England, the proportion of the population who could sign their name rose from about 6 per cent in 1500 to 53 per cent in 1800. A reading public of this size was unprecedented in world history and led to new ways of thinking in many areas.

Numeracy also increased in early modern England, although its spread is harder to measure. Commercial developments were the primary cause. While many people wanted to read as an aid to devotion or for simple pleasure, very few people learned long division for fun. Arithmetic was studied for its utility (Thomas 1987). Knowledge of arithmetic and geometry was important to keep accounts and navigate ships. The much greater level of human capital in the eighteenth century than in the middle ages is an important reason why the Industrial Revolution did not happen earlier.

Consumerism and hard work

The evolution of the economy also increased the incentive to work hard. This was a theme of eighteenth-century writers, who contended that the availability of new consumer goods – both English manufactures like books and clocks and imports like sugar and tea – gave people the desire to earn income. Sir James Steuart developed the argument in his *Inquiry into the Principles of Political Economy* (1767, pp. 53–4, 58, 199, 229). 'Where industry is made to flourish, the free hands . . . will be employed in useful manufactures, which, being refined upon by the ingenious, will determine what is called the standard of taste; this taste will increase consumption.' Why? 'Let any man make an experiment of this nature upon himself by entering into the first shop. He will nowhere so quickly discover his wants as there. Every thing he sees appears either necessary, or at least highly convenient; and he begins to wonder (especially if he be rich) how he could have been so long without that which the ingenuity of the workman alone had invented.' To buy these goods, people needed income, and that required them to work more. In the ancient world, 'men were . . . forced to labour because they were slaves to others; men are now forced to labour because they are slaves to their own wants'. As a result, 'in a trading nation every man must turn his talents to account, or he will undoubtedly be left behind in this universal emulation, in which the most industrious, the most ingenious, and the most frugal will constantly carry off the prize'.

These ideas have been developed by Mathias (1979) and de Vries (1993, 1994, 2003, 2008), who coined the term 'industrious revolution' for the changes that Steuart was describing. Historians of consumption have studied how new goods transformed spending patterns (McKendrick, Brewer and Plumb 1982, Brewer and Porter 1993, Berg 1998, 2002, 2004, 2005, Berg and Clifford 1999, Fairchilds 1993, Lemire 1991, 1997, Styles 2007, Weatherill 1996), and Voth (2000) has found evidence of the predicted increase in work intensity. England and the Low Countries were the heartlands of the Consumer and Industrious Revolutions, although similar patterns have also been observed in Paris and in other capital cities. Although the new consumerism was not sufficient to explain economic progress, it was necessary: the frenetic pursuit of income to buy novel consumer goods, many imported from abroad as the economy globalized in the seventeenth century, was a cultural basis of the Industrial Revolution.

Marriage and children

Northwestern Europe also developed a distinctive pattern of marriage that contributed to high living standards and a broader sphere of personal independence than prevailed in many societies. Hajnal (1965) found that early-twentieth-century censuses showed two patterns of marriage in the world. East and south of a line from St Petersburg to Trieste, virtually all women married, and many of them married in their teens. West and north of that line, as many as one-fifth of women never married, and most of those who did marry waited until their twenties. These tendencies were most pronounced in northwestern Europe. The first marriage pattern led to high fertility and low living standards. The second, which Hajnal called the European marriage pattern, implies a lower level of fertility and one that responded to economic conditions through shifts in the proportion of women marrying and the average age of women at first marriage. The European marriage pattern implied a persistently higher standard of living for the mass of the population, and that high standard facilitated savings and economic growth (Jones

1981). Malthus believed that the standard of living of most people was higher in England than in China because the English deferred marriage when incomes were low, while the Chinese did not.

What explains the European marriage pattern? In a paper evocatively called 'Girl Power', De Moor and van Zanden (2005) have traced it back to England and the Low Countries in the late middle ages. While developments in religious doctrine that emphasized the role of personal (rather than family) choice of marriage partner played a background role, the decisive factor was the high wage economy following the Black Death. High wages and the corresponding strong demand for labour meant that young people – and young women in particular – could support themselves apart from their parents and control their lives and marriages. Women put off marriage until it suited them, and they found the right partner. The wage decline of the sixteenth century threatened this independence, but the high wage economy of northwestern Europe guaranteed its existence, and, indeed, marriages in that part of Europe were the most independent from parental influence and exhibited the characteristics of the European pattern most fully. We should not overestimate the freedom enjoyed by women in the eighteenth century. Nevertheless, personal autonomy was promoted in the long run by the high wage economy.

The emergence of modern culture

The popular culture of England and northwestern Europe generally was transformed in the centuries leading up to the Industrial Revolution. Culture possibly became more secular and more concerned with economic success. People could read and calculate. They chased after new products and worked to get the money to buy them. They refrained from marriage and limited their families when they were not economically appropriate. While the eighteenth century was not the same as the twenty-first, modern attitudes and attributes were ascendant. Many had economic roots, and they furthered the growth of the economy.

An economic approach to the Industrial Revolution

The modern culture facilitated the Industrial Revolution, but it was not enough to bring it about. Like capitalism, minimal government and the Scientific Revolution, modern culture has a fatal weakness as an explanation. These developments may have been necessary conditions for the Industrial Revolution, but they were not sufficient. Getting the institutions right, increasing knowledge of the natural world, and focusing people's minds on an empirical approach to production may have increased the *supply* of technology, but they would have had little impact on invention without a *demand* for new techniques. This book explores how Britain's high wages and cheap energy increased the *demand* for technology by giving British businesses an exceptional incentive to invent techniques that substituted capital and energy for labour. I do not ignore supply-side developments like the growth of scientific knowledge or the spread of scientific culture. However, I emphasize other factors increasing the *supply* of technology that have not received their due, in particular the high real wage. It meant that the population at large was better placed to buy education and training than their counterparts elsewhere in the world. The resulting high rates of literacy and numeracy contributed to invention and innovation. Since high wages and cheap energy were consequences of Britain's success in the global economy, the Industrial Revolution can be traced back to prior economic success.

My view of Britain in the eighteenth century is reminiscent of Habakkuk's (1962) analysis of technical progress in nineteenth-century America. American inventions had a labour-saving bias that accelerated the growth in output per worker. Habakkuk attributed the labour-saving bias to high American wages, which led inventors to economize on labour. High wages, in turn, were the result of the abundance of land and natural resources. In this book, I argue that Britain's extensive coal fields played a similar role in the eighteenth century. Cheap energy made it possible for businesses to pay high wages and remain competitive. High wages and cheap energy made it profitable to invent technologies that substituted capital and energy for labour. Eighteenth-century Britain was, thus, the prequel to nineteenth-century America.[2]

Britain's unique wage and price structure was the pivot around which the Industrial Revolution turned. Logically, the next question,

[2] Paul David (1975) proposed a formulation and extension of Habakkuk's views based on local learning, and David's approach has strongly influenced my own views. Temin (1966) studied the general equilibrium implications of the argument and emphasized the importance of distinguishing different senses of the 'real wage'. I have followed his lead in this regard.

therefore, is how to explain Britain's wages and prices. They turn out to have been the result of the country's great success in the international economy in the early modern period. This success was partly due to changes in factor endowments and partly to commercial policy. These themes will be developed in Part I of the book. Here is a thumbnail sketch of what happened.

The transformation of the European economy, 1500–1750

Between 1500 and 1750, the economy of Europe was transformed. The manufacturing and commercial centre of Europe in the middle ages had been the Mediterranean with a small offshoot in what is now Belgium. Most of the British population lived in the countryside, and most depended on agriculture. Productivity and incomes were low. Much of the rest of Europe was similarly backward. By the eighteenth century, the economic centre of gravity shifted to the North Sea. The Mediterranean economies were in serious decline, and the Belgian economy was slipping. In the sixteenth and seventeenth centuries, the Dutch Republic pulled ahead and became the economic wonder of the age. British advance was slower but steady. By the seventeenth century, British incomes pushed past those of its chief continental rivals – France and the Habsburg Empire. By the eighteenth century, Britain extended its lead and overtook the Dutch. The Industrial Revolution was the capstone to this advance.

The reconfiguration of the European economy was precipitated by an increase in international trade. In the sixteenth and seventeenth centuries, greater market integration led to a shift in the location of cloth production from the Mediterranean to the North Sea. In the seventeenth and eighteenth centuries, intercontinental trade expanded. The great gainers were the English and the Dutch, who established world empires that fuelled their manufacturing and commerce. At first, the Spanish looked like the biggest winners due to the Latin American silver they acquired, but it proved their undoing for it unleashed inflation that rendered their manufacturing and agriculture uncompetitive (Drelichman 2005).

Success and failure in the early modern economy show up dramatically in economic structure. Table 1.1 divides the populations of the leading economies of Europe into three groups: agricultural, urban, and rural non-agricultural. Countries are defined in terms of modern

Table 1.1 ***Percentage distribution of the population, 1500–1800***

	1500			1800		
	Urban	Rural non-agriculture	Agriculture	Urban	Rural non-agriculture	Agriculture
Most successful over the period						
England	7%	18%	74%	29%	36%	35%
Moderately successful over the period						
Netherlands	30%	14%	56%	34%	25%	41%
Belgium	28%	14%	58%	22%	29%	49%
Small advance over the period						
Germany	8%	18%	73%	9%	29%	62%
France	9%	18%	73%	13%	28%	59%
Austria/ Hungary	5%	19%	76%	8%	35%	57%
Poland	6%	19%	75%	5%	39%	56%
Little change over the period						
Italy	22%	16%	62%	22%	20%	58%
Spain	19%	16%	65%	20%	16%	64%

Notes: The first thing to notice in this table are the percentages of the population in agriculture. In 1500, many were about 75 per cent, which was also the share of the population in agriculture in less-developed countries early in the twentieth century. Notice which countries had lower shares in 1500 and how the shares decreased between 1500 and 1800. England had the biggest drop and Spain the least. Then notice how the urban and rural non-agricultural shares take up the slack. England had the biggest urban revolution between 1500 and 1800 and, next to Poland, the biggest increase in rural, non-agricultural share.

Source: Allen (2000, pp. 8–9).

boundaries. This is necessary because of data availability, and it is desirable to investigate the effect of policies and constitutions, but it is also artificial since many of these countries were fragmented.

In 1500, most Europeans lived in backward economies. This is indicated, in the first instance, by the fraction of the population engaged in agriculture. About three-quarters of the people were agricultural in England, Austria–Hungary, Germany, France and Poland. This proportion was also characteristic of the less developed countries of Asia, Africa, Latin America and eastern Europe early in the twentieth century (Kuznets 1971, pp. 203, 249–55). In terms of economic structure, western Europe was at a similar – low – level of development at the end of the middle ages.

The counterpart of a large fraction of the population in agriculture was small cities that included less than 10 per cent of the population. In 1500, for instance, only 50,000 people lived in London; other English cities were little more than market towns. Non-agricultural employment in the countryside was also limited, especially in comparison to later developments.

The leading economies of Europe in 1500 were Italy, Spain and present-day Belgium. The Dutch economy also showed advanced proportions, but its population was so small that its figures are more a portend of the future than an indicator of economic importance at the time. The urban fraction ranged from 19 per cent to 30 per cent in these economies, and those cities housed the great manufacturing industries of the middle ages. The agricultural fraction was correspondingly reduced to about 60 per cent.

The economies of Europe followed a variety of trajectories between 1500 and 1800, and the countries in Table 1.1 are grouped to emphasize these divergences. England was the most successful country by far. The fraction of its population in agriculture dropped to 35 per cent – this was the biggest decline and the lowest value reached in Europe. In 1800, each person in agriculture had to feed almost three people (2.86 = 1 / 0.35), while his predecessor in 1500 had only fed one and a third (1.35 = 1 / 0.74). An agricultural revolution was part of the transformation of the English economy.

The drop in the agricultural share was matched by rises in both the urban and the rural non-agricultural proportions. The latter corresponds to the 'proto-industrial' revolution (Mendels 1972, Coleman 1983). This was a phenomenon of the early modern period. In many parts of Europe, manufacturing industries developed in the countryside. Production was carried out either in workshops or in people's homes. Merchants signed up rural residents as piece rate workers, brought them raw materials and collected the finished products. These were often sold in large market halls to other merchants who shipped them across Europe. Regions were intensely specialized. Woollen cloth industries developed around Norwich and in the West Riding of Yorkshire, metal buttons, fittings and implements were made in Birmingham, stockings were knit in Leicestershire, and blankets were woven near Oxford and shipped to Canada by the Hudson Bay

Company. Rural industries were found in many parts of Europe, but they were particularly dense in England.

The expansion of rural industry in northwestern Europe was associated with the emergence of new economic leaders because it came at the expense of established producers. In the middle ages, Italian and Flemish cities produced woollen cloth that was exported across the continent. The English also produced and exported heavy broadcloths made from short staple wool. By the sixteenth century, the English and the Dutch began to imitate the lighter Italian worsteds. These clothes were the 'new draperies'. They proved so popular that the Italians were driven out of the woollen business in the seventeenth century (Rapp 1975, Harte 1997). England was successful in this competition largely because the fall in the population after the Black Death led to the reversion of much good farmland to pasture. The improved feed supply for sheep meant that their wool was longer and better suited for worsted than the shorter wool of poorly fed medieval sheep. In addition, refugees from the continent brought skills that improved the quality and variety of English products (Goose 2005).

Urbanization was also rapid in early modern England. Some of the urbanization was due to the improvement of agriculture. The state taxed some of the income generated in the countryside and spent it in the capital or in towns like Portsmouth where arsenals and naval dockyards dominated the economy. Cities like Bath were also supported by the agricultural income of landed society. Some of the urban growth was due to manufacturing; London was the centre of English publishing and furniture-making from an early date. Most of the growth of cities, however, was due to trade and commerce. In the seventeenth century, intra-European trade was the basis of London's expansion. There were close connections to rural manufacturing. The new draperies were woven in East Anglia and exported to the Mediterranean through London. Between 1500 and 1700, the population of London increased ten-fold. The export of new draperies made a significant contribution to that growth (Davis 1978, p. 390, Wrigley 1987, p. 148).

Intercontinental trade became more important in the seventeenth and eighteenth centuries. Portugal was the most successful European power in South Asia in the sixteenth century. It monopolized the spice trade and seized important colonies including the Moluccas, the 'Spice Islands' that were the source of cinnamon and nutmeg. The Netherlands, in turn, took these islands from Portugal in the early seventeenth century and established its Indonesian empire. This imperial success contributed to Amsterdam's becoming Europe's wholesaling centre for tropical produce. A vigorous colonial policy, the navigation acts and three wars with the Dutch helped London wrest that trade from Amsterdam. Trade with India added tea and cotton textiles to the list of Asian imports. As the eighteenth century progressed, intercontinental trade loomed larger in England's international accounts, and the growth of that trade contributed to the growth of Britain's cities.

The Low Countries were the second most successful economies in the early modern period. Less than half of their populations were engaged in agriculture, and the urban and rural, non-agricultural shares were also very high. Flanders in present-day Belgium had been highly urbanized and a leading manufacturing centre in the middle ages. Its economy failed to grow as rapidly as the leaders in the early modern period, but it still retained a more modern structure and higher incomes in 1800 than most of the continent.

The Dutch economy was the most advanced in Europe in the seventeenth century; indeed, the main question in economic policy was how to emulate the Dutch. Like the English, the Dutch had an agricultural revolution, which facilitated the growth of the urban and manufacturing economies. Trade was critical to the progress of the Netherlands. The new draperies were first established in the Low Countries in villages like Hondschoote. The manufacture of light cloth spread into other rural areas including the Ardennes, but, more significantly, was re-established in the cities like Leyden, Delft, Gouda, Haarlem and Utrecht (Pounds 1990, pp. 235, 293). The Dutch took over the Portuguese empire in Asia, and Amsterdam became the great wholesale market in Europe. Dutch manufacturing and rural industry were also formidable. The English did not overtake the Dutch before the late eighteenth century.

The third group was the rest of continental Europe north of the Alps and Pyrenees. France and Austria were major military powers, Poland was united in 1500 but dismembered in the next three centuries, and Germany remained divided into many states throughout the period. Prussia, however, was an actor on the international stage.

These countries showed modest development in the early modern period. Their agricultural shares dropped to about 60 per cent – rather like Italy and Spain in 1500. This decline was matched by a rise in the share of people in proto-industry. These countries developed important rural manufacturing industries that rivalled those of the leading economies in terms of the fractions of the population employed. Their urban shares, however, scarcely increased, and that sets them apart from England and the Low Countries. For a time, the French had some valuable colonies, but they were lost in the Seven Years War and the Revolution.

Italy and Spain comprise the final group. What is remarkable about these economies is the absence of structural change between 1500 and 1800. They had larger urban shares and smaller agricultural shares than most of the continent at the end of the middle ages, and these shares hardly budged. A corollary was the absence of growth in rural manufacturing. The proto-industrial revolution did not extend south of the Alps or the Pyrenees. The Italians never had foreign possessions. Spain did, but they did her no good, for they brought inflation that wrecked the peninsular economy rather than stimulating industrial expansion.

From early modern expansion to Industrial Revolution

The Industrial Revolution was the result of a long process of social and economic evolution running back to the late middle ages. The commercial and imperial expansion of Britain was a fundamental feature of this evolution, but not its totality.

The path to the Industrial Revolution began with the Black Death. The population fall increased labour mobility by generating many vacant farms, and that mobility undermined serfdom (Allen 1992, pp. 37–77). The low population also created a high wage economy. The benefits of high consumption were not confined to people: sheep ate better as well, and their longer wool was the basis for England's early modern worsted industry – the new draperies. The enormous export of these fabrics through the port of London led to rapid growth in the city's population and the rise of the coal industry to provide the capital with fuel. The trade boom was extended to the Americas and Asia in the seventeenth and eighteenth centuries by England's mercantilist expansion of trade and acquisition of colonies. More trade led to larger cities, and their growth was an impetus for advances in agricultural productivity. Larger cities sustained a more refined division of labour than smaller towns, so urbanization also led directly to greater efficiency and higher wages (Crafts and Venables 2003).

The expansion of the early modern economy was underpinned by favourable institutional and cultural developments. The end of serfdom and the establishment of a stable legal environment favourable to capitalist enterprise undoubtedly promoted growth. The gradual decline in superstition and medieval religion and the corresponding rise of a scientific attitude inclined more and more people to look for practical solutions to life's problems rather than trying to solve them by manipulating supernatural agents. The demands of trade and the enormous drop in the price of books spread literacy and numeracy. New products, many obtained from abroad like cotton, tea, sugar and tobacco, enlarged the aspiration to consume and increased the incentive to work and earn high income. Political institutions favourable to capitalist development, as well as the growth of literacy, numeracy and hard work, followed from the expansion of international commerce and cities (Brenner 1993, Hill 1966, Acemoglu, Johnson and Robinson 2005). Urbanization may also have undermined medieval superstition.

The upshot of the commercial expansion of the early modern economy was the unique wage and price structure that Britain enjoyed in the eighteenth century. Wages were high and energy was cheap. These prices led directly to the Industrial Revolution by giving firms strong incentives to invent technologies that substituted capital and coal for labour. The famous technologies of the Industrial Revolution – the steam engine, mechanical spinning and coke smelting – had these characteristics. The evolution of law and culture created a favourable supply response to these incentives. Since the evolution of culture and law had commercial roots, the international expansion of Britain's economy in the early modern period made a decisive contribution to the Industrial Revolution. These themes define the agenda for the rest of the book.

PART I

The pre-industrial economy

2 *The high-wage economy of pre-industrial Britain*

> The working manufacturing people of England eat the fat, and drink the sweet, live better, and fare better, than the working poor of any other nation in Europe; they make better wages of their work, and spend more of the money upon their backs and bellies, than in any other country.
>
> Daniel Defoe, *The Complete English Tradesman*, 1726, Chapter XXII

One of the most distinctive features of the British economy in the eighteenth century was the high level of wages. This finding is unexpected in view of the literature on the standard of living during the Industrial Revolution, much of which emphasizes the poverty of the period. British workers certainly were poor by today's standards; however, the main point of this chapter is that British workers were more prosperous than their counterparts in most of continental Europe and Asia during the eighteenth century. While British workers did not share fully in the economic expansion of the Industrial Revolution,[1] they had already reached a high income position in international terms.

The view that British workers were extremely poor during the Industrial Revolution runs back to the fierce nineteenth-century debates about 'the poor', and, in particular, to the views of the classical economists. Their language is part of the problem, for they usually spoke of wages being at 'subsistence'. The term is loose and misleading. To the modern ear, it suggests that wages were only enough to buy a physiologically minimum diet, rags for clothes and a bit of thatch for

1 This is the view of Feinstein (1998). It has recently been challenged by Clark (2005) on the basis of a new consumer price index. Clark's index, however, places far too little weight on carbohydrates and uses a wheat price series as a proxy for bread prices even though there is abundant evidence respecting the latter. Eliminating these procedures produces a pessimistic real wage series along the lines of Feinstein's. See Allen (2007b, 2007c)

a roof. If all wages were at this 'subsistence', then workers around the globe led a uniformly miserable existence. In fact, classical views were more nuanced because 'subsistence' was an elastic term. Sometimes, it meant the physiological minimum that barely kept a family alive; sometimes, it was 'socially determined' and meant a higher standard of comfort.

Rather than seeing everybody at the bare bones minimum needed for survival, the classical economists saw the world in terms of a wage ladder on which workers in northwestern Europe had the highest standard of living and workers in Asia had the lowest. Adam Smith (1776, pp. 74–5, 91, 187, 206) put it like this: 'In Great Britain the wages of labour seem, in the present times, to be evidently more than what is precisely necessary to enable the labourer to bring up a family.' Workers' living standards were even a bit better in the Low Countries: 'The wages of labour are said to be higher in Holland than in England.' Within Britain, England was above Scotland: 'Grain, the food of the common people, is dearer in Scotland than in England . . . The price of labour on the contrary, is dearer in England than in Scotland.' Hence, a day's work bought more food in England than north of the border. However, in Scotland, 'labour is somewhat better rewarded than in France'. Asia lagged far behind Europe: 'The real price of labour, the real quantity of the necessaries of life which is given to the labourer . . . is lower both in China and Indostand . . . than it is through the greater part of Europe.' Smith saw the maritime centres of southern England and the Low Countries as having the highest real wages. Real wages were lower on Britain's Celtic fringe. Most of continental Europe also lagged behind the mercantile leaders, and Asia was at the bottom of the wage ladder. That was where wages were at the physiological minimum in the classical view.

During the nineteenth century, the mainstream explanation of these facts was demographic. Malthus believed that population expanded until birth and death rates were equal. The wage that corresponded to that outcome was the 'subsistence' wage since it was just enough to allow parents to raise children, and for the population to reproduce itself without expanding. In the original, positive check version of his theory, the birth rate was always at its maximum while mortality declined as wages rose. Under these circumstances, the subsistence wage had to be low enough to push mortality up to equal the high birth rate. In the later, preventive check version of the theory, fertility also declined as income dropped, and this modification meant that births and deaths equalled each other at a higher 'subsistence' wage. The wage in a society, therefore, depended on whether the positive or the preventive check predominated. That was a question of marriage customs, law, and what Malthus called 'habit'.

Malthus (1803, pp. 116, 124, 251–2) applied the model by arguing that 'habits' differed between Europe (in particular England) and Asia. In England, 'the preventive check to population operates with considerable force throughout all the classes of the community'. The sons of farmers and tradesmen deferred marriage 'till they are settled in some business or farm, which may enable them to support a family'. Even the labourer 'will hesitate a little before he divides that pittance [of a wage] among four or five' family members. Late marriage restrained fertility and kept the English wage high. In Asia, on the other hand, several customs led to early and universal marriage, and that practice meant that the positive check reigned, and wages were lower than in Europe. Ancestor worship, the expectation that children would support their parents in old age, and infanticide all meant that China was 'more populous, in proportion to its means of subsistence, than perhaps any other country in the world'. Malthus entertained the possibility that Hindu asceticism depressed fertility (a preventive check) but concluded, 'from the prevailing habits and opinions of the people there is reason to believe that the tendency to early marriages was still always predominant'. As a result, 'the lower classes of people were reduced to extreme poverty . . . The population would thus be pressed hard against the limits of the means of subsistence, and the food of the country would be meted out to the major part of the people in the smallest shares that could support life'. Disaster was never far away. 'India, as might be expected, has in all ages been subject to the most dreadful famines.'[2]

The generalizations of Smith and Malthus about European and Asian wages are supported by the reports of contemporary travellers and by

[2] Malthus' view of China has been challenged by Lee, Campbell and Tan (1992), Laveley and Wong (1998), Lee and Wang (1999) and others. Lee and Wang propose that infanticide in China was the functional equivalent of the preventive check in Europe. This interpretation, however, presupposes that Chinese living standards were on a par with those in Europe. The evidence in Allen, Bassino and Ma *et al.* (2007) calls that assumption into question, for it shows that real wages in the advanced parts of Europe (England and the Netherlands) were higher than those in the advanced part of China (the Yangtze Delta).

historians who have reviewed the evidence on diet and consumption. We are particularly concerned with people who were regularly employed and at the bottom of the earnings distribution – peasants and unskilled labourers. Skilled workers, of course, did better everywhere. The aged, the disabled, the ill and infirm all fared worse, but their circumstances depended on public welfare, private charity and the church rather than the labour market. Travellers' accounts suggest that it was Chinese, Indian, French and Italian workers who were at rock bottom subsistence, while English workers enjoyed a far higher standard of living.

We need a standard to interpret this evidence, which becomes very detailed. A key benchmark is the subsistence income defined as the 'physiological minimum'. A family with that income spends virtually all its resources on food. The diet has to be nutritionally adequate in the sense that it supplies enough calories and protein for the family to survive – but no more. The cheapest way to get that level of nutrition is generally to buy the least expensive grain and boil it into a gruel. Bread (especially wheat bread) is usually avoided as too expensive, and, if any bread is taken, it is usually made with inferior grains that are often ground at home to avoid the loss entailed by commercial milling. Some legumes are also eaten for protein. Meat is a rare treat and is often obtained from some natural source like fishing rather than animal husbandry. Small amounts of butter or oil are eaten for their fat. The physiological minimum diet is, thus, a quasi-vegetarian diet based mainly on the cheapest grain prepared in the way that minimizes the loss of food value in milling and cooking. The physiological minimum diet lacks wheat bread, meat, alcohol and many dairy products. These are all expensive ways to get nutrients. In addition, very little else is purchased.

It is important to distinguish the 'physiologically minimum' standard from a pleasing or a respectable standard of living. While people can, by definition, survive on the physiological minimum diet, they generally prefer more food and a greater variety of highly processed foods (as well, of course, as more non-food items). Meat was an important preferred food. Engels (1845, p. 85), for instance, described how 'the normal diet of the individual worker . . . varies according to his wages'.[3] The best-off workers 'have meat every day and bacon

[3] Somerville (1843, pp. 12–13) provides a numerical summary of similar consumption patterns.

and cheese for the evening meal'. Less well-off are workers who 'have meat only two or three times a week, and sometimes only on Sundays'. They substituted potatoes and bread for meat. Below these workers are those 'who can afford no meat at all and they eat cheese, bread, porridge and potatoes'. Finally, there were 'the Irish for whom potatoes are the staple diet'. The emphasis on potatoes as the cheapest food marks this as a nineteenth-century hierarchy, for potatoes came into wide consumption only around 1800. Before that, the cheaper grains like rye, barley, and especially oats, played that role. Meat, however, was always a food with a high income elasticity of demand, and so the amount of meat consumed was an important dimension along which working-class living standards varied.

Budget studies from the Industrial Revolution confirm the high standard of living that Engels described. The high grain prices of the 1790s prompted Sir Frederick Eden's famous three-volume inquiry into *The State of the Poor*, in which he detailed the income and consumption of many working families across the country. By the middle-class standards of the day, the people were poor, but their circumstances look better than those of many of their counterparts across Europe and Asia, as we will see. A typical example is the forty-year-old gardener living in Ealing (at the time just outside London) with a wife and four young children (Eden 1797, II, pp. 433–5). By combining several jobs, he managed to earn about 30d per day, which was a labourer's wage in London in the 1790s. On this income, the family could afford per day: one quatern loaf of wheat bread, about one half pound of meat, a few ounces of cheese, a pint of beer, tea and sugar. The family bought new shoes and clothes and sent the eldest two children to school. They bought coal in the winter for heat and paid rent for a house and garden, which doubtless provided them with vegetables and perhaps some animal foods. This family was living towards the top of Engel's meat scale and far above bare bones subsistence.

The representativeness of budgets like this is, of course, a question. We will address this later by calculating what people could afford to buy with the incomes they earned. The calculations confirm that the lifestyle of the Ealing gardener was within the reach of many Brits.

Was life as good across the Channel? The situation depends on where we land. The diet in the Low Countries looks prosperous. De Vries and van der Woude (1997, pp. 621–7) reviewed the history of orphanage diets, which, they contend, are representative of consumers as a whole.

From the sixteenth century through the eighteenth, most of the money spent on orphans' food went for rye bread, meat and beer. In the eighteenth century, average consumption was about 140 kg of bread per orphan per year, 20 kg of meat and 14 kg of butter. These figures compare well with the English diets discussed, especially bearing in mind that the orphans were children. The main difference between the orphanage diets and the consumption of the general public was in the type of bread consumed – the general public ate more wheat bread.

When we look to France rather than the Low Countries, conditions look worse. Hufton (1974, pp. 44–8) summarized many studies of eighteenth-century worker and peasant diets. They were restricted to a narrow range of foodstuffs of which at least 95 per cent were cereals. These were eaten either as bread or 'some kind of liquid broth or gruel'. Generally, the cereals were 'rye, barley, oats, buckwheat, maize, or chestnuts' rather than the wheat eaten by English agricultural labourers. The cereal was supplemented with vegetable soup made from 'cabbages and turnips, onions, carrots, and greenery from the hedgerows', and it might be thickened with more grain. Milk was added if the family had a cow. 'In fact, milk, an occasional egg, scraping of cheese, a little pork fat' and fish along the sea coast were the only sources of animal protein. They had meat only if they were in a position to raise their own stock. Not surprisingly, nutritional deficiency diseases were widespread. Hufton concluded that, 'if outright starvation vanished with the seventeenth century, permanent undernourishment was the lot of the poor'. If this was, indeed, the norm for French labourers, their standard of living was certainly lower than the English or the Dutch, and the French were consuming a diet like the physiologically minimum subsistence wage.

The situation was similarly grim in Italy where living standards declined to a very low ebb in the late eighteenth and early nineteenth centuries. This was marked by the spread of maize cultivation, which provided a much cheaper source of calories than wheat bread, which had been the medieval norm. Bread gave way to polenta as the staple food.

> In short, a labourer, a countryman who only ate two pounds of bread during the day would still need a soup in the evening: whereas, for the same price as two pounds of bread, he could buy at least six to seven pounds of polenta, which takes the place of both soup and bread and is more than enough for a man's sustenance.
>
> Quoted by Wolf 1986, p. 59

'Meat had vanished from the peasant diet' (Wolf 1986, p. 59). Tobias Smollett, in his *Travels through France and Italy*, 1766, remarked: 'The nourishment of these poor creatures consists of a kind of meal called Polenta, made of Indian corn, which is very nourishing and agreeable' (quoted by Langer 1975, p. 59). In fact, polenta lacks niacin, so the all-maize diet led to endemic pellagra and chronic diarrhoea. Wolf (1986, p. 58) concluded that 'during the eighteenth century the frontier between subsistence and poverty was shifting, in both city and countryside, to the detriment of the former'. Not only was the trend downward, but the level was far below that of workers in England.

What about the other end of Eurasia? The common diet in most of Asia was based on the cheapest available grain. 'It appears from contemporary accounts that the articles in the diet of the common people in most parts of India consisted chiefly of rice, millets and pulses' (Raychaudhuri and Habib 1982, vol. I, p. 164). Palsaert, who visited India in the early seventeenth century, called the Indian diet 'monotonous'. In the Delhi–Agra region, the people 'have nothing but a little kitchery [kedgeree] made of green pulse mixed with rice . . . eaten with butter in the evening, in the day time they munch a little parched pulse or other grain'. The workmen 'know little of the taste of meat'. Indeed, pigs, cattle, chickens and eggs were all taboo. Where available, fish was the only source of animal protein. It was a similar story in western India. Wheat was not eaten by the labouring population, whose main source of carbohydrates was millet. This was ground into a coarse flour and fried up as chapatis that were eaten with pulses and vegetables. Charles Lockyer (1711, p. 258), who toured Asia in the early eighteenth century on the East India Company ship, *Streatham*, observed of the Arab sailors in the Indian Ocean: 'They serve for small Wages, and are Victual'd at a much cheaper Rate than our Ship's Companys: Salt-fish, Rice, Gee, and Doll, with a few Fowls, being all the Provisions they care for. Doll is a small Grain, less than Fetches, contains a Substance like our white Peas, and being boil'd with Rice makes Kutcheree.'

The restricted character of consumption was also pronounced in other areas. Generally, Indians went barefoot. Contemporary accounts emphasized 'the scantiness of clothing'. For much of the year, men wore little more than a loin cloth and women a sari. Houses were mud huts with thatched roofs. The peasants and workers had few furnishings besides bamboo mats and cots. Metal pots and utensils were rare, and much cooking was done in earthen pots (Raychaudhuri and Habib 1982, vol. I, pp. 459–62). It was hard to spend less money on your lifestyle than this.

As with India, travellers to China described a quasi-vegetarian diet. Sir George Staunton (1798, vol. II, pp. 55, 213), in his account of the famous Macartney expedition, observed that 'the labouring poor' of Beijing 'are reduced to the use of vegetable food, with a very rare and scanty relish of animal substance'. (Minimalism in consumption extended beyond food: 'The inhabitants along the Pei-ho bore strong marks of poverty in their dwellings and apparel.') Lockyer (1711, p. 173) gave a more enthusiastic account of the same diet as consumed by the more prosperous in Canton. 'Rice is the general Diet.' The Chinese also have 'a Cup of Shamshoo, Pouchoo, or other Liquor at Meals, to sup off when their Chops are full.' They ate little meat. 'It is not brought to the Table in Joints, or large Pieces, as with us, but minced, and served up in Cups, or Small Bowls; whence they take it very dextrously with a couple of small Chop-sticks . . . They are great lovers of Broth, and will drink even the Liquor their Fish is boil'd in.' Historians of China accept that 'Europeans certainly ate more meat and far more dairy products than most peoples in Asia' (Pomeranz 2000, p. 35). In his reconstruction of agricultural output in the Yangtze, Li (1998, p. 111) reviewed the uses of farm goods. 'For food, rice was basic.' In addition, wheat, which was boiled up as porridge, 'was also used in the lean summer seasons to survive rice shortages'. Some beans were consumed, as was rice wine. Scarcely any animal products were produced. Since the diet consisted mainly of rice, the standard methodology used by historians of China to assess living standards is to estimate per capita rice consumption.

The history of diet suggests that there really was a range of living standards around the globe. Northwest Europe stands out as having the highest standard of living in view of the apparent widespread consumption of expensive and highly refined foods like white bread, meat, dairy products and beer. In contrast, workers and peasants in France, Italy, India and China ate a quasi-vegetarian diet of grain, often boiled, with scarcely any animal protein. Diets like these were consumed only by the poorest people in Britain or the Low Countries. The contemporary accounts on which these conclusions are based are not as abundant as one would like, and are necessarily generalized in their descriptions. How representative were the accounts of eighteenth-century travellers?

Fortunately, we can address the questions with different evidence that points to the same conclusion.

Wages and prices

We can be more systematic in the comparison of living standards by asking what people could afford to buy with their wages. Our calculations require databases of wages and prices. Since the mid-nineteenth century, historians of Europe have been writing price histories of cities, and these provide the necessary raw material. Typically, the historian finds an institution like a college, hospital or monastery that has existed for centuries. The historian then searches its financial records abstracting the price of everything it purchased. The results are time series of the prices of foodstuffs, textiles and building materials, as well as the wages of people like masons, carpenters and labourers who worked for the institution. Comparable work for Asia has barely begun, and the available data do not yet run as far back into the past. Nonetheless, enough is at hand to assess pre-industrial living standards around the globe.

The study of wages and prices shows that Britain was a high wage economy. This is true in at least four senses:

1. At the exchange rate, British wages were among the highest in the world.
2. British wages were high relative to the cost of consumer goods, i.e. British workers could buy more with their money than workers in many other countries, so living standards were higher in Britain than elsewhere.
3. Wages were higher relative to the price of capital in Britain than elsewhere.
4. Wages were higher relative to the price of energy in Britain than elsewhere.

The third and fourth points are particularly relevant for the incentive to invent coal-powered, mechanized technologies and will be considered when we come to those topics. Here, we will take up the first two points.

Figure 2.1 shows the wage rates of building labourers in leading cities in Europe and Asia from the middle ages to the nineteenth century. The original sources record wages in the monetary units of the countries concerned, and these have been converted to the weight

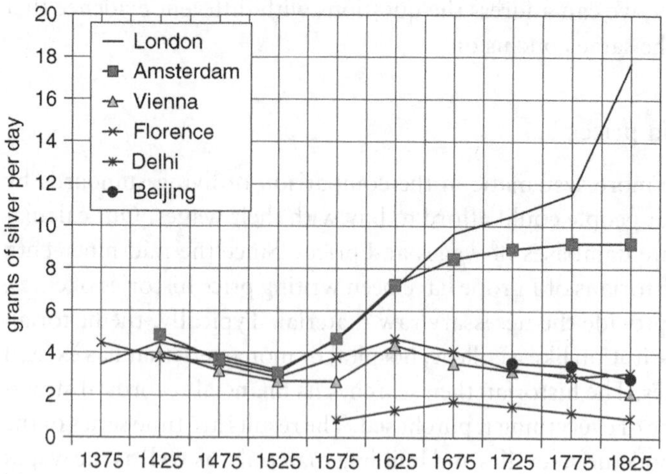

Figure 2.1. Labourers' wages around the world

of silver they could buy. Since silver coins were the principal medium of exchange for most countries in this period, this procedure amounts to comparing wages at the exchange rate.

Figure 2.1 shows that wages were similar across Europe in the late middle ages. Whatever the currency, labourers earned about 3.5 grams of silver per day. This uniformity broke down during the sixteenth century when European wages and prices inflated as silver was imported from the Americas. The inflation in wages was greater in northwestern Europe, however, than in eastern Europe or even in Spain, where most of the silver arrived. The history of wages has been studied for many cities on the continent, and they were uniformly like those in Vienna and Florence. By the end of the seventeenth century, wage inflation ceased in the Low Countries but continued unabated in London. The result was that London wages were the highest in the world during the eighteenth century.

Asian wages were very much lower. The history of Asian wages has not yet been pushed back before the late sixteenth century, but from then onwards Asian wages were consistently below European wages. The gap between northwestern Europe and Asia was very large. Continental wages were probably marginally above Asian wages, but the differential was less. Asia, in other words, looks a lot like the lagging parts of Europe.

Did the high wages earned in northwestern Europe translate into a high standard of living? The answer depends on the prices of consumer goods. It is unrealistic to assume that there was only one consumer good (for instance, bread), so instead we specify 'baskets of goods' that correspond to different lifestyles. The basket must be complete and specified in terms of goods whose prices can be measured or inferred, so that its cost can be worked out around the globe. Taking the earlier discussion of diets and subsistence wages as a guide, I define two baskets of goods. The more expensive is a 'European respectability' basket,[4] and is inspired by budgets that Eden and other observers report for 'respectable' labourers in Britain and the Low Countries. Table 2.1 shows that budget. It is replete with meat, bread, cheese and beer. The respectability budget provided 2,500 calories and a whopping 112 grams of protein per day.

The respectability budget was not the kind of diet that workers in most of Europe and Asia were consuming – as we will see, it was just too expensive. Instead, they got their calories and protein in the least costly way from the cheapest available cereal. Since maize was eaten in Italy and rice in Bengal, different diets have been specified for different regions, but they have all been tailored to yield a bit over 1,900 calories per person per day. This was about the level of calories available in many poor countries in the 1950s before the Green Revolution increased their food supplies. 1,900 calories is not enough sustenance for a full day of hard work. These subsistence spending patterns are shown in Tables 2.2 and 2.3.

Protein supply varied considerably among the subsistence diets. The oat-based diet of northwestern Europe gave more protein (84 grams per day) than the Asian rice diet, which supplied the least (45 grams per day). However, even that was enough to meet modern nutritional norms. The US recommended daily allowance of protein is 0.8 grams per day per kilogram of ideal body weight. A man of average height in the early modern period (about 165 cm) with a body-mass index of 20 (in the ideal range) would have weighed 54 kg and required 44 grams

[4] This basket is a variant on the basket used in Allen (2001). The main difference is that bread consumption has been increased from 182 kg to 234 kg per year to boost the calorie content from 1,914 calories to 2,500 calories. This seems more appropriate for 'respectability'. Increasing bread consumption raises the cost of the basket 5–10 per cent depending on relative prices. These adjustments lower the welfare ratios (now called respectability ratios) by 5–10 per cent everywhere and so have a negligible impact on relative living standards or their trends.

Table 2.1 *The respectable lifestyle: basket of goods*

	Quantity per person per year	Price, grams of silver per unit	Spending share	Nutrients/day	
				Calories	Grams of protein
Bread	234 kg	0.693	36.0%	1,571	64
Beans/peas	52 l	0.477	5.5%	370	28
Meat	26 kg	2.213	12.8%	178	14
Butter	5.2 kg	3.470	4.0%	104	0
Cheese	5.2 kg	2.843	3.3%	54	3
Eggs	52 each	0.010	1.1%	11	1
Beer	182 l	0.470	20.0%	212	2
Soap	2.6 kg	2.880	1.7%	–	–
Linen	5 m	4.369	4.8%	–	–
Candles	2.6 kg	4.980	2.9%	–	–
Lamp oil	2.6 l	7.545	4.3%	–	–
Fuel	5.0 M BTU	4.164	4.6%	–	–
Total		450.956	100.0%	2,500	112

Notes:

[1] Where oil and wine were consumed instead of butter and beer, 5.2 litres of olive oil were substituted for the butter and 68.25 litres of wine for the beer. 5.2 litres of olive oil yields 116 calories per day and no protein; 68.25 litres of wine gives 159 calories per day and no protein. In Strasbourg, the average prices 1745–54 were 7.545 grams of silver for olive oil and 0.965 grams of silver for wine.

[2] M BTU = millions of BTUs

[3] Prices are in grams of silver per unit. Prices are averages for Strasbourg in 1745–54. The total shown in the price column is the total cost of the basket at the prices shown.

[4] Nutrients are computed assuming the following composition: bread: 2,450 calories per kg, 100 grams of protein per kg; beans/peas: 2,592 calories per litre, 199 grams of protein per litre; meat: 2,500 calories per kg, 200 grams of protein per kg; butter: 7,286 calories per kg, 7 grams of protein per kg; cheese: 3,750 calories per kg, 214 grams of protein per kg; eggs: 79 calories each, 6.25 grams of protein each; beer: 426 calories per litre, 3 grams of protein per litre; wine: 850 calories per litre, 0 grams of protein per litre.

of protein per day according to the US recommended daily allowance. The contrast between the 44 grams required for health and the 112 grams supplied by the European respectability diet highlights the extravagant consumption of protein by English labourers.

Table 2.2 *Subsistence lifestyle: baskets of goods*

	Indian rice			Indian millet		
	Quantity per person per year	Nutrients/day		Quantity per person per year	Nutrients/day	
		Calories	Grams of protein		Calories	Grams of protein
Rice	162 kg	1,607	33			
Millet				205 kg	1,698	62
Beans/peas	20 kg	199	11	10 kg	100	5
Meat	3 kg	21	1	3 kg	21	1
Butter/ghi	3 kg	72	0	3 kg	72	0
Sugar	2 kg	21	0	2 kg	21	0
Cotton	3 m			3 m		
Total		1,920	45		1,912	68

Table 2.3 *Subsistence incomes: baskets of goods*

	European oats			Beijing sorghum		
	Quantity per person per year	Nutrients/day		Quantity per person per year	Nutrients/day	
		Calories	Protein		Calories	Protein
Sorghum				179 kg	1,667	55
Oats	155 kg	1,657	72			
Beans/peas	20 kg	187	14	20 kg	187	14
Meat	5 kg	34	3	3 kg	21	2
Butter/oil	3 kg	60	0	3 kg	67	0
Soap	1.3 kg			1.3 kg		
Cotton/Linen	3 m			3 m		
Candles	1.3 kg			1.3 kg		
Lamp oil	1.3 l			1.3 l		
Fuel	2.0 M BTU			2.0 M BTU		
Total		1,938	89		1,942	71

The spending patterns in Tables 2.1 to 2.3 apply to a single adult male. To analyze subsistence income, we need to inflate them to include the living expenses of wives and children. Since the recommended calorie intake of a woman is less than that of a man, and since, of course, children need even fewer calories, we can say – reasoning rather loosely – that three 'baskets' like those in Tables 2.1 to 2.3 were needed to support a family with a father, a mother and some children. In addition, the reader will have noticed that none of those baskets includes the cost of renting housing. This, however, amounted to only about 5 per cent of spending. With these considerations in mind, we can estimate the annual cost of supporting a family as 3.15 (= 3 x 1.05) times the cost of the subsistence baskets shown in Tables 2.1 to 2.3.

We can check the balance of income and expenditure by computing the ratio of full-time annual income to annual subsistence cost. The latter is 3.15 times the cost of the baskets in Tables 2.1 to 2.3, while the former is the wage rate multiplied by the time employed. In Europe, most of the wage information refers to daily wages, and we assume that a full year was 250 days – the balance was accounted for by Sundays, religious holidays, illness and slack time. In India, many of the wage contracts we know of were monthly, so we take annual earnings to be twelve times the monthly figure. Dividing income by the cost of the respectability budget gives the 'respectability ratio', while dividing income by the cost of a subsistence budget gives the 'subsistence ratio'. In either case, a value greater than one indicates that the worker had enough money to buy the lifestyle in question with something to spare; values less than one indicate that the lifestyle was beyond his reach on the maintained assumptions.

Figure 2.2 shows the history of living standards in leading European cities from the late middle ages to the nineteenth century and in Delhi and Beijing from the seventeenth or eighteenth century into the nineteenth. Figure 2.2 uses the European respectability basket as the standard. The fifteenth century was a peak for labourers across Europe. If they worked 250 days per year, they earned about 50 per cent more than the cost of the respectability basket (i.e. the respectability ratio equalled 1.5). Wages sagged everywhere in the sixteenth century as population grew (Rappaport 1989), but there was a rebound in London and Amsterdam, so workers in those cities maintained high living standards with full-time earnings that were ample enough to

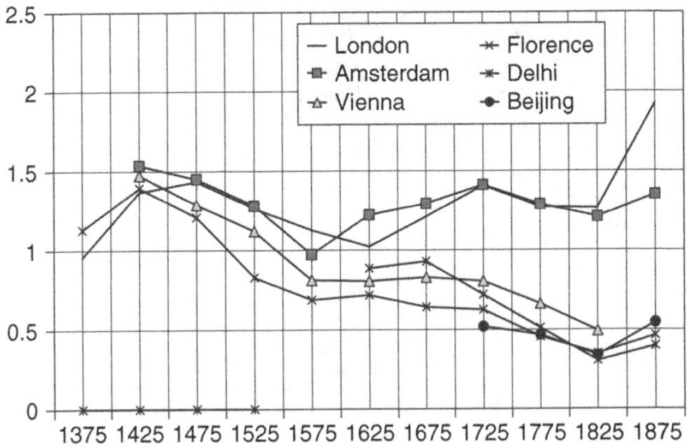

Figure 2.2 Respectability ratio for labourers: income/cost of respectable basket

buy the respectability basket (Schwartz 1985, 1992). It was a different story for workers in Vienna and Florence, and, indeed, their experience was the norm for most European workers. The real income slide continued steadily, so that, by the mid-nineteenth century, full-time annual earnings amounted to half or less of the cost of the northwestern respectability lifestyle.

Starting in the seventeenth century, we can add Asian wages to the comparison. The experience of India and Beijing looks like the pattern in Vienna and Florence. In the seventeenth century, wages in Delhi were almost enough to buy the European respectability basket. Would Indian workers have done even better if we could look further back in time? At the moment, we do not know. What we do know is that, by the eighteenth century, Asian workers did not earn enough to buy a respectable European standard of living. They earned only 30–40 per cent of that cost.

How did Asian and European workers survive when they only earned 30–40 per cent of the cost of a respectable lifestyle? Could they buy enough to eat? Figure 2.3 sheds light on this question by summarizing subsistence ratios (full-time annual earnings divided by a family's cost of the subsistence lifestyle). The rankings and basic patterns are the same as in Figure 2.2, although there are some interesting differences. Basing the diet on oats means that workers in Amsterdam generally had greater – as well as less volatile – purchasing power than

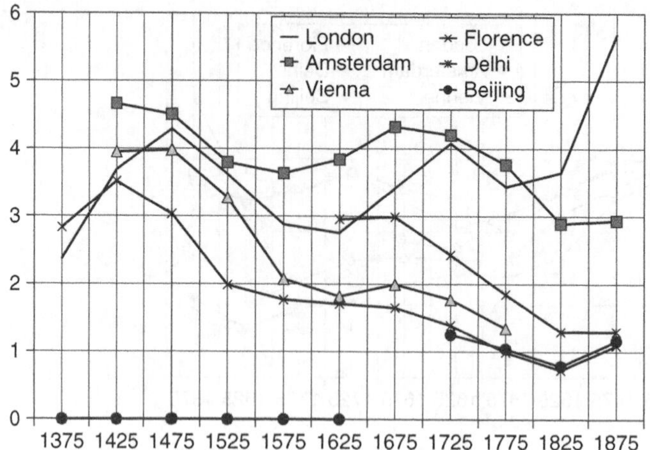

Figure 2.3 Subsistence ratio for labourers: income/costs of subsistence basket

their counterparts in London.[5] But both groups of workers were very well off, by this measure, earning three to four times the cost of a bare bones subsistence income. In the late middle ages, workers in Vienna and Florence – indeed in other continental cities – enjoyed that high standard of living, but their good fortune did not last, for their incomes in the nineteenth century were barely enough to purchase the physiological minimum. Indeed, the wages of Italian and Chinese men were not quite enough to buy even that – the meagre earnings of the wife or the garden produce of a scrap of land were necessary for family survival. Lefebre (1962, I, pp. 216–19) came to the same conclusion in an early study of mens' wages in France: 'The wife's earnings must have been barely enough to keep the family from starving.' The income and expenditure calculations confirm the observations of the nineteenth-century observers of the 'polenta economy'.

India does better in comparisons using subsistence standards of living. In the seventeenth century, workers in north India could earn three times the cost of the subsistence basket if they worked full time for the full year. This income was on a par with the prosperity of their

[5] Basing the bare bones diet in northwestern Europe on oats probably understates the subsistence ratio for workers in those countries during the late eighteenth and early nineteenth centuries, for potatoes were a cheap source of calories and consumption was growing. However, oatmeal still remained common.

counterparts in London (at its trough) but below that of Amsterdam. In this respect, the calculations provide some support for the revisionist historians who see little difference between pre-industrial Europe and Asia (Parthasarathi 1998, 2001, Pomeranz 2000). By the nineteenth century, however, this prosperity had slipped away, and north Indian workers were barely able to purchase the subsistence basket. Our information about wages in Beijing only begins in 1738, and, for the next two centuries, average earnings hovered around the cost of the subsistence basket just as they did in Delhi, Florence and Vienna. In this period, there was little difference in real income between Asia and the backward parts of Europe.

Aside from the advanced parts of Europe, there was one region in the world where living standards exceeded these rock bottom levels, and that was the east coast of North America. Figure 2.4 shows the subsistence ratio for labourers in Massachusetts at decade intervals between the 1750s and the 1840s.[6] In the mid-eighteenth century, the ratio was just over three, i.e. below the London level but above that in most English provincial towns. The western periphery of the Atlantic economy was booming, and that prosperity attracted immigrants from Europe and drew slaves from Africa. The comparative advantage of the future United States lay in primary products, and the country exported agricultural goods and imported manufactures. In 1790, 95 per cent of the American population was rural, and the largest city was New York with a population of 33,000 – less than that of London in 1500. High real wages in the eighteenth century were indicative of the dynamism of the Atlantic economy, which was transforming Britain, but had little immediate import for the evolution of industrial technology, for there was little industry in America. As the United States expanded in the nineteenth century, however, American wages pulled ahead of those in Britain and took on great significance by prompting the invention of labour-saving technology. America's ascendancy stands out in Figure 2.4. Real wages grew very little in Britain during the Industrial

[6] The basket used to compute the Massachusetts cost of living is identical to those shown in Table 2.2 except that the grain is 165 kg of maize (American corn). Wages and prices are ultimately from Wright (1885) but were taken from the tabulation by Lindert and Deitch and posted on the website (http://gpih.ucdavis.edu) of the Global Price and Income History Group at the University of California, Davis. Some gaps were interpolated. The price of firewood was assumed to be a price per cord despite Wright's indicating the unit was the 'ft'.

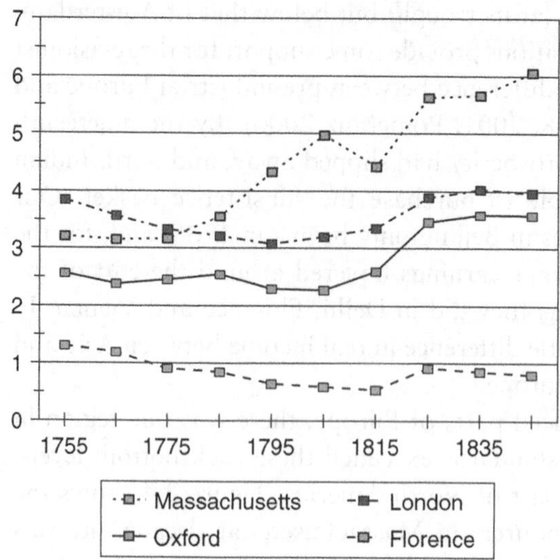

Figure 2.4 Subsistence ratio for labourers in Europe and the United States: annual earnings relative to the cost of the subsistence basket

Revolution, but they increased sharply in America after independence,[7] and American real wages exceeded British wages by about 50 per cent. By the nineteenth century, the American high wage economy, which was the impetus to Habakkuk's theorizing, had emerged. In the mid-eighteenth century, however, it was the high wages in Britain, in the core of the Atlantic economy, that played the important role of imparting a labour-saving bias to technical change.

Wage convergence in Britain

Within Britain, the geographical boundary of the high wage economy shifted over time. In the fifteenth century, real wages were high in all parts of the country. This was a legacy of the Black Death in 1348–9. So many people died that there was a labour shortage everywhere until population growth resumed in the mid-sixteenth century. After 1550,

[7] The literature on the history of US real wages is very large. Recent contributions include Williamson (1976), David and Solar (1977), Williamson and Lindert (1980), Margo and Villaflor (1987), Goldin and Margo (1992), Sokoloff and Villaflor (1992) and Margo (2000).

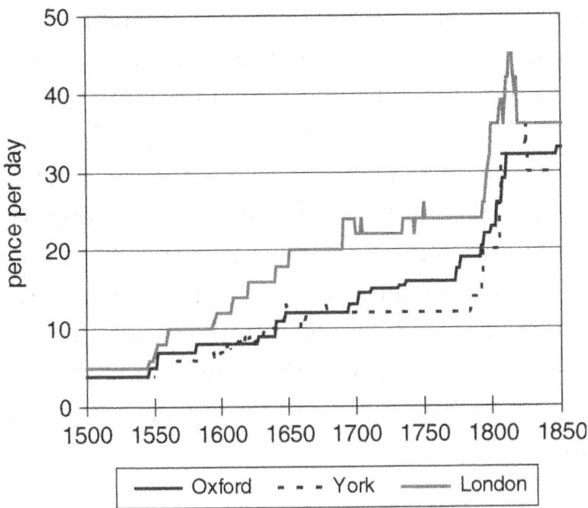

Figure 2.5 Labourers' wage across England

real wages fell everywhere. The drop was attenuated in London whose population exploded from 50,000 in 1500 to 200,000 a century later. The rapid growth of the city's economy led to tight labour markets and rising wages that attracted a flood of migrants from adjoining counties. This is manifest in Figure 2.5 as London's wages pulled above wages in Oxford and York after 1550: by the early seventeenth century, the earnings of fully employed unskilled workers in rural England dropped to only 60 per cent of the respectability budget. Geographical differentials were then at their greatest, and the high wage economy was confined to London.

By the late seventeenth century, the high wage economy began to spread north as provincial wages began to close the gap with London. Figure 2.5 shows the daily wage in Oxford rising towards the London level from the late seventeenth century. Throughout the eighteenth century, fully employed labourers in Oxford were earning enough to buy the respectability budget. Incomes also rose in the North, but less rapidly. In York, labourers earned only 80 per cent of the respectability budget in the eighteenth century. This gap was not closed until the Industrial Revolution when northern wages and southern provincial wages again approached London levels. It was only after 1800 that unskilled workers in York earned enough to buy the respectability budget.[8]

[8] This issue was first addressed by Gilboy (1934).

The northern spread of the high wage economy was matched by a corresponding spread of the consumption of white bread. In the early eighteenth century, the predominant carbohydrate in northern Britain was oats, eaten as both bread and porridge (Smith 1776). Dr Johnson exaggerated only a little when he remarked that oats were 'a grain which in England is generally given to horses but in Scotland supports the people'. Petersen (1995, pp. 220–35, 284–316) calculated that wheat accounted for 60 per cent of the value of British bread in the 1770s, 81 per cent in the first decade of the nineteenth century, and 90 per cent in the middle of the century. Much of the growth took place in northern manufacturing towns where more and more workers shifted from oats to wheat bread.

Skilled workers

Thus far, we have spoken only of unskilled workers, people generally described as 'labourers'. Skilled workers always earned more. In Europe, the wage of a carpenter or a mason was about 60 per cent higher than the wage of a labourer. Our information about Asian wages is fragmentary and not entirely consistent. Some information for early modern India suggests that the skill premium was about 100 per cent; fuller information for eighteenth-century China points to a skill premium of 60 per cent as in Europe (van Zanden 2004a). For the moment, I will concentrate on the European pattern, which is better established and helps delineate the high wage district on the continent.

Figure 2.6 shows respectability ratios for building craftsmen across Europe. These ratios were all higher than the corresponding ratios for labourers. Indeed, in most cases, the ratios were greater than one indicating that carpenters and masons who were employed full time could purchase the respectable lifestyle with some money to spare. There were important differences in trend, however. In London and the Low Countries, the real incomes of craftsmen remained high throughout the early modern period, while living standards fell on the rest of the continent. In contrast, by the second half of the eighteenth century, the real incomes of craftsmen in Valencia and Florence had dropped just below one. They had no surplus income (indeed, a slight deficit) if they bought the respectable lifestyle. This was a common pattern in Europe. The situation in Paris and Vienna was not quite as dire, although the respectability ratio for Viennese craftsmen dropped below one in the

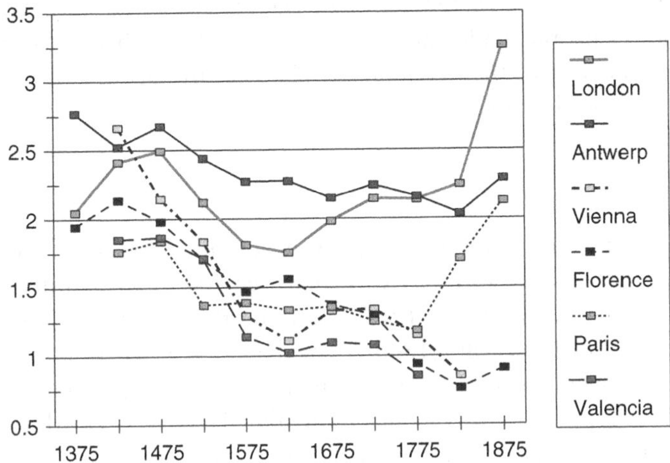

Figure 2.6 Respectability ratio for masons: income/cost of respectable basket

first half of the nineteenth century. In eighteenth-century Paris and Vienna, masons and carpenters could buy the respectable lifestyle with a little left over.

We can now see the boundaries of the high wage economy. Its core was always the maritime ports – London and the cities of the Low Countries. In the core, even unskilled workers always earned enough to buy the respectability budget. Skilled workers, of course, did better. In the course of the seventeenth and eighteenth centuries, the high wage economy advanced north through England, so that unskilled workers in northern cities could buy the respectability lifestyle early in the nineteenth century. On the continent, there was no evidence of geographical spread, but there were pockets of moderately high incomes in cities like Paris and Vienna. In Paris, for instance, skilled workers certainly earned enough to buy the respectable lifestyle, and the earnings of the unskilled came close, although they were noticeably less than in London or Amsterdam. As a result, some of the consequences of the high wage economy extended to Paris in attenuated form.

What the high wage economy meant for the quality of life

One reason that high wages and high subsistence ratios were important is because they indicate the presence of purchasing power beyond that required for basic needs. There were many ways to spend that surplus, and the choices people made had a big impact on the quality of their lives and the growth of their economies. Here are five aspects of life that were influenced by real incomes:

Food quantity

People living at bare bones subsistence were usually hungry, so the usual response to rising incomes was increased food consumption. Table 2.4 summarizes budgets of workers in northern England compiled by Alexander Somerville (1843).[9] The highest wage corresponds to skilled tradesmen like masons or carpenters. The next highest (186d per week or 31d per day) corresponds to building labourers. The third highest (120d per week) represents the average earnings of a cotton mill operative. The lowest income corresponds to the intermittently employed. Calories consumed per adult male rose from 1,605 per day in the poorest paid job, a rate which barely sustains basal metabolism, to 3,937 calories among the skilled trades. This is a twenty-first-century level of intake. With more money, people ate more food.[10]

The patterns in Table 2.4 apply internationally and, thus, highlight the connections between wages and diets that we discussed earlier. The low consumption of meat by French and Italian workers was the result of their low wages. More broadly, Fogel (1991, p. 45) has estimated the average calorie consumption in England and France in the late eighteenth century, and his results are consistent with these patterns. He found that the average Englishman consumed 2,700 calories per day, while the average Frenchman had only 2,290. Forty per cent of the French population received less than 1,958 calories, while only 20 per cent of the English were in a similar situation. While Fogel's calculations are founded on a high ratio of assumptions to reliable data, the tenor of the results is consistent with the differences in consumer purchasing power in the two countries.

9 Horrell and Humphries (1992) provide a statistical analysis of many budgets spanning the Industrial Revolution. Their work focuses on spending categories rather than food quantities and, in that regard, supports the conclusions from the Somerville budgets.

10 Budgets collected by social investigators often look stylized or censored – in this case by under-reporting alcohol consumption.

Table 2.4 ***How food consumption varied with income: Somerville's budgets***

	Weekly income			
	66d	120d	180d	318d
Pounds of food and pints of milk consumed per week				
Flour	8.54	12.20	17.08	19.53
Oatmeal	7.50	13.75	11.25	15.00
Potatoes	17.39	34.78	36.52	34.78
Milk	7.33	4.00	6.00	6.67
Butter	0.00	0.00	0.80	1.28
Meat	0.00	0.00	1.09	2.55
Bacon	0.29	1.14	0.57	0.43
Cheese	0.00	0.00	0.56	0.80
Sugar	0.00	0.57	1.26	2.40
Tea	0.00	0.00	0.12	0.23
Percentage of income spent on food	85%	76%	74%	61%
Calories per day per adult male	1,605	2,806	3,219	3,937
Grams of protein per day per adult male	64	106	119	147
Index of food cost per calorie	1.00	0.92	1.23	1.41

Notes:

[1] The income class of 318d is also shown consuming 6d per week of beer. I have ignored this.

[2] The calculations of calories per day and protein per day per adult male assume that the family consisted of three adult male equivalents, the same assumption used in the subsistence and respectability ratios.

[3] The index of food cost per calorie is based on the cost of food divided by the calories it contained.

[4] The food quantities were obtained by dividing the expenditure on each item by their prices.

Source: Somerville (1843, pp. 12–3).

Food quality

Not only did people in the high wage economy eat more food, they ate more expensive food. During the fifteenth century, when real wages were very high, desirable diets emphasized bread, meat and alcohol (Dyer 1989, pp. 158–9). During the seventeenth and eighteenth centuries, imported commodities like sugar and tea were added to the list of preferred foods. Potatoes came to be widely consumed by workers, but the spud was regarded as an inferior source of calories.

The preference for these foods is shown by the increased expenditure on them shown in Table 2.4. The poorest workers did not consume the tropical goods like tea and sugar. Protein consumption increased from 64 grams per day for the poorest men to a staggering 147 grams per day for the best paid. An index of the shift in preferences is the rise in the cost of a calorie shown in Table 2.4. As food consumption was tilted towards expensive sources of nutrition like meat, the cost per calorie rose almost 50 per cent.

Physical well-being, health and stature

The higher level of food consumption in northwestern Europe led to better health, longer life and a more productive workforce. A prime indicator is stature. Historians have followed its history by analyzing military recruitment records. In the late eighteenth century, the heights of British army recruits imply an average height of about 172 cm for the male population (Floud, Wachter and Gregory 1990, pp. 140–9, Cinnirella 2007). French records indicate that Frenchmen were only 162 cm tall in the seventeenth century. Their average height jumped to 168 cm in the 1740s and dropped again to 165 cm in the 1760s (Komlos 2003, p. 168). The heights of men in Lombardy dropped from 167 cm in the 1730s to 164 cm in the early nineteenth century. In the late eighteenth and early nineteenth centuries, men in the Austrian empire were even shorter – about 162 cm (A'Hearn 2003, pp. 370–1). Heights are determined by net nutritional intake during childhood. To the degree that low real wages implied restricted food consumption, one would expect Frenchmen and Italians to be shorter than their English counterparts, as they were.

The income and diet differences may have had implications for economic performance. One was work intensity. People subsisting on low calorie diets had less energy to work. On the basis of his calorie estimates, Fogel (1991, p. 46) claimed that 20 per cent of the French population could do no more than three hours of light work per day. The corresponding proportion was smaller in England. Many jobs in the eighteenth century entailed a full day of hard labour – building work or mining, for instance. People doing this work had to be well nourished. Other jobs – spinning, framework knitting or tending machines – required much less physical effort. Whether differences in average nutrition affected aggregate economic performance, therefore, depended on the distribution of job requirements.

Consumer revolution

The 'consumer revolution' has been an important theme in recent writing on the eighteenth century.[11] McKendrick, Brewer and Plumb (1982, p. 1) first proclaimed: 'There was a consumer revolution in eighteenth-century England.' Two sorts of evidence point to the change (Shammas 1990, Brewer and Porter 1993). One is contemporary discussions of trade and 'luxury' consumption; the second is statistical evidence of the increased consumption of 'luxuries' and novelties. These goods included tropical foodstuffs (tea, sugar, coffee and chocolate), imported Asian manufactures (cotton textiles, silk and Chinese porcelain) and British manufactures (imitations of the Asian imports and a wide range of other items like clothing, books, furniture, clocks, glassware, crockery and metal products). While the consumer revolution was regarded by contemporaries as a British phenomenon (Berg 2005, pp. 7–8), it also characterized the Low Countries and extended to cosmopolitan centres like Paris (de Vries 1993, Fairchilds 1993).

Who was buying these consumer goods? There is no doubt that the upper and middle classes were major purchasers, but workers were also an important source of demand. Table 2.5, which is a reworking of Gregory King's famous social table of England in 1688, shows the potential for non-subsistence spending for broad social groups. King assigned an income of £2 per person per year to vagrants, paupers and cottagers, the poorest 18 per cent of the population. As it happens, the bare bones subsistence basket including rent cost £2.07 when valued in the average prices of 1683–94. The correspondence both validates King's £2 and shows what it implied for consumption. Evidently, cottagers and paupers had no surplus income for the consumer revolution.

[11] Kowaleski (2006) has argued that many features of the early modern consumer revolution were anticipated in fifteenth-century England when real wages had also been high in most parts of the country.

Table 2.5 *England in 1688*

	Number in class	Percentage of population	Income per head	Income relative to subsistence	Percentage income above subsistence
Landed classes	200,358	3.5%	£46.4	23.2	21%
Bourgeoisie	262,704	4.6%	£40.2	20.1	23%
Commercial	1,190,552	20.9%	£9.0	4.5	19%
Farmers	1,023,480	18.0%	£10.4	5.2	20%
Workers	1,970,895	34.7%	£5.6	2.8	17%
Cottagers, poor	1,041,344	18.3%	£2.0	1.0	0%
Total/ average	5,689,322		£9.6	4.8	

Note: I have altered Lindert and Williamson's figures in one way. When King reported a household with more than 4.5 people, I assume the excess were servants and tally them among the workers. I also assign £9 income to each servant and deduct it from the income of the person they worked for. This is along the lines of calculations made by Lindert on his website.

Subsistence income is taken to be £2 per head. A direct calculation of the bare bones subsistence income of an adult man using 1680s prices is £2.07. Women and children could survive on a somewhat lower amount, and that refinement is not included here. Income above subsistence is computed for each group by multiplying the number of people by income per head less £2. Summing this for all groups gives the total, and the 'Percentage of income above subsistence' for each group is computed accordingly.

Landed classes includes the various lords, gentlemen, clergy and practitioners of sciences and the arts.

Bourgeoisie includes merchants, office-holders, lawyers, artisans with incomes of at least £200 per year, and naval and military officers.

Commercial includes shopkeepers, tradesmen and manufacturers.

Farmers includes farmers and freeholders.

Workers includes labourers, the building trades, miners, domestic servants, common seamen and soldiers.

Cottagers, poor includes cottagers, paupers and vagrants.

Source: Lindert and Williamson (1982).

All other social groups, however, did have some surplus purchasing power. Setting subsistence at £2 per year implies that the gentry, aristocracy, rich merchants, lawyers and other members of the richest two groups had 43 per cent of the surplus purchasing power, although they comprised only 8 per cent of the population. The middle strata of shopkeepers, proto-industrialists and workers made up almost three-quarters of the population and had command over 57 per cent of the income beyond subsistence. This group did, indeed, comprise a large market for consumer goods.

Their purchases show up in probate inventories, which list possessions at the time of death. Weatherill (1996, pp. 76, 78, 168) has studied the ownership of seventeen manufactured goods in English inventories between 1675 and 1725. Some are traditional (tables, cooking pots, pewter plates and dishes, silver or gold), and some were novel like saucepans, earthenware, books, clocks, pictures, looking glasses, window curtains, table linen, china, knives and forks, and utensils for hot beverages. Not unexpectedly, Weatherill finds that people with more money and status were more likely to own these items. Nonetheless, the English market for imported and novel consumer goods extended down to the working class. The skilled workers earning the highest wages were the most active buyers, and their purchases extended to many new and imported goods. Less well paid labourers were more modest buyers, but even they were purchasing some of the British products. Many working people bought stylish clothing (Lemire 1991, 1997, Styles 2007). Unlike India, almost everyone had a table, cooking pots and some pewter. In his tours of England in the late 1760s, Arthur Young (e.g. 1771b, vol. III, p. 276) frequently reported that the poor 'All drink tea'. Inventory evidence for the Low Countries and eighteenth-century Paris suggests a similar pattern. Outside of these areas, there is not much evidence of working-class purchases of these kinds of goods.

These patterns make very good sense in terms of the wage history developed here. The high wage economy was centred on England and the Low Countries with some lesser offshoots in capital cities like Paris and Vienna. These, indeed, were the places where the consumer revolution occurred. Desire for consumer goods may have been more widespread, but it was the high wage economy that gave the workers, shopkeepers and proto-industrialists the cash to turn their dreams into reality.

Education and learning, skill differentials

Workers in northwestern Europe could enjoy their new-found affluence in ways other than eating or consuming; in particular, they could acquire learning and skills. Sometimes this was done for pleasure and sometimes for gain. Economists usually assume the second motivation was primary and call education 'human capital' since schooling involves expending resources at one time in order to realize a higher income at a later date. Three aspects of 'human capital formation' were literacy, numeracy, and trade skills.

Start with literacy. Its spread has been studied by measuring the proportion of people who could sign their names (rather than make a mark) to marriage registers and other official documents. The ability to sign one's name is an imperfect indicator both because it does not indicate great skill and because many people learned to read without learning to write. Nonetheless, signing can be observed for many people over long periods and – historians presume – was correlated with a wider range of literacy skills.

The signature information indicates that literacy increased dramatically during the early modern period especially in the high wage economies of northwestern Europe. In the late middle ages, literacy was mainly confined to the cities. In Venice, for instance, 33 per cent of the men and 13 per cent of the women were literate in 1587 (Grendler 1989, p. 46), and other cities were similar. Only about 5 per cent of the rural population could read. Based on these proportions and the urban–rural breakdown of the population, the literacy rates for 1500 have been estimated (Table 2.6). At that time, literacy was very low in England – about 6 per cent.

By 1800, literacy had increased everywhere. It was highest in northwestern Europe – the Low Countries, the Rhine Valley in Germany, northeastern France, and England where over half of the population could sign their names. These districts were high wage regions or ones linked to them by migration. In the poorer parts of Europe, only about one-fifth of the population was literate.

People probably learned to read for two reasons – economics and pleasure. Literacy was much more valuable in trade and business than in small-scale farming – at least during the middle ages – which is why literacy was higher in medieval cities than in the countryside. This motive persisted through the early modern period. Some of the

Table 2.6 *Adult literacy, 1500–1800*

	Proportion of the adult population that could sign its name	
	1500	1800
England	0.06	0.53
Netherlands	0.10	0.68
Belgium	0.10	0.49
Germany	0.06	0.35
France	0.07	0.37
Austria/Hungary	0.06	0.21
Poland	0.06	0.21
Italy	0.09	0.22
Spain	0.09	0.20

Note: Data for 1500 are estimated from rural–urban breakdown.

Rural population assumed to be 5 per cent literate. This is suggested by later data from Nalle (1989, p. 71) and Houston (1988, pp. 140–1, 152–3) for Spain, Wyczanski (1974, p. 713) for Poland, Le Roy Ladurie (1974, pp. 161–4) for Languedoc, and Graff (1987, p. 106) for England.

Urban population assumed to be 23 per cent literate generalizing from Grendler's (1989, p. 46) estimate for Venice in 1587 that 33 per cent of the men and 12.2–13.2 per cent of the women were literate for an overall average of 23 per cent. The proportion was of the same order in Valencia (Nalle 1989, p. 71), among the nobles and bourgeoisie of Poland (Wyczanski 1974, p. 713), and perhaps a bit lower in fifteenth-century London (Graff 1987, p. 106). The small urban shares in countries besides Spain and Italy at this time mean that the urban literacy rate had no discernible impact on the national average.

Data for 1800 are fuller for the seventeenth and eighteenth centuries and include: Nalle (1989), Houston (1988), Graff (1987), Cressy (1980, 1981), Fraga (1990), Grendler (1989), Ruwet and Wellemans (1978), Wyczanski (1974), Francois (1989), Furet and Ozouf (1977), Gelabert (1987), de Vries and van der Woude (1997), Park (1980), Chartier (1987), Cipolla (1969), Kuijpers (1997) and Larguie (1987).

rise in literacy in northwestern Europe reflected the urbanization of the period. But urbanization was not enough to explain the upsurge in literacy after 1500, for more people were reading in both town and country in the eighteenth century. Gutenberg's invention of printing with movable type quickly cut the real price of a book by two-thirds. Declines continued, so by 1800 the real price of a book had dropped to

10 per cent of its 1450 value, and books were within the reach of many more people (van Zanden 2004b, p. 13). Protestantism put a premium on reading God's word, and that may have played a role. Catholics in northwestern Europe, however, learned to read and write just like Protestants. The agrarian world was transformed by the legalistically justified reorganization of private estates and by state-sponsored reforms like the enclosure movement, both of which put a premium on being able to navigate through written documents. Economic change raised the value of reading and writing; and, indeed, many eighteenth-century books were legal, technical or otherwise functional. Religion and work were not the only inducements to reading: the early modern period saw the publication of cheap scatological tracts on religion and politics. Irreverence may have been a motive as well as religion (Reis 2005).

Greater numeracy was another aspect of human capital formation. The proportion of people with command of arithmetic and geometry is more difficult to gauge than the proportion who were literate since there was no analogue to marriage registers where a broad swath of the population had to sign their names. Thomas (1987, p. 128) has reviewed much impressionistic evidence and concluded that 'there can be little doubt that numerical skills were more widely dispersed' in England 'in 1700 than they had been two centuries earlier'. Landed gentlemen in 1500 could rarely add or subtract, while their successors two centuries later generally could. By the eighteenth century, there was a voluminous trade in arithmetic books, which suggests that many people were learning the skills. Arithmetic, indeed, had become more powerful: arabic numerals had replaced Roman, while logarithms and slide rules sped calculation. Unlike reading, where pleasure may have been a motive, very few people learn maths for fun: the incentive was instrumental. Geometry was necessary for navigation and surveying that grew in demand as England's merchant marine expanded and its agriculture was reorganized. The examples in the arithmetic texts were drawn from trade and commerce, which must have been the main application of these skills. It was the growth of the urban, commercial economy that generated the demand for mathematical skills that prompted their acquisition.

Craft skills were the third aspect of human capital, and they were usually acquired by apprenticeship. Apprenticeships were contracts in which the master agreed to house and feed the apprentice and to teach him the trade. The apprentice agreed to work for the master, usually without any pay beyond the room and board, for the duration of the contract. In addition, the apprentice gave the master a payment at the beginning of the apprenticeship. Successful completion of the apprenticeship allowed the apprentice to practise the trade and, in England, conferred important social benefits such as a settlement under the Poor Law. We do not know how common apprenticeship was in the low wage parts of Europe, but it was high in England where two-thirds of the boys in the seventeenth and eighteenth centuries completed apprenticeships (Humphries 2009). The accumulation of these craft skills was an important contributor to the Industrial Revolution.

Masters did not take on apprentices gratuitously. The master charged the apprentice's parents a large sum at the beginning of the apprenticeship. They had to save the money themselves or raise it from relatives. The capital requirements did not end there. To become a master, a boy had to raise the capital to start a business even after he completed the apprenticeship, and that usually required saving part of his pay as a journeyman.

These financial considerations highlight the importance of the high wage economy, which underpinned all three types of human capital accumulation. Charitable support aside, parents had to pay for schooling and apprenticeships. The Ealing gardener we met earlier was spending 6d per week to educate his two children – as much as he spent on beer. Had he been poorer, he might have found school 'too expensive'. Literacy and numeracy were everywhere highest among the wealthy. It was only in England and the Low Countries that a majority of workers could sign their names. In the low wage parts of Europe, peasants and labourers were little more literate than they had been in the late middle ages (Reis 2005, pp. 206–7). A similar situation probably applied to numeracy. High wages facilitated all forms of skill acquisition: the ability of parents to come up with the cash to pay the master for taking on their son was eased if they were in receipt of high wages, and the ease with which a journeyman could save the money to start a business was helped if journeymen earned more than it cost to survive. Widespread literacy, numeracy and craft competence reflected the demand for skills in the advanced economies, and the high wages those economies generated gave workers the money to pay for schooling and apprenticeships.

High wages and economic growth

High wages were a remarkable feature of English life in the seventeenth and eighteenth centuries. They led to high levels of consumption and education. High wages were a consequence of the vigorous economic growth of the period and led to further growth as new technologies were invented to economize on expensive English labour.

3 *The agricultural revolution*

> The English are still imbued with that doctrine, which is at least debatable, that great properties are necessary for the improvement of agriculture.
>
> Alexis de Tocqueville, *Journey to England*, 1833, p. 72

Agriculture played an important role in the expansion of northwestern Europe. In the successful economies of England and the Low Countries, the share of the workforce in farming dropped from about 75 to 35–40 per cent. Since the British and the Dutch were being fed mainly with domestically grown food, each farm worker in these countries had to raise his productivity enough to feed more mouths than before. Not only that – in Chapter 2 we saw that British and Dutch farmers put more food on the table than farmers in other parts of Europe. How and why did they do it?

There is a well-established answer to this question, at least in so far as English agriculture is concerned, and it not only explains the agricultural transformation but also the development surge of the English economy as a whole (e.g. Brenner 1976, Cohen and Weitzman 1975, Ernle 1912, Marx 1867, McCloskey 1972, Overton 1996, Shaw-Taylor 2001, Young 1774, etc.). This theory is summarized in Figure 3.1. In this model, the modernization of agrarian institutions – the enclosure of the open fields and the replacement of peasant cultivators with large-scale capitalist farms operated by wage labour – was the prime mover that drove the economy forward (box one). Large-scale enclosed farms are supposed to have produced more food and – in some accounts – employed fewer people per acre than peasants (box two). Greater food production and lower farm employment led to an expanded urban population (box three). The result was greater manufacturing production and economic growth (box four).

This chapter agrees with the established model in affirming the reality and importance of the agricultural revolution. The chapter

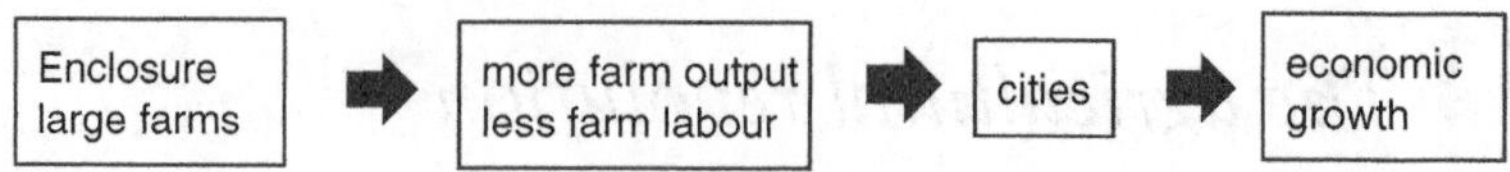

Figure 3.1 The standard model of agriculture and English economic development

disagrees with the established model, however, in regards to causation. The burden of this chapter is that the causal arrows pointing to the right were very small. Much larger causal arrows should be drawn in the opposite direction. There were agricultural revolutions in the Netherlands and England, and they were integral to the economic expansion. Most of the causation, however, ran from expanding world trade, to the growth of urban manufacturing, to rising agricultural productivity, and, finally, to large farms and enclosures. The city drove the countryside – not the reverse.

The macro story: how were the people fed?

The growth of agricultural output was an important feature of the agricultural revolution. More food was essential to support the growing population at a high standard of living, and the timing of output growth highlights the changes that really mattered.

In the absence of agricultural censuses, the only way to gauge farm output across early modern Europe is from consumption. The simplest approach is to extrapolate agricultural output from changes in the population by assuming that per capita food consumption was constant and making an allowance for imports and exports (e.g. Deane and Cole 1969, Overton 1996).[1] Applied to England, this procedure indicates static output between 1650 and 1750 (since the population was not growing) followed by rapidly rising output as population growth accelerated after 1750. The apparent surge in farm output beginning in 1750 suggests that enclosure had a large impact on productivity since the parliamentary enclosure movement began in the 1750s and continued into the nineteenth century.

[1] These reconstructions employ the identity that agricultural output (Q) equals the population (N) multiplied by per capita consumption of agricultural productions (c) and by the ratio of agricultural production to agricultural consumption (t): $Q = tcN$. The factor t incorporates the role of international trade in farm goods: if imports were 10 per cent of consumption, for instance, t would equal.9. Before the nineteenth century, it played only a small role in most cases.

The argument, however, is nothing but population history projected onto the realm of agriculture. The problem is that per capita food consumption was not a constant, as we saw in the last chapter. Higher incomes led people to consume more calories and protein, and their consumption also responded to changes in the price of food. These behaviours must be incorporated into the projections for them to have any reliability.[2] Several investigators (Crafts 1976, Jackson 1985, Clark, Huberman and Lindert 1995, Allen 1999) have done that using estimates of the income and price elasticities of demand for farm goods derived from English budget surveys and studies of consumption in developing countries.[3] The usual assumptions in the historical literature are an income elasticity of demand equal to 0.5, an own price elasticity of –0.6, and the cross price elasticity between food and manufactures of 0.1 (other reasonable values give similar results).

Once demand is made a function of income and prices, we can calculate the growth in farm output that would have cleared the agricultural product markets. For England, this shows three phases. The first lasted from the early sixteenth century through to the 1730s. Output approximately doubled in this period. This was the era when yeomen farmers were at their apogee. The second ran from 1740 to 1800. Output grew only 10 per cent in this period. The meagreness of this increase calls into question the claim that enclosure increased farm output in these years. The third phase extended from 1800 to 1850. Yields rose significantly (Allen and O'Grada 1988), and output jumped 65 per cent. This period of advance was short-lived, however, for the growth of farm output and productivity ground to a halt after mid-century (O'Grada 1994).

The pause in farm output growth between 1740 and 1800 deserves a closer look. Population and income were growing rapidly in the period, pushing up the demand for food. However, prices in Britain rose more rapidly than those on the continent.[4] The obvious explanation for the rapid rise in English prices was that English demand was

2 Crafts (1976) first made this argument, and it has since been reworked by Jackson (1985) and others.

3 The easiest way to make the per capita consumption of agricultural products a function of wages and prices is with the equation $c = ap^e i^g m^b$, where p is the price of farm products, i is income per head, m is the price of manufactured consumer goods, and a sets the units of measurement. The own price, income, and cross price elasticities of demand are e, g and b.

4 Divergent price movements were possible only because international food markets were not yet fully integrated.

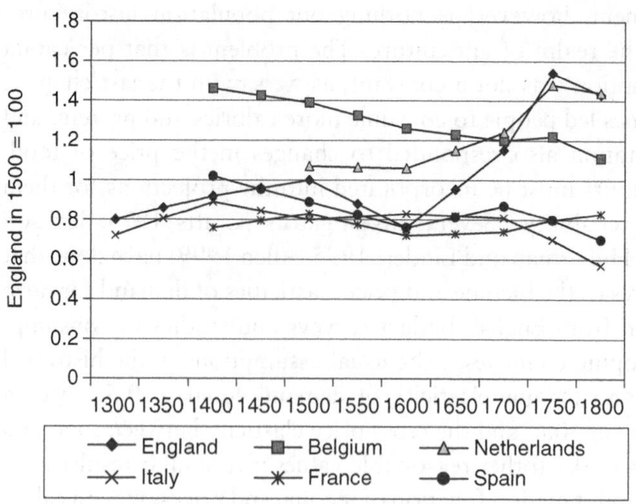

Figure 3.2 Agricultural labour productivity

growing faster than English supply. That insight is given mathematical expression by making consumption a function of income and prices. The procedure, in turn, extracts the history of supply from the trajectories of population, income and price by backing out the growth of supply that implies the rise in prices.

Output per worker in agriculture

Not only did English farms produce a large volume of food per person, but by 1800 each English farm worker produced enough to support two workers in manufacturing and services. Output per worker in agriculture is obtained by dividing the estimates of farm production by the agricultural population figures presented in Chapter 1. Figure 3.2 shows the resulting figures for leading countries in Europe. Three different patterns are apparent.

The first is exemplified by present-day Belgium. Medieval Flemish agriculture was renowned for its efficiency, and the high labour productivity of the province meant that the farmers could support a large urban population. Pockets of high productivity were also found elsewhere in Europe, notably in northeastern Norfolk (Campbell 1983, 2000). Output per worker declined slowly in Belgium as the population grew and farms were subdivided during the early modern period. Nevertheless, Belgium continued to set a high standard that took centuries for Europe's other farmers to meet.

The Dutch and the English exemplify the second pattern. Seen in their totality, neither country exhibited impressive productivity in the middle ages (Allen 2005). Between 1600 and 1750, each experienced an agricultural revolution in which output per worker reached and exceeded Belgian levels. Both countries are famous for their agricultural revolutions, and they show up dramatically in the graph of labour productivity.

The third group is all the rest. Italy, for whom the figures start in 1300, is a paradigm case. The Black Death cut the population in the middle of the fourteenth century. As a result, output per worker rose between 1300 and 1400. In the next hundred years, renewed population growth began to cut productivity back to pre-plague levels. The English series shows the same rise and fall, but the difference is that Italian labour productivity continued to decline throughout the early modern period. There was no agricultural revolution there. All the major continental countries showed a similar drop in productivity between 1400 and 1800 as the expansion of the farm population ran into diminishing returns.

Why did output and productivity rise?

We can sort out the sources of the Dutch and English agricultural revolutions by splitting output per worker into components with the equation:

$$\frac{\text{output}}{\text{labour}} = \frac{\text{output}}{\text{improved area}} \times \frac{\text{improved area}}{\text{total area}} \times \frac{\text{total area}}{\text{labour}}$$

This is revealing since the components were determined by different factors. We can analyze the components from left to right.

Output per improved area

'Improved area' includes the acreage of arable, meadow and pasture. Output per improved area rose in the early modern period since the productivity of both crops and livestock increased. Milk per cow, for instance, grew from about 100 gallons per year in 1300 to 380 gallons in 1800. A sheep's fleece rose from 1.5 lbs to 3.5 lbs, and its carcase weight jumped from 22 lbs to 60 lbs. Likewise, the yield of wheat almost doubled from about 10 bushels per acre in most of England in 1300 (although there were some districts where it was higher) to about 20 bushels in 1700 and then increased by only a further 10 per cent over the course of the eighteenth century (Allen 1992, 1999, Turner, Beckett and Afton 2001, Brunt 1999, 2004). Yields of other grains increased proportionally.

Yields rose because of both genetic and environmental improvements. Farmers controlled the reproduction of their plants and animals by selecting seed corn from the best plants – this was first observed during the seventeenth century – and by choosing the best animals for breeding. The productivity of the genetic material was enhanced by improving the growing environment. In the case of animals, that meant feeding a diet of more abundant and nutritious grass (the result of improvements in pasture) and of cultivated beans, clover and turnips. The yield of corn was also boosted through improved nutrition, although much of this must have been unintended. The increased cultivation of peas, beans and clover, which was largely dictated by the desire to expand animal production, augmented the stocks of nitrogen in the soil by fixing atmospheric nitrogen. The build-up of soil nitrogen was a very slow process, but it pushed up the yield of wheat by about 5 bushels per acre over several centuries, and, thus, accounted for a considerable proportion of the rise in yield. The rest was due to improvements in seed and to better tillage from improved ploughs and so forth that made it easier for corn to absorb nutrients (Allen 2008).

Improved area relative to total area

Productivity also increased because land was improved. This process was most dramatic in the Netherlands where so much land was reclaimed from the sea. Reclamation was also undertaken in England where Dutch engineers were employed to supervise the draining of the fens. Improvements in grazing land, already alluded to, were of great importance to English productivity. In 1300, there were perhaps 2 million acres of improved meadow and pasture and 20 million acres of common grazing. By 1700, about 7 million acres of common had been improved, and, in the eighteenth century, a further 8 million acres of 'waste' were converted to 'pasture' (Allen 1994, p. 104). These were not simply changes in nomenclature but involved real improvements in the quality of the land. In northern England, for instance, the enclosure of common pasture meant surrounding fields with walls, the stone for which was collected from the surface of the newly enclosed land. Removing surface rock in itself increased the growth of grass.

Total area per worker

This is more easily thought of in terms of its reciprocal, labour per acre. This term was affected by offsetting trends. On the one hand, the increase in improved area pushed up employment since enclosed pasture was tended more intensively than common grazing. On the other hand, labour per improved area fell in England during the early modern period. Enclosure that involved the conversion of arable to grass cut farm employment. The shift from small-scale family farms to large-scale farms also reduced agricultural employment. The declines were particularly sharp for women and children, but the number of full-time male jobs per acre also fell (Allen 1988, 1992). Finally, employment was also affected by the price of farm products relative to wages. For instance, when grain prices were very high during the Napoleonic Wars, farmers hired extra workers to get the most they could out of the land.

Agricultural labour productivity depended on the balance of these factors. Output per improved acre and improved acres relative to total agricultural land both tended to push up output per worker in the centuries after 1500. Employment per acre, on the other hand, had a variable effect depending on whether employment-creating or employment-reducing changes predominated.

Did enclosure raise output and productivity?

The oldest explanation for the rise in efficiency in early modern English agriculture is the enclosure of the open fields. Arthur Young, for instance, denounced open field farmers as 'goths and vandals'. This assessment was amplified by Lord Ernle (1912, p. 248) in a sweeping and highly influential interpretation: 'The agricultural defects of the intermixture of land under the open-field system were overwhelming and ineradicable', and 'no increased production or general adoption of improved practices could be expected under the ancient system.' Likewise, the large-scale tenant farmers were supposed to have been more innovative than yeomen farmers since the former had to generate the cash to cover their wage bill and their rent, while the latter often owned their land and relied on family labour so they lacked the need for money that pushed the large-scale tenant forward.

It is easy to show that, at best, this critique is hopelessly overstated. Consider, for instance, Ernle's (1912, p. 199) extravagant claim that open field farmers were 'impervious to new methods'. This can be tested by comparing the cropping patterns in open and enclosed villages. Such comparisons generally show that open field farmers adopted many features of improved practice. This is quite clear for the seventeenth century when peas and beans were coming into widespread usage, for open field farmers adopted them wherever they were appropriate. The late eighteenth century shows a mixed pattern. Open field farmers adopted the new crops, clover and turnips, to a great extent. However, enclosed farmers retained the lead, for they adopted these crops more completely than open field farmers, who tended to preserve elements of the old system along with the new (Allen 1992, pp. 107–29). The greatest difference in land use between open field and enclosed farming was in areas where grazing was the most profitable use of the land. Enclosed farmers typically had most of their land under grass. Open farmers retained a higher proportion under crops, although less than their counterparts in arable districts.

The differences in cropping between open fields and enclosures in the eighteenth century were not of great consequence since they did not involve much loss in output or productivity. The difference in efficiency between the middle ages and c. 1800 is an important yardstick, since it shows how much progress the two systems had made from the medieval baseline.

Crop yields have been one of the most frequently used indicators of agricultural productivity, and Table 3.1 summarizes the results for the English south midlands c. 1800. The yield data are arranged in three districts reflecting the agricultural potential of the soil. The greatest difference between open and enclosed farming was in the heavy arable district. It was characterized by clay that required subsoil drainage for high yields. Enclosure facilitated draining, and, indeed, in this district spring grains in enclosed villages yielded about one-third more than open villages. The yield differential for wheat, however, was negligible

Table 3.1 *Crop yields and enclosure, c. 1800*

	Open bushels per acre	Enclosed bushel per acre	Enclosed relative to open	Gain relative to yield increase from middle ages to nineteenth-century enclosures
Heavy arable district				
Wheat	19.7	20.2	2.2	5.3
Barley	26.5	31.8	20.0	35.3
Oats	23.5	33.0	40.4	44.6
Beans	18.8	22.2	18.1	27.9
Average	21.2	24.1	14.7	23.8
Light arable district				
Wheat	20.0	19.7	-1.5	****
Barley	27.0	29.3	8.5	18.4
Oats	26.5	32.5	22.6	28.8
Beans	19.9	18.1	-9.0	****
Average	23.4	24.7	5.6	10.9
Pasture district				
Wheat	20.9	21.9	4.8	8.9
Barley	28.0	32.2	15.0	27.3
Oats	36.9	38.1	3.3	4.5
Beans	22.4	23.4	4.5	7.5
Average	24.7	26.7	8.1	14.2

Source: Allen (1992, p. 136).

and the overall advantage of enclosed farming only 15 per cent. This differential corresponded to about 24 per cent of the gain that enclosed farmers had made since the middle ages. In the light arable district, where clover and turnips were the road to improvement, the yield difference between open and enclosed villages was about 6 per cent, and, in the pasture district, where a high proportion of land was laid down to grass following enclosure, yield differences were also moderate – about 8 per cent. These differentials corresponded to 11 per cent and 14 per cent of the advance made by enclosed farmers over medieval corn yields. Ernle's judgment that open field farmers were 'impervious to new techniques' is wide of the mark since they accomplished 76 per cent, 86 per cent and 89 per cent of the advance of the enclosed competitors depending on the natural district (Allen 1992, pp. 133–7, 2002, p. 19). This conclusion is not unexpected since open field farmers were leaders in cultivating peas and beans in the seventeenth century, and legumes were an important source of the nitrogen that pushed up crop yields.

We can also compare open and enclosed farming in terms of labour productivity. This has been done for the districts in the south midlands just discussed. Labour productivity equals output per worker, and in these calculations 'output' is the value (in 1806 prices) of farm production net of seed and feed. The workforce is measured by the cost of farm labour including the value of the farmer's time.

As with yields, the comparisons show enclosed farming to have been slightly more productive. In the heavy arable district, output per worker was 11 per cent higher under the enclosed system. In the light arable district, the advantage dropped to 3 per cent. In most pastoral areas, the differential ranged from a 6 per cent lead for the open fields to a 12 per cent advantage for enclosures. The only case where enclosed farming had a substantial advantage was some old enclosures where productivity was 81 per cent greater than in the open fields. The basis of this performance was the intrinsic superiority of the grasslands rather than the character of the farming. Parliamentary enclosures could not match it.

These differentials need to be interpreted in terms of the aggregate growth in labour productivity, which jumped over 50 per cent from 1500 to 1750. As with yields, enclosure accounted for little of the advance. In other words, open field farmers accomplished most of the growth in productivity that occurred in the country as a whole.

Total factor productivity (TFP) is a third way to compare open and enclosed farms, and it has become widely used. TFP is the ratio of farm output to an index of all of the land, labour and capital employed in production. One reason for its popularity is that it can be inferred from land rents, which are abundantly documented. Some additional economic assumptions must be made, however: if land markets are in equilibrium, then rent differences (adjusted for differences in input and output prices) indicate TFP differences since more efficient farmers generated more surplus than less efficient farmers, and the surplus accrued to landlords as rent. Enclosed farms generally rented at higher rates than open field farms, but the implied TFP differences were small both in absolute amount and compared to the rise in TFP between the middle ages and the nineteenth century. Moreover, the rent differential between open and enclosed farms may have overstated the efficiency differential since the assumption that rental markets were in competitive equilibrium was particularly problematic for early modern agriculture. In that case, the rent increases at enclosure may have involved income redistribution as well as income creation (Alien 1992, pp. 171–87).

How did open field farmers modernize?

One of the most powerful critiques of open fields was advanced in 1766 by H. S. Homer (1766, pp. 7–8): 'The necessity of universal agreement among proprietors especially where they are numerous is an almost insurmountable obstruction to any improvements being made in lands during their open field state.' The adoption of new crops by open field farmers, of course, calls this judgment into question. How can their innovativeness be squared with Homer's view that unanimity was required to introduce new crops? How was agreement achieved? Was unanimity really required or could change be introduced without universal consent? How were decisions taken in the open fields?

Innovation in the open fields raises further questions about the institutional basis of technical change. Agricultural innovation involves costs of research and development in each locality since the culture of new crops has to be tailored to local conditions. Not only does this principle operate across great distances (Mediterranean farmers, for instance, could not raise output by simply copying English and Dutch practices), but it also operates over short distances and between districts with seemingly similar natural conditions. In the modern world, regional agricultural colleges and government extension services carry out the necessary experimentation. In the classic landlord model of the English agricultural revolution, R&D was performed by owners of great estates who devoted their home farms to agricultural experiments. The methods they pioneered were then adopted by their tenants, who were free to innovate since they operated enclosed farms. Landlords realized a return on their experiments through the higher rents paid by their tenants. This model has run into two road blocks. First, agricultural historians have found very few home farms operating as experimental stations and even fewer that discovered anything profitable (Beckett 1986, pp. 158–64). Secondly, innovation was occurring in the open fields, so they must have developed institutions that performed the same function. What were they?

These questions about the open fields can be answered only through case studies of decision-making. One village where we can do this is Spelsbury in Oxfordshire. It is only a single example, but it provides a glimpse into the inner workings of an open field village and shows the farmers performing experiments, innovating and making decisions in ways that contradict Homer's condemnation. Joan Thirsk (1985, pp. 547–58) has described a group of seventeenth-century agricultural improvers centred around Samuel Hartlib. These were gentry living around England who were actively engaged in experiments on crops like clover that were being introduced from the Netherlands. The cultivation of clover involved many practical problems. The members of Hartlib's circle experimented on different approaches and wrote to him about them. He published some of this correspondence and distributed other information in letters to his associates. The members of the group could build on each other's research. A process of collective invention brought clover cultivation to England.[5] The introduction of sainfoin, turnips and clover into the open fields of Spelsbury presented comparable problems, and they were solved in ways reminiscent of Hartlib's circle.

Spelsbury is a particularly large parish (3,900 acres) and consisted of three distinct villages – Taston, Fulwell and Spelsbury itself. Each had its own field system. Most farms were small enough to be operated by families and were held as traditional copyhold tenures. Consequently, the farmers had a long-term, proprietary interest in the soil, so they benefited financially when they found ways to raise its productivity.

The first new crop we can track is sainfoin, which was a grass that diffused across Oxfordshire at the beginning of the eighteenth century. It was adopted in Taston in 1701 when the copyholders agreed to withdraw some strips from the open fields and combine them into an improved meadow. The agreement calls this 'inclosing', and it was in the sense that the land was removed from the fields and fenced with walls or a hedge. Many features of open field organization, however, were preserved in its management. The land, for instance, was not

[5] See Allen (1983) for a discussion of collective invention in industry.

consolidated – each farmer retained his strips, which were mowed, in the first instance, for hay. Later, the meadow was grazed in common by the village herd. Each copyholder was responsible for maintaining the field's boundary where it crossed his property. Three fieldmen were chosen from among the copyholders to establish when the meadow would be planted and when the village herd would be pastured on it. Violations of the agreement were punishable by fines paid to the lord. The Taston sainfoin agreement created an improved meadow operated in the manner of the open fields.[6]

How much agreement was required for the meadow's creation? Unanimity was apparently needed, for the agreement was signed by all the copyholders of Taston as well as William Canning, the estate's steward.[7]

While the existence of the agreement shows that unanimity was not the impossible hurdle that Homer suggested, unanimity clearly involved strains that were difficult to overcome. We have no record of the discussions preceding agreement, but there was clearly dissension in the following year that threatened its continuation.

Canning summarized the situation in a letter to the Earl of Litchfield on 3 April 1703. 'At the Court I found a great disturbance a Mungst them of Tastone and Fullwell about Settling their Methods of Managing the sainfoine Grass that they had Sowed.' It was not surprising that the management of the sainfoin was debated in the manorial court since it was the body which normally administered the fields. Canning saw the cultivation of sainfoin as 'like to be a great Improvement if it be inCouraged, & carryed on as it should be'. Not all of the copyholders agreed, however. 'I found so much Crossness . . . a Mong the Mainuagers of it; that, if they be not overawed, the designe will soon be destroyed.' There were two dissidents. 'Therefore, I took upon me to force Wilt. Rooke & John Hull of Tastone to a better Comployance, and the way that I took was the next day after the Court, I took John Freeman [another copyholder in Taston] with me & went to them both.' Canning 'told them that, if they wold not Imedially Comploy

6 Havinden (1961) was the first to study these sainfoin agreements and the first to realize their importance in assessing open field farming.

7 This conclusion is based on a comparison of the Spelsbury quit rental for 1703 (DIL II/b/33) and the Taston Inclosure Agreement (DIL II/n/1). All documents referenced in this section are deposited in the Oxfordshire County Record Office.

to the Well ordering of all those Matters we had on foote, I wold forthwithe Report to ye Losp, their Ill Manners & misbehaviour at the Court Thursday that their should be such a course taken with them as to have them severely punished'. In addition, Canning threatened them in other ways, for instance by punishing them 'for leting their Houses run to Ruin'. In addition, 'for every little offense which they should commit against ye well ordering of the Sainfoine I would have a writ on their Backs, and as for Hull if he did not Imediably pay me 20s for the Tree he cut down I wold serve him with a Writ the next day'. These threats worked. 'So then they bothe agreed with me that they Wold comply to any orders I should make.'[8]

Coercion by manorial authorities was one solution to Homer's problem. But the usual solution in Spelsbury was to make the introduction of new crops voluntary. An example was the 1708 agreement to enclose land in Spelsbury. The purpose of the agreement was to make 'a certain quantity of land Every years Land', that is, land that was continuously cropped. As in Taston, communal grazing was practised after the harvest, fieldmen were chosen to regulate the grazing, and fines were assessed for violations of those rules. The main difference with the Taston agreement was that each copyholder could use his Every Year's Land as he liked – 'to soo Corne or Sainfine or What they please'.[9] The sensible use of this enclosure was to cultivate sainfoin as in Taston, but that was not required of everyone at the outset. It is likely that it became the usual practice, however. Court records later in the eighteenth century refer to the 'old sainfoin' field,[10] as does the field map prepared at enclosure.[11] By providing flexibility at the outset, the kind of disputes that occurred at Taston were avoided, the entrepreneurial copyholders could proceed with experiments, and the others could adopt the sainfoin culture after it was proved in their village.

Sainfoin was not the only crop to be introduced into Spelsbury's open fields. Clover and turnips were also adopted in the mid-eighteenth century. The first reference to turnips is in the 1751 manorial court rolls, and the voluntary approach was used at the outset: 'we do order and agree that the Over Furlong Shooting into Chipping Norton Road in a field called Sinquefoil field in Spelsbury be sowd with turnips this next Season.' Significantly, turnip culture was not introduced into the open fields themselves but into the sainfoin enclosure created in 1708

[8] DIL I/k/1h. [9] DIL II/n/26. [10] E.g. DIL II/w/134. [11] Misc. Sta. I/1.

as Every Year's Land. It was being used as an experimental field to test out the new crop. In the original agreement, everyone was allowed to decide what to grow on his strips in that field, and the principle of voluntarism was explicitly recognized in the 1751 order: 'every person shall make his own mind.'[12]

In later years, the procedures were modified. Although the cultivation of turnips was still confined to the 'sainfoin enclosure', cultivation became obligatory. Unanimity was not required, but the majority ruled. Thus, the 1758 field orders state that: 'We do order and agree to Sow White Turnips the next Season in such part of Spelsbury Field called Old Saint Foyne Field as the Landholders or Major part of them shall by next May Day Agree.'[13] Presumably, the management of the field was more efficient if everyone's cropping was the same, and that was the motivation for this change. The open fields were mixtures of private ownership and communal control. In this instance, giving precedence to the collective rather than the individual facilitated innovation.

The year 1762 witnessed two momentous changes in cropping. First, turnip cultivation was shifted from the sainfoin enclosure to the open fields themselves: 'We order & agree that the Barley quarter shall be sowed with Turnips.'[14] The orders for the next year were more explicit in indicating that the turnips were to be planted in Briar furlong and Witner Beer furlong.[15] Secondly, clover was introduced into the fields.

> Also We agree to plant almshouse Furlong and Winter Bere with Clover and that the same shall be hained [fenced] from Christmas Day to tenth of April under the penalty of ten shillings for each person who shall turn in any Cattle between Christmas and the said Tenth of April.[16]

In this case, there was no experimental period when clover was tried out on Every Year's Land. Instead, it was introduced directly into the fields, indeed, in an obligatory fashion. Cultivation, however, was confined to only part of the fields.

The 1760s and 1770s were decades of experimentation in which the villagers perfected the rotation scheme that was best for the soil. The 1760s saw a rotation of clover and turnips over a small number

[12] DIL II/w/108. [13] DIL II/w/108. [14] DIL II/w/134.
[15] Ms summary of Spelsbury court rolls. [16] DIL II/w/134.

of furlongs. In 1765, for instance, winter beer furlong was planted with turnips, and briar furlong with grass seed.[17] This was a reversal of the practice in 1762. Gradually, the cultivation was spread to other furlongs. By the 1780s, the rotation had been perfected:

At this court it is agreed to sow Clover on Costar Hill and Dean Field side and that the same shall be hained at Michaelmas and broke the twelfth of July with Sheep and the Sheep to be stocked as usual And, to sow Turnips from Jack's Brake to Slate Pits and to hain the same as soon as they are up & that they shall be mounded by the Occupiers. And that the Clover shall lie two years at Coom Road to be hained the first of January and broke the twenty-sixth of April.[18]

The villagers had settled on a scheme in which land was planted for one year with turnips but two years with clover before rotating to other crops. Twenty years of experimentation underlay this decision.

Convertible husbandry, the systematic alternation of land between arable and pasture, was one of the most famous inventions of the agricultural revolution. The Taston court rules suggest that Taston farmers experimented with this practice from the 1760s onwards. For instance, the court rolls for 1766 recorded the conversion of field land to sainfoin for a twelve-year period:

Ordered . . . that the Field of Taston from the old St Fine wall down to Guys Close and as far as the Landholders can agree shall be planted with St Fine in the Spring of 1767 and mounded by the Michmas following by the Yard Land to continue for Twelve Years to be hained at Christmas and broke at Michmas but no sheep to go thereon at any time.[19]

The minutes for 1788 prescribe the planting of an old sainfoin field with turnips, the reverse sequence: 'Also it is agreed and ordered that Turnips shall be sowed on part of the Old Saint Foin down Deadman Hill as far as each tenant thinks proper and that the same shall be hained as soon as they are up.'[20] This was common practice in the Cotswolds at this time. Russell (1769, vol. I, p. 23) reports that:

Sainfoine is much sown in all this country, and lasts generally about ten years, some longer; and their method of breaking it up, as well as sheep

[17] DIL II/w/18. [18] Ms summary of Spelsbury court rolls.
[19] Ms summary of Spelsbury court rolls.
[20] Ms summary of Spelsbury court rolls.

pastures, after they have laid about ten years, is by paring and burning; they take off the surface about half an inch thick, and plough in the ashes for turnips, sometimes for wheat.

Converting field land to sainfoin enclosures for a dozen years, and then converting the land back to cultivation of turnips, clover and corn, amounts to convertible husbandry. These shifts were required of all occupiers. The need for unanimity did not prevent this. Perhaps the voluntary – presumably selective – incorporation of turnips, clover and sainfoin into the cropping system had both proven the worth of these crops and provided farmers with the opportunity to learn to cultivate them.

Homer was wrong in claiming that the need for unanimity prevented open field villagers from innovating. Indeed, the history of Spelsbury shows they supported agricultural experimentation. This was essential since, in 1700, no one knew the optimal way to integrate clover, turnips and sainfoin into an efficient farming system; that knowledge was developed by trial and error everywhere. Spelsbury was no exception.

What is perhaps more surprising is that the open fields were a suitable environment for this evolution, for two reasons. First, furlongs rather than fields were the fundamental operating units, so land could be shifted to new or experimental uses in small quantities. Secondly, not everyone in each furlong had to do the same thing. The first Spelsbury sainfoin enclosure was set up so that each person could grow what he wanted. The aim of the enclosure was certainly to grow sainfoin, and ultimately it did, but uniformity waited until the gains became obvious to everyone. (Failure to follow this procedure resulted in disputes like those in Taston. While manorial authority could force a minority to comply with a majority, voluntary procedures could achieve similar ends without coercion.) The voluntary principle was also applied again when turnip cultivation was tried. 'Every person shall make his own mind.' By letting those eager to try the new crops take the first steps, small-scale experiments were undertaken to establish whether and how the new crop should be cultivated. Other farmers soon followed. Eventually, majority rule replaced individual decision-making. Even then, however, the open fields catered to many tastes. By the end of the eighteenth century, the majority had not forced all the land to a four-course Norfolk rotation. Instead, a complicated system evolved incorporating the new crops but also retaining old practices like the use of the fallow. The inclusiveness of the decision-making process in Spelsbury helps to make the late eighteenth-century survey data intelligible. The flexibility of the open fields, which had a strength at the outset when it allowed enterprising individuals to try out new crops, became a weakness later since it continued to find a place for the least enterprising.

Why did farmers improve their methods?

In the classic model of the English agricultural revolution, innovation is caused by institutional change – enclosure, capitalist agriculture and so forth. We have seen, however, that all types of farmers – open and enclosed, large-scale and small – were improving their methods, so institutional change cannot have been the cause. Some other factor was responsible, and the growth of the urban economy is the obvious candidate. Campbell (2000, pp. 424–30) has recently argued that it was a lack of urban demand that held back agriculture in the middle ages. This thesis will be explored in the next chapter, as well as the view that inefficient institutions were the problem. Here we see what we can learn from price and wage history.

If the growth in the urban economy was causing agriculture to modernize, the influence must have been transmitted through markets, which were the main way the rural and urban economies were linked. The von Thünen (1826) model is commonly cited. In this model, urban demand raises the prices of goods that are expensive to ship and leads to their cultivation near the city. Yields per acre are high in all activities near the city since it paid to apply labour intensively to the land. Campbell (2000, pp. 424–30) argued that London affected the home counties in this way and suggested that corn yields would have been higher throughout England had there been more urban demand. Looking across the Channel, Grantham (1978, 1989) has argued that the growth of Paris raised agricultural prices near the French capital, and farmers responded with a more intensive, higher productivity agriculture.

There are examples of the growth of London affecting adjacent counties in this way in the seventeenth and eighteenth centuries. In England, markets were reasonably well integrated, and shipping costs for grain were small so its price did not vary greatly. Animal products were another story, however. While markets were integrated, transport costs were large, so the price of meat, for instance, was highest in London and lowest in Scotland and Wales (Young 1771b, 1771c). This differential led landowners near London to convert arable to pasture, and some seventeenth-century enclosure can be explained in this way (*Victoria County History, Cambridgeshire*, vol. XX). However, there is nothing to suggest that grain was cultivated more intensively in Hertfordshire than in Yorkshire nor were yields higher near London than in the hinterlands. Certainly, the rise in yields between the middle ages and the nineteenth century occurred in most parts of England and cannot be explained by London or any other urban demand.

Expanding cities affected agriculture through the labour market as well as through product markets. London was a high wage city throughout the early modern period. The growth of the Metropolis was so rapid – and mortality in the city was so high – that it was absorbing half of the natural increase in the English population (Wrigley 1987, p. 136). The result was a high rate of rural–urban migration that drew labour from many farming villages. By the end of the seventeenth century, the high wage economy spread to other towns and cities in southern England, and by the end of the eighteenth century the North was also drawn into the high wage orbit. The question is how agriculture was affected by the high wage economy.

One way to see the implications is to add farm incomes to the graphs of urban wages discussed in the last chapter. This is done in Figure 3.3, which includes the wages of farm labourers. Their earnings fell behind those of London building labourers in the seventeenth century, and the income gap was the reason so many farm workers moved to London. The difference between London and rural wages could have emerged because London wages were unusually high or because the rural wages were unusually low. International comparisons show that it was the former rather than the latter; in other words, the income gap did not emerge because enclosures flooded rural labour markets with dispossessed farmers who drove down wages, but rather because the expansion of the Metropolis increased demand and pulled up wages.

The incomes of farm employees, however, are less pertinent than those of farm operators, who were making the decisions that cumulated into the agricultural revolution. Figure 3.3 also plots the net income of a small-scale yeoman farm. The farm assumes 15 acres of arable land and typical numbers of animals, as indicated by probate

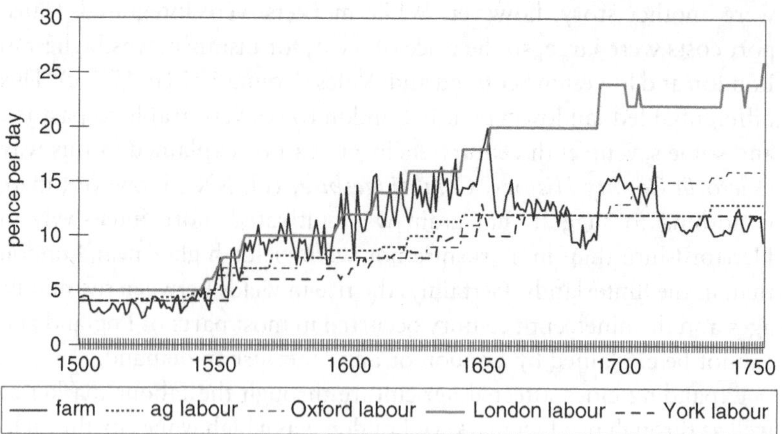

Figure 3.3 Farm and labourers' daily earnings

inventories. The annual net income is converted to a daily rate based on the number of days it took to work a farm of the specified acreage, crop rotation, animal numbers and yields. A key feature of the calculation is that it assumes medieval crop and livestock yields. The farm income shown in Figure 3.3, therefore, shows how well small farmers would have done if they did not modernize their methods.

Figure 3.3 suggests why open field farmers increased their productivity in the seventeenth century. During the price revolution – roughly 1550 to 1620 – agricultural prices rose more rapidly than any others. In this period, London was exploding, and the wages of London labourers leaped ahead of those elsewhere in the country. The rising farm prices meant that small farmers kept up with London living standards and moved ahead of labourers in the county towns. There was no great incentive to modernize in this period.

After 1620, the situation changed. Agricultural prices stopped rising, and farm incomes stagnated. As the ripples of growth spread to the small towns of southern England in the mid-seventeenth century, yeomen found themselves falling behind not only Londoners but also their neighbours in the towns. These gaps were particularly distressing due to the spread of the consumer revolution. The high real wages of the seventeenth century allowed artisans in the leading cities of northwestern Europe to enlarge their consumption beyond the bread, beer and meat that marked affluence in the late middle ages. Well-off workers could consume the newly abundant products of the tropics – pepper and other spices from the Indies, coffee, tea and sugar. In addition, 'luxury' manufactures were also added to the normal standard of consumption. These luxuries included books, clocks, cutlery, crockery, better furniture and so forth.

Farmers wanted this standard of living, too. They had several options. One was to sell the farm, move to London, and join the urban economy. Many yeomen did that. In the eighteenth century, great estates grew, in part, by buying up small freeholds and copyholds (Habakkuk 1940). The sellers of these properties were the yeomen leaving agriculture.

Another option was to raise productivity. There were two ways to do that, and they define the yeomen and the landlord agricultural revolutions. The former involved raising the income of the farm to keep pace with London consumption.[21] Sir James Steuart had the essential insight: 'a farmer will not labour to produce a superfluity of grain relative to his own consumption, unless he finds some want which may be supplied by the means of the superfluity.' Sixty years later, Gibbon Wakefield spelled out the global context:

> In England, the greatest improvements have taken place continually, ever since colonization has continually produced new desires among the English, and new markets wherein to purchase the objects of desire. With the growth of sugar and tobacco in America, came the more skilful growth of corn in England. Because in England, sugar was drank and tobacco smoked, corn was raised with less labour, by fewer hands.
>
> Quoted by Eagly 1961, pp. 55, 60

Higher crop and livestock yields could, indeed, keep the small farms viable. Figure 3.4 shows the daily income that a small farm could generate if real output increased smoothly by 50 per cent between 1630 and 1730. This was the order of magnitude of yield increases in this period. With this rise in productivity, the income of small farmers kept

[21] Weisdorf (2006) has developed a model in which rising productivity in commercial manufacturing lowers the price of manufactures, thereby increasing the desire of farmers to purchase them. Farmers respond by reallocating their effort from the home production of manufactures to the production of food to sell in order to buy commercially produced manufactures. In aggregate, labour moves from the farm sector to commercial manufacturing, and agricultural output per farmer rises. Weisdorf shows that the model describes early modern England.

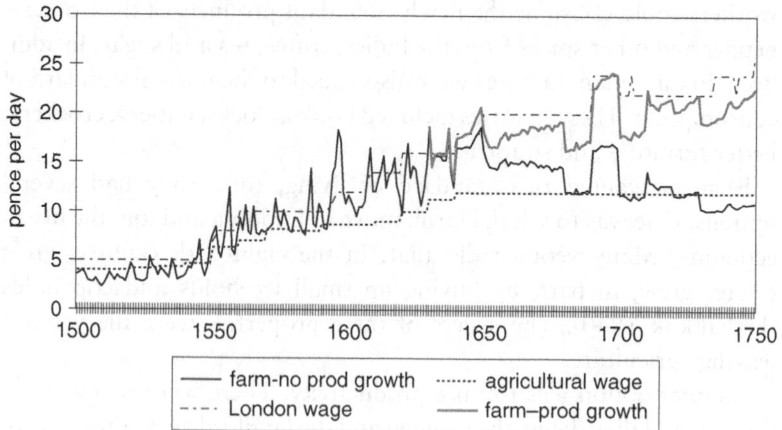

Figure 3.4 Alternative farm incomes with and without productivity growth

pace with labourers in London. That was a motive for an agricultural revolution, and it was a viable course of action.

Another way to respond to the high urban demand for labour was by farming with fewer people. This was done by amalgamating small holdings into large farms and enclosing open field arable and converting it to pasture. Kulak peasants followed this strategy by buying up the farms of their neighbours – many of whom were doubtless moving to London – and realizing the labour savings of large-scale operation. Enclosure and farm amalgamation were also the main strategies of the landlord's revolution. Whether pursued by landlords or kulaks, these strategies were effective in meeting the needs of the urban economy and pushed up agricultural productivity.

Conclusion

In the standard story of the agricultural revolution, the prime mover was the modernization of agrarian institutions – the enclosure of open fields and the replacement of peasant cultivation by capitalist farming. These changes increased output and (in Marxist accounts) reduced farm employment. The extra output made it possible to feed a larger urban or proto-industrial population and so fostered the growth of manufacturing. Institutional change in the countryside caused the growth of the city and propelled the economy forward.

There is some truth in the standard narrative, but causation ran more strongly in the opposite direction. London and the proto-industrial sectors were the engines of growth. Their expansion raised wage rates and drew labour out of agriculture. Small farmers either sold out and moved to the city or improved their methods and raised their yields in order to keep up with high urban incomes and participate in the consumer revolution. Landlords consolidated farms and converted land to pasture in order to economize on labour. Some yeomen who remained in farming did the same thing by buying up the small farms of their neighbours who moved to London. The result of these mechanisms was a substantial rise in farm output and an increase in labour productivity. The agricultural revolution was the result of the growth of cities and manufacturing.

4 *The cheap energy economy*

> Coal is one of the greatest sources of English wealth and plenty [and] the soul of English manufactures.
>
> Monsieur Ticquet, 1738[1]

In Chapter 2, we saw that eighteenth-century Britain was a high wage economy. That was one way in which it was distinctive and which helps explain the technological innovations of the Industrial Revolution. But expensive labour was not the only way in which Britain stood apart from other countries. Even more striking was the price of energy. The early development of the coal industry in Britain meant that it had the cheapest energy in the world. Learning to use that energy was an important incentive to technical change, and one which distinguished Britain from other high wage countries in Europe like the Netherlands.

Coal is making a comeback. Great nineteenth-century works like Jevons' *The Coal Question* (1865) attributed Britain's industrial pre-eminence to abundant coal, and the theme was developed in John Nef's classic, *The Rise of the British Coal Industry* (1932). Later in the twentieth century, however, coal was eclipsed by macro-aggregates like capital accumulation and residual productivity growth. With attention returning to the micro-bases of economic growth, coal is coming back into prominence. Environmental historians were the first to emphasize its role. 'The ecological roots of the English industrial revolution are not difficult to find. The initial stimulus to change came directly from resource shortages', pre-eminently a timber shortage due to 'an economic system expanding to meet the needs of a population growing within a limited area' (Wilkinson 1973, p. 112). Coal was the solution and made the Industrial Revolution possible. Some writers expand this insight into a series of historical stages defined by the pre-eminent fuel

[1] As quoted by Hatcher (1993, p. 547) citing Nef (1932, vol. I, pp. 222–3).

– wood, peat, coal, oil, hydroelectricity, nuclear energy (Boyden 1987, Smil 1994). Wrigley (1988) has popularized this paradigm among economic historians with his distinction between the 'organic' economy and the 'mineral fuel' economy.

Coal has also received attention from historians trying to understand why the Great Transformation occurred in Europe rather than Asia. Pomeranz (2000, p. 62), for instance, has pointed to coal as an exogenous factor that explains why Europe forged ahead of China in the nineteenth century. 'When we compare England to the Yangzi Delta where similar incentives existed to relieve pressure on the local wood supply, and where advanced technology and a highly commercialized economy were also present, Europe's advantage rested as much on geographic accident as on overall levels of technical skill and much more than on any (probably nonexistent) advantage in the market efficiency of the economy as a whole.' A fixed point at last: Britain was first because Britain had coal – a fact of nature, not an artifact of history.

Indeed, coal was one of the success stories of early modern Britain. The medieval economy was propelled by animals, humans, water and wind. Wood and charcoal were the main sources of thermal energy for heating and industrial processes. A little coal was taken from all the major fields but did not account for a significant share of the energy supply. There was a national market for coal for lime burning and blacksmithing – two uses for which it was especially well adapted. There were also some small, local markets as on the northeast coast where coal was used to boil down sea water for salt (Hatcher 1993, p. 430). The situation was broadly similar in other countries, for small amounts of coal were scratched from outcrops on all of the major coal fields. Nowhere was the coal industry large, and Britain was certainly not in the lead.

All this changed after the mid-sixteenth century. Between 1560 and 1800, output increased sixty-six-fold (Table 4.1). Half of the growth was accounted for by mines in Northumberland and Durham, and the bulk of that coal was shipped to London, which was growing rapidly. The rest of the coal was mined in the coal fields of western Britain, Scotland and Wales and generally served more local markets. The only other place in the world with a large industry was what is now southern Belgium. The mines around Liège and Mons were producing about 2 million tons a year around 1800 – about as much as Scotland and 13

Table 4.1 *British coal production, 1560–1800*

	Coal production (thousands of tons)		
	1560	1700	1800
Scotland	30	450	2,000
Cumberland	2	25	500
Lancashire	7	80	1,400
North Wales	5	25	150
South Wales	15	80	1,700
Southwest	13	150	445
East Midlands	20	75	750
West Midlands	30	5,10	2,550
Yorkshire	15	300	1,100
Northeast	90	1,290	4,450
Total	227	2,985	15,045

Source: Hatcher (1993, p. 68) for 1560 and Flinn (1984, pp. 26–7) for 1700 and 1800. Hatcher also gives figures for 1700. His total is 2,640 thousand tons. The figure for the northeast is similar to Flinn's. There are significant and offsetting discrepancies elsewhere. I have used Flinn's since he also provides estimates of consumption by sector (pp. 252–3).

per cent of Britain's total (Pounds and Parker 1957, p. 97). Elsewhere in the world, output was very low, scarcely above medieval levels. There is no doubt that Britain's coal industry took a commanding lead before the Industrial Revolution. In 1800, Britain was producing the vast preponderance of the world's coal.

This abundant coal made energy very cheap – at least in the mining districts. We will examine many energy prices in this chapter, for they are crucial for understanding the expansion and significance of the coal industry. Figure 4.1 gives a taste of the main results. The most striking is the low price of energy (based on coal) in Newcastle. Coal was, of course, mined near there and shipped to London. The Newcastle price was one-eighth of the London price, which indicates the burden of transportation. The Newcastle price was not unusual for British mining districts. Everywhere the pithead price in the eighteenth century was about four or five shillings per ton – about 0.75 grams of silver per million BTUs. These prices highlight two things: (1) Britain's cheap energy economy, which was located in the mining districts; and (2)

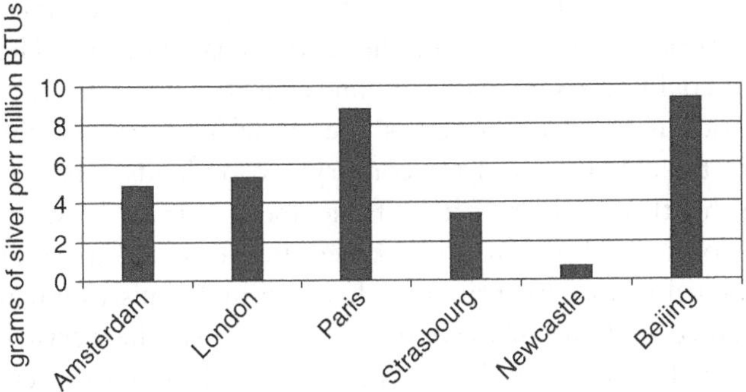

Figure 4.1 Prices of energy, early 1700s

the two-tier structure of prices in Britain with low prices in the coal-producing counties and higher prices in the consuming counties.

Even in the consumption centres, however, the prices were not exorbitant. The price of energy in London shown in Figure 4.1 is also derived from the price of coal. This price was moderate by international standards, and close to the price in Amsterdam, which is based on peat. With their abundant wood supplies, prices were lower in central Europe (on the order of Strasbourg's). Even these prices, however, were quadruple those in northern and western Britain. Fuel was expensive in Paris, which was very large and dependent on wood. Madrid and Valencia were close seconds in Europe. Both lacked coal and abundant forest cover. Fuel was also expensive in Asia, as Beijing shows.

Did the cheap energy economy matter? Coal was, indeed, critical for British industrialization because it provided an inexhaustible (*pace* Jevons) supply of cheap energy. Coal was also important, as we shall see, for its technological spin-offs, the steam engine and the railway. Combined with metals, coal was the basis of the engineering industries that mechanized manufacturing and integrated the world economy in the nineteenth century. In all of these ways, coal separated Britain from the rest of the world, including, in particular, the high wage economy of the Low Countries.

The present chapter is concerned with explaining how and why the cheap energy economy emerged in Britain. It is not simply a question of coal being in the ground, for Britain's coal deposits were largely ignored at earlier dates and the exploitation of the coal resources of other countries – Germany and China are important examples – occurred centuries after the rise of the British coal industry. The exploitation of coal had social and economic causes. The most established explanation is Nef's 'timber crisis' theory, which attributes the shift to coal to the exhaustion of the country's wood lands. There is some truth in this theory, at least in so far as the coal trade between the northeast coast and London is concerned, but it fails to account for what happened in western Britain and, surprisingly, misses much of the significance of London's economy. I argue that the decisive factor explaining the growth of the coal industry was Britain's success in the world economy. This led to the expansion of London with its high wage economy and, in consequence, an enormous growth in the demand for fuel in southeastern England. Coal met that demand. For that response to occur, however, residential housing had to be redesigned so that coal could be used in the home. The high rate of house construction in London was a fertile ground for those design innovations. Once the coal-burning house was invented, it spread to western and northern Britain where coal had always been a cheap – but unusable – fuel. Growing residential demand (rather than the exhaustion of woodlands) led to growing output outside of the northeast coast.

The growth of London and the rise of the coal trade

The problem is to explain why the British coal industry grew so enormously after 1560 and why a parallel process of expansion did not occur elsewhere. We shall first look at the growth of coal production on the northeast coast, which was intimately tied in with the growth of London, the main market for this coal. Then we will consider the growth of output on other British coal fields. Finally, we will consider why Dutch urbanization did not lead to a parallel expansion in the continental coal industry.

The most venerable explanation for the growth of British coal production was proposed by John Nef in his classic, *The Rise of the English Coal Industry* (1932). The trigger for adopting coal was a 'timber crisis' in the Tudor period. 'Between the accession of Elizabeth and the Civil War, England, Wales, and Scotland faced an acute shortage of wood, which was common to most parts of the island rather than limited to special areas, and which we may describe as a national crisis without laying ourselves open to a charge of exaggeration' (Nef

1932, vol. I, p. 161). England cut down its forests first, which is why it developed its coal before France or Germany. Continental countries followed suit a century later. 'By the end of the seventeenth century . . . the timber crisis had become general in all the countries of western Europe' (Nef, 1932, vol. I, p. 162).

Many have questioned the reality of the timber crisis (Flinn 1959). Hammersley (1957), for instance, argued that 'the much-vaunted fuel shortage . . . was always a strictly local and limited phenomenon'. In support of his view that there was abundant timber in Britain, Hammersley pointed to surveys of Crown Forests that showed difficulty in selling timber and – even – timber rotting for lack of buyers, as well as the lower value of land as forest than as farm. While acknowledging objections of this sort, however, Hatcher (1993) endorses an updated version of the timber crisis theory in his magisterial history of the early modern coal industry. Nef would certainly have approved his key chapter: 'From Abundance to Scarcity: Fuel Shortage and the Rise of Coal, 1550–1700'.

Prices are the litmus test for the timber crisis: if there really was a crisis, then the prices of firewood and charcoal should have been rising and, indeed, rising faster than prices in general. Nef recognized this and supported his thesis with *one* London price series. It is the wood price series shown in Figure 4.2. The figure also plots two series of charcoal prices for London and vicinity compiled since Nef wrote. All prices are expressed in grams of silver per BTU. At first glance Figure 4.2 supports Nef's view: wood fuel prices rose substantially after 1550 when the coal industry took off.

The facts are a little murkier, however. First, Nef's wood series[2] rose more rapidly than the charcoal series up to the 1630s and thus overstates the growth in wood fuel prices generally. Secondly, as Nef recognized, the period 1550–1640 was marked by inflation, so wood

[2] Drawing on Wiebe's *Zur Geschichte der Preisrevolution des 16 und 17 Jahrhunderts* (1895, p. 375), Nef (1932, vol. I, p. 158) contrasted an index of the price of firewood between 1451 and 1632 and a general price index. The former rose much more rapidly than the latter. Wiebe took his firewood index from Thorold-Roger's *A History of Agriculture and Prices in England* (1866–1902). Later writers have relied heavily on this comparison with only minor emendations. Wilkinson (1973, p. 112), for instance, reprints Wiebe's series through 1702, and Sieferle (2001, p. 86) reprints Wilkinson. Various odd prices are discussed in support of the view that wood was becoming scarce on the continent in the eighteenth century, but the data are unsystematic and very patchy.

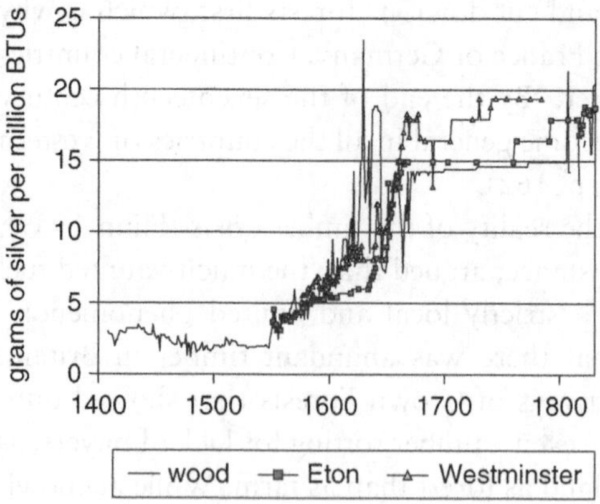

Figure 4.2 Prices of wood fuels in London

Source: wood: Thorold-Rogers (1866–1902); Eton: Beveridge (1939, pp. 144–7), price of charcoal; Westminster: Beveridge (1939, pp. 193–5), price of charcoal.

fuel prices must be compared to a general price index and to coal prices to test their significance. Figure 4.3 plots the 'real price' of coal, i.e. its price divided by a general price index,[3] and the real price of wood fuel based on intermediate values of the various series shown in Figure 4.2.

Figure 4.3 confirms Nef's view in an attenuated way:

1. The real price of wood fuel was higher in the second half of the sixteenth century than it had been before, and it rose again to a new plateau after 1650.
2. There was little difference between the prices of coal and wood fuel before 1550.
3. There was a slump in the real price of coal in the next half-century. This is not unexpected since transport facilities were dramatically improved in this period. Perhaps the slump in the coal price was not significant, however, since it was reversed in the seventeenth century. The overall impression is that the real price of coal in London was trendless for several hundred years. This suggests that the industry could vastly increase its output at constant cost.

[3] The general price index is the consumer price index used in Allen (2001). It shows prices relative to the average prices in Strasbourg in 1745–54. 'Real prices' measured in this way are interpreted as the prices that would prevail at the price level of Strasbourg in the mid-eighteenth century.

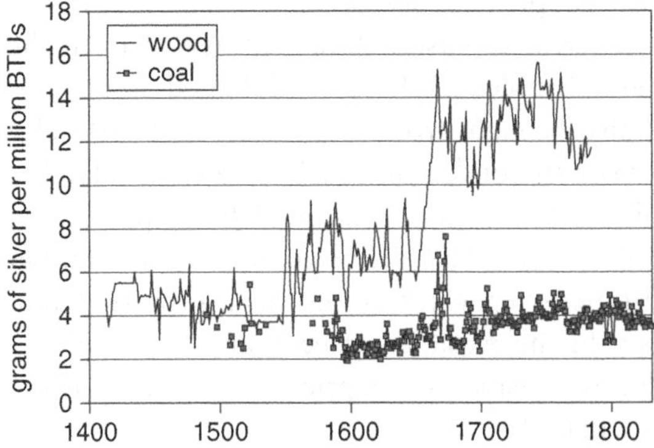

Figure 4.3 Real prices of wood and coal in London

Sources: wood: composite of the wood and Eton series in Figure 4.3; Coal: price delivered to London destinations from Mitchell and Deane (1971, pp. 479–80); both series deflated by the London consumer price index described in Allen (2001).

4. The price of charcoal was double the price of coal after 1550. Wood fuel prices lurched upwards in the 1650s, and the premium over coal became even greater. It was this gap between the prices of coal and charcoal that led to the surge in coal consumption.

The increase in wood fuel prices in London was the result of the city's enormous growth. In 1520, London's population was only about 55,000 (down from perhaps 75–100,000 before the Black Death). By 1600, it had jumped to 200,000. The population exceeded half a million by 1700, and almost one million at the beginning of the nineteenth century (Wrigley 1985). An exploding population combined with a high wage economy generated extraordinary growth in the demand for fuel in an extremely small area.

While the demand for fuel was geographically concentrated, the supply was necessarily dispersed. Much wood came from woodlands that were coppiced to maximize the sustainable yield. Under this system, trees were cut back to their stumps for timber. Then new shoots grew from the stumps to be harvested after about fifteen years when the cycle was repeated. Coppicing meant that land produced about one cord of wood per year. To supply London with wood required a vast and growing acreage to be harvested. Wood was very expensive to shift overland, less expensive by water. As a result, there was a timber supply area surrounding London that was defined by the costs of river and coastal shipping.[4] Wood from the upper Thames valley was assembled in Henley and floated down river to London. Wood was also brought from along the coast 120 miles from Mettingham in Suffolk to London and perhaps further (Hatcher 1993, p. 34, Campbell, Galloway and Murphy 1993, pp. 49, 86, 117). Increasing the volume of wood delivered to central London meant increasing the distance over which wood was transported and, thus, increasing the cost. In the parlance of economists, the supply curve of wood in London was rising, so the price of wood rose as the city grew and demand increased.

The transition from wood to coal was complicated by differences in the properties of the fuels. Coal was superior to wood for lime burning and blacksmithing, but in other uses wood was preferable. When coal and charcoal sold at the same price per BTU, as they did in the late fifteenth and the first half of the sixteenth centuries, the market for coal was confined to lime burning and blacksmithing; firewood or charcoal were purchased for other uses (Figure 4.3). Coal, of course, burnt with a foul smell and introduced objectionable impurities into manufactured goods, and so was regarded as an inferior product for those purposes. 'Coals are a less agreeable fewel than wood: they are said too to be less wholesome. The expence of coals, therefore, at the place where they are consumed, must generally be somewhat less than that of wood' (Smith 1776, p. 165). This is manifest in Figure 4.3 by the fact that coal sold at half the price of firewood in the first thirty years of extensive coal use. A 50 per cent discount was what it took to induce most buyers to choose the inferior fuel. After 1650, coal sold at an even greater discount to wood fuels.

Coal was what ecologists call a 'backstop' technology, that is, an energy source that can provide vast amounts of power at constant cost. Solar energy is a modern-day example. According to backstop theorizing, conventional energy is cheaper, which is why it is used initially. As conventional sources are depleted, the price of energy rises. When it reaches the cost of the backstop energy, then the latter comes on stream, and its cost caps the price of energy for the indefinite future. The backstop technology 'solves' the energy crisis by

4 Galloway, Keene and Murphy (1996) have mapped this region for medieval London, and the early modern pattern was similar.

providing unlimited supplies but at a higher price than the conventional alternatives.

Coal was a backstop technology that set a ceiling to the price of energy but in a curious way. We can see this ceiling in Figure 4.3. Coal could be delivered in vast quantities to London at the 'real price' of four grams of silver per million BTUs shown in Figure 4.3. Charcoal and firewood sold at higher prices per BTU since they were cleaner fuels, but price increases in those markets were limited by the steady price of coal in conjunction with the discount that made buyers willing to accept its undesirable features. Seen from this perspective, the steady price of wood fuel in the seventeenth and eighteenth centuries reflected the steady price at which the flood of northeastern coal reached London. Furthermore, unlike the usual backstop model, the price per BTU of energy did not rise in London as the backstop technology came into play. The supply of energy expanded at the late medieval price, although its quality declined.

The discount applied to coal also played an integral role in explaining when the east coast coal trade took off. The price of coal in London had to be high enough to cover the cost of mining the coal and shipping it to the metropolis. This was about 4 grams of silver in 'real' prices. In the fifteenth century, wood was so cheap that the coal market was limited to lime burning and blacksmithing. As the price of wood rose, the possibilities of using coal in other activities increased. By the 1580s, wood was selling at twice the price per BTU of coal. That discount was great enough to induce attempts to substitute coal for charcoal. As those attempts proved successful, the east coast coal trade took off. The timing is perfect: the coal trade took off when London got big enough to drive the price of wood fuel high enough to make it profitable to mine coal in Northumberland and ship it to London. The growth of the coal trade was the result of the growth of the capital – not of a general shortage of wood.

Stepping back from the details of the fuel market, we can now see the take-off of England's coal industry in global perspective. In Chapter 1, we argued that British urbanization – including the growth of London – was the result of the expansion of international trade. In the seventeenth century, the expansion was within Europe and based on wool; in the eighteenth century, the expansion became intercontinental and broader in its composition. The growth of London, in turn, drove the growth of the coal trade. Combining these propositions implies that Britain's early exploitation of coal was due to her success in the international economy. We habitually describe coal as a 'natural' resource. It is true that there would have been no coal trade had there been no coal in the ground. That much was a fact of nature. But the mere presence of coal was not sufficient to cause the coal trade. It was only activated by the growth of the international economy. Coal was a social artifact as well as a natural fact.

Learning to heat a house with coal

The discussion in the last section skims over an important feature of the coal market: The technology of energy consumers had to be reinvented in order to use coal. In some cases – evaporating sea water to extract the salt is an important example – the technical difficulties were slight, but in most applications they were serious. Had the technical problems not been solved, the market for coal would not have expanded as it did. Some purchasers of energy were manufacturers of glass, bricks, porcelain, beer, bread, metals and so forth. How some of them addressed their energy problems will be discussed when we consider the evolution of industrial technology. The most important use of coal in the seventeenth century, however, was residential heating. Flinn (1984, pp. 252–3) estimated that over half of Britain's net coal consumption was used for this purpose in 1700. Converting from wood to coal was not, however, simply a question of chucking one fuel rather than the other onto the fire. Switching fuels, in fact, presented complex design problems.[5]

These began with the layout of the house. The typical medieval house had a large hall or room that extended from the ground to the rafters. The fire for heating and cooking was built on a low hearth in the centre of the room. Smoke from the fire filled the space above the hearth and exited the dwelling through a hole in the roof. The smoky atmosphere was useful for curing bacon but not entirely salubrious. This design did have two advantages, however. First, the family could gather round the fire, and, secondly, the fire was away from the flammable walls making it less likely that the house would be burnt down. Had one put coal rather than wood on the fire in this house, two

[5] My discussion of the technical issues draws extensively from Hatcher (1993, pp. 409–18).

outcomes were in train. First, the sulphurous fumes of the coal smoke would have rendered the structure uninhabitable. Secondly, and much more likely, the fire would have gone out. For efficient combustion, coal must be confined in a small, enclosed space rather than the open hearth of the medieval house.

Burning coal, therefore, required an entirely new style of house. Chimneys were essential, and they were being built in great houses by the fifteenth century. Initially, stone or masonry walls were built in the house, and the open fire lit against them. A hood above the fire gathered the smoke and led it out through a chimney. Often a small room was built around the fire to husband the warmth.

The hooded fire was a first step towards coal burning but was not sufficient. An enclosed fire place or metal chamber was necessary to confine the coal for high temperature combustion. The coal had to sit on a grate so a draft could pass through. A tall, narrow chimney (rather than the wide chimney used with wood fires) was needed to induce a draft through the burning coal. This was necessary both to increase the oxygen supply to the fire as well as to vent the smoke upwards and out of the house rather than having it be blown back into the living quarters. To work well, the chimney had to narrow as it got taller. The termination of this design trajectory was the house designed around a central chimney with back to back fireplaces on the ground and first floors. It could burn coal and warm the house without filling it with smoke.

It took a long time and a great deal of experimentation to develop this style of house. Each element had to be perfected. That required trying out many different variants to see what worked best. Grates, for instance, could be made from metal or brick. Which was better? How big should the holes be? Such prosaic questions arose with all elements of the heating system. How big should the fireplace be? Should it be made with brick or metal? How could it be designed so that heat projected into the room rather than escaping up the chimney? How tall should the chimney be? How wide? Should there be a taper? How many twists and turns could there be in the flues? How could several fireplaces be connected to a central chimney without smoke passing from one room to the next? And so forth. Not only did the individual elements have to be perfected, but they had to be balanced against each other. Records of some of this work have survived, since some designs were patented and some people wrote books and pamphlets promoting their work. Much experimentation was surely done without any records being kept. Most of this experimental work was done in London, and the architectural results were destroyed when the city burnt down in 1666.

The one innovation whose adoption can be roughly dated is the chimney. John Aubrey remarked: 'Anciently, before the Reformation, ordinary men's houses . . . had no chimneys but flues like louver holes.' In 1576–7, William Harrison called 'the multitude of chimneys lately erected' one of the 'three things to be marvelled in England' in recent decades. Old men could remember that, in their youths, 'there were not above two or three' chimneys in the ordinary dwellings 'in most uplandish towns of the realm'. In the early sixteenth century, 'each one made his fire against a reredos in the hall, where he dined and dressed his meat' (quoted by Hatcher 1993, p. 411). Aubrey and Harrison indicate that the chimney was not common before the middle of the sixteenth century when chimney construction began in earnest. Harrison, at least, was talking about Essex. This is not very precise evidence, but it does indicate that the proliferation of chimneys occurred at the same time the market for coal took off in southern England.

Inventing the coal-burning house presented economic challenges that paralleled the engineering challenges. Consider what did not happened: had a modern economy faced the challenge of shifting from wood to coal, there would likely have been a large and coordinated research and development programme to solve the design problem. Nothing of the sort happened in the sixteenth and seventeenth centuries. Design innovation was left to the decentralized market. Since most of the innovations were unpatentable (the taper of a chimney was not a legal novelty), no one could recoup the cost of experiments through patent royalties. As a consequence, experiments were piggybacked onto commercial building. A builder erecting a house could change the design of a chimney to see if it worked better without any great cost or risk. His motive was to build a house that was more efficient to heat and would not fill with smoke since he could sell such a house for more money. If a design innovation proved successful, he or someone else could extend it and try to make it even better. Copying and elaborating innovations was the way the coal-burning house evolved. In this model, which is called 'collective invention', the rate of experimentation depended crucially on the rate of house building since commercial construction was the activity that financed the experiments.

The economics of collective invention highlights another way in which the growth of London was critical to the shift to coal. The first way, of course, was the rising price of wood, which motivated the shift. The second was the building boom, which was underpinning collective invention and which solved the problem. In the sixteenth and seventeenth centuries, London was growing very rapidly, and a very large number of new houses were being built in a small area. The high volume of construction provide innumerable opportunities to tack design experiments onto projects that were being undertaken for ordinary commercial reasons. The proximity of this building facilitated the sharing of information and allowed builders to extend each other's innovations and perfect the coal-burning house. Despite cheap coal in the ground, this sort of experimental work would not have taken place in small towns in the west midlands since not enough building was going on. London's boom created the incentive to shift to coal and subsidized the experiments that were needed to solve the technical problems that arose.

The growth of coal production outside the Northeast coal field

Half of Britain's coal was mined in Northumberland and Durham. Some of that coal was used by local, energy-intensive industries like salt and glass. Most of the expansion, however, was accounted for by the growth of London. Western England, Wales and Scotland accounted for the other half of the coal industry. This makes them important in their own right, and they are doubly important since they (not the northeast coast) were the centres of the Industrial Revolution. One reason that the Industrial Revolution occurred further west was that the coal was interspersed with metallic ores in those districts, while metals were unknown on the northeast coast.[6] Metal was not an important part of the story before the eighteenth century, however. Domestic heating absorbed most of the coal mined in western Britain in the seventeenth century, just as it did in eastern and southern Britain. We can ask why output grew rapidly in the midlands or Scotland in the seventeenth century, but the answer is bound to be different from the London story for geographical reasons. The enormous concentration

6 Iron ore was present in the Cleveland Hills but the main seam was not discovered until 1850 (Birch 1967, p. 334).

of people in the capital meant that wood prices shot up in London after 1550 due to the great distances wood had to be shipped to fuel the giant city. That same mechanism did not operate in the west midlands since there were no great cities: the centres of consumption were small and interspersed with the centres of production of both coal and wood.

The difference between London and western Britain stands out in the history of fuel prices. Figure 4.4 plots the 'real' prices of charcoal and coal (i.e. the actual prices divided by a consumer price index) in non-metropolitan England from the early sixteenth century to 1800. This graph must be regarded with great caution due to the disparate nature of the component material. Despite the scattered nature of the evidence, however, it shows some strong and powerful trends. First, in contrast to early sixteenth-century London where coal and charcoal sold at about the same price per BTU, coal in western Britain was always half as expensive as charcoal. Secondly, there is no evidence of a change in the relative prices of coal and charcoal before the Restoration in 1660. In particular, London's great increase in wood prices is absent. Thirdly, this situation changed in the late seventeenth century as charcoal prices rose rapidly and the real price of coal declined slowly. It was only then that western England was at last running short of wood.

The price patterns outside London point to a conclusion and to a puzzle regarding the growth of coal production. The conclusion is that rising wood prices were not the cause of coal expansion before the late seventeenth century. With the relative price of the fuels unchanging and steady compared to prices in general, the explanation for the growth in coal output must be a shift in demand rather than changes in the supply of fuels.

The puzzle is this: as early as 1538 when our data begin, coal was already half the cost of wood fuel. We do not have data for earlier years, but there is no reason to believe that the situation was different. Coal was always cheap to mine. Why did the shift to coal not occur earlier, in the middle ages for instance? One cannot say that medieval people did not know that there was coal to be had, for it was mined throughout the region. Without medieval coal and charcoal prices for western England we cannot definitively reject the possibility that wood was so cheap that no one had reason to use coal. However, a more likely explanation is the absence of demand for coal.

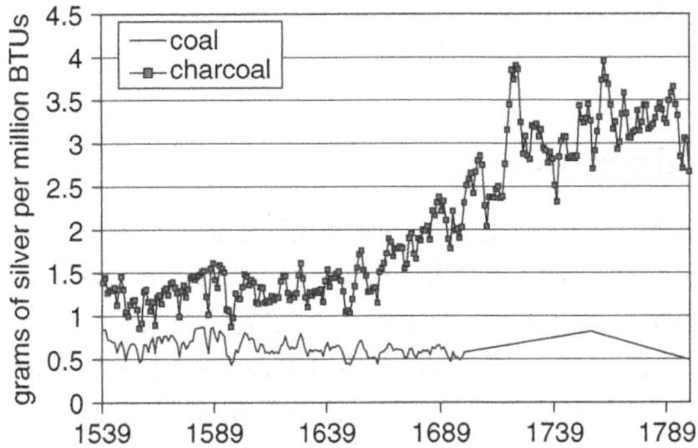

Figure 4.4 Real prices of wood and coal in the midlands

Why was there no demand for coal in the middle ages and why did demand for coal increase so much from 1538 onwards? Most coal in this period was used for domestic heating, and the answer to both questions is the invention of the coal-burning house. Before it was invented, people in western England or Scotland might well have thought, in an abstract sort of way, that they could cut their heating costs by burning cheap coal instead of wood. That was not feasible with their medieval hearths, however. One might ask why they did not invent the coal-burning house, but that was a complex and multifaceted problem, as we have seen. It was only solved through collective invention and that presupposed a high rate of house construction in a small area where builders could observe each other and exchange information. In western Britain, the population was too dispersed and too few houses were built for collective invention to be sustained. The use of coal throughout the British isles awaited the building of London, the laboratory that brought coal into the home.

Once the coal-burning house was invented, it spread across Britain. The replacement of medieval houses with these 'modern' structures, which generally had chimneys and fire places adapted for coal, is known as the 'Great Rebuilding' after Hoskins (1953). He thought it occurred mainly between 1570 and 1640, but it is now recognized that the Great Rebuilding ran into the early eighteenth century. This means that the Great Rebuilding was coterminous with the rise of the coal industry in western England, Scotland and Wales. Indeed, there was a reciprocal relation between the two: cheap coal was an incentive to replace old wood-burning houses, and building new housing increased the output of coal.

British energy in world perspective

The rise of the coal industry meant that Britain's energy situation was unique in the eighteenth century (Malanima 2000, 2006). This is apparent in terms of both the quantities of fuels and their prices.

We have already noted that Britain produced the vast proportion of the world's coal in the eighteenth century. Coal also loomed large from the British perspective. In the eighteenth century, most thermal energy consumed in Britain was probably produced by burning coal. This is seen most clearly in the case of England.

Thermal energy was produced by burning wood, coal or peat. Some peat was burnt in England, but its use was restricted to remote fringes of the kingdom. Wood and coal were the major sources of thermal energy. How much energy did they provide?[7] Around 1700, there were approximately 3 million acres of woodland in England, and this declined to 2.5 million acres in 1800. According to Gregory King, half of this acreage was used for fuel – i.e. 1.5 million acres in 1700 and, let us say, 1.25 million in 1800. An acre of woodland could produce about one cord of wood per year on a sustainable yield basis. The energy conversion coefficients used in this chapter imply that a cord of wood gave as much energy as 1.3 tons of coal, so the woodlands of England yielded the energy of 1.95 million tons of coal in 1700 and 1.625 million in 1800. These figures can be compared to the production of coal in those years – about 3 million and 15 million tons respectively. Coal was already more important than wood in 1700 and almost certainly supplied over half of the thermal energy including that derived from peat. By 1800, almost all thermal energy was derived from coal as well as a small amount of mechanical energy. No other country in the world was in this situation.

The abundance of coal was also manifest as a low price of energy in Britain. Tables 4.2 and 4.3 summarize much information about

[7] This discussion follows Hatcher (1993, pp. 54–5, 549) but uses somewhat different energy conversion figures. The conclusions are similar. Warde (2007, pp. 115–22) estimates that coal became a more important source of energy than wood during the seventeenth century.

worldwide energy prices between 1400 and 1800. The following points stand out:

1. The price of energy in most European and Asian cities was fairly stable. In Europe, the extremes were Spain, where wood fuels cost 10–12 grams of silver per million BTUs, and central Europe, where abundant forests kept prices down to 2–4 grams of silver per million BTUs. Most cities, however, had prices of the order of 5–6 grams of silver per million BTUs. In Asia, prices were on the high side. Prices in Puna were like prices in Spain, and Beijing was not much lower. The price of charcoal in Canton was close to the European norm. These prices did not trend upwards over time in real terms. There is no evidence here to support Nef's claim that continental Europe was experiencing a timber crisis.
2. The explosion of wood fuel prices in early modern London was almost unique. The rise of the coal trade did provide a solution to this problem. Coal did not, however, give London cheap fuel. The price of energy in the capital was about the same as in most European cities.
3. The gains to Britain from the rise of the coal trade showed up on the coal fields in northern and western Britain. Transport costs were so high that Britain had a two-tiered price structure. On the British coal fields, energy from coal cost less than one gram of silver per million BTUs and was only a fraction of the cost of energy elsewhere. This was the cheapest energy in the world. Even energy from charcoal was cheap in the west midlands.[8] The benefits of this cheap energy were reaped during the Industrial Revolution.
4. North America is well known for the abundance of its natural resources, but this advantage did not extend to energy, once the forests were cleared. Certainly, energy was not cheap on the east coast of the United States at the end of the eighteenth century. Around 1800, anthracite coal in Philadelphia cost 7 grams of silver per million BTUs. This was about the same as in London and many times the cost of energy in British cities on the coal fields. The price of anthracite on the eastern seaboard dropped in

[8] Of course, the cheap price of English coal depressed the price of charcoal, but for most of the period it remained high enough to pay the costs of coppicing. The supply of English wood fuel was not expandable to any degree, but it still paid to exploit the land to its full potential.

the 1830s as canals were built to link the coal fields to the coast (Chandler 1972). In the 1840s, anthracite cost about 15 shillings per ton in Philadelphia and New York – three times the cost of coal in Manchester or Edinburgh (von Tunzelmann 1978, p. 96). Early American industrialization, unlike British, was not based on cheap coal.

Dutch urbanization and the 'timber crisis'

The Low Countries were a particularly important counterpoint to Britain, for they also experienced intense urbanization based on international commerce in the early modern period, and, for that reason, they were the other high wage economy. One of the enduring mysteries is why they did not have an Industrial Revolution in the eighteenth century and why Britain overtook them. Coal is a big part of the answer.

Tables 4.2 and 4.3 report several price series for Antwerp and Amsterdam that throw light on these issues. The price history of Antwerp was the closest counterpart to London's. Antwerp experienced a similar increase in charcoal prices starting in the late sixteenth century. Coal was quoted sporadically in Antwerp starting in 1576. At that time, coal and charcoal were selling at about the same price per BTU. At these prices, the demand for coal was very limited. The continued rise in charcoal prices in the early seventeenth century, however, broadened the market for coal, and, from 1621, coal was regularly quoted. Antwerp's coal came from both the northeast coast of England and down the Meuse from Liège (Pounds and Parker 1957, pp. 129–30). Although Antwerp is not much further from Newcastle than London, coal was more expensive in the Low Countries. Nonetheless, coal in Antwerp cost about half the price per BTU of wood, just as in London. Evidently, a similar discount was required to induce consumers to buy the more troublesome fuel.

The history of Antwerp differs from that of London in one important way – demographic development. While the population of London ballooned, that of Antwerp fell. What then was driving up the price of firewood? It may, indeed, be that Antwerp was suffering from a decline in its timber supply. Possibly, the warfare surrounding the revolt of the Netherlands and trade reorientation following their independence disrupted supply routes.

Table 4.2 *The price of energy*

	Average cost of energy (grams of silver per million BTUs) for half-century beginning								
	1400	1450	1500	1550	1600	1650	1700	1750	1800
London, coal		1.68	1.57	2.67	3.26	5.00	5.26	6.47	8.16
London, charcoal	3.74	2.18	1.86	4.36	6.25	14.38	14.90	16.36	18.04
Northeast UK coast, coal			0.13	0.45	0.73	0.70	0.72	1.18	
Western UK, coal			0.24	0.51	0.77	0.81	0.81	1.13	1.13
Western UK, charcoal			0.44	0.94	1.61	2.53	3.25	5.34	6.17
Amsterdam, peat			1.81	2.64	4.48	4.47	4.88	6.39	11.61
Amsterdam, wood					2.92	4.05	4.24	5.44	8.91
Amsterdam, coal									7.52
Antwerp, charcoal	4.00	3.45	3.14	6.41	9.06	9.16	13.09	15.23	19.04
Antwerp, peat						6.71	20.94	23.82	22.89
Antwerp, coal				6.71	6.03	7.12	7.95	7.20	7.37
Paris					8.62	8.51	8.84	9.64	
Florence			3.17	4.69	6.36		5.63	5.58	10.23
Naples				7.61	9.03		5.37	6.13	8.75
Valencia	7.45	6.41	6.70	11.27	13.26	12.81	8.54	11.28	
Madrid				10.86	14.31	11.91	7.58	10.14	14.25
Strasbourg	1.94	1.30	1.22	2.38	2.98	3.01	3.41	5.46	11.28
Leipzig				3.43	4.78	2.96	4.12	3.62	
Vienna	1.42	1.15	1.01	1.61	2.07	2.10	2.35	2.82	2.98

Table 4.2 (*cont.*)

	Average cost of energy (grams of silver per million BTUs) for half-century beginning								
	1400	1450	1500	1550	1600	1650	1700	1750	1800
Gdansk			2.00	3.49	3.59	3.79	3.58	6.00	9.79
Warsaw				3.07	6.46	5.44	5.16	8.84	
Lwow			4.02	4.83	5.09	4.78	4.47	6.68	
Beijing							9.33	8.99	8.08
Canton							4.15	7.15	
Puna								15.26	11.03
Philadelphia									7.14

Sources: Allen (2003b, 2007a), Allen *et al.* (2007), and the sources cited there. Philadelphia computed from *Historical Statistics of the United States, Millennial Edition Online*, series Cc235, anthracite, average 1795–1805.

Table 4.3 *The real price of energy*

	Average real price of energy for half-century beginning								
	1400	1450	1500	1550	1600	1650	1700	1750	1800
London, coal		3.76	3.36	3.08	2.63	3.56	3.93	3.96	3.84
London, charcoal	6.35	4.50	4.14	5.91	5.08	10.21	11.15	10.08	
Northeast UK coast, coal			0.35	0.57	0.60	0.48	0.54	0.75	
Western UK, coal			0.69	0.69	0.63	0.58	0.63	0.65	0.50
Western UK, charcoal			1.30	1.26	1.30	1.80	2.49	2.97	2.67
Amsterdam, peat			4.04	3.01	4.09	3.70	4.21	4.87	7.08
Amsterdam, wood					2.55	3.39	3.57	4.23	5.67
Amsterdam, coal									4.57
Antwerp, charcoal	8.01	8.57	7.25	7.50	9.96	10.49	12.61	13.94	12.31
Antwerp, peat						15.31	20.28	23.15	15.92
Antwerp, coal				6.53	4.92	6.41	7.61	6.60	5.51
Paris					5.50	5.39	6.95	6.65	
Florence			4.73	4.79	5.02		6.10	5.13	6.38
Naples				7.88	8.45		7.01	5.85	5.39
Valencia	9.97	9.04	9.03	7.80	6.64	6.90	5.53	6.58	
Madrid				7.17	6.49	7.06	6.16	5.98	6.28
Strasbourg	2.82	2.25	2.08	2.54	2.38	2.69	3.34	4.30	5.93
Leipzig				4.18	3.73	3.05	4.21	3.69	
Vienna	2.87	2.58	2.34	2.65	2.15	2.72	3.20	3.31	2.76

Table 4.3 (*cont.*)

	Average real price of energy for half-century beginning								
	1400	1450	1500	1550	1600	1650	1700	1750	1800
Gdansk			5.35	6.06	4.60	4.54	4.96	6.99	6.01
Warsaw				6.70	9.50	9.99	8.78	10.81	
Lwow			6.34	6.26	7.83	6.09	7.03	6.38	
Beijing							10.85	9.41	7.11
Canton							5.14	7.66	
Puna								13.12	10.78

Source: Allen (2003b), Allen *et al.* (2007), Allen (2007a).

The history of Amsterdam differs from that of both London and Antwerp. The growth of the cities of the Dutch Republic led to a large increase in the demand for fuel just as the growth of London did. The supply of wood was governed by the same high transport costs as in England. Nevertheless, Dutch wood prices do not show the increases seen in the London and Antwerp series. The reason is that peat was the backstop technology of the Dutch. Peat was an organic fuel and was not suffused with sulphur like coal. Table 4.2 shows that the two fuels sold at similar prices per BTU. Evidently, consumers and industrial customers regarded peat and wood as equally valuable.

The vast reserves of peat in the Dutch Republic meant that the fuel was available in elastic supply. The canal system meant that it could be delivered to urban customers at low cost. The abundant supply of peat put a lid on wood prices. As a result, the shift from wood to peat took place without the wood price increases seen in London and Antwerp.

It was not inevitable that Dutch expansion relied on peat; it was only a matter of cost (Unger 1984). Coal was available from several sources – Newcastle, from where it could have been delivered to Amsterdam at the same price as to Antwerp, the mines in what is now southern Belgium, from where it could have been shipped down the Meuse to the Low Countries, and, potentially, from the Ruhr in Germany. Coal would have had to sell at a discount to peat to compensate for its lower quality, but, if the price of peat were high enough, or if the costs of mining coal low enough, it would have paid to fuel the Dutch cities with mineral fuel. This is what happened in the nineteenth century on a large scale.

What is most intriguing is whether it would have paid to float Ruhr coal down the Rhine to power Amsterdam. As it was, the transportation costs were too high and political divisions impeded movement. The Ruhr itself had to be improved and that was not done until the end of the eighteenth century. Political unity was not achieved until 1815 (Pounds and Parker 1957, pp. 98–9). It would take a detailed cost–benefit study to determine whether improving the Ruhr would have paid a century earlier. Perhaps it would have, in which case Amsterdam's reliance on peat was the result of political division and 'policy failure'. Alternatively, peat may have been so cheap – and British coal so affordable – that there was no point turning to inland coal until the nineteenth century.

The fates of Britain and the continent diverged because of their different fuel trajectories. The two-tier price structure was the secret to Britain's success, and it reflected the core–periphery orientation of the economy: London was the core and grew because of international trade. This growth led to rising fuel demand, and it was met by the development of coal mines on the northern and western peripheries of England. High transport costs meant that coal was extremely cheap on the periphery, and that is where the steam engine and coal based metallurgy were developed.

The parallel trajectory of development that might have unfolded – but did not – would have featured the cities of the Dutch Republic as the core. Their growth was, indeed, founded on success in the international economy, and it did result in a rise in fuel demand. Most of this demand was met, however, by Dutch peat. The alternative source of energy that was not tapped was the coal field of the Ruhr. An economic corridor running from Amsterdam up the Rhine to the Ruhr was the continental counterpart of Britain. It was the counterpart whose development was choked off by cheap peat. The peat precluded the development on the continent of the two-tier pricing structure of Britain. And it was those low fuel prices on the coal fields that motivated so much new technology in the eighteenth century.

Only in Antwerp, where peat was too expensive for ordinary use, did a development pattern like England's unfold. Coal mining in southern Belgium developed to meet the city's needs. Coal prices were low at the mines near Liège just as they were at Coalbrookdale, and, indeed, this was the part of the continent that most quickly adopted the technological breakthroughs of the British Industrial Revolution. The region was too small to make these breakthroughs on its own, however. Moreover, some of the development benefits of the Low Countries' demand for coal accrued to Britain since coal was imported from Newcastle as well as Liège. The early development of the north-east coast coal field gave England a 'first mover advantage' in this regard.

Conclusion

The cheap energy economy was a foundation of Britain's economic success. Inexpensive coal provided the incentive to invent the steam engine and metallurgical technology of the Industrial Revolution

– a theme we will develop in Part II of this book. The cheap energy economy also sustained the high wage economy.

One of the puzzling features of the high wage economy was how British firms could pay more for their labour than French firms, for instance, and yet remain internationally competitive. One reason is that British firms developed labour-saving machinery even before the Industrial Revolution. A second is that cheap energy offset the burden of high wages. (This relationship is the 'factor price frontier' of neo-classical economics.) Contemporaries were aware of this advantage. Glass-making was one industry where the French were still ahead of the English in the late eighteenth century. Delaunay Deslandes, the director of Saint-Gobain, the leading French firm, was initially sceptical that the English could successfully compete against the French since English wages were one-third higher than French and the standard of living was accordingly superior:

> Given the manner in which the French and English lived . . . they could never make plate [glass] which could enter into competition with ours for the price. Our Frenchmen eat soup with a little butter and vegetables. They scarcely ever eat meat. They sometimes drink a little cider but more commonly water. Your Englishmen eat meat, and a great deal of it, and they drink beer continually in such a fashion that an Englishman spends three times more than a Frenchman.
>
> Quoted by Harris 1975, p. 67, n. 42

The burden of high wages in England, however, was offset by cheap energy. In prospectuses of the 1770s, the fuel cost of glass production was estimated to be only one-sixth of the French (Harris 1975, p. 38). The same offset occurred in iron production. Richard Reynolds of the Coalbrookdale Iron Company wrote to Earl Gower, President of the Privy Council, in 1784, to object to a proposed tax on coal on the grounds that 'coal . . . is the only article that, in any degree compensates for our high price of labour' (quoted by Raistrick 1989, p. 97). The shift from charcoal to coal in industrial processes during the seventeenth and eighteenth centuries – a shift that required the solution of many technical problems – gradually lowered the average price of energy in the English economy and underpinned the rise in the average wage.

5 *Why England succeeded*

> Philosophy is written in this grand book, the universe, which stands continually open to our gaze. But the Book cannot be understood unless one first learns to comprehend the language and read the characters in which it is written. It is written in the language of mathematics, and its characters are triangles, circles, and other geometric figures without which it is humanly impossible to understand a single word of it; without these one is wandering in a dark labyrinth.
>
> Galileo Galilei, *Il Saggiatore*[1]

The British economy leaped forward after 1500: cities grew, London's wages were high, agriculture improved, and manufacturing spread across the countryside. The specifics of change suggest that cities and commerce were the responsible agents. High wages, for instance, were maintained in London in the sixteenth century while they were collapsing elsewhere; in the seventeenth century, the rest of the country began to catch up as provincial cities began to grow rapidly. London's growth unleashed the flood of northeastern coal as wood prices soared.

This chapter will develop the idea that the growth of the urban, commercial economy drove the English economy forward in the centuries before the Industrial Revolution. The matter is complicated by two issues. The first relates to ultimate causation. The growth of cities may have pushed the national economy forward, but what made the cities grow? I will shift the analysis back a stage by attributing city growth to other factors. The second relates to reciprocal causation. The growth of cities, for instance, caused agricultural productivity to rise, while a more productive agriculture encouraged urbanization. Two-way causation must be addressed.

1 Quoted by A. C. Grayling, *Towards the Light*, 2007, pp. 95–6.

The only way to sort out these relationships is with a mathematical representation.[2] Galileo's realization that the natural world is mathematical applies to the social world as well. In this chapter, I follow his lead, except that simultaneous equations take the place of triangles and circles in representing social and economic development. The model developed here applies to all of the countries in Europe whose economic structures were summarized in Table 1.1. The time frame for the analysis runs from 1300 to 1800. In this model, the prime movers responsible for economic changes are population growth, the reorganization of agrarian institutions, technological innovation, empires and the associated intercontinental trade, constitutional structure, and the evolution of energy prices.[3] They affected urbanization, agricultural productivity, proto-industrialization and the real wage, which, in turn, affected each other.

The importance of these prime movers has been extensively debated, usually in terms of internal coherence. The enclosure argument, for instance, has been called into question by historians who have denied that enclosure led to much agricultural productivity growth, as we saw in Chapter 3. Empires and intercontinental trade have been attacked on the grounds that the extra-European markets were too small to matter, as were the profits earned on slavery and colonial trades.[4] The representative government argument has been disputed by those who assert that France did not have particularly high interest rates or taxes.

This chapter takes a different approach by simulating a four-equation simultaneous equation model of European development.

[2] The model discussed in this chapter is the same as the model in Allen (2003a) except for the addition of the price of energy. Allen (2003) contains further information regarding the sources of variables and estimation issues.

[3] In Allen (2003a), literacy was also included as a prime mover. However, it was so statistically insignificant that it was not included in the simulations reported there, and I do not discuss it here.

[4] The debate is enormous. A few relevant works showing the diversity of approaches includes Davis (1973, 1978, 1979), Minchinton (1969), Williams (1944), Wallerstein (1974–91 (1979)), Frank (1978), Findlay (1990), Darity (1992), Engerman (1972, 1994, 1998, 2000), Ferguson (2003), Thomas and Bean (1974), O'Brien (1982, 1999), O'Brien and Engerman (1991), O'Brien and Prados de la Escosura (1998), McCloskey (1970–1, 1980), Solow (1991) and Solow and Engerman (1987). Morgan (2001) is a survey of some important aspects, and Inikori (2002), O'Rourke and Williamson (2002a, 2002b), Findlay and O'Rourke (2003), McCusker and Morgan (2000), Ormrod (2003) and Findlay and O'Rourke (2007) are recent contributions.

Models of this sort are required when causation goes two ways. The model explains four variables – the wage rate, urbanization, agricultural productivity, and the proto-industrial revolution. We can use the model to simulate economic development and find out why some countries were successful and others not.

The model is based on a database of fifty-five observations of European countries at roughly century intervals, for example Spain in 1400, Spain in 1500, Poland in 1750, etc.[5] The database is used to estimate statistically the equations of the model, and it provides the information for simulations. The database includes information on economic structure like that shown in Table 1.1, real wages as in Chapter 2, agricultural output and productivity as explained in Chapter 3, and the energy prices tabulated in Chapter 4. In addition, international trade volumes and political and institutional variables have been added as discussed in this chapter. Other than the price of energy shown in Table 4.3, the database was published in Allen (2003a, pp. 436–9), where detailed descriptions and sources are also given.

A very serious issue is whether countries are appropriate units of analysis. One question is whether they were homogeneous enough. Was there an 'English' or an 'Italian' wage, for instance? In many respects, the countries were internally heterogeneous, and I represent them with averages. However, if world empires or agrarian institutions were powerful enough to remake societies, their effects should show up in the average experience of the nations concerned. And they do.

A second question is whether the same model fits all countries; in particular, does a single, four-equation model summarize the variety of development experiences seen in early modern Europe or do we need specific, different models for each country to capture the divergent paths of development on the continent? The surprising answer is that one model does fit all, and it indicates why some countries were more successful than others.

The method of analysis followed here is statistical, but it is not incompatible with a narrative approach to early modern history.

[5] The countries are defined in terms of post-World War II boundaries and include England and Wales, Belgium, France, the Netherlands, Spain, Italy, Germany, Poland and Austria/Hungary/Czechoslovakia. The years include 1300, 1400, 1500, 1600, 1700, 1750 and 1800, although observations in 1300 are available only for England and Italy, while the Netherlands does not enter the dataset until 1500.

Indeed, the purpose of the analysis is to choose between competing narratives. One narrative, for instance, emphasizes differences in agrarian institutions as the cause of different development trajectories. Another narrative emphasizes the emergence of representative government as the source of economic success. The analysis of this chapter discounts the importance of both of those narratives. Instead, the model tested here emphasizes the importance of the commercial revolution and international trade.

Commerce plays three roles in the narrative. The first and most important concerns the new draperies. The commercial revolution of the seventeenth century was an intra-European affair, and the changing locus of textile production was central to it. In the middle ages, woollen cloth was produced in the cities of Italy and Flanders and exported across the continent. The English were also successful in exporting heavy broadcloths. By the sixteenth century, the English and the Dutch were beginning to make the 'new draperies', which were light worsteds. These were patterned after Italian fabrics. The northern imitations were so successful that English and Dutch exports drove Italian producers out of business in the seventeenth century (Rapp 1975, Harte 1997). The new draperies were established in the Low Countries and in East Anglia, where they built on a long tradition of worsted manufacture (Coleman 1969). The Norwich industry was boosted by an influx of Flemish refugees fleeing war and oppression in the middle of the sixteenth century (Gwynn 1985, Munro 1997, Holderness, 1997, Martin 1997, Goose 2005, Luu 2005). By the end of the seventeenth century, about 40 per cent of England's woollen cloth production was exported, and woollen fabrics amounted to 69 per cent of the country's exports of domestic manufactures (Deane 1957, pp. 209–10, Davis 1954, p. 165). Wool was even more important for London. The new draperies flowed out of the capital: cloths amounted to 74 per cent of London's exports and re-exports in the 1660s (Rapp 1975, p. 502) and made a large contribution to the growth of that city. By the early eighteenth century, one-quarter of London's workforce was employed in shipping, port services or related activities (Boulton 2000, p. 320).

England's success in the new draperies had roots in the population crisis of the late middle ages. Before the Black Death, England's comparative advantage lay in the production of raw wool, the exports of which were very large. In the first half of the fourteenth century, increasingly heavy duties were levied on wool exports (but not on domestic sales). By 1347, these duties amounted to one-third of the value and conferred great protection on the production of cloth in England, the exports of which expanded steadily (Carus-Wilson 1952). In 1348–9, the Black Death slashed populations everywhere in Europe. The decline was at least as great in England as anywhere else. In most of Europe, the population began to recover by the fifteenth century, but the English population remained very low until the mid-sixteenth century. During this period, England's comparative advantage shifted even more strongly towards wool, and millions of acres of arable reverted to pasture. Real wages were very high. Sheep shared in the prosperity as well as people, for in the midlands especially, much high quality land, which had grown corn before the Black Death, was laid down to grass. With superior nutrition, the wool grew to greater length. 'The staple of the wool, like every other part of the sheep, must increase in length or in bulk when the animal has a superabundance of nutrient' (Youatt 1883, p. 70) and, indeed, the typical weight of a fleece doubled between the fourteenth and the seventeenth centuries (Trow-Smith 1957, pp. 166–8, 245–7). While the short wool of poorly nourished medieval sheep was well suited to making broad cloth, the long wool was best suited to making worsted. This was the material basis of the new draperies, and the expansion of the industry can be seen as the inevitable response to changes in the available wool supply (Bowden 1962, Kerridge 1972, Ramsay 1982). The new draperies also depended on the export tax on raw wool, for, in the absence of that tax, England's high wages would have meant that cloth production was uncompetitive, and unprocessed wool would have been exported instead of worsted cloth.

In the eighteenth century, international trade gave the economy a second boost via successful mercantilism and colonialism. Many European countries chartered companies to trade with Asia and the Americas, and these companies competed in trade with India and China. However, trade with colonies was usually restricted to nationals of the colonizer. Spain and Portugal were the first European states to acquire large territories in Asia and the Americas. The Dutch seized the Portuguese territories in the first half of the seventeenth century. They kept the Asian colonies like Indonesia for centuries but only managed to keep the American colonies for a short time. English colonization also began in the seventeenth century, and the English economy benefited from the enormous trade generated by these possessions in the eighteenth. London grew in the seventeenth century because it was the export point for the new draperies, and the city's growth continued in the eighteenth century as trade with the Americas, Africa and Asia expanded.

Commercial expansion promoted growth in a third way – via cheap energy. As we saw in the last chapter, coal mining in Northumberland was precipitated by the growth of London in the late sixteenth century, and that growth was due to commerce. The coal trade provided the capital with unlimited fuel at a reasonable price, but energy in southern England was not much cheaper than in many continental cities. The situation was very different on the coal fields where energy was extremely cheap. Cities like Birmingham and Sheffield expanded in the eighteenth centuries as coal was applied to more and more industrial technologies. Metal refining and fabricating industries, among others, took off and provided a basis for economic development outside of London. Wages rose rapidly in northern Britain since cheap coal meant that industries in that region could compete internationally while paying a high wage. By the second half of the eighteenth century, wages throughout Britain were converging upwards to London levels.

Modelling progress and poverty

To establish that this is the right narrative for early modern England, we use a model of the early modern economy. The model distinguishes the explanatory variables from those that are explained. The model developed here explains four variables – the real wage, the urban and proto-industrial shares of the population, and agricultural productivity. Each of these variables influenced the other. A productive agriculture, for instance, promoted large cities, while urbanization induced agricultural productivity growth. The view of development is, thus, one in which living standards, urbanization, proto-industrialization and agricultural revolutions were mutually reinforcing. Neither was a prime mover pushing all of the others forward. These four variables are all ultimately explained by other variables in the model – the enclosure of the open fields, for instance, and the establishment of world empires. Other prime movers include an index of productivity in woollen cloth production, previous levels of urbanization, and the land–labour ratio.

The model contains four equations to explain the four variables – the real wage, the urban and proto-industrial shares of the population, and agricultural productivity – in terms of the other variables.

The model works as a recursive system. In each time period (century), the four equations are solved to determine the values of the real wage, the urban and proto-industrial shares of the population, and agricultural productivity in terms of the prime movers of the economy. Figure 5.1 is a flow diagram that shows the logic of this solution. The diagram shows the links between variables that emerge as important in the statistical analyses: many more links were examined but failed to be statistically or historically significant. The four variables determined by the model are shown in rectangles and the prime movers that ultimately explain them are shown in ovals. The variables determined by the model influenced each other in many ways. Higher urbanization, for instance, led to higher agricultural productivity. Causation worked in the opposite way as well with higher agricultural productivity increasing the share of the population living in cities. In the model developed here, agricultural and urban revolutions are both a cause and a consequence of economic development. The model is linked from period to period by the change in population and the previous level of urbanization.

The model is specified by the equations shown in the appendix to this chapter. I review them in turn.

Wage equation

The wage equation is critical, for we want to explain why northwestern Europe had high wages while wages fell to low levels in the rest of Europe. The standard explanation for falling real wages in the sixteenth and seventeenth centuries is population growth in the context of a fixed supply of land (Abel 1980, Le Roy Ladurie 1974, Postan 1950, 1975, Wrigley and Schofield 1981, Wrigley 1988). This diminishing returns effect is represented in the model by making the wage depend on the land–labour ratio. Figure 5.2 makes the point theoretically. In that figure, D represents the demand curve for labour in pre-industrial society. Since the land area was fixed, diminishing returns implies that a larger population could be employed only if the wage fell. For that reason, the demand curve sloped downward. Statistical analysis confirms that more people depressed wages in early modern Europe,

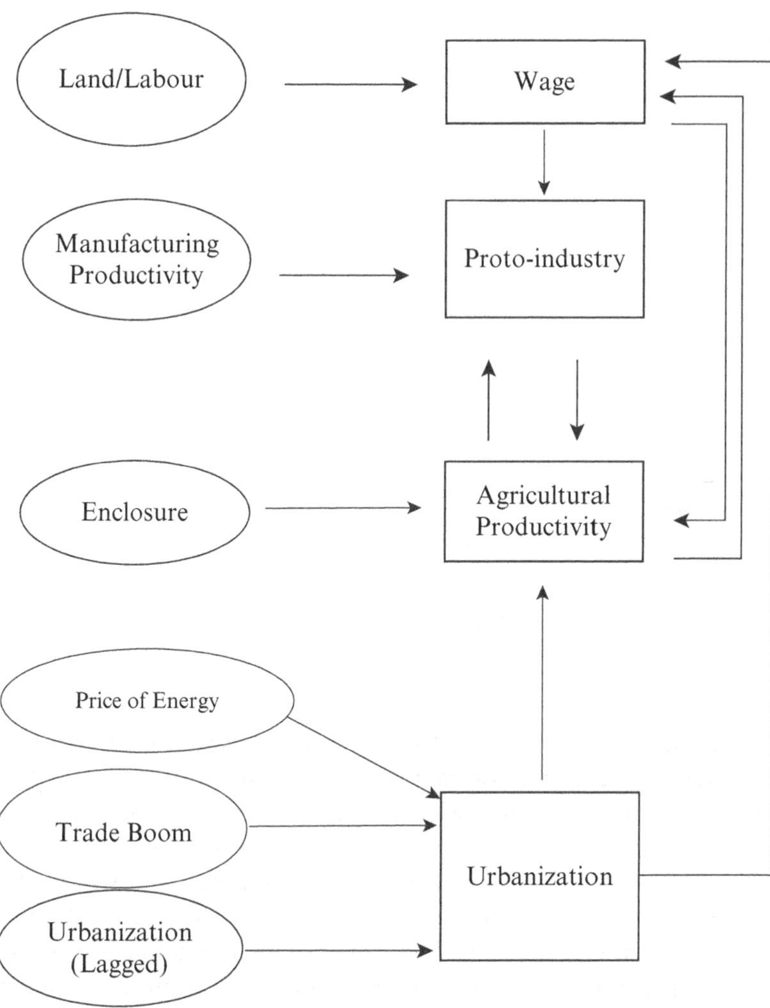

Figure 5.1 Flowchart (one period) of the model

all other things being equal. S indicates the supply of labour, which is represented by the population. With S at a low level, the wage was high at w. In most of Europe, the population expanded between 1500 and 1800, and the wage fell from w to w_1 as was shown in Figure 5.2. In the successful economies, however, the story was different. There, the demand curve for labour shifted to the right (to D_1) in step with the population growth. As a result, the wage remained at w.

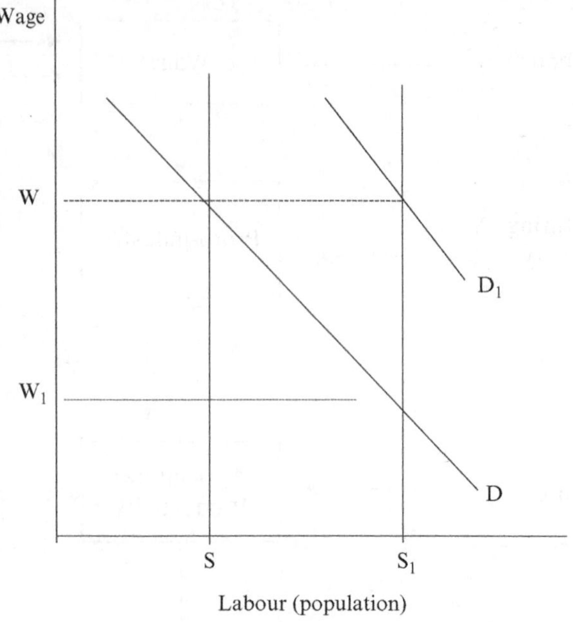

Figure 5.2 Supply and demand for labour

The key question is why the demand curve for labour grew in a few countries and remained constant in the rest. Statistical tests show that the demand for labour rose when agricultural efficiency increased and cities expanded. One reason that larger cities mattered is because they gave rise to economies of scale that raised efficiency and with it the demand for labour (Crafts and Venables 2003). Better farming and urban growth were the immediate causes of high wages in northwestern Europe, and their absence in France, Italy and Spain led to falling living standards.

Agricultural productivity equation

Logically, the next questions are why did agricultural productivity rise and why did cities grow? I begin with farming.

There are two approaches to explaining the growth in agricultural productivity. The traditional view, discussed in Chapter 3, attributes agricultural revolutions to the 'modernization' of rural institutions. The second approach attributes high agricultural productivity to the growth of the non-agricultural economy. Large cities and rural industries increased the demand for food, flax, wool, leather and labour, thereby providing an incentive to farmers to modernize their methods. In the statistical analysis, both agrarian institutions and the non-agricultural economy proved important in explaining agricultural productivity.[6]

Statistical analysis of the European database confirmed that urbanization, the growth of proto-industry, and high wages all contributed to higher agricultural productivity. Larger values for the first two variables indicate greater demands on agriculture for food and fibre, while higher wages provided an incentive to shed low productivity jobs or to increase efficiency in other ways in order to generate enough net income to keep the farm labour force from migrating to the city. These variables instantiate the view that a larger non-agricultural economy induced an increase in farm efficiency.

The role of agrarian institutions in limiting the response to these demands was ascertained by including two additional variables in the statistical analysis. One was a variable representing eighteenth-century England. At that time, England's distinctive agrarian institutions – its great estates, large-scale farms and landless labourers – reached their fully developed form. If they mattered, presumably, they would have pushed English efficiency above the level implied by the other variables. However, the variable representing these institutions was never statistically significant and, indeed, had a negative coefficient suggesting they were counterproductive. This finding calls into question the importance of England's great estates as a source of agricultural improvement.

The second variable was the proportion of farm land that was enclosed, and this provides a focused test of the importance of England's most distinctive rural institution. In England, that proportion increased over time as the open fields disappeared, and Wordie's (1983) estimates (with slight adjustments) have been used to measure the progress of enclosure. While England is famous as the only country with an enclosure movement in this period, it was not the only country with enclosed farms. Indeed, there was considerable variation in the

6 The measure of agricultural productivity used in the simulation of this chapter is the index of agricultural total factor productivity used in Allen (2003). That index is a transformation of the agricultural labour productivity index in Chapter 3, and graphs of the two indices look similar.

fraction of land enclosed as shown by a map drawn up by Pounds (1990, p. 335), and, for countries besides England, the fraction of land enclosed is taken from this map.

In the event, the proportion of land enclosed had only a marginal effect on agricultural productivity. The enclosure variable had a coefficient that was usually about 0.18, and it was statistically significant at about the 15 per cent level, which is low by most standards. There is, however, much to be said in favour of the coefficient. The value of 0.18 implies that the total factor productivity of enclosed farms was 18 per cent higher than that of open fields. If rent accounted for one-third of revenues, then enclosure boosted rent by 64 per cent, for example a rise from 12 shillings to 20 shillings per acre. This result is consistent with rent differences in many parts of England (Allen 1992, p. 172, 1999). Arthur Young would have been enthusiastic about the regression coefficient, for it is close to the doubling he often spoke of. Despite its borderline statistical significance, enclosure is included in the model both as a tribute to Young and to make sure that enclosure gets its due.

Urbanization equation

Growing cities was another immediate cause of high real wages. The fraction of the population living in cities changed very little in many countries during the early modern period, while rising in the Netherlands and, especially, in England.[7] Five variables account for this divergent pattern.

A variable that was robust in all statistical tests was the urbanization rate of a country in the previous century. Its coefficient of 0.79 means that the urban fraction would have been 79 per cent of its value a century earlier if nothing else had caused it to change. This variable measures the persistence of the urban system.

Persistence represents several social processes. The most common case was countries like Austria or Germany where the urban fraction was low and remained so – in other words where growth was modest. A more interesting case is Italy where the accumulation of social capital allowed cities to renew themselves even when their

[7] De Vries (1984) and Bairoch (1988) provide magisterial overviews of European urbanization. See Sweet (1999), Chalklin (2001) and Ellis (2001) for recent surveys of English urbanization in this period.

economic base collapsed. In the middle ages, a major Italian industry was woollen cloth. Its manufacture was destroyed by the exports of the new draperies from northern Europe. The Italian cities did not disappear, however. Instead, their economies were recreated on the basis of silk. This involved raising silkworms in the countryside as well as weaving silk cloth in the city. While different technical skills were involved, business skills and networks carried over from wool production. Italians showed tremendous enterprise in the seventeenth century, but it was one step forward for two steps back, and the economy as a whole did not advance.

The urban fraction also remained high in Spain throughout the early modern period, but the reason was different. The manufacturing industries that sustained the medieval cities were destroyed by the inflation caused by American bullion imports. Their population losses were counterbalanced by the growth of Madrid as American treasure was used to build the capital (Ringrose 1983). These very different histories are summarized by the inclusion of the lagged urbanization rate.

Persistence does not, of course, explain the urban revolutions in England and the Netherlands. Four more variables were responsible for urbanization in those countries. The first was agricultural productivity, which has already been discussed. Not only did bigger cities lead to more efficient farms, but better farming led to bigger cities. The second was intercontinental trade. The volume of this trade was related to mercantilism and the acquisition of colonies. Some countries were successful in the race for empire, while others were not. Spain seized a vast empire in Latin America and the Philippines, England acquired much of North America, some rich sugar islands in the Caribbean, and Bengal, the Netherlands conquered Indonesia, the original Spice Islands and Surinam, and France had important possessions in North America, the Caribbean and India. Portugal had a substantial empire in Brazil, Africa and South Asia but is not in the database analyzed here. The other European countries were not in the running.[8]

[8] The role of empire as a source of capital and a market for manufactures has since been emphasized by 'world system theorists' like Wallerstein (1974–91), Arrighi (1994) and Frank (1978, 1998). Acemoglu, Johnson and Robinson (2005) also emphasize the importance of Asian and American trade, as does Inikori (2002).

The effect of empires is measured by the volume of intercontinental trade per capita.[9] London's exports of cloth in the early seventeenth century were balanced by the import of colonial products, and their re-export in the eighteenth century further expanded the capital's trade (Boulton 2000, p. 321). All of the countries were mercantilist and tried to reserve trade with their colonies for their nationals. The experience of the Dutch is the exception that proves the rule. They were highly efficient in shipping and the closest to free traders in the Atlantic economy (but not in the Asian). However, the Dutch were squeezed out of most Atlantic colonial trade by the regulations of the English, French and Spanish. Only in times of war could the Dutch make much headway (De Vries and van der Woude 1997, pp. 476–9). Many factors affected trade volumes, but the experience of the Dutch shows the primacy of politics in this period, which is why trade is treated as the result of imperial advantage in this model.

It should be noted that trade volumes are measured exclusive of shipments of gold and silver. This affects the measurement of Spanish trade where bullion was the main cargo. While the Dutch and, especially, the English empires offered trade and markets, the Spanish may have been too successful in generating loot: the gold and silver from the Americas inflated prices and wages in Spain, rendering much manufacturing unprofitable (Hamilton 1934, 1936, 1947, Dreilichman 2002).

The third variable that promoted urbanization was the price of energy. The biggest change in this regard was the development of the coal economy. The question is how much that mattered for the English economy. Much of Britain's urban growth in the eighteenth century occurred outside London in cities located near coal fields. The availability of cheap fuel was accelerating urbanization and economic growth in northern and western Britain in the eighteenth century.[10]

9 This trade variable excludes shipments of gold and silver. Trade volumes were derived from Deane and Cole (1969, p. 87), Levasseur (1911, vol. I, p. 518, vol. II, pp. 20–2, 94–6), Haudrère (1989, vol. 4, p. 1201), Villiers (1991, p. 211), De Vries and van der Woude (1997, pp. 393, 445, 460, 474, 478), Garcia Fuentes (1980), Morineau (1985, pp. 267, 494), Hamilton (1934, pp. 33–4) and Fisher (1985, pp. 67–8, 1997, pp. 164–70, 201–6). The English imports and exports for the eighteenth century were valued with c. 1700 prices, so they are quantity indices. Linen and sugar prices were used to convert the values of exports and imports, respectively, for other countries to 1700 sterling values comparable to the English values. See Allen (2001) for the sources of the prices.

10 English coal production grew because the growth of London raised the price of wood. That suggests that the price of energy was endogenous. However, coal

The final variable that affected urbanization was constitutional structure. Eighteenth-century liberals contrasted the absolutism of France with England's 'mixed monarchy' and the constitution of the Dutch Republic. Representative institutions were alleged to be economically superior, as evidenced by lower interest rates in England and the Netherlands compared to France. These arguments have been restated by recent theorists like North and Weingast (1989) and De Long and Schleifer (1993), who contend that absolutist kings expropriated property and raised taxes in ways that discouraged business enterprise. Ekelund and Tollinson (1997) have proposed complementary explanations in terms of rent seeking.

In the model discussed here, I have represented constitutional structure with a variable called Prince. It is a so-called 'dummy variable' that equals one for a country with an absolutist government and zero for a republic or a country with a representative government. I have followed the classification of De Long and Schleifer (1993). Medieval Italy, the Dutch Republic and eighteenth-century England were the classic 'representative' states. Most of the rest were absolutist 'princes'.[11]

De Long and Schleifer did not categorize Poland, and it is necessary to do so for the present analysis. Poland is an interesting case, for its government was representative with an exceptionally weak monarch up until its dismemberment, which was completed in the 1790s. Before 1800, I have put Poland in the 'non-prince' category. In 1800, I have assigned it to the 'prince' category, for Russia, Prussia and Austria were all absolutist states. Eighteenth-century Poland is an object lesson in how a government can be too 'minimal' for anyone's good.

Despite being statistically insignificant in most cases, the Prince variable has been included in all of the equations in the model to give the constitutional argument its due (see the appendix to this chapter). The Prince variable, however, was statistically significant in the urbanization equation, but it had a positive sign indicating that absolutism increased the rate of economic growth. The effect, however, was small.

was supplied to London at a constant real price throughout the period since coal was available in unlimited supply at that cost. The price of coal was, therefore, exogenous, and it was used in model estimation.

[11] Implicitly, they have categorized Napoleon as a prince, and I have followed that lead, so France in 1800 is put in the 'prince' category. Likewise, the Netherlands in 1800 are classified the same way since the country was a dependency of France.

Proto-industry equation

Proto-industrialization was the third development that promoted high wages. It did not enter the wage equation directly, but it affected wages since it affected agricultural productivity. Indeed, proto-industry is crucial for understanding England's high wage economy since it includes the new draperies, whose expansion was the motor of English development in the seventeenth century.

Proto-industry had contradictory causes that reflect its ambiguous role in early modern development. On the one hand, there were large rural manufacturing industries (e.g. the new draperies) in the leading economies, and these industries played an important role in economic growth. On the other hand, many rural industries developed in backward regions and left no legacy for industrialization.

The two faces of proto-industry are reflected in its equation. On the one hand, the fraction of the population in rural industry was a negative function of agricultural productivity and of the wage rate. These negative effects show that proto-industrialization was a consequence of low agricultural productivity rather than high productivity. In other words, it was often the occupation of poor peasants practising a backward agriculture as in central Europe (Table 1.1).

On the other hand, the size of the proto-industrial sector was a positive function of productivity in textile production. This productivity growth was a feature of the development of the new draperies. People had to learn how to process the supply of long staple wool that became abundant as pasture was improved in the fifteenth century. The influx of refugees from the continent brought skills and commercial knowledge that contributed to these advances. As their skills were assimilated and methods improved, the price of worsted cloth fell with respect to the prices of wool and labour. These cost savings signal the rise in efficiency and provide a basis for measuring textile productivity across Europe (Figure 5.3 contrasts the rise in the efficiency of new drapery production with the static efficiency of the English broad cloth sector). Productivity was highest in England and the Low Countries, and high productivity in textile production increased the size of the proto-industrial sector in the statistical investigations. In the seventeenth and eighteenth centuries, the high productivity of textile production in England and the Low Countries offset their high agricultural productivity and high wages, which would otherwise

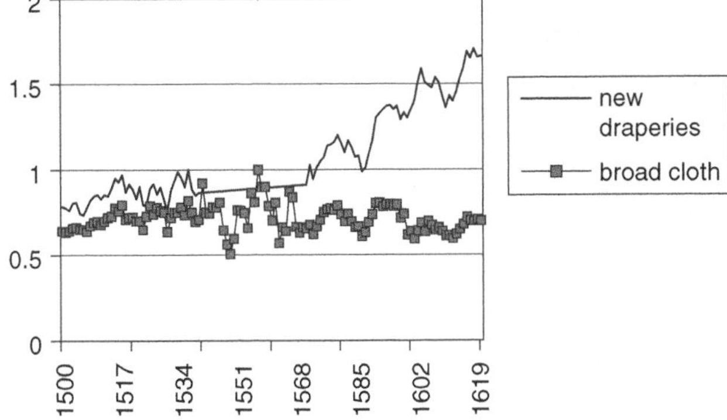

Figure 5.3 Total productivity in English cloth

have reduced rural manufacturing. The causes of rural industry in England and the Low Countries, therefore, were the reverse of the causes operating in central Europe.

The proto-industry equation includes the Prince variable representing absolutist government. In the statistical estimations, its coefficient was negative, large and almost significant. This is the strongest evidence that absolutism depressed economic development.

Divergent paths to the nineteenth century

How can we tell if the model is any good? An important test is whether the equations can account for the different paths of development followed by different parts of Europe. If the model is simulated from 1400 onwards, do Italy and France show falling wages and limited structural transformation? Do the Netherlands and England maintain their wages and exhibit urban and agricultural revolutions?

Figures 5.4 to 5.6 compare simulated trajectories for urbanization, agricultural productivity and wages for England, Italy, France and the Netherlands. The simulations for France are very similar to those for Germany, Austria and Poland. They show little cumulative urbanization, static agricultural productivity and falling real wages. For France and the major countries of central Europe, the model predicts little economic development. The simulations for Italy and Spain are almost as bleak, although their initially higher urban shares are largely maintained.

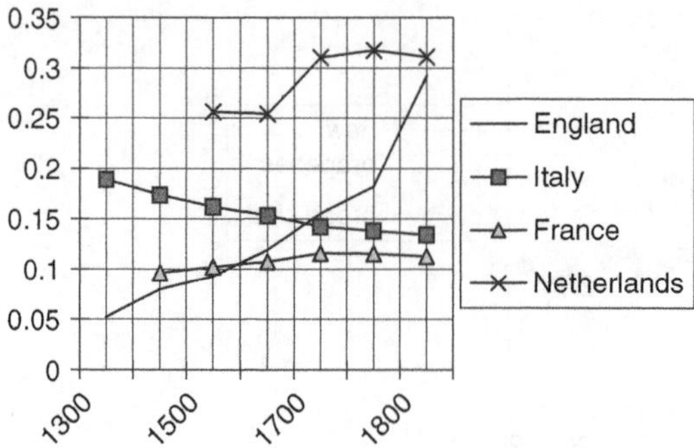

Figure 5.4 Simulated urbanization rate, 1300–1800

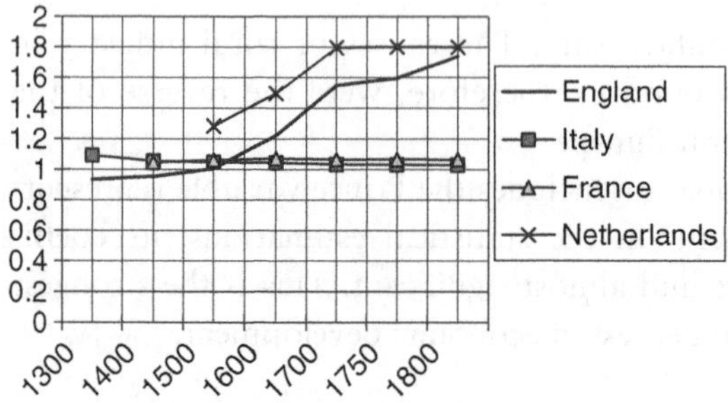

Figure 5.5 Simulated agricultural total factor productivity, 1300–1800

The simulations for the Netherlands and England, on the other hand, show successful patterns of economic development. In the first place, urbanization was much more extensive. The Dutch were already more highly urbanized in 1500 than much of the continent, and the development of commerce and empire built on that base to produce the highest rate of urbanization in 1800. The English started from a much lower level of urbanization in 1500, surpassed France and Italy, and almost caught up to the Dutch by 1800.

The difference between successful and unsuccessful economies is dramatic in the case of agricultural performance, and the equations reproduce that difference. England and the Netherlands both had agricultural revolutions, and the model simulates these. It also replicates the stagnation that gripped the rest of Europe.

Urbanization, greater farm efficiency, and proto-industrialization

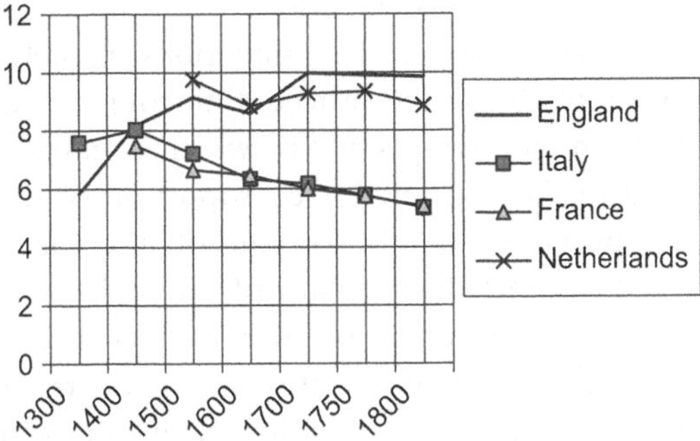

Figure 5.6 Simulated real wage, 1300–1800

had a pronounced impact on wages. In northwestern Europe, the simulated wage remains high during the early modern period. The simulation for England shows a drop in the sixteenth century and then a rebound in the seventeenth and eighteenth as economic development tightened up the labour market. This was escape from the 'Malthusian trap' through rapid development. The contrast for most of the continent is impressive. There, simulated real wages fell as population grew and the economy stagnated.

The sources of England's success

The simulation model can be used to factor out the differences between successful and unsuccessful economies. I concentrate on the comparison between England and her large continental rivals like France and Austria. How did England maintain a high wage despite rapid population growth, while continental wages fell even though the population grew little? The possibilities – as incorporated in the model – include: the replacement of absolutist by representative government in the seventeenth century, the enclosure of the open fields, the productivity advantage associate with the new draperies, the growth in intercontinental trade consequent upon the British empire, and the price of energy. By successively removing these sources of growth and resimulating the model, the fundamental differences between England and the continent are identified. These simulations include the ramifications of the changes throughout the economy and not simply in the sector concerned.

One implication of the simultaneous equations must be highlighted since it plays an important role in the simulations, namely, that all of the prime movers in the system affected all four of the variables determined by the model irrespective of which equations the prime movers appeared in. For instance, the proportion of the population living in cities depended on the volume of intercontinental trade. Trade was not a direct determinant of the real wage, agricultural productivity, or the size of the proto-industrial sector. Nevertheless, when the model is simulated, intercontinental trade affects all of these variables since trade increased the size of cities and larger cities led to more productive farming and so forth. Likewise, the proportion of farm land that was enclosed only entered the agricultural productivity equation, but enclosure affected urbanization, etc., since enclosure boosted farm efficiency and a more productive agriculture led to larger cities.

Figures 5.7 to 5.9 show alternative simulations for England of agricultural total factor productivity, the urbanization rate, and the real wage from 1300 to 1800. Near the top of all figures is the 'simulated actual' history of the variable, that is, the value implied by the model when it is simulated with the historical time paths of the variables describing the fraction of the land enclosed, relative textile productivity, and so forth. If the model were perfect, the simulated values would equal their historical time paths. In the event, the main features are replicated.

The other, gnerally lower, lines show the simulated value of the variables as growth-promoting factors are removed from the calculations. The line marked 'not representative' shows the course of the variable if England had remained an absolutist monarchy in the eighteenth century. The removal of explanatory factors cumulates as one moves down the graphs. Thus, the line marked 'no enclosure' keeps the fraction of enclosed land at its 1500 level, while also eliminating representative government. The difference between the 'no representative' line and the 'no enclosure' line, therefore, shows the impact of enclosure. By the same reasoning, the bottom line labelled 'no intercontinental trade' shows the result of eliminating all five growth-promoting factors.

Figures 5.7 to 5.9 make several important points about England's success. First, the bottom lines trace out a no-growth trajectory like that of the large continental countries: little growth in agricultural productivity or the urban share and a falling real wage. In the absence of

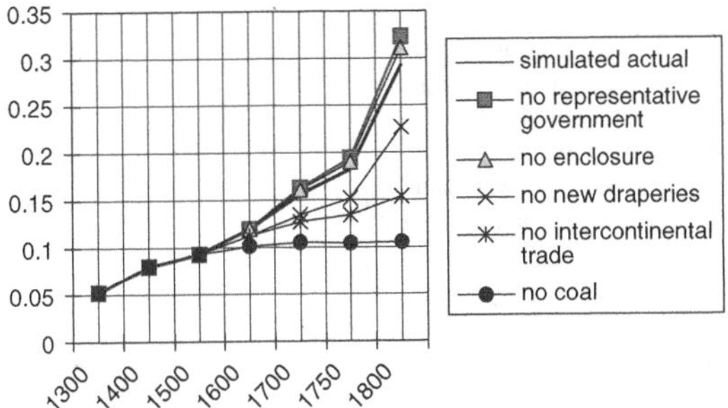

Figure 5.7 Simulated urbanization rate, 1300–1800

Figures 5.7 to 5.9 show the cumulative effects of removing growth-promoting factors from English history. Thus, 'simulated actual' shows the simulation of the urbanization rate using the actual, historical values of all of the growth-promoting factors. 'No representative government' shows the simulated urbanization rate if the country had been an absolutist monarchy. Notice that cities would have been even larger. 'No enclosure' shows that keeping the share of land enclosed at its 1500 value would have reduced city size slightly. The 'no enclosure' line includes the effect of both eliminating post-1500 enclosures and retaining an absolute monarch, so the difference between the two shows the effect of enclosure. Reading down the graph shows the effect of removing more and more growth-promoting factors: 'no new draperies' removes the productivity growth due to the new draperies, 'no intercontinental trade' removes intercontinental trade, and 'no coal' sets the energy price at twice the prevailing price of charcoal. The 'no coal' line shows the effect of removing all of the growth-promoting factors and eliminates the urban revolution: England has been turned into France.

the growth-promoting factors, in other words, the history of England would have been like that of France, Germany or Austria.

Secondly, the ascendancy of parliament in the eighteenth century made little contribution to England's development. Several studies of interest rates have failed to detect any growth-promoting result of the Glorious Revolution of 1688 (Clark 1996, Epstein 2000, pp. 12–37, Quinn 2001), and the present study supports that view.

It is not surprising that representative government did not accelerate growth. Property was secure in all the leading European countries, whatever their constitution. Indeed, as Rosenthal (1990) has shown, one of France's problems was that property was too secure: the state, for instance, could not push forward profitable irrigation projects in Provence because landowners could block these initiatives in the courts. Parliamentary ascendancy in England led to higher taxes than

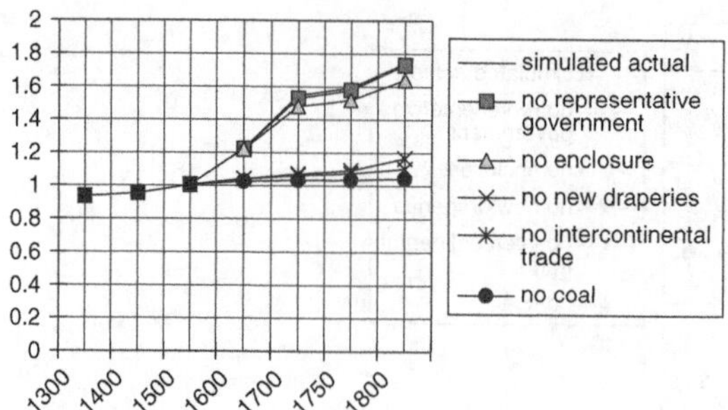

Figure 5.8 Simulated agricultural total factor productivity, 1300–1800

See the note to Figure 5.7.

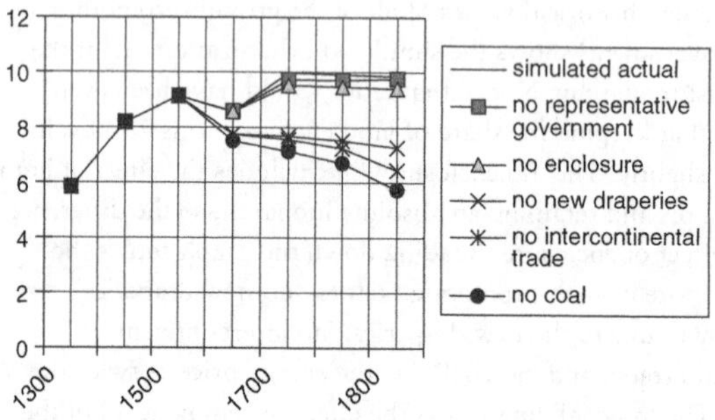

Figure 5.9 Simulated real wage, 1300–1800

See the note to Figure 5.7.

in France, contrary to the views of liberals then or now (Mathias and O'Brien 1976, 1978, Hoffman and Norberg 1994, Bonney 1999). And, while representative government could provide good government – England's local improvement acts are a case in point – it could also provide spectacularly bad government. The concentration of power in the diet emasculated the Polish state and ultimately destroyed it. It would be a great surprise if there were a straightforward statistical relationship between absolutism and underdevelopment, and there was not in these tests.

Thirdly, the enclosure movement made little contribution to England's progress. In all cases, the 'no enclosure' trajectory grows almost as rapidly as the 'simulated actual'. Figures 5.7 to 5.9 extend the findings of agricultural historians who downplay the importance of enclosure by showing that it had only a small impact on urbanization, the real wage and, even, agricultural total factor productivity (TFP). This simulation includes not only the direct effect of enclosure on farm efficiency but also the feedback effect when the impact of rising farm efficiency on city growth, for instance, is taken into account. In this broad framework – as well as in the more narrowly defined study of farming methods – the enclosure movement was peripheral to English development.

The converse of this conclusion needs underlining. The success of English agriculture was a response to the growth of the urban and proto-industrial sectors and to the maintenance of a high wage economy. Farmers responded to these challenges by increasing output and by economizing on labour. The latter was effected by increasing the size of farms and by enclosing land to convert arable to pasture. To the degree that these changes, the hallmarks of the English agricultural revolution, increased productivity, they should be seen as responses to an urbanized, high wage economy rather than as autonomous causes. (Dutch agriculture, it should be noted, developed along similar lines for similar reasons.) The traditional historiography, in other words, should be stood on its head.[12]

Fourthly, the productivity rise underlying the success of the new draperies in the seventeenth century was of great importance for England's success. Success in that industry was based on the abundance of pasture after the Black Death and to its favourable impact on the health of England's sheep and the length of their fleece. Success also depended on the export tax on raw wool. The growth of the new draperies provided a strong boost to urbanization, and the growth of rural industry. Through these effects, the success of the new draperies was responsible for a large fraction of the growth in agricultural TFP as farmers successfully responded to the greater demand for food, wool and labour. Without seventeenth-century success, wages, agricultural productivity and city size would all have been lower in 1800.

Fifthly, the empire established in the seventeenth and eighteenth centuries also contributed to growth. The greatest impact was on city size. Over half of England's urban expansion is attributed to empire in these simulations.

[12] This view is not shared by Crafts and Harley (2002), who argue that capitalist agriculture played an important role in explaining the growth of industrial employment in the British Industrial Revolution.

Sixthly, coal also mattered. In the counterfactuals, the price of energy from 1600 onwards is set at twice the average real price of energy from wood fuels. This trajectory is conjectural, but represents the sort of appreciation that might have occurred had even more wood been cut than was the case historically. Such a price increase would have checked the growth of the economy. The greatest impacts would have been on urbanization, which would have declined slightly from its 1500 value, and on the wage rate, which would have dropped as it did in France. The check to urbanization would also have suppressed agricultural productivity growth. The shift from the organic to mineral fuel economy (in Wrigley's terms) prevented these adverse developments.

Implications and questions

The simulations show that a simple model captures the factors responsible for success and failure in the early modern economy. The intercontinental trade boom was a key development that propelled northwestern Europe forward. This conclusion has also been advanced by many commentators including Pomeranz (2000), Frank (1998), Inikori (2002) and Acemoglu, Johnson and Robinson (2005). However, this chapter emphasizes that northwestern Europe's ascent began in the century before the American and Asian trades became important. This emphasis extends the work of historians like Davis (1954) and particularly Rapp (1975), who have noted that the commercial revolution began in the seventeenth century before the Atlantic trades became significant and was an intra-European reorganization in which northwestern Europeans out-competed Mediterranean producers in woollen textiles. The ascendancy of northwestern Europe and the eclipse of Italy, on this reading of the evidence, predated the rise of the Atlantic economy. Northwestern Europe's success was based on a two-step advance – the first within Europe, the second in America and Asia.

This success, it might be noted, marked the first steps out of the Malthusian trap. High wages were sustainable even with pre-industrial fertility so long as the economy grew fast enough. The reason is that the population growth rate was limited to about 2 per cent per year, the difference between the maximum observed fertility rate, 5 per cent per year, and the mortality rate, which was about 3 per cent per year in the early modern period. If the demand for labour grew faster than 2 per cent per year, then wages could rise even without the fertility restraint of twentieth-century Europeans. This favourable conjuncture first occurred in England and the Low Countries in the early modern period when high wages were maintained even as the population expanded at a brisk rate. In the rest of Europe, where population grew less rapidly, wages sagged as the economy stagnated. Rapid economic development, rather than fertility reduction, was the basis of continued high wages.

The simulations in this chapter also call into question the constitutional explanations of England's success. The establishment of representative government had a negligible effect on development in early modern Europe. The stress placed on its importance concatenates the form of the constitution, the security of property, low taxes and good government. These could come in many combinations, however. In England, for instance, most agricultural producers acquired the secure property that was a precondition for the agricultural revolution when royal courts created copyhold and beneficial leasehold tenures in the late fifteenth and sixteenth centuries (Allen 1992, pp. 55–77). This was judicial activism by royal officials rather than the action of parliament. Much of England's rise to pre-eminence occurred before the Glorious Revolution of 1688. The English had displaced the Italians in woollen cloth production by then, and the population of London had exploded from 55,000 in 1520 to 475,000 in 1670 (Wrigley 1985). The development of the coal industry was a mega-project that demanded investment on a grand scale. In eighteenth-century France, property was secure enough for the Atlantic ports to boom based on intercontinental trade. Would representative government have made them grow faster? Perhaps by voting higher taxes, France could have contested mastery of the seas more successfully and expanded its empire rather than losing it. The possible gains are doubtful, however, since the French population was three or four times that of England (and ten times greater than the Dutch), so that intercontinental trade would have had to have been larger by the same proportion to have had the same per capita effect. (It is a subtle point, but England's success depended on her population being neither too large nor too small.) French development was not held back by high taxes, the inability to enforce commercial contracts, or royal interference with private credit (Hoffman, Postel-Vinay and Rosenthal 2000). Good government was not cheap nor did it require a parliament.

Economic success in the early modern economy was not due to limited government, high literacy, efficient agrarian property rights or slow population growth. Ecological factors deserve considerable credit, for they were responsible for the population decline that led to the conversion of arable to pasture and the improved feeding of sheep. This resulted in heavier fleeces with longer staple wool and, ultimately, for the new draperies, which were the manufactured realization of that raw material. The export tax on raw wool also played a role, for it ensured that it was worsted cloth rather than sacks of wool that England exported. These cloth exports propelled the English economy forward. In the seventeenth and eighteenth century, it received further powerful boosts from the expansion of intercontinental trade, whose growth was largely dependent on aggressive mercantilism and empire, and the availability of low cost fuel, which maintained living standards and industrial competitiveness. It may, indeed, have been the case that the availability of new consumer goods imported from Asia and America was stimulating consumer demand and leading to an 'industrious revolution' of harder work and more vigorous entrepreneurship. The success of the British economy was, thus, due to long-haired sheep, cheap coal and the imperial foreign policy that secured a rising volume of trade.

Appendix Equations describing the early modern economy

Wage equation

LNWAGE = 0.23 LNURB + 0.54 LNAGTFP + 0.40 LNTL – 0.03 PRINCE – 0.66

Agricultural productivity equation

LNAGTFP = 0.23 LNURB + 0.50 LNPROTO + 0.44 LNWAGE + 0.18 ENCL + 0.06 PRINCE + 0.40

Urbanization equation

LNURB = 0.40 LNAGTFP + 0.10 TRADEPOP – 0.14 LNPENERGY + 0.79 LNURBLAG + 0.05 PRINCE – 0.28

Proto-industry equation

LNPROTO = – 0.93 LNAGTFP – 1.00 LNWAGE + 1.27 MANPROD – 0.18 PRINCE – 0.80

Variables whose values are determined by solving the model

LNWAGE	logarithm of the real wage
LNURB	logarithm of the urbanization rate
LNAGTFP	logarithm of agricultural total factor productivity
LNPROTO	logarithm of the fraction of the population in proto-industry

Variables that characterized economies and determined the variables listed above

LNTL	logarithm of the land–labour ratio
PRINCE	dummy variable that equals 1 for absolute monarchs and 0 otherwise
ENCL	fraction of land enclosed
TRADEPOP	real intercontinental trade per capita
LNPENERGY	logarithm of the price of energy
LNURBLAG	logarithm of the urbanization rate 100 years previously
MANPROD	productivity in textile production

Source: the simulations use equations estimated in Allen (2003a). The wage equation is regression 2 in Table 3 of Allen (2003a), the agricultural productivity equation is regression 3 in Table 4 of Allen (2003a), and the proto-industry equation is regression 2 in Table 6 of Allen (2003a). The urbanization equation is adapted from regression 5 in Table 5 of Allen (2003a).

PART II

The Industrial Revolution

6 *Why was the Industrial Revolution British?*

Invention is 1% inspiration and 99% Perspiration.

Thomas Edison

The Industrial Revolution was one of the great, transformative events of world history. Part I explored the high wage, cheap energy environment from which it emerged. Part II will show how and why that environment caused the Industrial Revolution. But what was the Industrial Revolution? Its essential characteristic was technological innovation. In the words of Ashton's famous schoolboy: 'About 1760 a wave of gadgets swept over England.'[1] Some are well known (the steam engine, the spinning jenny, the water frame and coke smelting), and others less so (devices to lay out and cut the gears of watches, and foot-powered trip hammers to stamp the heads on nails).[2] In the remainder of this book, I concentrate on the famous inventions because they unleashed trajectories of technological advance that drove the economy forward. If we can explain the breakthroughs that started these sequences of progress, we can explain the Industrial Revolution. The basic principles have broader application, however, and governed minor inventions as well. In the remainder of this book, I tackle the question of why the steam engine, mechanical spinning and coke smelting were invented in Britain, in the eighteenth century.

The famous inventions had a life course, and I shall tell their biographies, for they give the Industrial Revolution a natural unity. The inventions began with a conception and were born through difficult labour. In their youth, they were decidedly British in their biases. As

1 Ashton (1955, p. 42).

2 There has been a lively debate about the importance of productivity growth in the famous 'revolutionized' industries versus productivity growth in industries where inventions were less dramatic. See McCloskey (1981), Temin (1997, 2000), Harley (1999), Crafts and Harley (2000, 2002), Berg and Hudson (1992, 1994), Bruland (2004).

they matured, these biases wore away, and the inventions were adapted to any circumstances. At that point, the Industrial Revolution diffused to the continent, to North America, and then to the rest of the world. This lifespan took a century and a half, and it sets the natural limits of the Industrial Revolution. I shall tell the history of the Industrial Revolution in two stages: first, the birth and youth of the great inventions when they were useful in Britain but nowhere else, and, secondly, their maturation into globally useful technologies that spread from Britain to other countries.

My analysis is based on two distinctions. The first is between macro-inventions and micro-inventions.[3] Newcomen's steam engine and Hargreaves' spinning jenny, for instance, were macro-inventions. They set in train long trajectories of advance that resulted in great increases in productivity. Fundamentally for my analysis, they also radically changed factor proportions, substituting energy and capital for labour. For this reason, the macro-inventions of the Industrial Revolution were only cost-effective in Britain. Micro-inventions, on the other hand, refer to all of the improvements in the trajectory of advance that elaborated macro-inventions and realized their possibilities. Economies were made across the board – in the use of inputs with which Britain was abundantly endowed (e.g. coal) as well as in the use of inputs that were scarce in Britain (e.g. labour). As a result, the stream of micro-inventions made steam engines, cotton mills and coke blast furnaces cost-effective in more and more countries and eventually spread the Industrial Revolution around the world.

The second distinction concerns the nature of invention itself, namely, Edison's observation that 'invention was 1% inspiration and 99% perspiration'. Invention involved both leaps of imagination or scientific discovery (inspiration) and research and development (perspiration). Usually, 'inspiration' is emphasized,[4] but both need to be explained, and Edison's weighting suggests that we should concentrate on research and development. I will consider both inspiration and perspiration, but I will follow Edison's lead and concentrate more on

[3] The distinction is Mokyr's (1990, p. 13), although my understanding is different. Mokyr (1991), however, does discuss the relationship between macro- and micro-inventions in a similar way to that used here. The distinction between the two types of invention was anticipated by Rosenberg (1982, pp. 62–70).

[4] MacLeod (2007) deconstructs the view that the inventors of the Industrial Revolution were inspired geniuses.

the latter than has been customary. This perspective is rewarded with a deeper understanding of why the Industrial Revolution happened when and where it did.

I analyze the search for better methods in terms of the demand and supply of new technology. Britain's success in the early modern global economy gave her expensive labour and cheap energy. These prices affected the *demand* for technology by giving British businesses an exceptional incentive to invent technology that substituted capital and energy for labour. The high real wage also stimulated product innovation since it meant that Britain had a broader mass market for 'luxury' consumer goods including imports from east Asia.

This view of Britain and British technology has an important precedent, namely, Habakkuk's (1962) explanation of American technology in the nineteenth century. The United States emerged as the world's leading economic power after 1870, and the basis of American success was the remarkable degree to which its technology increased the productivity of labour. Habakkuk attributed the labour-saving bias of American inventions to the high wages of the American economy, which, in turn, were due to the abundance of land and natural resources in north America.[5] Eighteenth-century Britain was the prequel to nineteenth-century America.[6] In Britain, cheap energy underpinned a high wage economy that induced the invention of labour-saving technology, just as abundant land led to high wages and the labour-saving bias of American inventions in the nineteenth century.

High wages increased the *supply* of British technology as well as the demand for it. High wages meant that the population at large was better placed to buy education and training than their counterparts elsewhere in the world. The resulting high rates of literacy and numeracy contributed to invention and innovation.

The supply of technology was also affected by other developments. Jacob (1997), Stewart (2004) and Mokyr (1993, 2002) have emphasized the importance of Newtonian science, the Enlightenment and

[5] Hahn and Matthews (1964, pp. 852–3) summarize standard objections to the Habakkuk view, including the observation that profit-maximizing firms are indifferent between saving capital or labour. See also Salter (1960) on this point. My emphasis on the cost of R&D and the expectations about the bias of the resulting technology are meant to address this.

[6] Fremdling (2004, pp. 168–9) entertains this possibility, as does Mokyr (1993, pp. 87–9), who also raises many objections to it.

genius in providing knowledge for technologists to exploit, habits of mind that enhanced research, networks of communication that disseminated ideas, and sparks of creativity that led to breakthroughs that would not have been achieved by ordinary research and development. Mokyr's influential interpretation conceptualizes these elements as the Industrial Enlightenment. These developments would have boosted the rate of invention at any level of wages, prices and human capital. That is also their weakness. The Scientific Revolution and the Industrial Enlightenment were Europe-wide phenomena that do not distinguish Britain from the continent. That is appropriate in some contexts: France was in the lead in many industries with new techniques to her credit in paper, clocks, glass and textiles, for instance (Hilaire-Pérez 2000). Any theory that explains British success by positing a British genius for invention is immediately suspect. Instead, we must explain why Britain invented the technologies she did. The solution turns on the demand for technology and the price structure of the British economy.

Britain: a high wage, cheap energy economy

In Chapter 2, we saw that British wages were very high by international standards, both at the exchange rate and in terms of the standard of living that they bought. In Chapter 4, we saw that British energy prices were exceptionally low, especially near the coal fields of northern and western Britain. These are important features of the economy, but they are not the critical ones in so far as the demand for technology is concerned. The demand for technology depended on the price of labour relative to the prices of other inputs in production, i.e. the price of labour relative to the prices of capital and energy.

The price of labour relative to capital is shown in Figure 6.1, which plots the daily wage of a building labourer divided by an index of the rental price of capital in the English midlands, Strasbourg and Vienna. The rental price of capital is an average of the price indices for iron, non-ferrous metals, wood and brick, multiplied by an interest rate plus a depreciation rate. Strasbourg and Vienna were chosen since there are long series of wages and prices for those cities, and their data look comparable to those of most of Europe apart from the Low Countries. The series are 'PPP adjusted' so that we can compare across space as well as over time.

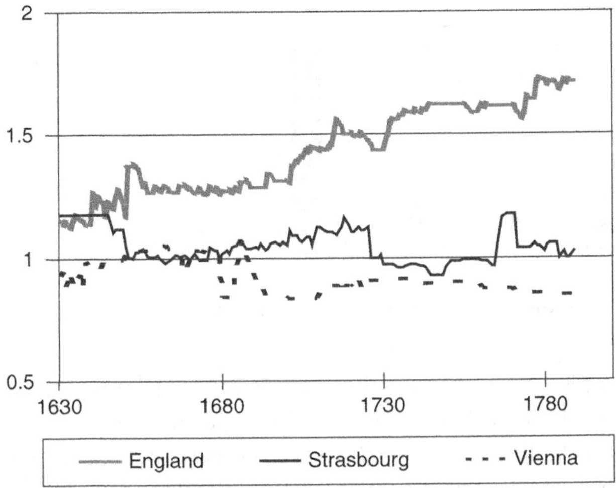

Figure 6.1 Wage relative to price of capital

The ratio of the wage relative to the price of capital was trendless in the early seventeenth century, and the differences between the cities were small. English labour was relatively cheap. The positions were reversed in the mid-seventeenth century when the series diverged, and English labour became increasingly expensive relative to capital. In contrast, the ratio of the wage to the price of capital declined gradually in Strasbourg and Vienna across the seventeenth and eighteenth centuries. The divergence in trends reflects the trajectories of nominal wages, which increased much more rapidly in Britain than elsewhere (e.g. Figure 2.1), rather than the cost of capital. This is a further blow to the institutionalists who maintain that Britain's superior institutions gave it cheaper capital. In the event, the incentive to mechanize production was much greater in England than in France, Germany or Austria.

The differences between Britain and other countries were even more pronounced in the case of energy. Figure 6.2 shows the ratio of the building wage rate to the price of energy in the early eighteenth century in important cities in Europe and Asia. For this calculation, the price of fuel was stated in terms of its energy content in millions of BTUs. The ratio is calculated for the cheapest fuel available in each city – coal in London and Newcastle, peat in Amsterdam, charcoal or firewood in the other cities.

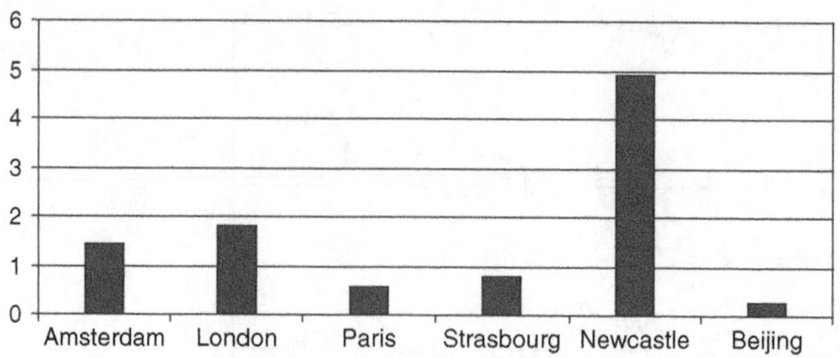

Figure 6.2 Price of labour relative to energy, early 1700s

Newcastle stands out as having the highest ratio of labour costs to energy costs in the world. To a degree, the high ratio reflects high British wages, but the low cost of coal was the decisive factor. Indeed, a similar ratio characterized the situation on all of the British coal fields and in the industrial cities (Sheffield, Birmingham and so forth) built on them. The only place outside of Britain with a similarly high ratio of labour to energy costs was probably the coal mining district around Liège and Mons in present-day Belgium. The high cost of labour relative to fuel created a particularly intense incentive to substitute fuel for labour in Britain. The situation was the reverse in China where fuel was dear compared to labour.

Why Britain's unique wages and prices mattered: substituting capital for labour

The British Industrial Revolution was the unfolding of a particular pattern of technical change. It was a path-dependent trajectory in which each step is explained (in part, at least) by the step that came before (David 1975, 1985, Dosi 1982, 1988, Arthur 1994). To understand why the technology of the British cotton industry or iron industry developed as it did, we must explain the first step in the trajectory. Those first steps were the famous macro-inventions of the eighteenth century.

The macro-inventions were made in Britain in the eighteenth century since Britain's high – and rising – wage induced a demand for technology that substituted capital and energy for labour. At the end of the middle ages, there was little variation across Europe in capital intensity. As the wage rose relative to the price of capital in Britain, it was increasingly desirable to substitute capital for labour and that is what happened. Sir John Hicks (1932, pp. 124–5) had the essential insight: 'The real reason for the predominance of labour-saving inventions is surely that . . . a change in the relative prices of the factors of production is itself a spur to innovation and to inventions of a particular kind – directed at economizing the use of a factor which has become relatively expensive.'[7]

We can clarify the influence of prices on invention, if we recognize that it involved the two stages that Edison called 'inspiration' and 'perspiration'. The important thing about the inspiration of the macro-inventions is that the idea they embodied came from outside the experience of the industry concerned. The idea of using coke as a blast furnace fuel was borrowed from industries like malting where it had been innovated as a fuel. Roller spinning was the adaptation of a technology (rollers) that was used in metallurgy and paper-making. The atmospheric steam engine was the application of knowledge discovered by seventeenth-century natural philosophers. Because the idea came from elsewhere, it could – and did – represent a radical change in practice, and that is why these ideas resulted in radical changes in factor proportions – the hallmark of macro-inventions. Hargreaves' spinning jenny is the exception that proves the rule. He thought it up by watching a spinning wheel. The invention of the spinning jenny looks like 'local learning' rather than an idea imported from elsewhere. While one expects local learning to result in minor changes, the spinning jenny, nevertheless, embodied a far-reaching change in factor proportions and, thus, qualifies as a macro-invention despite its origin.

The second stage of invention was research and development – the perspiration that turned a concept into a new product or a process. Leonardo da Vinci is famous as an 'inventor' since he sketched hundreds of novel machines, but his reputation is overblown in that he rarely did the hard work to turn drawings into functioning prototypes. Our interest is in the technologies that were *used* in the Industrial Revolution, and use required R&D as well as a eureka moment. While new ideas may not have been economically conditioned, R&D certainly was since the decision to incur costs to operationalize a technical idea was an economic one. As Machlup (1962, p. 166)

[7] Economists have since debated how to formalize these ideas (David 1975, pp. 19–91, Temin 1971, Ruttan 2001, Ruttan and Thirtle 2001, Acemoglu 2003).

remarked, 'Hard work needs incentives, flashes of genius do not.' Prices influenced technological development through their effect on the profitability of R&D.

The essential idea is that inventors spent money to develop ideas when they believed the inventions would be useful, in particular, when their social benefits exceeded the costs of their invention. When this condition was satisfied, an inventor with an enforceable patent could recoup the development costs through royalties. Even when private gain was not the object – for instance, Abraham Darby II figured out how to make coke pig iron that was suitable for wrought iron but refused to patent the discovery – social utility was still the aim, so our analysis has force. Whether or not an inventor got a royalty, a mundane point is crucial: an invention was socially useful only if it was used. If it was not used, there was no point in inventing it. Invention, thus, depended on adoption. Adoption, in turn, depended on factor prices, and that meant that factor prices influenced R&D and hence invention.

Implicit in this analysis is the idea that firms undertaking R&D knew what they were aiming at, at least in economic terms. It would be hard to argue with this assumption in the case of the inventions that increased the use of coal, for they were clearly aimed at changing factor proportions in the direction of a cheaper input. The assumption is not as immediately obvious in the case of machines. Was Hargreaves aiming at saving labour with the spinning jenny and Arkwright with the water frame? MacLeod (1988, pp. 158–81) notes that patent applications rarely specified 'saving labour' as the goal, but also adds that such a declaration might have only caused trouble. In the case of machines, however, the assumption must be that the invention was aimed at saving labour. In 1757, the Reverend John Dyer described Wyatt and Paul's roller spinning machine with the lines:

A circular machine, of new design
In conic shape: It draws and spins a thread
Without the tedious toil of needless hands.[8]

Twenty years later, Adam Smith (1776, p. 271) generalized the view that machines were *intended* to raise the capital–labour ratio and output per worker:

[8] Quoted in the article, 'John Wyatt (Inventor)', www.wikipedia.org (2008).

> The intention of the fixed capital is to increase the productive power of labour, or to enable the same number of labourers to perform a much greater quantity of work . . . In manufactures the same number of hands, assisted with the best machinery, will work up a much greater quantity of goods than with more imperfect instruments of trade.

This idea was popularly accepted: anti-machine riots in the eighteenth century were based on the idea that machines cut jobs. Bentley (1780), who believed that the rioters were short-sighted (they failed to recognize that higher labour productivity would create more jobs in the long run by making Britain more competitive), nevertheless accepted their assumption that machines reduced employment per unit of output, for he called his book *Letters on the Utility and Policy of Employing Machines to Shorten Labour*. If this was the conventional assumption among the population at large, can we imagine that saving labour was far from the thoughts of the inventors of machines?

Eighteenth-century comments like these bear on a red herring in the analysis of factor prices and technical change: a high wage might not imply high labour costs if the high wage workers were more productive than the low wage workers. If true, the incentive to mechanize might then be reduced. In the modern world, workers in poor countries may be less productive than their better fed and better educated counterparts in rich countries, so the difference in wages overstates the difference in production costs. The same may have been true in the eighteenth century if high wage British labour was better nourished, for instance, than lower wage French labour. But clearly there are limits to this effect: the higher productivity of manufacturing workers in rich countries has not been enough to prevent firms from relocating factories to the developing world to take advantage of the low wage, nor has it stopped them from raising the capital–labour ratio in the developed world. Comparisons between rich and poor countries depend critically on the characteristics of particular workers and the requirements of the jobs at issue. And, by replacing human power with machines, mechanized factories reduced the importance of nutrition in job performance.

Eighteenth-century commentators suggest that nutritional or other differences between workers in England and her competitors were not enough to offset the higher wage earned by English workers. Bentley (1780, p. 4) said that the 'advancing price of manual labour' in British manufacturing was offset 'by adopting every ingenious improvement the human mind could invent' rather than by an improvement in the intrinsic productivity of British labour that rendered mechanization unnecessary. The French glass manufacturer Delaunay Deslandes was particularly convincing on this point, for he recognized that high British wages led to a better diet than their French counterparts could afford: the English ate meat and drank beer, while the French only had soup, vegetables and water. In reflecting on these facts, Deslandes did not wonder how the French could hope to compete against such well-nourished foreigners. Instead, he asked how the English ever hoped to compete against the French when British wages were so high. The answer was cheap coal that offset the high cost of English labour.[9] Either a cheaper input (e.g. coal) or a more mechanized technology was needed to offset the high British wage if the British ever hoped to compete internationally.

It is important to bring out another feature implicit in my analysis. Even though a macro-invention might have had revolutionary consequences, the first models were very inefficient from a commercial point of view. They scarcely turned a profit even under the most favourable circumstances, and they did not earn enough income to cover costs in most situations. For the same reason, their social savings (contribution to economic growth) was negligible in the beginning. Wyatt and Paul spent decades trying to make roller spinning pay, and never did succeed. Abraham Darby I could not produce pig iron that was suitable for refining into wrought iron, but he did succeed in developing a specialized niche market of thin-walled castings. The inefficiency of the early models of macro-inventions is the reason that their adoption was very sensitive to factor prices. R&D can be thought of as the process of designing a prototype that was efficient enough to cover its costs. Then it could be operated commercially and further knowledge gained through observation and modification (local learning). At that point, the phase of micro-improvements was reached. The great virtue of this phase was that it did not require specific finance since R&D was effectively funded through normal business operations. In time, the macro-invention might be so improved that it could be used everywhere and revolutionize the world. But that was not the state of play at the outset.

[9] I quote Deslandes' comments in Chapter 4. See also Harris (1975).

Applying the model to Britain and China

Before seeing how macro-inventions were improved, we can look at two examples of how factor prices guided invention. The first relates to pottery kilns in England and China. In Britain, pottery was fired in round, up-draft kilns shown in Plate 6.1. These kilns were cheap to build but did not use energy efficiently. Much heat was lost as the draft left the kiln through the holes in the top. In Asia, on the other hand, kilns were designed to conserve energy. A common design was the 'down-draft climbing kiln' shown in Plate 6.2. These kilns were built on the slope of a hill. The kiln was a series of domes ('beehives') that were connected at the bottom. The walls were built thick to prevent heat loss. Each beehive had a firebox (but in the illustration only the first is shown). The hot air in the first chamber was not allowed to vent immediately into the second but was first forced down to ground level before leaving. As a result, much of its heat remained in the chamber, which reached an exceptionally high temperature. When the cooler (but still hot!) air entered the second chamber, the heat was passed on to the next batch of pottery. Another fire added more energy. The

Plate 6.1 English kiln (image courtesy of Dianne Frank)

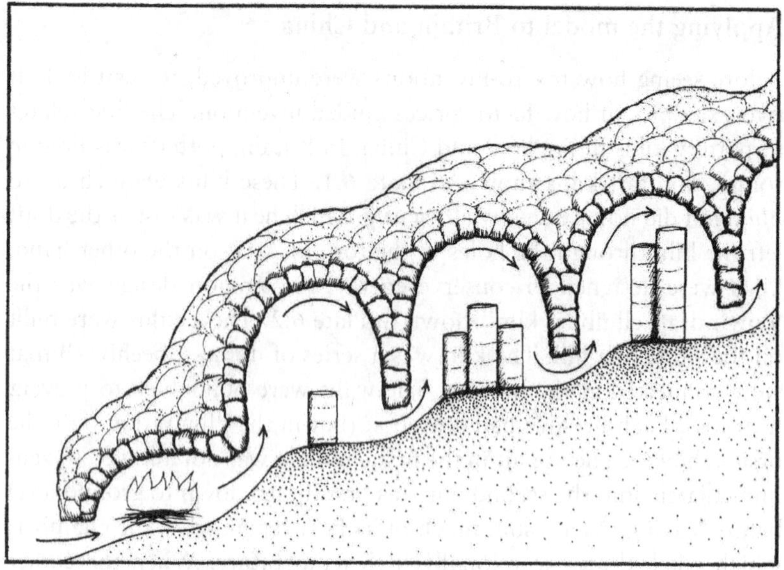

Plate 6.2 Chinese kiln (image courtesy of Dianne Frank)

process continued from chamber to chamber. In this way, very high temperatures were reached, and energy was conserved. Much capital was used, however, and many workers were employed stoking the various fires.

Neither the English nor the Chinese design was 'better' in an absolute sense. The best choice of design varied with the circumstances and depended on the prices of fuel, capital and labour. The Chinese developed a fuel-efficient design because energy was expensive, while the English saved capital and labour instead of energy because coal was so cheap.

Applying the model to Britain and France: the pin factory

We can see the same principles operating closer to home in the most famous production process of the eighteenth century – the pin factory described by Adam Smith in *The Wealth of Nations*. Smith argued that high productivity was achieved through a division of labour among hand workers. It is very likely that he derived his knowledge from Diderot and d'Alembert's *Encyclopédie* (1765, vol. V, pp. 804–7, vol.

XXI, 'épinglier') since both texts divide the production process into eighteen stages, and that cannot be a coincidence.[10] Indeed, Smith seems to have used the *Encyclopédie* for the exact purpose that Mokyr (2002, pp. 68–72) suggests – to find out about the latest technology.

There is a difficulty, however. The *Encyclopédie*'s account is based on the production methods at L'Aigle in Normandy. This was not the state-of-the-art practice as carried on in Britain. The first high-tech pin factory in England was built by the Dockwra Copper Company in 1692, and it was followed by the Warmley works near Bristol in mid-century (Hamilton 1926, pp. 103, 255–7). The latter was a well-known tourist destination (Russell 1769), and Arthur Young visited it. Both mills were known for their high degree of mechanization, and they differed most strikingly from Normandy in the provision of power. In L'Aigle, machines were propelled by people turning flywheels that looked like spinning wheels. In contrast, the Warmley mill was driven by water power. Since the natural flow of the stream could not be relied on, a Newcomen steam engine was used to pump water from the outflow of the water wheel back into the reservoir that supplied it. 'All the machines and wheels are set in motions by water; for raising which, there is a prodigious fire engine, which raises, as it is said, 3000 hogsheads every minute' (Young 1771a, p. 138). Powering the mill in this way immediately eliminated the jobs of the wheel turners (their wages amounted to one-sixth of the cost of fabricating copper rod into pins) and probably other jobs as well. Many French workers, for instance, were employed scouring pins. This activity was done with large machines driven by water power at English needle factories at the time.[11] Arthur Young observed that the Warmley works 'are very well worth seeing'. It is a pity that Adam Smith relied on the French *Encyclopédie* to learn about the latest in technology rather than travelling with Arthur Young.

Why did the English operate with a more capital- and energy-intensive technology than the French? L'Aigle was on a river, and water power drove a forge in the town, so geography was not a bar (indeed, the steam engine at Warmley shows that water power was

[10] Peaucelle (1999, 2005, 2007) has examined Smith's sources very carefully and identified several additional French publications that he argues Smith relied on. All of these sources describe production in Normandy.

[11] Early eighteenth-century water-driven scouring machinery is still in operation and can be seen at the Forge Mill Needle Museum, Redditch.

possible almost anywhere if you were willing to bear the cost of a steam engine). The Swedish engineer R. R. Angerstein (1753–5, p. 138) visited Warmley in the 1750s and noted that 'the works uses 5000 bushels of coal every week, which, because they have their own coal mines, only costs three Swedish "styfwer" per bushel', which was about half the Newcastle price.[12] In addition, English wages were considerably higher than French wages. Innovation in pin-making is an example of factor prices guiding the evolution of technology.

The second phase: a steam of micro-inventions

If innovation had stopped with the macro-inventions of the eighteenth century, the results would have been limited. While the Newcomen steam engine, for instance, was the technological marvel of 1712, it could do little more than pump water and was grossly inefficient by later standards. It took almost a century before a steam engine could directly drive machinery and a century and a half before steam was cheaper than sail on the tea route from China to Britain. This progress was the result of a vast stream of micro-inventions.

Micro-inventions differed from macro-inventions in three respects. First, micro-inventions were not generally biased technical changes that increased the demand for inputs that were abundant and cheap in Britain. Instead, micro-inventions were likely to be neutral technical improvements. In some cases, they even reversed the bias of the macro-inventions and saved inputs that were abundant in Britain. Thus, Newcomen's steam engine increased the demand for coal, but subsequent improvements like Watt's separate condenser were aimed at reducing energy consumption.

The gradual improvement of the macro-inventions had implications that we observe in the eighteenth and nineteenth centuries. At first, as the micro-inventions were made, Britain increased her technological lead over other countries. Moreover, countries with lower wages and more expensive energy still did not adopt the new British technology even though it was more modern, indeed, increasingly so. Thus, the coke blast furnace of the 1780s was more efficient that the furnace of the 1730s, but the French still did not use it. This reluctance has given rise to debates about the quality of French entrepreneurs and

[12] I thank Martin Dribe for help in deciphering the Swedish styfwer.

engineers, but the reality was that the blast furnace of the 1780s still used too much coal to be profitable in France where coal was very dear. In the next seventy years, British engineers reduced the use of all inputs – coal, ore, labour and capital – so much that coke smelting became more profitable than charcoal smelting in France. At that point, the French shifted to mineral fuel smelting very quickly: a 'tipping point' was reached. The French jumped directly to the most advanced blast furnace technology and skipped all of the intermediate stages through which the British progressed. Britain's competitive advantage had been based on the invention of technology that benefited it differentially. It is ironic that the success of Britain's engineers in perfecting that technology destroyed the country's competitive advantage.

A second difference between macro- and micro-inventions was in the inspiration for the inventions. While the ideas behind most macro-inventions came from outside the immediate industrial experience, the ideas for micro-inventions often originated in the study of that experience. Such ideas are called local learning. When Watt, for instance, invented the separate condenser, he began with a model of the Newcomen engine to see how it could be improved. He was also involved in erecting several engines, so he saw how they worked in practice and could try out his improvement. Learning in this way meant that the inventor was as likely to find an improvement that saved capital as one that saved labour. Since any change that cut costs was an improvement, there was no selection mechanism that generated a bias to save one input rather than another.[13] Of course, the possibilities of invention were affected by the characteristics of the materials themselves – no one has yet contrived to make a pound of cotton yarn with less than a pound of raw cotton – and by extraneous scientific discoveries and economic developments that created new factor price configurations, but reliance on local learning imparted a tendency towards neutrality in the second, micro-improvement phase of technological progress.

The third difference between macro- and micro-inventions lay in business behaviour. Because macro-inventions involved radical departures from existing practice, the R&D they entailed was expensive. Unless one was rich and prepared to spend his fortune like Edmund

[13] The essays collected in David (1975, pp. 1–191) are the most penetrating analysis of learning and technical change in economic history. My analysis draws on them.

Cartwright, the inventor of the power loom, external sources of finance had to be found. Venture capitalists, known as 'projectors' in the eighteenth century, usually became partners and received a share of the profits of the business. The invention was patented to secure those profits. Thus, the macro-inventions of the eighteenth century gave rise to the modern trilogy of R&D, venture capital and patent protection (Dutton 1984, MacLeod 1988, Sullivan 1990).

Micro-inventing was often a more collective enterprise (Rosenberg 1976, 1982). Since learning was local, it was often cheaper than macro-inventing, so the needs for external finance and patent protection were reduced. By sharing information, inventors could learn from each other and become more efficient. An important case in point was the perfection of the Cornish pumping engine in the nineteenth century which pointed the way to fuel economy in steam engines generally. These improvements were effected by the exchange of technical and economic information among all of the mines in Cornwall (Nuvolari 2004a, 2004b). Even when inventors patented their improvements, there was often also an exchange of knowledge and a cooperative approach to technical progress. Engineering societies played an important role in this regard. As collective learning became institutionalized, the tendency for technology to improve neutrally was increased.

The biographies of three macro-inventions

In the next three chapters, I will use the framework of this chapter to tell the stories of three of the great inventions of the Industrial Revolution: the steam engine, mechanical spinning, and smelting iron with coke.

First, I tell the story of the macro-invention. I begin with conception: what was the inspiration for the invention? Was it local learning, scientific discovery, or copying? How much genius was involved? Then I analyze birth: how much perspiration was required? How was R&D organized and financed? Then I consider the pay-off to this exertion in terms of the growth in productivity. How did the invention affect input requirements? Was it a biased technical change? Was it profitable to use the technique in Britain but not abroad? Does invention look sensible in terms of the economics of R&D?

Secondly, I analyze the long history of improvements to the macro-invention. What were the significant engineering improvements? Were they due to local learning? Did they lead to neutral technical progress in which all inputs were saved? Indeed, they were and did. And, by the middle of the nineteenth century, the macro-inventions of the Industrial Revolution lost their British bias and became globally useful technologies.

Appendix

Invention and the evolution of technology can be illustrated with a standard isoquant model.[14]

Phase I: macro-inventions

Macro-inventions are characterized by a radical change in factor proportions. This bias of the technical change interacted with factor prices and affected the incentives to undertake research and development. There are five important points to make:

1. A biased technical change saved one input disproportionally and reduced costs the most where that input was most expensive.
2. Techniques were worth inventing only if they were used.
3. A new technique was not worth using everywhere.
4. Countries with high wages found it profitable to develop a broader range of techniques with high capital–labour ratios than did low wage countries.
5. Larger markets increased the profitability of R&D and led to more invention.

These points are illustrated in Figure 6.3, which contrasts high wage and low wage countries. The curved isoquant through H and L connects the quantities of capital and labour needed to produce one unit of output. H is the input combination used by the high wage country, and it has a higher capital–labour ratio than the input combination L used by the low wage country. The straight lines tangent to the isoquant at H and L connect equal cost combinations of capital (K) and labour (N) where the unit cost of production is $C = rK + wN$ and where r and w are the rental price of capital and the wage rate. Each straight line

[14] Harley (1971) and David (1975, p. 89) use similar diagrams and Harley (1973) emphasizes 'the persistence of old techniques'.

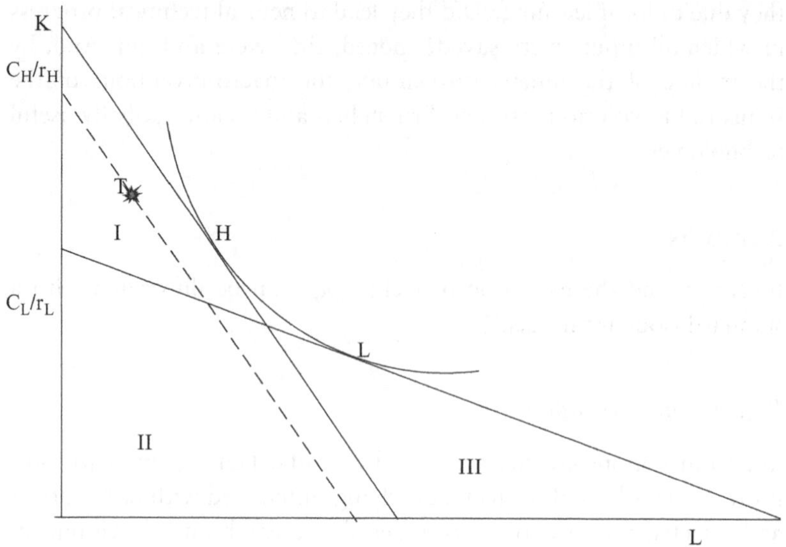

Figure 6.3 Phase 1: macro-inventions

plotted in Figure 6.3 is of the form K = C/r + (w/r)N. Its slope equals the wage relative to the price of capital (hence a steeper line denotes the high wage country) and C/r is the point where the line intersects the K axis. Hence, a higher intersection point indicates higher production cost (C). In Figure 6.3, C_H/r_H indicates the unit cost in the high wage country, and C_L/r_L the cost in the low wage country.

Now consider a potential new technology represented by the point T connecting a new combination of capital and labour that can produce one unit of output. T is a biased technical change: It uses more capital and less labour than either H or L. Would T be used? It would if and only if it lowered costs, and that is the case for the high wage country. We know this since a straight line through T that is parallel to the isocost line through H (hence, represents the same w/r) has a lower intersection point on the K axis and, hence, represents lower unit costs. For the low wage country, T would raise costs by the same argument. A technology like T is worth using – and hence worth inventing – only for the high wage country.

The two isocost lines divide the area below them into three spaces. New technologies in I would be adopted only by the high wage country, technologies in III only by the low wage country, and technologies like

II by either country. Some new technologies are useful to any country, while others are useful only to countries in particular factor price situations. Factor prices affect technological evolution because the adoption and invention of new techniques in sectors I and III depends on factor prices.

The high wage and the low wage countries had opposite incentives to invent technique T. It would be pointless for the low wage country to invent it since it would not be used. It might be worth inventing in the high wage country, but the incentive depends on benefits net of development costs. A technique like T in sector I would lower operating costs for high wage countries, and that saving generates the demand for the technology, i.e. creates a return for someone to invent it. But invention requires research and development to actualize the idea. Whether the demand for the technology is enough to motivate its development depends on the balance between the saving in operating costs and the cost of the R&D. Scale plays a role here since the R&D cost must be amortized over the output and compared to the reduction in unit operating costs. The total cost of production (inclusive of R&D) with the new technique is $C^* = C + D/q$ where D is the development cost and q is total production. The total cost line inclusive of R&D costs is $K = C^* + (w/r)N = C/r + (D/q)/r + (w/r)N$, i.e. the K intercept shifts up by the amortized R&D cost, so the total cost line is above the old one. The larger is q, the less is the upward shift in the isocost line inclusive of R&D cost. Two possibilities need to be distinguished at this stage. The first is that the isocost line rises but remains below the isocost line with the old technique. In that case, it is profitable to develop (i.e. invent) the new technique T. The second possibility is that the new isocost line rises above the original isocost line. In that case, it is not profitable to invent the new technique because the market is too small. Of course, if some other country or countries paid the R&D costs and the new technology were freely available, it would be adopted because it cuts operating costs. The size of the market affected the profitability of invention through the amortization of R&D costs.

Figure 6.3 identifies the conditions under which R&D was profitable, and they drove much private sector R&D. They also highlight the shortcomings of non-commercial R&D like some well-known technology initiatives of the French state. One was Cugnot's fardier, a steam tractor developed by the military to pull cannon across fields. Cugnot built a high-pressure steam engine and installed it on a vehicle. The fardier was a technical success, but the project was abandoned since it consumed too much fuel and sank into the mud. High-pressure steam engines were successfully used for traction only when both problems were solved by putting them on rails to pull wagons in British coal mines. A second example was Vaucanson's fully automated silk loom. This was a tremendous technological achievement, but it was never used commercially since it was far too capital intensive (Doyon 1966). These technologies show the force of Figure 6.3 in that they were not profitable to invent because they were not profitable to use.

Phase II: micro-inventions

Figure 6.4 shows the path of development if the British macro-invention unleashed a stream of micro-improvements that were neutral.[15] Neutrality means that all inputs would be saved in equal proportion, and technology would evolve along the straight line from T towards the origin.

The trajectory of micro-improvements in Figure 6.4 has important features that resonate with the industrial history of the last two hundred years. These include:

- Initially, the high wage country, which is the world's technological leader, builds up its lead. Invention and R&D are occurring there, and productivity is rising.
- In contrast, nothing much happens in the low wage country. They do not adopt the modern technology of the high wage country. Questions inevitably arise about the quality of their entrepreneurs and engineers.
- There is a 'tipping point', however, once the technology is improved to the point X where the path of technical improvement crosses the price line of the low wage country. At that point, it becomes suddenly profitable to adopt British technology. (A dotted isocost line for the low cost country is drawn through an input combination on the line from T to the origin and below X. The dotted isocost line is below the original isocost line for the low wage country and, therefore, represents cheaper production.)
- The low wage country finds that it pays to leap over many stages of technological development and go directly from L to the latest British

[15] Harley (1971) and David (1975, pp. 66, 71, 75) use similar diagrams.

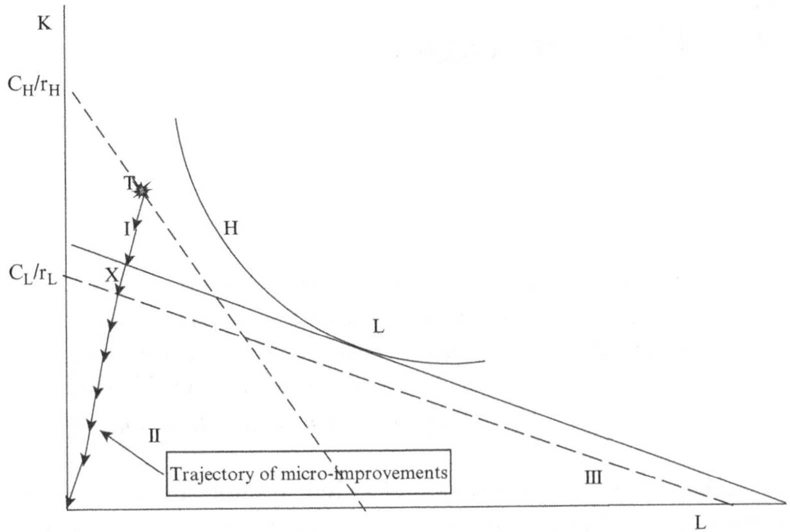

Figure 6.4 Phase 2: the trajectory of micro-improvements

technology. Catch-up is very rapid – a great spurt (Gerschenkron 1962). The Industrial Revolution spreads around the globe.

- Britain's competitive advantage had been based on the invention of technology that benefited it differentially. It is ironic that the success of Britain's engineers in perfecting that technology destroyed the country's competitive advantage.

7 *The steam engine*

> The high state of wealth and civilisation which the English people have attained within the last half century, has been greatly promoted by the application of the power of the steam-engine to various purposes of the useful arts, in aid of manual labour.
>
> John Farey, *A Treatise on the Steam Engine*, 1827

For most of human history, muscles (human and animal) were the main sources of power. In the ancient world, wind and water were also harnessed to the task. The steam engine was the next great step forward. Its impact on economic output in the eighteenth century was modest (von Tunzelmann 1978), but the use of steam to power industry increased dramatically in the nineteenth, and it was applied to transportation where the railway and steamship created a tightly integrated world economy. Between 1850 and 1870, steam technology accounted for two-fifths of the growth in British labour productivity (Crafts 2004, p. 348). By freeing the economy from dependence on wind, water and muscle, the energy that each worker could deploy increased dramatically and with it the productivity of labour.

The history of the steam engine goes through the two phases described in the last chapter.[1] The first phase was the macro-invention by Thomas Newcomen. His atmospheric or fire engine, as it was called in the eighteenth century, was a biased technical change in which the demand for fuel increased dramatically. His first engine was put into operation in Dudley in 1712 where it drained a coal mine. The Newcomen engines were only cost-effective in coal mines where fuel was effectively free and where the engine's uneven, reciprocating motion was suited to raising and lowering pumps, the main application.

The atmospheric steam engine is a good illustration of Edison's

[1] Standard works on the history of the steam engine include Farey (1827), Dickinson (1939, 1958), Forbes (1958), Cardwell (1963), Hills (1970, pp. 134–207, 1989), Nuvolari (2004a) and von Tunzelmann (1978).

distinction between 'inspiration' and 'perspiration'. The inspiration for the steam engine was unusual, for it was an application of scientific discoveries of the seventeenth century. Historians have remarked on several other applications of scientific knowledge during the Industrial Revolution such as chlorine bleach and the extraction of alkali from kelp (Clow and Clow 1952, pp. 65–90, 186–98). The steam engine was by far the most important. While scientific discoveries were necessary for the invention of the steam engine, they were not sufficient, they did not lead inexorably to the engine. It required a ten-year R&D programme. Much of the basic scientific research was done in Italy and Germany. Had the British coal industry not existed, there would have been no point going to the expense of developing the steam engine, and the scientific discoveries would not have flowered into the technology of the Industrial Revolution.

Newcomen's steam engine was a paradox: it was a scientific wonder and a very inefficient device. As soon as it was built, engineers studied it and sought to improve it. The process lasted a century and a half. This was the second phase of the steam engine's history. Many of Britain's most illustrious engineers like John Smeaton, James Watt and Richard Trevithick played leading roles. This development trajectory was broadly neutral: all inputs were saved, particularly in the case of rotary engines. The upshot were engines that were highly fuel efficient and that produced regular power that could drive locomotives, ships and machines. When engines became this good, the technology went global, and the steam engine diffused around the world. The tipping point was reached in the middle of the nineteenth century, towards the end of the second phase.

Phase I: Newcomen's macro-invention

The atmospheric engine that Newcomen brought into service in 1712 was a low-pressure engine. In these engines, the steam was condensed to form a vacuum in the cylinder, and the piston was pushed into it by the pressure of the atmosphere. This design was based on the idea that the atmosphere had weight, which was a discovery of seventeenth-century science and then a hot topic in experimental physics.

The link from science to the steam engine was direct.[2] The science began with Galileo, who discovered that a suction pump could not

[2] Dickinson (1958) provides a useful summary.

raise water more than about 28 feet – despite a vacuum existing above the column of water that had been drawn up to that height. Aristotle had said that nature abhorred a vacuum but only, it seemed, for 28 feet! Galileo suggested to Evangelista Torricelli, his secretary, that he investigate this problem. In 1644, Torricelli inverted a glass tube full of mercury and placed its bottom in a bowl of mercury. The mercury stabilized in the tube forming a column 76 centimetres high with a vacuum above it. This was the world's first barometer, and Toricelli concluded that the atmosphere had weight and pushed the mercury up the column. This was confirmed in 1648 by placing the barometer in a larger container and pumping the air out of it – the column of mercury collapsed and then reappeared as air was readmitted into the larger container.

A particularly important set of experiments was performed in Magdeburg by Otto von Guericke. In 1655, he put two hemispheres together and pumped the air out of the space they enclosed. It took sixteen horses to pull them apart. In another portentous experiment in 1672, von Guericke found that, if the air was pumped out of cylinder A (Plate 7.1), the weights D rose as the atmosphere pushed the piston down into the cylinder. Evidently, the weight of the air could perform work.

This idea had been anticipated by Christiaan Huygens in 1666, who used exploding gunpowder to drive a piston up a cylinder. When it reached the top, the gases from the explosion were released creating a vacuum. Air pushed the piston down and raised the load. While there was some scientific interest, exploding gunpowder was never going to be practical. However, his assistant, Denis Papin, realized that filling the cylinder with steam and then condensing it accomplished the same purpose. In 1675, Papin built the first, very crude, steam engine.

The first practical application of steam technology was Thomas Savery's steam vacuum pump patented in 1698. It created a vacuum by condensing steam in a reservoir; the vacuum then sucked up water. The purpose of Savery's device was draining mines, but it was not widely used, and it was not a steam engine.

But still an R&D project

The first successful steam engine was invented by Thomas Newcomen. Like Savery's device, it was intended to drain mines. Newcomen's

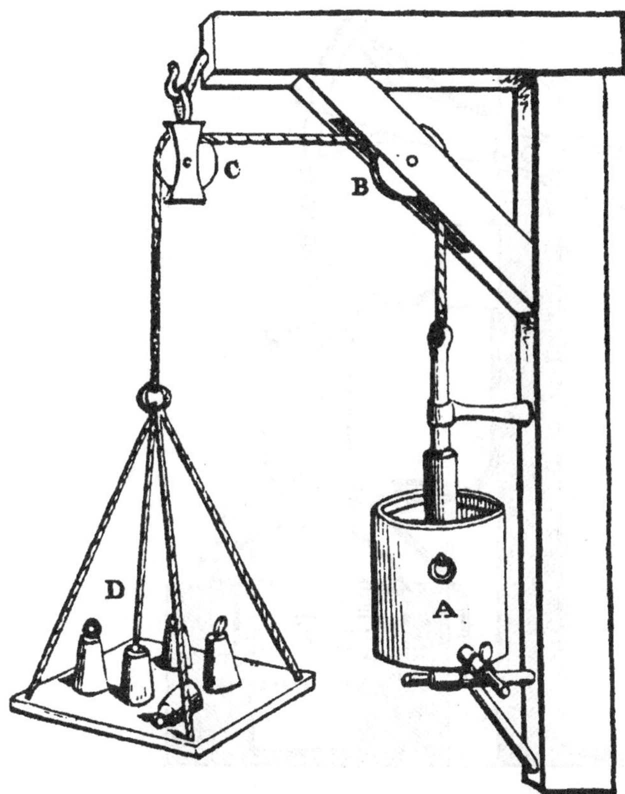

Plate 7.1 Abstraction of Von Guericke's illustration

engine applied the discovery that the atmosphere has weight (Rolt and Allen 1977, pp. 37–8, Cohen 2004). That application required a major R&D project, and that project meant that the invention was an economic commitment as well as a scientific spin-off.

Newcomen's design (Plate 7.2) was suggested by von Guericke's apparatus. First, replace the weights with a pump (I). Secondly, construct the 'balance beam' so it is slightly out of balance and rests naturally with the pump-side down (H). Then, if a way were contrived to create a vacuum in the cylinder (B), air pressure would depress the piston (E) and raise the pump. Next, if air were reintroduced into the cylinder, the vacuum would be eliminated and the pump would drop since the beam is slightly out of balance. Finally,

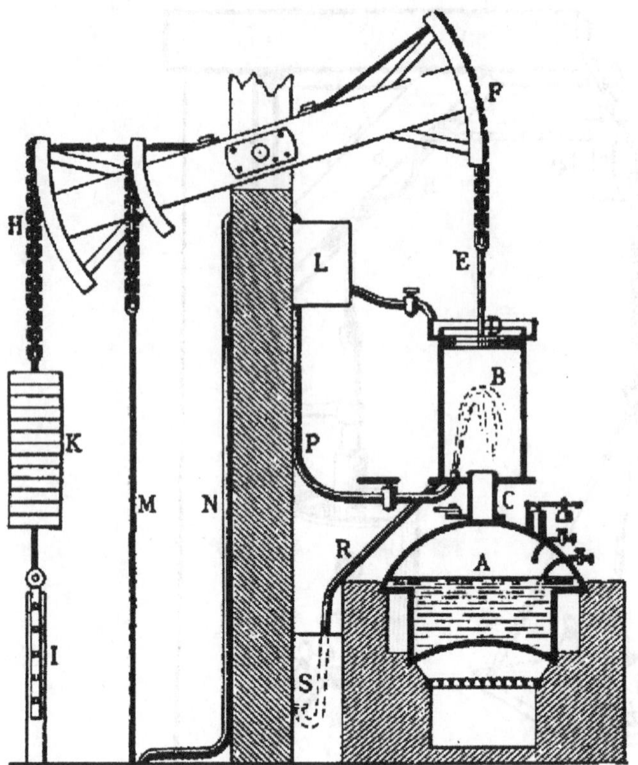

Plate 7.2 Thomas Newcomen's steam engine

recreating the vacuum would raise the pump again since the pressure of the atmosphere would again depress the piston. Thus, creating a vacuum and relieving it raises and lowers the pump. This apparatus becomes a 'steam engine' when steam is made by boiling water (A) and drawing it into the cylinder when the piston is raised, and the vacuum is created when cold water is injected into the cylinder (B) to condense the steam. This is a low-pressure engine since it is not steam pressure that pushes the piston up: the point of the steam is simply to provide a gas that fills the cylinder and which is condensed to create the vacuum. At the heart of the Newcomen engine was seventeenth-century science.

While the Newcomen engine differed from other eighteenth-century inventions in its scientific basis, it was similar in the engineering challenges it posed. Twentieth-century engineers who have built Newcomen engines have found it difficult to make them work (Hills 1989, pp. 20–30). That Newcomen could resolve the engineering problems was a remarkable achievement. He began experimenting around 1700 and apparently built an engine in Cornwall in 1710, two years before his famous engine at Dudley.

In this decade of R&D, Newcomen learned many things. He discovered by accident that the steam could be condensed rapidly if cold water was injected into the cylinder (B). He found that the water supply tank (L) for the injector worked best if it was placed at the top of the engine house, so the injection water entered the cylinder at high pressure and volume. The pipe (R) that drained the condensed water from the cylinder had to run far enough down into a hot well (S), so that atmospheric pressure could not force condensed water back into the engine. The top of the cylinder had to be sealed with a layer of water – nothing else worked. The dimensions of the balance and the weights of the engine's piston and the pump (K) had to be coordinated for smooth operation. Linkages between the beam and the valves had to be designed so that they would open and shut automatically at the correct moments in the cycle. No wonder it took Newcomen ten years to create an operating engine. It was a time-consuming and expensive undertaking.

Like many practitioners of R&D, Newcomen hoped for a pay-off through patenting his creation. In this he was frustrated because the Savery patent was extended twenty-one years to 1733 and construed to cover his very different engine! Newcomen was forced to do a deal with the Savery patentees to realize any income at all.

A biased technical improvement that favoured the British

R&D costs meant that the link between Galileo and Newcomen was mediated by economics. Scientific curiosity and court patronage may have been reason enough for Torricelli, Boyle, Huygens and other scientists to devote their time and money to studying air pressure (David 1998), but Newcomen was motivated by prospective commercial gain. What was that gain? The object of the engine was to drain mines, so the demand for the technology was determined by the size of the mining industry. In 1700, England's lead was immense: it produced 80 per cent of the tonnage in Europe and 59 per cent of the value. Germany, which had been Europe's mining centre in the late middle ages, produced only 4 per cent of the tonnage and 9 per cent of the value in 1700.[3] The change was all down to coal. Servicing the drainage needs of England's coal industry is one reason why steam engine research was carried out in England.

Coal mattered for a second reason as well. There were alternative ways of powering pumps – water wheels or horse gigs – so there was effective demand for steam power only if it was cost-effective. The early steam engines were profligate in their consumption of fuel, so they were cheap sources of power only if fuel was remarkably cheap. Desaguliers (1734–44, vol. II, pp. 464–5), an early enthusiast of steam power, put the matter succinctly:

> But where there is no water [for power] to be had, and coals are cheap, the Engine, now call'd the Fire-Engine, or the Engine to raise Water by Fire, is the best and most effectual. But it is especially of immense Service (so as to be now of general use) in the Coal-Works, where the Power of the Fire is made from the Refuse of the Coals, which would not otherwise be sold.

The Newcomen engine was a biased technological improvement that shifted input demand away from animal feed and towards combustible fuel.

Free fuel overcame high fuel consumption, but, by the same token, the energy intensity of the Newcomen engine restricted its use to the coal fields. Since most of the coal mines were in Britain, so were most of the engines. At the expiry of the Savery–Newcomen patent in 1733, there were about 100 atmospheric engines in operation in England. By 1800, the total had grown to 2,500 in Britain, of which 60–70 per cent were Newcomen engines.[4] In contrast, Belgium, with the largest coal-mining industry on the continent, was second, with perhaps 100 engines in

[3] Production of coal, copper, lead, mercury, silver, tin, zinc and iron from Nef (1932, vol. I, p. 129, n. 4), Flinn (1984, p. 26), Schmitz (1979, pp. 61, 92, 126, 143, 160, 182, 328) and Pounds and Parker (1957, pp. 21–52). Prices from Schmitz (1979, pp. 268, 275, 282, 289, 293, 290) and Hyde (1973, pp. 402–4). The metal ores were valued at half the price of the refined metal. The calculations are only approximate, since the figures come from a mix of years near the beginning of the eighteenth century.

[4] Kanefsky and Robey (1980, p. 171). The uncertainty depends on how one classifies the engines of unknown type. As the production of Watt engines is reasonably well established, the unknown engines were probably Newcomen, and that choice yields the higher percentage.

1800.[5] France followed with about 70 engines of which 45 were probably Newcomen (installed mainly at coal mines) and 25 were Watt. The first steam engine in the Netherlands was installed in 1774, in Russia in 1775–7, and in Germany at about the same time. None seem to have been installed in Portugal or Italy (Redlich 1944, p. 122, Tann 1978–9, pp. 548, 558). The Newcomen engine 'was adopted in numbers only in the coal fields . . . The machines were, until well into the nineteenth century, so symbolically linked to the coal-fuel matrix in which they had come to maturity that they could not readily pass beyond its limits' (Hollister-Short 1976–7, p. 22). The diffusion pattern of the Newcomen engine was determined by the location of coal mines, and Britain's lead reflected the size of her coal industry – not superior rationality.

Why the steam engine was invented in Britain rather than France or China

Moreover, the diffusion pattern of the Newcomen engine indicates that it would not have been invented outside of Britain during the eighteenth century. Non-adoption was not due to ignorance: the Newcomen engine was well known as the wonder technology of its day. It was not difficult to acquire components, nor was it difficult to lure English mechanics abroad to install them (Hollister-Short 1976–7). Despite that, it was little used. A small market for engines implied little potential income for a developer to set against the R&D costs. The most likely alternative was Belgium, which had the largest coal industry on the continent. However, production around 1800 was only 13 per cent of Britain's and Belgium's steam engines amounted to only 4 per cent of the British total. The benefit–cost ratio was correspondingly higher for Newcomen than for any would-be emulator on the continent. This is an example of the effect of market size on the propensity to do R&D discussed in Chapter 6. Newcomen had to know about the weight of the atmosphere in order to design his engine, but he also needed a market for the invention in order to make its development a paying proposition. The condition was realized only in Britain, and that is why the steam engine was developed there rather than in France, Germany or even Belgium.

[5] The total is very poorly established and is surmised from an estimate of 200 engines installed in France (then including Belgium) in 1810 made by Perrier, the first important French steam-engine manufacturer (Harris 1978–9, p. 178).

Phase II: a century and a half of improvement

Newcomen's steam engine was the cutting-edge technology of its day, but, in hindsight, it was a primitive machine. Its fuel consumption was prodigious – that, of course, is why it was only worth developing in Britain – and its reciprocating action was too uneven to drive machinery. How engineers did it at all will be explained later. Newcomen's engine was only suitable for pumping water. Both of these limitations were removed in the next century and a half, and that improvement made steam power cost-effective in many countries where it had previously been too expensive and in many uses where it cost more than wind, water or animal power.

The process of technical change differed in important respects from Newcomen's breakthrough. One relates to 'inspiration'. While Newcomen's breakthrough was based on seventeenth-century scientific discoveries, science did not provide useful new knowledge until far into the nineteenth century. Carnot's *Réflexions sur la puissance motrice du feu* was not published until 1824 and had little immediate impact. Steam engines evolved as engineers varied current designs to improve performance. This was 'local learning'.

A second difference related to bias. The first atmospheric engine increased the demand for capital and coal. In the next century and a half, technical progress in rotary engines saved both capital and energy – it was, in other words, roughly neutral – while progress in pumping engines saved mainly coal. The bias in the pumping sector reflected new price incentives arising from the special circumstances of copper and tin mines in Cornwall where coal was relatively expensive (Burt 1969). Neutrality in rotary engines was the result of local learning, which tended to save all inputs, as argued in the last chapter. Finally, inventors learned from each other, so invention often had a collective character even when people tried to protect innovations that were patentable.

Improvements in engine design economized on fuel. The early Newcomen pumping engines consumed on the order of 45 pounds of coal per horsepower-hour of power.[6] This was cut to less than

[6] In the eighteenth century, the fuel-efficiency of a steam engine was measured by its duty, where duty was the work (in millions of foot-pounds) done by burning one bushel of coal. Thus, a duty of 5 meant that one bushel of coal performed 5 million foot-pounds of work. A Newcastle bushel weighed 84 pounds (Hills 1989, p. 36), so that coal consumption per horsepower-hour equalled 166.32

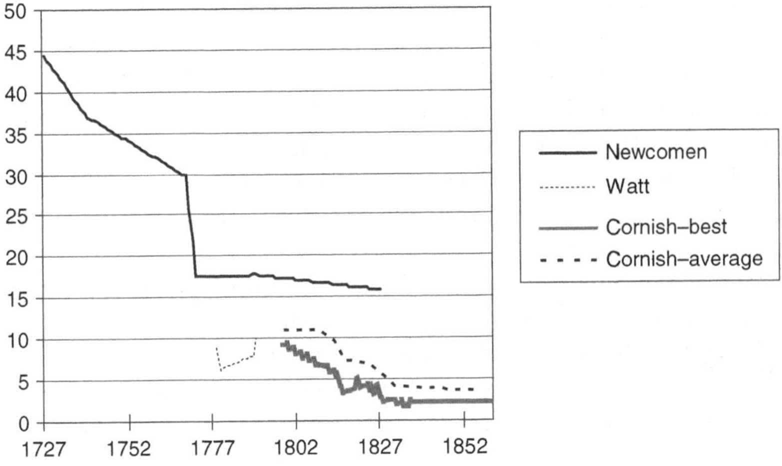

Figure 7.1 Coal consumption in pumping engines: pounds of coal per horsepower-hour

Sources: Hills (1989, pp. 37, 44, 88, 59, 111, 131), von Tunzelmann (1978, pp. 67–70), Lean (1839).

one pound in the most efficient marine engines manufactured late in the nineteenth century. Figure 7.1 plots the fall of coal consumption per horsepower-hour in pumping engines over this period. The points on the graph represent new design configurations rather than average practice. The most marked absolute improvement was achieved by Newcomen engines in the eighteenth century. Very little is known about the decline from 45 to 30 pounds per horsepower-hour that was realized before 1760. We do know, however, that variation among engines was very great. John Smeaton, for instance, studied fifteen atmospheric engines working near Newcastle in 1769 and found that coal consumption ranged from about as little as 22 pounds per horsepower-hour to as much as 47 pounds per

divided by the duty. (166.32 = 84 x 33,000 x 60/1,000,000). Thus, a duty of 5 implies a fuel consumption of 33.264 pounds of coal per horsepower-hour. For counties other than Cornwall, I have used this relationship to convert duty to pounds of coal per horsepower-hour, which became the measure of fuel efficiency in the nineteenth century. In Cornwall, a bushel of coal weighed 94 lbs, and the conversion was done accordingly for Cornish pumping engines. I thank Alessandro Nuvolari for bringing this to my attention.

horsepower-hour.[7] Information of this sort was not closely guarded, as Smeaton's success in collecting it shows. Indeed, openness had a long tradition, for Desaguliers and Beighton collected and published detailed technical data regarding Newcomen's original design (Dickinson 1958, pp. 176–7). Under these circumstances, engineers could compare performance, learn from each other, and make improvements. This was certainly the route taken in later, better documented examples.

Individual initiative, nonetheless, played an important role. The drop in fuel consumption from 30 pounds per horsepower-hour in 1769 to 17.6 in 1772 was due to Smeaton's efforts. He experimented with a model engine and fine-tuned each component of the design as well as the proportions among them to effect an atmospheric engine that was as efficient as possible. He treated this research as a scientific inquiry rather than an advance to be patented. (Of course, he was a consulting engineer, and, by raising his professional stature, he increased the demand for his services.) The improved engines that he built at the Long Benton Colliery in Northumberland and the Chacewater Mine in Cornwall were exemplars of best practice (Hills 1989, p. 37).

There were no further significant improvements in the efficiency of Newcomen engines. The next great reduction in fuel consumption was due to James Watt's separate condenser. In the early 1760s, Watt read the literature on steam engines and conducted some experiments on steam pressure.[8] In 1763–4, he was employed by the University of Glasgow to repair a model Newcomen engine. He noted that cold water injection chilled the cylinder, which then had to be reheated as steam was drawn in. Experiments and calculations on the energy needed to change water from a gas to a liquid organized his thoughts, although he only later learned of the theory of latent heat that Dr Joseph Black, also then at the University of Glasgow, had formulated around 1760. Watt realized that the loss of energy from chilling the cylinder could be avoided by leading the steam into a second chamber where it could be cooled. The separate condenser was born. In 1765 and 1766, Watt was involved in erecting several Newcomen engines,

[7] I infer this from von Tunzelmann's (1978, p. 18) report that the average duty measured by Smeaton was 5.59 million foot-pounds per bushel of coal and the maximum was 7.44.

[8] Details of Watt's life and business dealings from *Oxford Dictionary of National Biography*, online edition, 2008.

and in 1768 he recommenced experiments on model engines and then built the prototype of an engine with a separate condenser, which he patented in 1769. By then, he had spent almost £1,000 on the project. Commercial production was delayed until after 1776, when Watt's partnership with Matthew Boulton commenced and his 1769 patent was extended by parliament to 1800. In 1778, Smeaton measured the energy consumption of a Watt engine at 8.8 pounds of coal per horsepower-hour, a saving of 50 per cent over Smeaton's improved version of the Newcomen engine (Hills 1989, p. 59).

Watt's career epitomizes the private R&D model of technical change. His invention of the separate condenser and the detailed engineering to produce a commercial product entailed considerable effort and expense. He sought to realize a return on this investment by patenting the separate condenser in 1769. To finance this R&D, Watt needed venture capital, and he received it first from Joseph Black.[9] In 1768, John Roebuck, the inventor of the lead chamber method of making sulphuric acid and a founder of the Carron Ironworks, assumed Watt's debts and paid the costs of a patent in exchange for a two-thirds interest in it. Roebuck, in turn, went bankrupt, and Matthew Boulton purchased his share of the Watt patent. The Boulton–Watt partnership was the basis of a successful business that produced hundreds of steam engines and related machinery into the nineteenth century.

There were no further improvements in pumping engines due to James Watt. In this field, he became an impediment to progress. His vigorous enforcement of his patent stifled technical progress in the 1780s and 1790s. Jonathan Hornblower, for instance, invented a compound engine in which exhaust steam from the main cylinder was led into a second cylinder where it could do more work rather than being chilled (and its energy wasted) in a separate condenser. Watt claimed that the second cylinder was really a 'separate condenser' and infringed his patent. The threat of legal action dissuaded Hornblower from pursuing his idea, and this promising line of research was shut down until the nineteenth century (Hills 1989, pp. 147–8).

Further progress in the design of pumping engines occurred in Cornwall. Hundreds of steam engines, including Watt engines as well as Newcomen engines, had been installed to drain copper and tin

[9] Brunt (2006) has shown that some eighteenth-century 'country banks' functioned like venture capital firms – indeed, financing Boulton–Watt engines in Cornwall.

mines. When Watt's patent expired in 1800, he removed the engineers who had overseen his engines, and their performance deteriorated. The district was thrown back on its own devices, and the response was altogether different from private R&D. In 1811, a group of mine managers decided to publish each month details of their engines and their coal consumption, which was ascertained by independent audit. Eventually, most mines joined the consortium, and the details of performance were published in *Lean's Engine Reporter* until 1904. Engineers could study the sources of success and build on the initiatives of other firms (Lean 1839, Nuvolari 2004a, 2004b, Nuvolari and Verspagen 2007).

This way of organizing technological change is called collective invention (Allen 1983, Nuvolari 2004a, 2004b). It is particularly suited to situations where the effects of design innovations can only be ascertained by building a large and expensive production facility like a pumping engine. Each new engine became an experiment. By exchanging information, the costs of experimenting were shared among the mines. Collective invention was also suited to situations where the entry of new firms was limited, so that the benefits to design improvements were limited to the firms doing the experimenting. The restricted number of locations for copper and tin mines had that effect. By learning from the leaders, the followers could lower their costs by re-engineering old engines or eventually replacing them with new, efficient ones.

Cooperation among the Cornish mines was effective in reducing the fuel consumption of pumping engines. In the 1790s, Cornish engines were like other Watt engines and burnt just under 10 pounds of coal per horsepower-hour (Figure 7.1). By the mid-1830s, the average engine was burning 3.5 pounds per horsepower-hour and the best engines burned less than 2 pounds per horsepower-hour. This improvement was due to a long sequence of innovations (Hills 1989, pp. 64–6, 99–113). The first was the high-pressure steam engine, first built around 1800 by Richard Trevithick, who had long been a thorn in Watt's side. In high-pressure engines, steam at a pressure of about 25 pounds per square inch was injected into the cylinder and the force of that steam drove the piston. (In contrast, the function of steam in the low-pressure engine was to fill the cylinder and then be condensed. The pressure of the atmosphere drove the piston into the resulting vacuum.) High-pressure engines saved fuel and capital (they weighed less). They were the engines that eventually powered railway locomotives and steamships. The idea of high-pressure steam was not new – Watt's

1769 patent made reference to it, and he denounced it regularly – but Trevithick was the first to apply it. The use of high-pressure steam required high-pressure boilers, and Trevithick also designed one of the first successful models.

The second innovation was the use of steam expansively. In the high-pressure engine, one could keep injecting steam until the piston reached the end of the cylinder, and that would give maximum speed and power. Alternatively, one could stop the inflow of steam earlier in the cycle and let the pressure of the steam already in the cylinder push the piston to the end. Less steam meant less coal was burned, but the pressure dropped as the piston travelled, leading to irregular work. This problem was overcome by the adoption of the plunger pump, also invented by Trevithick and the third important innovation. The fourth key innovation was the 'double beat drop valve' that allowed the precise control of steam during expansion so that maximal energy could be converted to mechanical power.

Arthur Woolf developed the drop valve, and he was also responsible for the final major innovation in Cornish design – the use of compounding. Hornblower had patented this in 1781, but it had not been successfully applied. Woolf, in partnership with Henry Harvey, combined compounding with high-pressure steam and began selling engines in 1813. They set startling records for fuel economy. The improvement from Newcomen's original design was monumental. The early eighteenth-century limitation on the use of steam engines to draining mines in Britain had been broken. They were now cost-effective virtually anywhere.

Pumping water was only one application of steam power. Manufacturing (and later transportation) were others. The Newcomen engine suffered from a major liability in this regard, however. The rocking motion of the beam, which was ideal for raising and lowering a suction pump, was often irregular; the piston paused at its highest position waiting for the cylinder to fill with steam and then for the steam to be condensed; power, in any event, was only generated when the atmosphere pushed the piston down, not on the return stroke, which was effected by the counterweight of the beam and the drag of the machinery. These features of the Newcomen engine, which were fundamental to its operation, meant that it could not provide smooth power to machinery. The contrast with a water wheel, which turned continuously and which was widely used to drive machinery, was profound.

The first solution to the inadequacies of the Newcomen engine was to combine it with water power. Streams, which provided adequate flow to drive a water wheel in the winter, often dried up in the summer, and production was interrupted. The solution, first adopted at Coalbrookdale in 1742 (Raistrick 1989, p. 113) and ten years later at the Warmley brass works, was to use a Newcomen engine to pump water that had passed through the water wheel back into the upstream reservoir so it could pass over the wheel again. These 'returning engines' were widely used in the last half of the eighteenth century (Von Tunzelmann 1978, p. 143). They are usually thought of as steam engines supplementing inadequate water power, but they can also be analyzed as a technique to improve a Newcomen engine by adding to it a water system so that the engine produces smooth, rotary power. In addition, augmenting the Newcomen engine in this way saved coal per horsepower-hour at the cost of more capital.

Figure 7.2 shows the evolution of fuel consumption in rotary engines from the early eighteenth century to the mid-nineteenth. The trajectory for the Newcomen engine describes the combined result of the steam engine and the water wheel, so that coal consumption depends on the assumed efficiency of the water wheel and (more importantly) on the proportion of the annual water flow that was pumped back by the engine. Once again, John Smeaton makes an appearance. In the 1770s, he was hired to install a returning engine to drive the blowing engines for the Seacroft iron works. He studied an old water wheel on the stream to determine its power output and the flow at different seasons. He reckoned that the reversing engine would have to pump one-third of the annual flow, mainly during the summer. This produced a very efficient outcome (Farey 1827, pp. 279–80). A more representative case, however, would have the engine pumping half of the steam's flow over the year and using an overshot wheel, which was less efficient than the breast wheel that Smeaton installed. I have modified his calculations accordingly, and the implied trajectory of coal consumption is the line labelled Newcomen returning in Figure 7.2. There were very large gains in fuel efficiency during the eighteenth century because of the improvements, previously discussed, in the design of atmospheric engines.

In the late 1770s, the first steps were taken to drive machinery directly with Watt's steam engine. It suffered from the same erratic drive as the Newcomen engine. In a patent granted in 1779, Matthew Wasborough

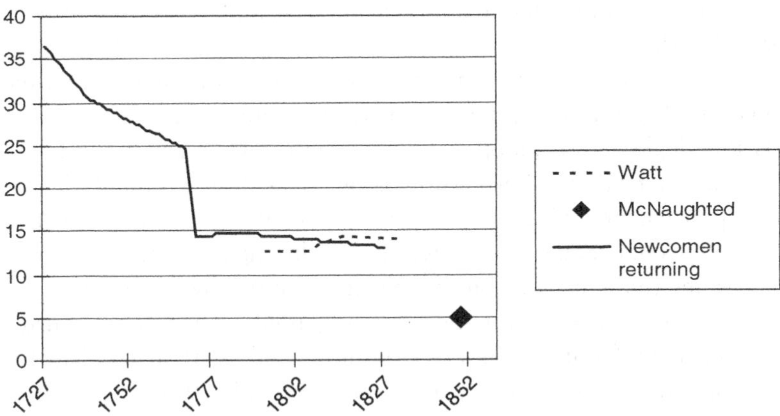

Figure 7.2 Coal consumption in rotary engines: pounds of coal per horsepower-hour

Source: Hills (1989, pp. 37, 44, 88, 59, 111, 131), von Tunzelmann (1978, pp. 67–70). See the text for the calculation of the coal required to operate the Newcomen engine as a returning engine.

addressed the problem by adding a flywheel to the engine, and the next year James Pickard patented the use of a crank to connect the engine to a factory power shaft (Hills 1989, p. 60).

The revolutionary breakthroughs, however, were made by Watt during the 1780s (Hills 1989, pp. 63–9, 85–6). He was reluctant to take up the problem, but did so at Boulton's urging: 'There is no other Cornwall to be found and the most likely line for the consumption of our engines is the application of them to mills which is certainly an extensive field' (quoted by Hills 1989, p. 62). Watt's inventions included, first, reorganizing the valves so that steam could be injected alternately into each end of the cylinder and vented into the condenser. In that way, power was created on each stroke, and the engine was said to be 'double acting'. Double action produced smoother, more regular power. Secondly, the chain that connected the piston to the beam was replaced by a system of rods called 'parallel motion', and this allowed the piston to push the beam as well as to pull it. Thirdly, to avoid infringing Pickard's patent, the 'sun and planet' gears were used to rotate the drive shaft with the reciprocating beam. A bonus was that the sun and planet gear doubled the rotation speed of the factory power shaft. Fourthly, the centrifugal governor, which had been used on windmills, was connected to a steam valve and used to stabilize the speed of the engine.

The result of these innovations was a rotary steam engine that did a good job powering machinery. It was not, however, as fuel efficient as the single action pumping engine: the rotary engine used 12–15 pounds of coal per horsepower-hour as against 8 pounds in the pumping engine. Indeed, the Newcomen engine-cum-water wheel used 15 pounds of coal per horsepower-hour, although performance varied according to the proportion of the water pumped by the engine.

To create a market for their engines, Boulton and Watt courted leading manufacturers. In 1784, Boulton and Watt invested in the Albion Mill, the first large-scale steam-powered factory, to promote their engines. In 1785, George and John Robinson of Papplewick near Nottingham were the first to install a Watt engine in a cotton mill. By 1800, Boulton and Watt had sold 308 engines to drive machinery and another 24 to power blowing engines (Hills 1989, pp. 60–72).

The use of steam power increased during the early nineteenth century, but, in 1830, still accounted for less installed power than water plus wind (Table 7.1). Indeed, explaining the slow adoption of steam power in the cotton industry is an important problem for the historians of its technology. Watt's rotary engine had been a great advance, but it was not subsequently improved. Low pressure remained the norm. The next step forward depended on importing some of the designs perfected in Cornwall – notably high-pressure steam and compounding. Rotary engines designed on these principles cut fuel consumption from 15 pounds per horsepower-hour to 5 pounds in the 1840s. In 1845, William McNaught patented a plan for adding a high-pressure cylinder to a beam engine and venting the steam from the new cylinder into the original one. This arrangement, called a McNaughted engine, allowed existing engines to realize the fuel savings from compound and high-pressure steam (Hills 1989, pp. 157–9, von Tunzelmann 1978, pp. 70, 86–8). Steam power then rapidly displaced water, and the general mechanization of British industry began.

So far, we have considered the effect of improved engines on fuel economy. What of other inputs? In terms of cost, the most important were coal and capital. Each accounted for about 45 per cent of cost, with labour accounting for most of the remaining 10 per cent (von Tunzelmann 1978, p. 74). Figures 7.3 and 7.4 throw light on the changing bias of technology, as well as the rate of technical progress.

Table 7.1 *Stationary power sources in Great Britain*

	1760	1800	1830	1870	1907
Steam	5,000	35,000	160,000	2,060,000	9,659,000
Water	70,000	120,000	160,000	230,000	178,000
Wind	10,000	15,000	20,000	10,000	5,000
Total	85,000	170,000	340,000	2,300,000	9,842,000

Source: Crafts (2004, p. 342) and ultimately from Kanefsky (1979). Internal combustion engines are excluded. Warde (2007, p. 75) presents alternative estimates for England and Wales that place the predominance of steam at an earlier date primarily by reducing the estimates of water power in 1800 and 1838 (he has no estimate for 1760). In addition, Warde estimates steam power in 1870 at about half of the value shown here – a large difference despite the variance in coverage.

They show the evolution of coal, capital and total cost per horsepower-hour of power.[10] All quantities are valued at 1795 prices, so the proportional fall in unit costs is the reciprocal of the increase in total factor productivity. The real cost of rotary power in the mid-1840s was about one-third what it had been in the early eighteenth century, while the real cost of pumping power had dropped by about half. The efficiency of the pumping engine had doubled and that of the rotary engine had tripled.

In both pumping and rotary engines, the evolution of technology reversed the bias towards coal that was inherent in Newcomen's original design. The reversal was most marked in pumping engines. Real coal cost per horsepower-hour dropped 90 per cent from the 1720s to the 1840s, while real capital costs declined only slightly. On the other hand, real coal and capital costs per horsepower-hour declined by similar proportions in rotary engines. The evolution of the rotary engine looks, therefore, like an example of neutral technological change.

On the economic plane, the different histories of the pumping engine and the rotary engine highlight the importance of economic incentives and institutions. Coal mines remained a market for pumping engines throughout the eighteenth century, but, from the 1760s onwards, improvements in their design were keyed to the Cornish mining

[10] Crafts (2004, p. 343) presents some calculations along these lines.

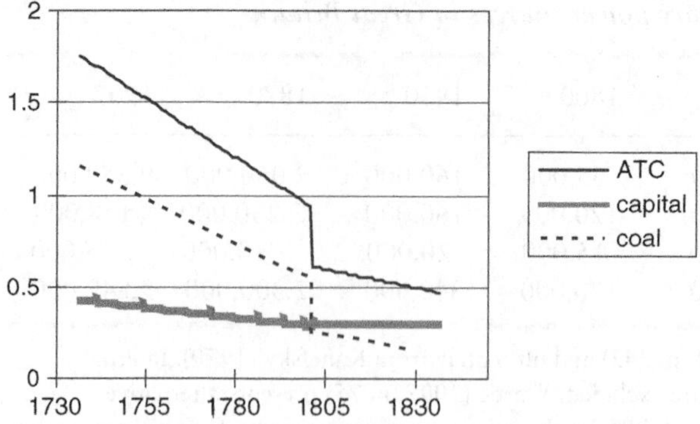

Figure 7.3 Pumping engine: costs per horsepower-hour

Note: costs for all years are computed with 1795 prices to show changes in input use and efficiency.

Source: Coal quantities as in Figure 7.1. Coal price assumed to cost 7.25 shillings per ton, the Manchester price in 1795 (von Tunzelmann 1978, p. 73).

Capital costs: Von Tunzelmann (1978, pp. 47–62, 145) reports the cost of the engine and boiler of an approximately 20hp pumping engine in 1736 (Newcomen), 1800 (Newcomen), 1801 (Watt) and 1836 (Cornish). These costs were increased by 45 per cent to make allowance for the cost of the engine house, framework, erection and pipes, which were not normally reported separately (von Tunzelmann 1978, pp. 50, 72). The total cost of the installed engine was converted to 1795 prices by deflating with an index of the prices of copper (10 per cent), wrought iron (20 per cent), coke pig iron (20 per cent) and skilled building labour (50 per cent). Division by engine horsepower yielded cost per horsepower. The costs were annualized by multiplying by an interest rate (5 per cent) plus a depreciation rate (7.1 per cent – the weighted average depreciation rate for the various components of installed engine costs according to von Tunzelmann 1978, p. 72).

Average total cost (ATC): on the assumption that capital plus coal cost equalled 90 per cent of total cost, their sum was divided by 0.9 (von Tunzelmann 1978, p. 74).

industry. Between 1775 and 1800, for instance, Boulton and Watt sold 164 pumping engines of which 49 went to Cornwall (Hills 1989, p. 70, *Dictionary of National Biography* entry for Watt). It had particular characteristics. The demand for drainage was great since the mines were deep and the ores valuable. Indeed, for that reason, Savery and Newcomen had entertained the possibility that Cornwall would be a market for their engines, but the promise was never realized. While Britain, in general, was a country of cheap coal, energy in Cornwall was actually expensive since coal had to be shipped from South

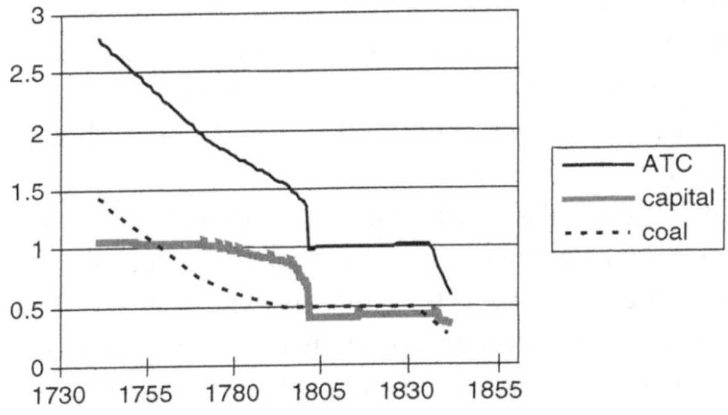

Figure 7.4 Rotary engine: costs per horsepower-hour

Note: Costs for all years are computed with 1795 prices to show changes in input use and efficiency.

Sources: the sources and methods were similar to Figure 7.3 with the following exceptions.

The figure plots costs for a Newcomen returning engine in 1722, 1772 and 1800 (in which half of the stream flow is pumped by the engine), a Watt rotary engine in 1795 and 1801, a Hick low-pressure engine in 1835, and a Hick high-pressure engine in 1841.

The Newcomen calculations assume the cost of a 30hp steam engine plus the cost of a water wheel capable of giving 20hp (at £15 per hp according to von Tunzelmann 1978, p. 146), which is the power output of the system as a whole.

The cost of the Hick engines is from Hills (1989, pp. 115, 119).

Wales. Early on, Newcomen shifted his attention from Cornwall to the coal fields. Indeed, around 1730, only 5 of the approximately 100 Newcomen engines in Britain were erected in Cornwall (Barton 1966, p. 16). While Watt's early experiments with the model Newcomen engine at Glasgow University may have been intellectually motivated, the development of the separate condenser took years and great finance. The obvious market for the engine was Cornwall where the separate condenser saved the expensive input coal and made the steam engine cost-effective in pumping. The separate condenser looks like another example of factor prices guiding research and development. In the nineteenth century, the story was repeated in a different institutional context as the high price of coal continued to guide the process of technical change during the period of collective invention. In *Lean's Engine Reporter*, fuel consumption was monitored because coal was expensive and engines were judged by their ability to economize on it

(Lean 1839). After its initial application to coal mines where energy was substituted for other inputs, the evolution of the steam engine was governed by the economics of Cornwall. The result was a trajectory of technological evolution in which energy was saved. In both phases, technology responded to input prices.

The situation was somewhat different with respect to rotary engines. Here, factor prices played a less important role because the main problem was producing smooth rotary power. This problem dominated technological evolution in the eighteenth century. Local learning was a key to progress, and discoveries were made by varying what was at hand. The marriage of the Newcomen engine and the water wheel is an obvious example. Watt's innovations that created his rotary steam engine are other examples. Double action was a simple enough variant on single action that produced more nearly continuous power. The replacement of the chain with a rod to connect the piston to the beam was not a great leap forward when the piston delivered push as well as pull. The other improvements made by Watt were small variants on existing practice that were clever but not profound modifications given the problem of regularizing the power output of the steam engine. Nor can compound cylinders have been much of an insight for someone working with steam engines every day.

Many of the engineers making steam engines patented their improvements. This secured them some return to their efforts while slowing down other inventors afraid of infringing their patents. Watt exercised a baleful effect in this regard. Despite the patents, however, invention in steam technology had a collective character, like that of the Cornish mining industry. Successful innovations by one engineer were adopted and extended by others. An important example was the application of compounding to rotary engines. Benjamin Hick, who had a foundry in Bolton, was a leader in this development. Charles Beyer, a designer for a firm making textile machinery that collaborated with Hick in equipping mills, wrote that: 'The engine is nominal 40 HP and Mr Hick warrants it capable to exert 90 indicated horsepower. It is on Wolfe's principle' (quoted by Hills 1989, p. 118). Woolf's principle was compounding. One engineer adapted the work of another. As discussed in the last chapter, this style of development tends to produce neutral technical progress, and that is what the history of the rotary steam engine illustrates.

The diffusion of the steam engine

The reversal of the bias of technical change had a profound effect on the utilization of steam engines. The reduction in the cost of power spread its use to more industries and to more countries. Table 7.1 shows the capacity of water wheels, wind mills and stationary steam engines in Britain. These engines drained mines and powered mills and factories. Steam capacity grew throughout, but water and wind remained the dominant sources of power until about 1830. It was only between 1830 and 1870 that steam became pre-eminent, and, even in that period, the capacity of water wheels continued to expand. The decisive shift to steam occurred in the middle decades of the nineteenth century after high-pressure compound engines cut costs, as we have seen. The effect of cheaper power on its spread can be seen in the diffusion of famous technical processes. Van Tunzelmann (1978, pp. 193, 200), for instance, has shown that the power loom[11] and the spinning of high count yarn with the self-acting mule became cost-effective as power costs dropped in the middle of the nineteenth century.

While the falling cost of power was the ultimate cause of the application of steam to more and more uses, this extension was not as smooth as a simple economic narrative might suggest. The improvements in the technology were due to local learning, and that implied that knowledge of the improvements was initially confined to the locality where the learning occurred. It took time for engineers in other districts or industries to become aware of the improvements and to be convinced of their utility. There were lags in which apparently profitable inventions were ignored. An important example is the Lancashire cotton industry, which relied on low-pressure steam engines until the late 1840s – several decades after high-pressure steam had cut fuel consumption in Cornwall (Nuvolari and Verspagen 2008). 'Non-economic' developments like the 1847 Ten Hours Bill could jolt entrepreneurs out of these ruts (von Tunzelmann 1978, pp. 209–25).

The use of steam also expanded in transportation as its cost fell. The railway, of course, depended on the steam locomotive, and that used high-pressure steam engines from the outset. Only these were light enough and efficient enough to pull trains. Improvements in engine design such as the tubular boiler cut their fuel costs further.

[11] However, see Lyons (1987).

Steam also displaced sail in the world's merchant marine during the nineteenth century. The transition was protracted and closely tied to reductions in the fuel used by engines (Harley 1971). All coal used by the British merchant marine, which was the largest in the world by a substantial margin, was mined in Britain because it was cheap and of high quality. As a result, fuel costs increased with distance from Britain since a ship had to devote more and more cargo capacity to carrying coal. The same effect obtained even if the coal was purchased abroad since the coal came from Wales, and the shipping cost was added to the Welsh price. Of course, a steamship could offer faster, more reliable service than a sailing ship, and that led to an early shift to steam in some services. In so far as bulk cargoes were concerned, however, cost per ton mile was the decisive factor, and the first routes to shift from sail to steam were the shortest, for which fuel was a minor consideration. By 1855, the trade between Britain and ports in France and the Low Countries was steam, and by 1865 steam had displaced sail on cargo voyages to the eastern Mediterranean, a journey of 3,000 miles. By the early 1870s, steam was established on trans-Atlantic routes of 3,000 miles, and the 5,000-mile voyage between Britain and New Orleans shifted to steam in the late 1870s. By the 1880s, steam displaced sail on trade between Britain and Asia. These transitions occurred when the cost of shipping freight by steam dropped below the cost by sail. The fall in steam costs was largely driven by improvements in the thermal efficiency of the engines. Efficiency was improved by extending the principles that cut the cost of rotary power in the 1840s, namely, by adding more compound cylinders and using a condenser. The pinnacle of efficiency was the triple expansion engine which burned less than 1 pound of coal per horsepower-hour (Forbes 1958, p. 164).

The improvements in the efficiency of steam engines that extended their use across the economy also spread their use internationally. The railway and the steamship were global technologies from their inception. They could be profitably adopted in many places at the same time they were profitable in Britain. Steamboats were used for river transportation and taken up by the (very much smaller) merchant marines of many countries at about the same time they became cost-effective for British firms. Railways were built almost as rapidly in western Europe and North America as they were in Britain. Even low wage economies like Russia and India built vast rail systems later in the nineteenth century.

Table 7.2 *Capacity of stationary steam engines*

	1760	1800	1840	1870
Britain	5	35	200	2,060
France		3	33	336
Prussia			7	391
Belgium			25	176
United States		0	40	1,491

Notes:

[1] The Prussian figure for 1840 is really for 1837 and the Belgium figure for 1840 is for 1838.

[2] The Prussian figure for 1870 is estimated by assuming a constant growth rate between the capacity in 1861 and 1878.

[3] The French figure for 1800 was estimated from Fohlen (1973, pp. 47–8). He reports that there were 200 steam engines in France in 1810 and many were out of date. I assume there were 200 in 1800. In 1830, there were 625 engines producing 10,000 hp (16 hp per engine) and, in 1839, 2,450 producing 33,000 hp (13.5 hp per engine). Using either 16 hp or 13.5 hp per engine implies 3,000 hp in total in 1800.

[4] United States: Hunter (1985, p. 415) for 1840 and 1870. According to Hunter (1985, p. 69), Latrobe reported half a dozen sizeable stationary engines around 1800. These could not have had more than a few hundred horsepower, which is rounded to zero in the table.

Sources: Britain: Table 7.1. British steam capacity in 1840 estimated on the assumption that capacity increased at a constant annual rate between 1830 and 1870. France, Prussia and Belgium: Landes (1969, p. 221), Table 7.1.

The improvements in engine efficiency that led the steam engine to be the dominant motive power in British mining and manufacturing in the middle of the nineteenth century also led to the widespread adoption of steam in western Europe and North America. Table 7.2 shows that there was very little steam capacity in France or Germany around 1800. Indeed, it was not until the second third of the nineteenth century that steam capacity expanded sharply, and steam came to play an important role as a power source for industry. The rapid take-up of steam for manufacturing outside of Britain followed immediately upon the use of compounding in rotary steam engines, a change which sharply cut the cost of power.

It was not until the middle of the nineteenth century that the stationary steam engine was widely used in American manufacturing, just as in France and Germany. However, the Americans showed a remarkable engineering capacity in developing steam power at an early date. Steam was such a revolutionary technology that there were experiments with it in many countries. In the 1760s, for instance, Cugnot, a French artillery officer, was commissioned to develop a steam-powered tractor to pull cannon across fields. He designed a high-pressure steam engine and mounted it on a three-wheeled tractor (the fardier) that is reputed to have knocked over a building in an early trial. The project was abandoned, however, since the tractor used so much fuel and would have sunk in mud had it been run across wet fields.[12] The solution to these problems in Britain was to mount the steam engine on rails in coal mines, and that experience led directly to the railway. Another solution to the road bed problem was to put the engine on a boat, and trials were made in many countries. Widespread commercial application was first realized in the United States as the conjunction of two developments. The first was Oliver Evan's independent invention of the high-pressure steam engine in 1789. He anticipated using it to power a road vehicle, but his plan was no more successful than anyone else's. Instead, success was realized on water. Experimental steam vessels were made in France in the late eighteenth century, and the American inventor, Robert Fulton, may have seen them. In 1803, he installed a Boulton–Watt engine on a boat on the Hudson River and began the world's first commercial steam service between New York and Albany. In 1811, the first steamboat left Pittsburgh for New Orleans. Steam travel took off on the Ohio and Mississippi Rivers. Demand for transportation was great, the rivers were free, and vast forests provided cheap fuel. Steamboat design evolved quickly and was one of the first great examples of American technological ingenuity (Hunter 1949). It was not until the mid-nineteenth century that stationary steam engines were adopted on a large scale as industrial powerplants in the United States – and that adoption was based on the Corliss engine, an American improvement to the high-pressure steam engine – but the independent invention of high-pressure steam and its application to river transport was more successful technically and commercially than the response of any other country to the British inventions.

[12] The most accessible information about Cugnot is found in the articles 'Joseph Cugnot' in www.wikipedia.org and www.wikipedia.fr.

Newcomen's invention had conferred a strong competitive advantage on Britain since it cut British costs by increasing the use of a resource that was cheap and abundant in England and Scotland. Present-day Belgium was the only other country to receive a comparable benefit. This competitive advantage was undone, however, when the bias of technical progress reversed, and engineers reduced the fuel consumption of steam engines. They became cost-effective in more applications and, most importantly, in countries where energy was more expensive. The elimination of Britain's advantage, moreover, made it profitable to spread the Industrial Revolution across Europe and America.

8 *Cotton*

> The cotton mill presents the most striking example of the dominion obtained by human science over the powers of nature, of which modern times can boast. That this vast aggregate of important discoveries and inventions should, with scarcely an exception, have proceeded from English genius, must be a reflection highly satisfactory to every Englishman.
>
> Edward Baines, *History of the Cotton Manufacture*, 1835, p. 244

Cotton was the wonder industry of the Industrial Revolution. From small beginnings, employment reached 425,000 in the 1830s and accounted for 16 per cent of jobs in British manufacturing and 8 per cent of British GDP (Deane and Cole 1969, pp. 143, 166, 187, Wood 1910, pp. 596–9). Giant cities were conjured where mill operatives lived and worked. Explaining how and why the cotton industry became so big is fundamental to explaining the Industrial Revolution.

Technological innovation was a central part of the story. In the middle of the eighteenth century, England had a small industry by world standards. About 3 million pounds of yarn were spun each year in England (Wadsworth and Mann 1931, p. 521). France was the other leading European producer, and it was about the same size as Britain. Both were dwarfed by Bengal, which produced about 85 million pounds per year[1] and was an important competitor for European

[1] Chaudhury (1999, pp. 143, 175, 188, 198, 211) indicates that about 60 million rupees of cotton cloth were consumed in Bengal in the middle of the eighteenth century, 10 million rupees were exported by Asian merchants and 6 million by Europeans. European exports in 1750/1 to 1754/5 amounted to 744,652 pieces. The average price of these cloths indicates that they were cheap, not luxurious. Scaling up in proportion to sales (76/6) implies that total production equalled 9,432,259 pieces. A piece was typically 40 x 2.25 covids and a covid was 18 inches, so 212,225,827.5 square yards were produced. Pomeranz's (2000, p. 318) figures indicate that Chinese cloth weighed about 0.4 pounds per square

producers in markets like Africa where cottons were exchanged for slaves.

All cotton was produced by hand technologies. Before any processing occurred, the cotton was cleaned and debris like seeds and stalks removed. The next stage in manufacturing was carding. The cotton was placed between two hand-held cards studded with pins, and the cards were pulled against each other, so that the pins combed the cotton fibres into alignment. A length of these fibres, called a roving, was assembled, and that was the material that was spun. The choice of spinning technique depended on the fineness of the yarn, which was measured by its 'count'.[2] Coarse yarn like that used in modern jeans was 16–20 count, finer yarn like that used in shirts was about 40 count, while the finest muslins were several hundred count. Counts below 50 were spun on wheels everywhere. The finest muslins were only made in India, and they were spun with the spindle-and-whorl. Whatever the count, the yarn was woven into cloth with a handloom.

The technological history of the cotton industry is the history of the mechanization of these processes.[3] Spinning was mechanized before weaving and is the focus of this chapter. The problem attracted attention throughout the first half of the eighteenth century. Indeed, Kerridge (1985, p. 269) claims to have discovered spinning machines in use in Norwich in the early 1700s. Lewis Paul and James Wyatt almost succeeded in inventing a successful spinning machine. Between the late 1730s and the late 1750s, they experimented with roller spinning. Two patents were secured, and they operated a mill in Birmingham, but they could not make money from it (Wadsworth and Mann 1931, pp. 419–48, Hills 1970, pp. 32–53). Success was first achieved by James Hargreaves, who invented the spinning jenny in the mid-1760s. He was quickly followed by Richard Arkwright who perfected roller spinning. Hand spinning had been organized as a domestic industry,

yard, which is plausible. That density implies that production was 85 million pounds per year.

2 The count was the number of 'hanks' of yarn that weighed one pound, where a hank was a piece of yarn 840 yards long.

3 Standard histories include Baines (1835), Aspin and Chapman (1964), Fitton (1989), Fitton and Wadsworth (1958), Wadsworth and Mann (1931), Hills (1970, 1979) and Rose (1986, 1996, 2000). Recent biographies of important figures are found in the *Oxford Dictionary of National Biography*, online edition, 2008, and summarize much important information.

and the spinning jenny quickly displaced hand spinning in that setting. From the outset, Arkwright's water frame was suited to factories. The jenny was best adapted to spin weft, while the water frame was better suited to manufacture warps.[4] Neither the jenny nor the water frame proved suitable for high count yarn. In the 1770s, Samuel Crompton combined elements of the jenny and the water frame to make a new machine called the mule. It could produce yarns that rivalled the finest in India, and it laid the basis for Britain's world dominance in cotton goods in the nineteenth century.

The spinning jenny, water frame and mule were key inventions in the mechanization of cotton spinning, but they were only part of the story. Not only were they themselves improved, but other processes – cleaning, carding and reeling – were also mechanized. In addition, the machines had to be spatially organized, the flows of materials coordinated, and the generation and distribution of power sorted out. A corresponding division of labour was needed. The cotton mill, in other words, had to be invented as well as spinning machinery *per se*.

The cost implications of these changes are shown in Table 8.1, which is a reconstruction of cotton manufacturing costs from the hand process of the 1760s to factory spinning in the 1830s. All costs are valued with prices from 1784, so changes in costs and their components indicate changes in input requirements and productivity. The table shows the cost of producing 16 count cotton and does not include the efficiency gains implied by the ability to spin higher counts. Even so, the growth in productivity was impressive. Factory production in 1836 cut the cost of yarn in half compared to the hand methods of 1760: overall productivity had doubled. There was some slight improvement in the reduction of raw cotton per pound of yarn, but most of the gain was due to savings in capital, materials and labour. Real value added per pound of thread dropped from over 18.12d per pound with hand methods to 1.52d with machine methods in 1836. The savings in labour, which fell from 17.19d to 0.5d, was particularly pronounced. Capital costs also declined but by much less – from just under 1d to less than 0.5d per pound. Innovation in the British cotton industry relentlessly saved labour, the scarce and expensive factor of production.

[4] A piece of cloth was anywhere from 12 to 30 yards long and 1 to 2 yards wide depending on type and specification. The yarn that ran the length was the warp, while the yarn than ran across the cloth was the weft.

Table 8.1 *Real cost of cotton (16 count) in 1784 prices (d/lb)*

	Hand method, 1760	24-spindle jenny, 1775	Arkwright mill, 1784	Glasgow (integrated) mill, 1836
Raw cotton	16.88	16.88	16.88	16.70
Preparatory	1.40	1.40	0.82	0.02
Carding	5.60	5.60	1.87	0.14
Spinning	7.00	2.33	2.57	0.34
Reeling, bundling	0.47	0.47	1.07	0
Craft and other			1.12	
Administrative	2.72	2.72	0.41	0.02
Materials	0	0	1.20	0.53
Capital	0.93	1.88	2.00	0.47
Average total cost	35.00	31.28	27.94	18.22

The figures in the table are of varying degrees of reliability.

Hand method, 1760

Following Ellison (1886, p. 61), 18 ounces of raw cotton were assumed as the requirement for a pound of yarn.

Guest (1823, p. 10) describes the income and expenses of a weaver who subcontracted for yarn to be spun. Guest reports that spinning, on the one hand, and carding, roving and picking, on the other, each cost 9d per pound, from which I conclude that each took the same length of time. Considerable evidence indicates that spinners could spin one pound per day of low count yarn (Muldrew 2007). The table assumes that spinning and carding, roving and picking each took one day per pound and a woman's daily wage in 1784 was 7d.

Picking was estimated to have cost 1.4d per pound and carding was estimated as 7d less 1.4d. Pinchbeck (1930, pp. 152–3) cites evidence from the early 1790s that picking cost 1.5d per pound when it was done domestically for cotton mills. The daily wage for women was about 7d, so picking took 1.5 / 7 = 0.21 days per pound. In this table, I round the labour requirement to 0.2 days per pound, which implies a cost of 1.4d per pound.

Reeling and bundling were estimated from the Papplewick accounts, as the operations at Papplewick were not highly mechanized. It is possible that this work was included in the spinning or was done by the putting-out merchant. However, it is shown separately as it did not amount to a great deal of money.

The costs of operating the putting-out system were estimated to be 25 per cent of the labour costs. Wyatt reports that James Livesey, 'a very considerable dealer

Table 8.1 (*cont.*)

in Manchester', told him in 1743 that 'though they gave but a penny a skein to the spinners' – payment that covered all of the direct labour costs since the spinners either did the work themselves or subcontracted it – 'yet the number of servants and agents that they were obliged to have about the country, made their yarn stand them in five farthings per skein' (as quoted by Baines 1835, pp. 131–2). Applying 25 per cent to the direct labour expenditure implies that the administration of the putting-out system came to 3.62d per pound. I report two-thirds of this as administrative labour (2.72d per pound) and the other one-third (0.90d per pound) as a capital cost on the ground that warehouses, carts and horses were required to operate the putting-out system and were implicit in Livesey's comment. The remaining component of capital (0.03d per pound) was the annual cost of the spinning wheel.

24-spindle jenny, 1775

All costs as for the 1760 hand method except that the cost of spinning was reduced to one-third of the hand value. This is the implication of the tripling of labour productivity discussed in the text.

Arkwright mill, 1784

The mill in question was the Papplewick cotton mill owned by George, John and James Robinson. A Watt steam engine was installed the next year. In 1784, the mill was a 2,000-spindle Arkwright water mill. Chapman (1971) describes it, and the costs are detailed in a document in the Nottingham Record Office, Portland Manuscripts, DD 4P 79/63. This document is detailed but incomplete. A breakdown of unit costs are given, and they can be related to the employment levels in most departments. However, some departments of the mill (e.g. carding) were not fully described and overhead labour (managers, craftsmen and so forth) was excluded. These lacunae were filled from the employment records of the Quarry Bank Mill given by Hills (1970, p. 237). Salaries of managers were taken from Pollard (1965, pp. 171–2).

Beyond incompleteness, the accounts raised two interpretive issues. The first was the number of shifts worked. The accounts made sense only if one assumed two shifts and round-the-clock operation. This was common in the 1780s (Fitton 1989, p. 152). This assumption reconciled my reconstruction of the employment levels and labour costs by department with the summary of costs given in the document. Secondly, the average count made in the mill was 25.6, and the table is intended to compare the cost of 16 count yarn. There were two ways to estimate the cost of 16 count yarn, which was one of the most common sizes. The document reports the price received for each count, so one could reduce overall unit cost per pound spun by the ratio of the price of 16 count yarn to the average price of all yarn. This calculation assumes that the ratio of price to cost was the same for all counts. Alternatively, a range of output is given for the mill. On the assumption that the production rate was higher for lower count yarn, one could compute a unit cost for low count yarn by assuming that the mill operated at its highest rate. This

Table 8.1 (*cont.*)

procedure gives a similar result to the calculation using prices, and is the basis of the cost structure shown in the table.

Glasgow (integrated) mill, 1836
Montgomery (1836, pp. 248–56). The mill was an integrated spinning and weaving mill. The yarn was all 16 or 18 count. The weaving costs have been excluded. This is straightforward for direct labour costs since employees and wage expenses are given by departments, as were most capital costs. The cost of the building and power plant, materials and overhead labour costs, however, were given for the mill as a whole. These costs were divided into carding and spinning, on the one hand, and weaving, on the other, in proportion to the ratio of capital in carding and spinning (62 per cent) to weaving (38 per cent).

Table 8.1 shows the fall in costs in the production of coarse yarn, but that was only part of the story. Finer yarn required more working, i.e. more labour, per pound, and wages were so high in eighteenth-century England that the production of yarn finer than 20 count was uncompetitive. Mechanization solved the problem, for machines cut the cost of high count yarn even more than coarse yarn. The average British count was said to be 27 in the late 1780s and rose to about 40 in the 1830s (von Tunzelmann 1978, p. 182). Figure 8.1 contrasts the reductions in the price of 18 count weft and 40 count warp. These prices have been deflated by an index of the prices of the inputs in cotton production that is meant to indicate how price would have evolved in the absence of technical progress. Declines in the price of cotton deflated by this index mean that product price was falling relative to the cost of the inputs and, therefore, indicate technical progress. The decline in the real price of 18 count weft is similar to the decline in the real cost of 16 count yarn shown in Table 8.1. Figure 8.1 shows that productivity growth in 40 count yarn was much more rapid. Gains were even more dramatic at higher counts, as we will see.

The cotton mill of 1836 was so efficient that it could out-compete hand spinning anywhere in the world. By the middle of the nineteenth century, cotton spinning mills were being built even in very low wage economies like India (Morris 1983, pp. 572–83). It was not always like that, however. In the middle of the eighteenth century when machine spinning was in its infancy, it was only profitable where labour was very dear. Without the innovations that took place in cotton textile production in Britain in the eighteenth century, the path

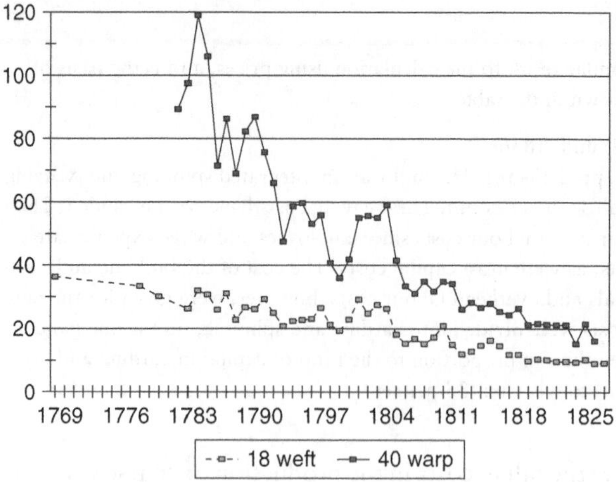

Figure 8.1 Real price of cotton yarn

Source: prices from Harley (1998, p. 74). The deflator uses four inputs weighted by their costs in the 1784 Papplewick mill. The inputs were raw cotton, labour, capital and materials. The price of raw cotton from Shapiro (1967, p. 261) and Mitchell and Deane (1971, p. 491). Labour is the wage of skilled building labour in northern England. Capital is an interest rate (5 per cent) plus a depreciation rate (5 per cent) multiplied by an index of skilled building labour, copper, iron and wood. The price index of steam-engine construction costs in Chapter 7 was used to deflate materials.

of development represented by Table 8.1 would not have taken place, and the worldwide industrialization of cotton textiles that began after Waterloo would not have occurred. To explain the trajectory, we begin by explaining the first step. Unusually, in this case there were actually two first steps, for the spinning jenny and the water frame were independent solutions to the same problem. We must analyze their inspiration, the research and development required, and the reasons that the invention occurred in Britain, in the eighteenth century.

Macro-invention I: the spinning jenny[5]

To gauge the creativity and hard work involved in inventing mechanical spinning, we must see how the spinning jenny and the water frame

[5] On the spinning jenny, see Baines (1835), Aspin and Chapman (1964), Hills (1970, pp. 54–60), Wadsworth and Mann (1931, pp. 476–82).

Plate 8.1 Woman spinning (from 'Costume of Yorkshire', by George Walker, 1814, Private Collection/The Bridgeman Art Library)

differed from the spinning wheel. Plate 8.1 shows a spinning wheel in operation. The raw cotton was first carded to produce a roving (a loose length of cotton fibres). The two key operations in spinning were drawing out the roving so it became thinner, and then twisting it to impart strength. In the late medieval period, this was done with a 'spinning wheel'. It consisted of three parts: the wheel itself, the spindle, and the string that acted as a belt to connect the wheel to the spindle. Sometimes, a treadle was connected to the wheel so that the spinner could turn it with her foot; otherwise, she used her right hand, as in the picture. She held the roving in her left hand, and its other end was attached to the horizontal spindle. The wheel was spun, and the spindle rotated. The spinner pulled back the roving so that it thinned out and then moved her hand to the left. This allowed the thread to slip off the end of the spindle each time it rotated. As that happened, the thread was twisted. When enough twist was imparted, the spinner moved her left hand to the right, so it was once again between her and the spindle. In this position, the thread was wound onto the spindle. The process was repeated as the next few inches of roving were pulled away from the spindle to be thinned out in turn.

Some inventions required strokes of genius, flashes of insight, or newly discovered scientific knowledge. The spinning jenny was not one of them. Many people had thought of devising an engine to spin fibre, and Hargreaves had tried to operate several wheels simultaneously by holding the threads from each in his left hand, but that proved impossible with horizontal spindles. He found the solution in 1764. The story, which is perhaps apocryphal, is that he was inspired by seeing a spinning wheel, which had toppled over on its side, continue to rotate and spin automatically. When the wheel was on its side, its spindle was vertical, and that made it feasible to draw and twist on many spindles. Vertical spindles became a fundamental feature of the jenny (Baines 1835, p. 157). If this story is true, it is an example of local learning leading to a macro-invention. That was unusual, since most macro-inventions were inspired by knowledge or practice from outside the industry, and that is why they led to major changes in factor proportions.

The spinning jenny had a row of spindles on one side and, on the other side, a parallel row of pins (Plate 8.2). The rovings were wound on these pins, and each roving extended across the jenny to the opposite spindle. The spindles were spun by belts from a single wheel. Between the spindles and the pins was a sliding bar called a clove with clamps that grasped the rovings and drew them out. Twist was then imparted by tilting the spindles forward, so the threads fell off the ends as they revolved. Finally, the yarn was wound onto the spindles as the clove was pushed towards them. At the same time, the clove pulled out more roving, and the sequence was repeated.

The spinning jenny was not rocket science. Hargreaves' first jenny was reportedly made with a pocket knife, but getting a design that operated satisfactorily took from 1764 to 1767 (Aspin and Chapman 1964, p. 13). The jenny mimicked the actions of a spinner and wheel but on an expanded scale. The difficulty, as with most eighteenth-century technology, lay in working out the details of the linkages and perfecting the sequences. An important feature was the deflection wire that ensured the yarn was wound evenly onto the spindle rather than bunching at one end. Inventing the spinning jenny was an engineering challenge, an exercise in R&D.

Compared to other inventions, the cost of the R&D was modest. Since Hargreaves was a hand loom weaver, his income could not be rated at more than £50 per year. There were certainly other expenses

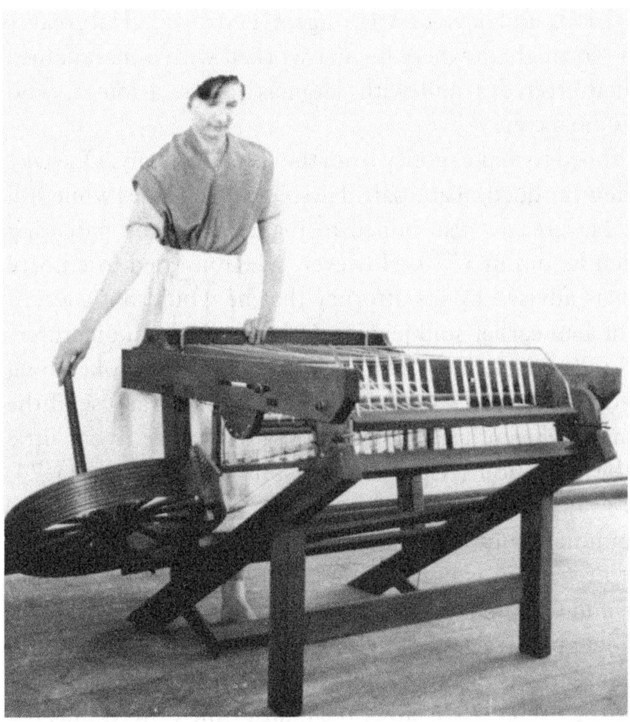

Plate 8.2 Reconstruction of Hargreaves' 'spinning jenny' of 1770 (Private Collection/The Bridgeman Art Library)

involved in buying materials for experimental machines. Perhaps sometimes, Hargreaves had assistance. By any reckoning, it is hard to see how the spinning jenny cost more than £500 to develop.

Nevertheless, someone had to come up with the money. At first, Hargreaves was supplied with accommodation in Ramsclough, a remote village in Lancashire, and support by Robert Peel, who was acting as his 'venture capitalist'. Peel sired a line of Sir Robert Peels including the prime minister, but Hargreaves' backer had no title and was not a cultivated man; rather, he was a small-scale farmer and putting-out merchant known as 'Parsley' Peel after the sketch of a parsley sprig he used as a trademark. When word got out that Hargreaves had made a spinning machine, neighbours broke into his house and destroyed the jenny and much of his furniture. In 1768, Hargreaves moved to Brookside where Peel paid for manufacturing premises. They were attacked by a mob, and jennies were again destroyed. Hargreaves then moved to Nottingham where he first worked with a man named Shipley and then erected a mill with Thomas James, a joiner, who became his new financier.

Hargreaves hoped to make money from the spinning jenny. One way was through their production and sale. He sold some jennies while still in Lancashire. Hargreaves also hoped to make money by patenting the jenny, which he did in 1770. However, when he tried to enforce his rights, he was advised by his attorney that he would not succeed in court since he had earlier sold jennies. Other cotton manufacturers offered him £3,000 to use the machine, but negotiations broke down since he insisted on at least £4,000. Despite the widespread use of the jenny in the late eighteenth century, Hargreaves realized very little money from the invention (Aspin and Chapman 1964, pp. 13–24, 34–5, Baines 1835, p. 158).

Since the spinning jenny was initially installed in cottages, there is a tendency to regard it as not being a capital-intensive production method. Aspin and Chapman (1964, p. 46), for instance, contrast 'the comparatively inexpensive jenny' to the mule, which was 'a costly machine'. 'Because it was driven by hand and because it was easier to make or far cheaper to buy than either the mule or the waterframe, the jenny was chosen by many men who set up in business with limited capital.' While it is true that buying a jenny was cheaper than building an Arkwright-style factory, nonetheless, the jenny had a big impact on input requirements in cotton spinning. Spinning wheels were far cheaper than jennies. Muldrew (2007, p. 8), for instance, reports that, in probate inventories he has examined, 'it is rare to find wheels valued at more than a shilling and some were worth considerably less'. In contrast, the spinning jenny with twenty-four spindles cost about 70 shillings. Since the wheel and the jenny were each operated by one woman, Hargreaves' invention raised the capital–labour ratio seventy-fold.[6] That was, indeed, a biased technical change.

The jenny was taken up very rapidly in England. Aspin and Chapman (1964) reported the use of jennies in many towns across northwestern England in the 1770s and 1780s. A historian in Manchester in 1783 recounted how the first 12-spindle jennies were 'thought a great affair'.

[6] The probate inventories predate the spinning jenny, but changes in the price level between the two data sources were not sufficiently great to change the tenor of the conclusion.

The spread of jennies, especially large ones in workshops, was punctuated by riots and arson as spinners protested against their use. By 1788, reportedly 20,070 jennies were spinning cotton in Britain (Aspin and Chapman 1964, pp. 48–9).

The situation was very different in India and in France. The French aversion to jennies was not due to lack of knowledge; indeed, the French government actively promoted them. John Holker was an English Jacobite, who fled to France in 1750 where he established himself as a cotton manufacturer. In 1754, he succeeded in being appointed Inspector General of Foreign Manufactures charged with importing foreign technology. In 1771, he sent his son to Lancashire to report on the new machines, and his son brought back a jenny. This was copied and made available to French producers; indeed, the state subsidized its use. It was installed in some large-scale factories but was otherwise ignored by the cotton trade. In 1790, there were about 900 jennies in France – less than 5 per cent of the number in England (Aspin and Chapman 1964, p. 49, Wadsworth and Mann 1931, pp. 195–9, 503–4).

The Indians also failed to adopt the spinning jenny. Ignorance may have been one reason, but there are grounds for believing that the cause was more fundamental. China provides a point of contact: a hemp-spinning machine was invented there in the thirteenth century, but it was never generally adopted and fell out of use (Elvin 1973, 1972, p. 137). Does this show a cultural or institutional failure, or were there rational economic reasons for continuing with hand processes? I shall argue that it would not have paid to use jennies in eighteenth-century India even if they had been known. This assessment, if true, is not a definitive solution to the Needham (1954) Problem (i.e. why did Chinese science and technology, which had been leading the world in the middle ages, stagnate in later centuries?), but it supports the view that Asia's not developing machine technology was a rational response to the economic environment and not a 'failure'.

Why were the French and Indians averse to the jenny? Was this bad entrepreneurship or cultural backwardness? An affirmative answer assumes that the profitability of adopting a jenny in France or India was just as high as it was in England, but this is doubtful in view of the bias of the technical change and the difference in factor prices. The spinners of Ramsclough and Brookside feared that it would pay their employers to buy jennies and cut jobs accordingly. Were they right?

And, if so, were the incentives greater in high wage England than in low wage France and India?

We can answer these questions by computing the rates of return that a putting-out merchant would have received from buying a jenny in the three countries. In accounting terms, the rate of return is the interest rate that equates the price of the jenny to the discounted present value of the annual savings of labour costs (less the additional costs of maintaining the jenny) over its economic life. The life of a jenny was about ten years. The labour saved by using a jenny instead of a wheel depended on the rise in labour productivity, and the number of days the spinner worked. There was variation in all of these, but the early 24-spindle jennies typically tripled labour productivity. Domestic spinners only worked about 40 per cent of full time since they often did agricultural work in the harvest, cared for children, cooked, and assisted their husbands in other businesses. Under these circumstances, the rate of return to buying a jenny was 38 per cent in England, 2.5 per cent in France and –5.2 per cent in India where it was a dead loss (see Appendix 1 to this chapter). These differences were due to the differences in wages relative to capital prices. Britain's high wage economy meant that a 24-spindle jenny cost 134 days of earnings in Britain compared to 311 days earnings in France and even more in India (Young 1792, p. 311, Chapman and Butt 1988, p. 107, Chassagne 1991, p. 191). On the figures, it is no wonder that putting-out merchants found the jenny irresistible in England but unattractive in France or India!

The adoption history also explains why the jenny was invented in Britain. As we have indicated, it took Hargreaves four years to perfect the jenny and the project cost hundreds of pounds. It would have been the same story in France or India had an inventor there considered trying to run many spindles off one wheel. Would this have been a worthwhile project outside Britain? No – the spinning jenny was not used in France or India; it brought no economic benefit in those countries in view of their low wages. Hence, it would not have been worthwhile to spend the time and money to develop the jenny. We need look no further to understand why the spinning jenny was invented in England rather than in France or India.

While the jenny is famous as the first successful spinning machine, its impact on cost and price was limited, as is clear from Table 8.1. The first column shows the cost of spinning one pound of 16 count cotton by the hand methods of the 1760s. The cost of spinning *per se* was 7d on the assumption that a spinner could spin one pound per day and might have earned 7d for a day's labour in 1784. In addition, however, there were costs for buying the raw cotton, cleaning and carding it, reeling the product, and operating the putting-out system. Some of those were capital costs, but most were labour costs. In total, one pound of 16 count yarn cost 35d, which was close to the market price. Spinning accounted for only one-fifth of the cost, and it was the only portion of cost, which was lowered to one-third of the hand value on the assumption that the spinning jenny tripled output per day. Since spinning costs were only a small share of the total, the adoption of the jenny cut average total cost by 11 per cent. The impact of the jenny also shows up in Figure 8.1, where the real price of 18 count yarn falls by about one-tenth during the 1770s when the jenny replaced the spinning wheel.

Richard Arkwright's inventions[7]

Roller spinning

Richard Arkwright may be the most famous entrepreneur of the Industrial Revolution. He was also probably the richest. He is credited with inventing the water frame – the machine that put roller spinning into practice. Table 8.1 shows that the water frame had a similar impact on productivity to the spinning jenny and cut the cost of spinning labour by about two-thirds. Arkwright's contributions went beyond the water frame, however. He also patented a carding machine that cut labour costs even more than the water frame cut spinning costs. In addition, he invented the cotton mill. This was a multi-storey structure in which the machines were arranged for efficient material flow and power transmission. Part-time work, and with it the part-time utilization of capital, were eliminated (Marglin 1976). The administrative labour associated with the putting-out system was also eliminated, although extra material and overhead labour costs were incurred that offset much of that gain. Overall, the Arkwright system reduced the real cost of coarse cotton production by 20 per cent compared to purely hand methods.

[7] On Arkwright and his inventions, see Baines (1835, pp. 147–96), Hills (1970, pp. 61–72) and Wadsworth and Mann (1931, pp. 482–503).

Plate 8.3 Arkwright's water frame, c. 1775 (© Science Museum/ Science and Society)

The water frame, which was patented in 1769, was the first of Arkwright's key inventions. Plate 8.3 shows a water frame, and Plate 8.4 is a close-up of the 'clockwork'. The rovings were coiled at the top. They then passed through three pairs of rollers. The rollers operated like mangles, pulling the cotton between them. The second pair spun at twice the speed of the first, and the third doubled the speed again. For this reason, the first pair of rollers pulled the roving into the mechanism and, at the same time, held it back with respect to the second pair, which was spinning faster and tugging it forward. The cotton was, thus, stretched and thinned out as it went between the two pairs of rollers. The stretching was repeated between the second and third pairs of rollers since the third pair spun faster than the second. In this way, the water frame accomplished the first task in spinning – drawing out the fibre.

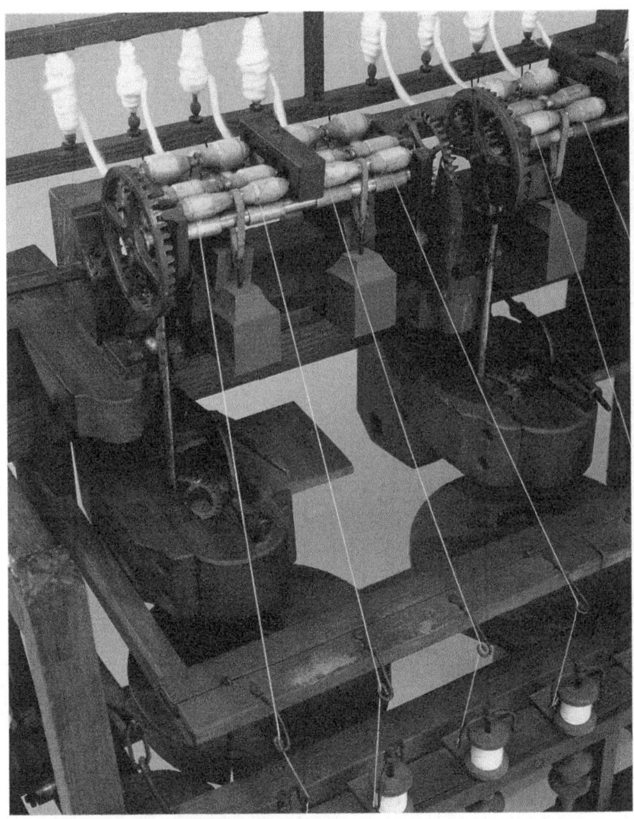

Plate 8.4 Arkwright's water frame, c. 1775, detail (© Science Museum/Science and Society)

The second task (twisting) was accomplished by the flyers, which spun around at the bottom of the frame, simultaneously twisting the fibre and coiling it on the bobbin.

Not much of this was original with Arkwright. The flyer, for instance was invented in the fifteenth century as an accessory for the spinning wheel. The novelty of the water frame lay in the trains of rollers that drew out the cotton. This idea, however, was not Arkwright's either: Wyatt and Paul conceived of using rollers to draw out cotton in the 1730s and pursued the idea until Paul's death in 1759.

While the spinning jenny was derived through local learning (observing a spinning wheel on its side), roller spinning was a technique copied

Plate 8.5 Rolling mill (courtesy of Uwe Niggemeier)

from other industries, and that source of inspiration contributed to its large impact on factor proportions. Using rollers to draw cotton was a clever application of a technique widely used at the time. Rollers had a long history in metallurgy where bars, ingots, plates and nails were shaped (Plate 8.5). Indeed, the similarities between a metal-rolling mill and roller spinning were so great that Rees (1819–20, vol. II, p. 173) reports that Arkwright conceived of roller spinning when looking at a rolling mill. There were sixteenth- and seventeenth-century designs for corn mills using rollers. In the late seventeenth century, cast glass was rolled at Saint-Gobain and polished with a roller. Cloth was pressed by rollers under enormous weight in the calendering process. In 1696, the Paris mint was using rollers. In the late seventeenth century, 'milled' sheet formed by rolling lead replaced cast lead sheet. In 1670, the Dutch developed a roller device with spikes to tear up rags for paper-

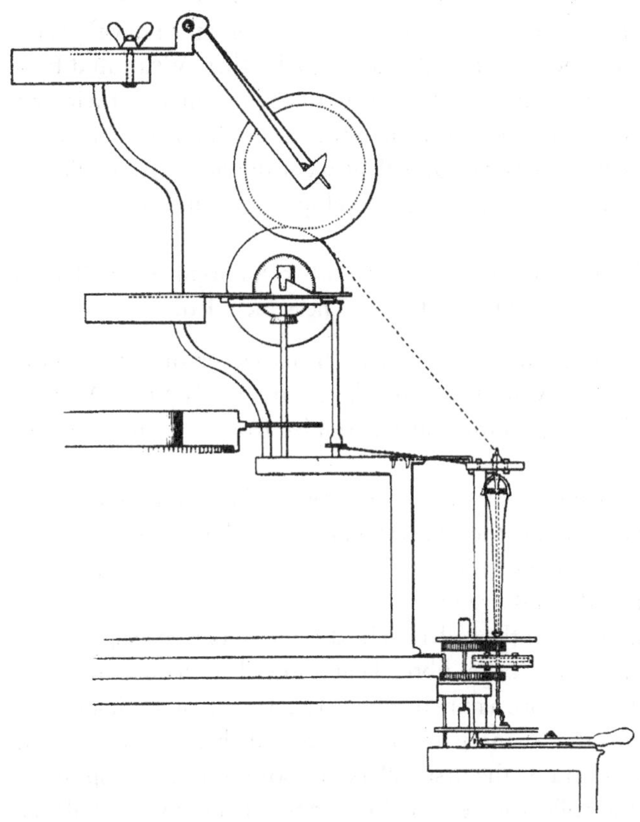

Plate 8.6 Enlarged view of the rollers, spindle and bobbin (Wyatt and Paul)

making and in 1720 applied rollers to pressing paper. Rollers were also used to crush rock.[8]

The challenge with roller spinning was making the idea work. Plate 8.6 shows Wyatt and Paul's diagram from their second patent, and it can be compared to the Arkwright machine to see the engineering problems involved. Both devices used a flyer to twist and wind the

[8] Singer, Holmyard, Hall *et al.* (1957, vol. III, pp. 16–17, 32, 45, 47, 177, 238–9, 340–4, 414–15), Raistrick (1972, p. 91), Rowe (1983, pp. 8–10), Beveridge (1939, pp. 191–2, 287–9, 485–9, 652–6), Mokyr (1990, p. 60) and Hunter (1930, pp. 170–1).

finished thread. Wyatt and Paul's diagram shows one pair of rollers, whereas Arkwright's frame had three. It was essential to have several in a series so that they could pull against each other. Wyatt and Paul did mention two pairs in the description of the machine in their first patent: deciding the number of rollers was a development challenge, and it looks as though Wyatt and Paul went down a wrong alley in their R&D programme by trying to develop a machine with only one set of rollers.

They never confronted, therefore, the other development challenges that Arkwright overcame in the 1760s. These included:

1. How much the speed should increase from one set of rollers to the next. In the early water frame displayed in Strutt's North Mill (in Belper, Derbyshire) rotation speed doubled from one pair of rollers to the next.
2. How to arrange the gears to connect the main power shaft to the rollers and coordinate their movements. The rollers and gears were produced as a module known as the 'clock work' in recognition of the apparatus that inspired it.
3. The spacing between the rollers. The distance had to be slightly less than the length of a cotton fibre. That allowed stretching and thinning of the thread since a fibre that was past the grip of the first rollers and caught by the second pair could be pulled ahead of an adjacent fibre that was held by the first rollers but not yet in the grasp of the second. If the rollers were too close, most of the fibres would be gripped by both pairs, so there would be no stretching. If the rollers were too distant, the thread would be pulled apart: proper operation required some fibres to be gripped by both rollers to prevent breakage, while others were held by one or the other pair for thinning. Thought and experimentation were required to work this out.
4. The materials with which to make the rollers. One was grooved metal and the other wood covered with leather. They had to pull the fibre without catching.
5. The pressure with which the top roller pressed down on the bottom one. The pressure was regulated by hanging weights from the top roller, as shown in Figure 8.4. The optimal weight could only be determined by repeated trials.

The point of this discussion is to emphasize the real issues involved in 'inventing' mechanical spinning. The originality was not in thinking up the roller; rather, the challenges were the practical issues of making the roller work in the application. Wyatt and Paul spent decades on this but did not succeed. Arkwright employed clock-makers over a five-year period to perfect the design. We have no record of exactly what they did, but the comparison of the Wyatt and Paul design with Arkwright's frame highlights the problems they faced. These challenges could only be met by constructing models or experimental prototypes. 'Inventing' the water frame involved a significant R&D programme.

The carding machine

Arkwright's second important invention was the carding machine. The success of roller spinning depended on the quality and uniformity of the roving fed into the machine. Perhaps for that reason, all of the inventors who worked on roller spinning also tried to perfect a carding machine. Early on, Hargreaves invented a contrivance for carding, which was described in Rees' *Cyclopaedia* (1808):

> A plain surface of wood was standing upright and was covered with wire cards which received the cotton, and the hand card which was applied to comb . . . was moved up and down against the cotton by means of a treddle on the floor . . . A wood board acting as a spring was affixed to the ceiling, being tied to the card in hand.
>
> Quoted in Aspin and Chapman 1964, p. 11

Wyatt and Paul patented two machines which were only minor modifications of hand cards. In 1748, Daniel Bourne invented a machine that he intended to be driven by water power, but he did not figure out how to feed material into the machine or how to extract from it a continuous roving. John Lees solved the feed problem in 1772, and Arkwright incorporated Lees' feeder into his carding machine. Arkwright also solved the problem of removing a continuous roving with his 'crank and comb'. These inventions were covered by Arkwright's 1775 patent. While the originality of Arkwright's patent was disputed in his patent trials, the effectiveness of the carding machine was not in question (Hills 1970, pp. 73–88). It cut the cost of carding by even more than the jenny or water frame cut the cost of spinning (Table 8.1).

Cromford Mill Number 2

Arkwright settled in Nottingham in 1767 to avoid the riots in Lancashire that had forced Hargreaves to leave. A small mill driven by a horse gig was built there, but it did not come into operation until the end of 1772. In the same year, Arkwright and his partners began building a water-powered mill at Cromford. It proved difficult to scale up the water frame for factory production. A further set of design issues emerged regarding the spatial location of the various machines, the flow of materials from one to the next, and the provision of power throughout a multi-storey building. The first mill was a learning experience, and its lessons were incorporated into a second mill opened in 1776. This mill was the prototype for cotton mills throughout Britain and the world. The first American mill built by Samuel Slater was patterned on Jedediah Strutt's copy of Cromford Mill Number 2, as was the first German mill, built in a new village near Düsseldorf known as Kromford.

Financial implications

Arkwright's R&D programme had very modern financial implications. First, the object was to make money, and patenting the invention seemed the essential step. The water frame was patented in 1769 and the carding machine in 1775. Many manufacturers used his machines without licences, however. In 1781, Arkwright tried to enforce his 1775 patent but was unsuccessful at trial. In 1782, he did secure a court victory upholding his 1769 patent but was unable to collect damages. As it was due to expire the next year, he sought a parliamentary act to extend the 1769 patent to 1789 but was unsuccessful in that, as well. In 1783, he again tried to enforced his 1775 patent and initially received a favourable judgment, but it was ultimately reversed. Despite these legal setbacks, which meant that he could not recover nearly as much royalties as he thought he deserved, he became very rich from the income he earned from his own mills. At the time of his death, Arkwright was worth half a million pounds (*Dictionary of National Biography*).

Secondly, there was the formidable problem of financing the R&D. Arkwright did what modern inventors do: he found 'projectors' (i.e. venture capitalists in today's terminology).[9] In 1768, he raised funds

[9] See Hudson (1986) for the parallel situation in the wool industry.

from two relatives, John Smalley, the landlord of a pub, and David Thornley, a merchant, who became equal partners. Quickly they ran out of money. In 1769, his attempt to raise a loan from two Nottingham bankers was turned down since they saw 'little prospect of the discovery being brought into a practical state' (Fitton 1989, p. 27). Samuel Need, a wealthy hosier, and Jedediah Strutt became partners for £500. Strutt was an established 'projector', who had already made a fortune financing improvements in frame knitting. Development work continued. Strutt himself suggested dusting the rollers with chalk to prevent the cotton from sticking to them. Several cam-operated devices were added to wind the thread, raise and lower the bobbins and move the thread back and forth along the rollers to prevent a groove's being worn in the surface. In 1774, Jedediah Strutt claimed that £13,000 had been spent on developing Arkwright's device. This included the construction of mills in Nottingham and Cromford, and it indicates the scale of the finance required to turn the idea of roller spinning into the reality of a working cotton mill (Hills 1970, pp. 60–71).

Why not France?

The British took up the water frame much more rapidly than the French or anyone else. About 150 large-scale mills were in operation in Britain in the late 1780s. In France, there were only four, and several of these were extremely small and not representative of British practice (Wadsworth and Mann 1931, pp. 193–208, 503–6, Chapman and Butt 1988, pp. 106–11).

As with the jenny, the difference in adoption reflected differences in profitability. The rate of return from an Arkwright-style mill can be computed by equating the cost of the mill to the present value of the savings in operating costs compared to spinning by hand (see Appendix 2 to this chapter). In Britain, the profit rate was 40 per cent per year, while in France it was only 9 per cent. The English profit rate was excellent. The French return, on the other hand, was unsatisfactory since fixed capital invested in business could earn 15 per cent.[10]

Indeed, profitability in France was probably much less than these figures suggest. The calculation assumes that capital was made of

[10] Symons (1839, pp. 203–4, 216) reports that French cotton manufacturers anticipated a gross profit rate of 16–18 per cent on fixed capital.

metal, wood and building labour. In addition, however, water frames required specialized engineering components, in particular, the 'clock work'. This was available in Lancashire but not in France.

The importance of watch-making for the textile industry cannot be overstated. The watch industry was the source of gears – brass gears in particular – and they were the precision parts in the water frame. Power was delivered to the rollers through gears, and gears controlled their speeds. Wyatt and Paul's patent specification showed gears at the base of the flyer (Plate 8.6). When Arkwright began developing the water frame, he hired John Kay, a clock-maker, and later negotiated with Peter Atherton, a Warrington machine-maker, who supplied him with a smith and a watch-tool-maker. Without watch-makers, the water frame could not have been designed.

The watch industry was a spin-off from the Scientific Revolution. A problem, which attracted the attention of the most famous scientists in the seventeenth and eighteenth centuries, was the determination of longitude. In principle, you could calculate your longitude if you knew the time difference between your location and Greenwich, and you would know the time difference if you had a clock set to Greenwich time. The problem was to design a clock that would keep accurate time for years on end. Galileo was the first to notice that a pendulum swung regularly and suggested incorporating it into a clock to improve its accuracy. Christiaan Huygens, who was also involved in developing the steam engine, independently discovered the pendulum principle and formulated the mathematical theory of the cycloid arc. Working with the Amsterdam clock-maker Salomon Coster, Huygens applied his theory and built the world's first pendulum clock. The inaccuracy of clocks was reduced from about 15 minutes in a day to 10–15 seconds (Landes 2000, pp. 118–35).

Unfortunately, the pendulum clock did not work well at sea, so Huygens improvised further. Around 1675, he invented the balance spring, which made an accurate watch possible and, indeed, installed it in a watch. Robert Hooke, the Curator for Experiments of the Royal Society and another scientific luminary, independently conceived of the balance spring perhaps as early as 1660, although he did not apply the idea until he heard of Huygens' work (Weiss 1982, pp. 111–12).

In themselves, clocks and watches were peripheral to the Industrial Revolution, but their large-scale production had important spin-offs. The improvements in clock and watch design made them more desirable, and their production grew rapidly. Their moving parts were systems of gears, and each had to be laid out and cut by hand. Hooke designed the first machine to do this (Weiss 1982, pp. 153–6). The growth of the watch industry prompted steady improvement in the design of these machines. Henry Hindley made a widely used machine that laid out and cut gears. Cheap, accurate gears were now mass produced.

Inexpensive gears revolutionized the design of machinery. Gears replaced levers and belts (as in the spinning wheel) to control, direct and transmit power. Mills had used gears in this way in the middle ages, but these gears were large, crude and made of wood. The gears of the Industrial Revolution were small, refined and made of brass or iron. 'Clock work' was used quite generally to control power in machinery in the nineteenth century, so gearing was the General Purpose Technology that effected the mechanization of industry (Lipsey, Carlaw and Bekar 2005).

The watch industry was a key to explaining Arkwright's success and the growth of the cotton industry in Lancashire. When Arkwright built his mills at Cromford, he hired clock-makers. One of his advertisements in the Derby *Mercury* in 1771 read: 'Wanted immediately, two Journeymen Clock-Makers, or others that understands Tooth and Pinion well' (Fitton 1989, p. 30). Arkwright did not sell water frames; entrepreneurs had to assemble their own engineering departments to construct them. In the late 1780s and early 1790s, the Quarry Bank Mill employed half a dozen clock- and watch-makers over the course of many years to construct the 'clock work' for the water frames (Hills 1970, p. 237). At the time, there were over 150 Arkwright mills, so of the order of 800 of these specialists were employed. Where did they come from? As it happens, most of the world's watch movements were made in one place – southern Lancashire. Landes (2000, pp. 238–9) believed the watch industry was British because the high wage economy of Britain created a large domestic market for clocks and watches.[11] One reason that cotton production was mechanized in Lancashire (rather than in the Netherlands, for instance) was because the supply of high-quality, cheap gears was far greater there than elsewhere, as

[11] It is more difficult to explain why the watch-making industry was located in Lancashire. Foster (2004, pp. 304–5) describes the watch-making industry, and his book as a whole offers an explanation for southern Lancashire's emergence as an important manufacturing region.

was the supply of skilled workmen to assemble them. In addition, the machinery for cutting watch gears was redesigned to produce gears for water frames – first from brass, later from iron. Standardized gears were made by specialist firms and sold to mills (Hills 1970, pp. 230–49). The 'clock work' of the water frame was a spin-off from the watch industry. The lack of a watch industry in France in the eighteenth century meant that the cost of capital (including gears) was even greater relative to labour than my calculations presuppose.

Why the British rather than the French invented mechanical spinning

As we have indicated, both the jenny and the water frame required considerable expenditures in R&D to make them work. The same would have been true in France. Would these expenditures have been worthwhile in France? No – mechanized spinning brought no economic benefit there in view of the low wage and the absence of a watch industry. Profitability considerations are sufficient to explain why the spinning jenny and the water frame were invented in England rather than France or, indeed, most other parts of the world.

Phase II: improvements to mechanical spinning[12]

By the 1780s, two mechanical spinning technologies were in use. Arkwright mills specialized in producing warp yarn, while spinning jennies produced weft. Technology was not, however, standing still: the achievements of Hargreaves and Arkwright were only the beginning of a long path of improvement. Jennies had already been enlarged to eighty spindles and located in workshops where they were operated continuously. The next half-century witnessed two further lines of development. One was improvements in the machines used at each stage of the production process. The second was the invention of the mule by Samuel Crompton. The latter was the more revolutionary.

Samuel Crompton grew up in a poor Lancashire family and learned spinning and weaving as a boy. In 1769, when he was sixteen, he began spinning with an 8-spindle jenny. In 1772, he set out to improve it, and,

[12] On Crompton, the mule and the later improvements, see Baines (1835, pp. 197–244) and Hills (1970, pp. 116–33).

by 1779, he had perfected the mule. He kept it secret, but rumours spread. He could not afford a patent and so made it public in 1780 in exchange for funds raised by a public subscription. This was financially disastrous, but it did make the mule generally available, and it was quickly integrated into the factory system and improved by many inventors.

The mule combined the best features of the jenny with those of the water frame, although Crompton always insisted that he was unaware of Arkwright's machinery and had conceived of rollers on his own. Both the jenny and the water frame produced uneven yarn since the rovings in the 1780s were uneven. In addition, the fineness of the yarn was limited since it had to be robust enough to be pulled by the clove of the jenny or by the flyer of the water frame. This problem was addressed by Crompton, who added several pairs of rollers to the jenny. As with the water frame, these rollers thinned the roving. In addition, the rollers paid out the roving as it left the spindle and at the same rate as the clove was pulled back. In this way, Crompton avoided ever putting the yarn under tension. It could, therefore, be drawn very fine. Once the clove had been pulled back to its full extent, its pins were tilted forward and turned so the yarn slipped off the end and was twisted. The yarn was also gently pulled and that evened out lumps. The result was exceptionally fine and uniform yarn.

The mule revolutionized spinning. The cost of producing high count cotton was slashed. This is apparent from Figure 8.2 which adds a graph of the real cost of 100 count yarn to Figure 8.1. The decline was so great, that reductions in the real prices of 16 and 40 count yarn, which had looked so impressive on their own in Figure 8.1, are almost obliterated. The mule also replaced the jenny at low counts: the 18 count weft produced in the 1836 mill whose costs are shown in Table 8.1 was spun on mules.

Since Britain was a high wage country, saving labour improved its competitive position disproportionally. With the invention of the mule, the British, for the first time, could compete against the Indians in the production of muslins. At first, the mule was used domestically, but it was soon adapted to factory use. In 1783, the wooden rollers Crompton had designed were replaced with metal rollers like Arkwright's. In the 1790s, the mule was driven first by water power and then by steam. In 1791, the technique of joining broken threads without stopping the machine was developed. In the 1790s, the gearing

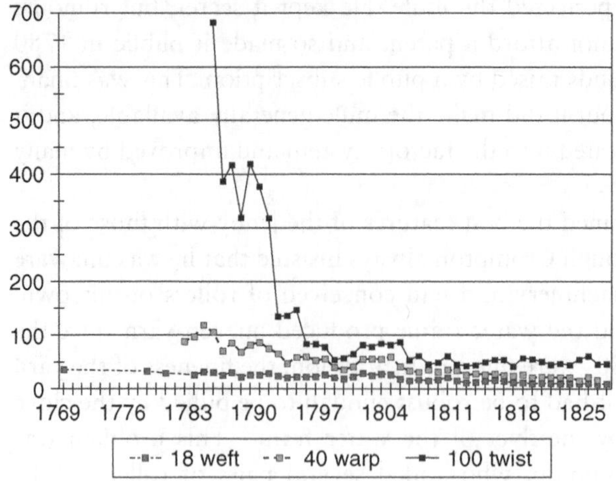

Figure 8.2 Real price of cotton yarn

See the note to Figure 8.1.

was reorganized, so that more and more spindles could be driven. The culmination was Robert's self-acting mule invented in the late 1820s (*Dictionary of National Biography* entries for Crompton and Roberts). His aim was to eliminate the jobs of the high wage spinners who had operated the mules, and in that he succeeded – thus providing a neat example of factor prices directing invention. The mule was the basis of Britain's pre-eminence in cotton production throughout the nineteenth century.[13]

While the mule was the most significant invention after Arkwright's, it was not the only one. A constant stream of improvements cut costs at all stages of production. Gear-cutting machines were made larger so that iron gears could be cut as well as brass (Hills 1970, pp. 243–6). With more robust gears, the water frame itself was redesigned, so that forty-eight spindles were run off one set of gears rather than a maximum of four with brass. The long-term result of this line of development was a great simplification in the transmission of power to the rollers. With this change, the water frame was rebaptized as the throstle (Baines 1835, pp. 208–9).

Machines were designed to accomplish even the most prosaic tasks. When the bales arrived at the mill, they had to be opened and the

[13] See Huberman (1996) for the ensuing labour relations.

cotton cleaned. In the 1780s, this was done without machinery by women and children who beat the cotton and picked out seeds and debris. Their work was eased by the invention of the cotton gin by Eli Witney in 1793, for the raw cotton arrived at British mills in a cleaner state. In 1801, a batting machine was invented. By 1810, it was being replaced by the willow, which also beat the cotton. Women still had to remove seeds and grit. This work was mechanized by the scutcher, a machine invented around 1801 and patterned after a grain thresher (Hills 1970, pp. 73–4, 85–7).

The stream of improvements had two economic dimensions. First, the real cost of producing coarse yarn dropped by another one-third between the 1780s and the 1830s. Since there was little saving in raw cotton costs, all of the decline was in value added. Secondly, the labour-saving bias of technical change that characterized macro-inventions was continued with these micro-improvements. All inputs were saved, but some more than others. Capital per pound of yarn was cut by three-quarters (the cost of erecting a spinning mill dropped from about £3 per spindle in the 1780s to as little as 16 shillings in the 1830s), while labour per pound dropped 90 per cent!

Improvements in the production process led to the construction of cotton mills in Europe and North America. In Europe, the spread of the industry was inhibited in the 1780s by Arkwright's licensing policy, which put the burden of building water frames onto would-be cotton-spinning firms. This policy favoured Lancashire producers because of their proximity to the watch industry. This constraint was eased by the establishment of firms that specialized in the production of textile machinery. The immediate impetus was the invention of the mule, which was too complex for do-it-yourself builders. Around 1790, McConnel & Kennedy, A & G Murray, and Dodson & Barlow all began to manufacture and sell spinning machines (Hills 1970, pp. 240–1). It was illegal to export machinery from Britain, but that did not stop people from trying. Charles Albert was sent to England in 1790 by entrepreneurs trying to set up a cotton mill in Toulouse. Albert was arrested in England and spent years in prison for industrial espionage, although, on his eventual return to France, he was successful as an inventor of textile machinery. Lieven Bauwens, a Belgian aristocrat, arrived in England in 1797 and purchased mules. He was caught smuggling them out of Britain, although eventually he became a successful textile magnate in Belgium and France. He even married the daughter of the Manchester businessman who sold him the mules (*Dictionary of National Biography*). The supply of textile machinery to France was eased as British engineers established manufacturing facilities on the continent. In 1799, William Cockerill began producing textile machinery in Verviers, Belgium. In 1807, he established a large works at Liège and shipped much machinery to France. In 1802, Cockerill's son-in-law, James Hodson, also established a machine-building business in Belgium. William Douglas was another serious competitor of Cockerill's in the French market for textile machinery (Henderson 1954, pp. 107–15). With the establishment of these firms, continental entrepreneurs were no longer shut out of the textile business by the need to manufacture their own machinery.

By the early nineteenth century, the factory production of cotton textiles was expanding rapidly in France.[14] This was not due to any change in relative factor prices. In the early 1830s, women earned about 1.1 to 2 shillings per day in Manchester cotton mills, and it cost about 17.5 shillings per spindle to erect a mill. In France at the same time, a woman earned about 1 franc per day, and it cost about 30 francs per spindle to build a mill. On these figures, the ratio of the wage to the price of capital in France was 39 per cent of the ratio in England – virtually the same as the proportion in the 1780s (Baines 1835, pp. 519, 524, Symons 1839, p. 203, Chapman and Butt 1988, pp. 116–17).

The profitability of cotton production by machinery rose in France because the productivity of English technology was improving, so factory costs were lower in comparison to hand spinning than they had been in the 1770s. Figure 8.1 suggests that productivity grew evenly between the 1780s and 1830s. The implication is that the average variable cost of one pound of 16 count yarn in 1810 would have been

[14] Thomson (2003) is an interesting study of the introduction of cotton spinning into Catalonia. Attempts with jennies in the 1780s were unsuccessful, i.e. unprofitable. Production only became profitable in the 1790s. Improved workshop jennies were being used, and the introduction of carding machines played a key role. The successful technology was advanced technology, in other words, and not the technology that had succeeded in England in the 1770s. Another ingredient of success was improved factory discipline, including the setting of output norms. For spinners, this was 1.5 pounds per day, a low value by English standards.

Table 8.2 Raw cotton consumption (thousands tons)

	UK	France	Germany	Belgium	United States
1781–90	8.1	4.0			2.2
1791–1800	13.9				3.6
1801–14	31.8	8.0			7.1
1815–24	54.8	18.9		1.6	14.1
1825–34	105.6	33.5	3.9	2.7	25.0
1835–44	191.6	54.3	11.1	6.6	46.8
1845–54	290.0	65.0	21.1	10.0	111.0
1855–64	369.4	74.1	42.0	12.8	126.0
1865–74	475.8	85.9	85.6	16.3	193.7

Sources: UK, France and Germany: Mitchell (1973, p. 780). Belgium: 1815–50 from Landes (1969, p. 165); 1845–54 is the 1850 figure and 1865–74 is the 1869 figure from Landes (1969, p. 194). The figure for 1855–64 is a geometric average. United States: Bruchey (1967, Table 3A) for 1790–1860; 1860–74 from *Historical Statistics of the United States, Millennium Edition Online*, series Dd843. Bales assumed to weigh 500 lbs.

21.85d,[15] which was 12.22d less than the average variable cost of the hand method. Likewise, the capital cost per spindle would have been reduced to £2. This was a much greater gain from mechanization (and at a lower capital cost) than with the 1784 mill, and the rate of return shot up to 34 per cent. This was very satisfactory, and the rise explains the shift to machine production in France and Belgium after 1815 (Table 8.2). The tipping point was reached earlier in cotton than in either steam power or coke iron.

The United States provides an important counterpoint to the continent, for the United States was a high wage economy. Massachusetts wages in the late eighteenth century were almost as high as London wages in terms of their command over consumer goods. By the 1830s, cotton wages relative to the price of textile capacity were equally high in Massachusetts and in Glasgow (Montgomery 1840, pp. 112–24). Under these circumstances, it would be surprising if there was much lag in the adoption of British textile technology in the United States, and,

[15] 1810 is halfway between 1784 and 1836, and 21.85 is the average of average variable cost in those years.

indeed, there was little. The first spinning jenny was manufactured in Philadelphia in 1775 on account of the high cost of labour. The 1780s saw numerous attempts to set up workshops with carding machines and jennies and efforts to build Arkwright-style mills. American craftsmen had no difficulty copying the equipment, but successful adoption required workers or managers experienced in the technology. In 1793, the first commercially successful mill was built and managed by Samuel Slater, who had worked in one of Jedediah Strutt's factories. The next breakthrough was the construction of an integrated spinning and power weaving mill by the Boston Manufacturing Company in Waltham, Massachusetts, in 1813. Francis Cabot Lowell founded the firm after visiting Britain and seeing power looms, which he sketched from memory. Production models were made by Lowell's engineer, Paul Moody. One of the most remarkable features of the Lowell–Moody system was the degree to which British technology was redesigned to make it suitable to American conditions. This engineering capacity portended much for the nineteenth century.[16]

Results

Cotton textile production was a global industry for centuries. Before the Industrial Revolution, China and India were the largest producers. In the late seventeenth century, the various east India companies began exporting cotton fabrics to Europe. They were a great success everywhere and showed there was a large European market. The Dutch accepted them without restriction, but traditional textile producers in other countries sought to curtail imports. Wool and linen manufacturers succeeded in 1701 in having printed cotton fabrics excluded from Britain. The import of white cottons was still permitted, and printing was done in England. A small British production of cotton cloth ensued. In 1721, the ban was extended to all cotton fabrics: the domestic production and consumption of purely cotton fabrics was made illegal. 'The Lancashire cotton industry . . . secured in 1736 a relaxation for goods of flax warp and cotton weft [called fustians], a relaxation which by custom (or subterfuge) came to cover the great bulk of

16 Jeremy (1981). There has been considerable investigation and discussion of relative British and American productivity, especially in the 1830s and 1840s. See, for instance, David (1975, pp. 95–190), Bils (1984), Temin (1988), Harley (1992), Irwin and Temin (2001), Harley (2001).

the industry's production and even, it is probable, the growing part of it that used hand-spun cotton twist for warps', i.e. all cotton cloth (Fitton and Wadsworth 1958, p. 68). English cotton producers, thus, received ambiguous protection from Indian imports. Similar restrictions were imposed in other European countries. France, for instance, prohibited the import of Indian cotton goods in 1686. While offering domestic protection, British laws did permit the importation of Indian cottons for re-export, and that market boomed with the growth of the slave trade in the mid-eighteenth century, for cotton cloth was bartered with African chiefs for slaves. Here, European and Indian producers faced each other in head-to-head competition (Inikori 2002). The Europeans were uncompetitive in fine cloths, which were labour intensive, because their wages were higher than those in India.

Broadberry and Gupta (2007) have argued that it was this competitive challenge that induced British producers to mechanize production. I have emphasized here, in contrast, that it was the wage relative to the price of capital that led the British to invent mechanical spinning. The international context remains crucial, however, because it was the reason that the British industry grew so large, so fast. Once mechanization lowered British costs, the British could undersell Indian producers in third markets and in India itself (Ellison 1886, pp. 61–3). As a result, British producers captured most of their world business. The increase in output was much greater than the output increases that could be induced by lowering production costs in an industry confined to a national market. The enormous increase in cotton output that followed mechanization was responsible for the growth of Manchester and the other centres of the cotton trade. It is the reason that so many people have equated the Industrial Revolution to the cotton industry.

Appendix 1 How profitable was the spinning jenny?

The rate of return to buying a jenny is found by solving the equation:

$$J = \Sigma\,(w\Delta L - m)/(1 + r)^t \text{ where the summation is over } t = 1, 2 \ldots n \quad (1)$$

Here J is the purchase price of a jenny, w is the daily wage of a spinner, ΔL is the number of days of labour saved per year, m is the additional maintenance costs associated with the jenny, t is time, n is the length of life of the jenny in years, and r is the internal rate of return, which is the variable to be computed. The savings in labour per year is computed as:

$$\Delta L = YD(1 - 1/P) \qquad (2)$$

where Y is the number of work days in a year, D is the 'part-time fraction' (the proportion of full-time that the jenny was actually operated), and P is output per hour worked with the jenny relative to the spinning wheel. Y and D enter the equation since the women who operated jennies were usually only part-time spinners. If a spinner worked 250 days per year but only for half a day each day, then YD = 125 full-time equivalent days of work that were paid at the rate of w. Now, if the jenny allowed the spinner to produce three times as much per hour as she could with a wheel, then P = 3, and she works one-third (1/P) as many hours as she did before to produce the same amount. So two-thirds of her time (1 – 1/P) has been saved.

To solve the equation, numerical values must be chosen for the parameters (Allen 2007d). I assume that jennies lasted ten years due to wear and obsolescence, that a full-time year was 250 days, that a 24-spindle jenny cost 70 shillings in England and 140 livre tournois in France (i.e. half the cost of workshop jennies according to Chapman and Butt 1988, p. 107 and Chassagne 1991, p. 191), and that a spinner working full time could earn 6.25d per day in England and 9 sou tournois in France (as reported by Arthur Young 1792, p. 311). Based on Indian experience with the Ambar Charkha, a machine comparable to a jenny that was widely used in India in the 1950s (Sen 1968, p. 107), annual maintenance costs were taken to be 10 per cent of the price of a jenny.

I assume that women worked 40 per cent of full time. Sir Frederick Eden (1797, p. 796) observed 'that a woman, in a good state of health, and not incumbered with a family, can [do] one pound of spinning-work the day, and [that] is the utmost that can be done: but if she has a family, she cannot . . . spin more than 2 pounds and a half in a week', which is about 40 per cent of full-time output. The same factors were in play in twentieth-century India where rural women spun for only 4–6 hours per day (Bhalla 1964, p. 613).

I assume that the jenny tripled labour productivity. Since spinners were paid by the hank, the impact of the jenny on labour productivity can be inferred from the increase in spinners' earnings. Contemporary commentaries give a range of values. Around 1780, women could earn 8–10 shillings per week on the jenny and 3–5 shillings per week on the wheel (Pinchbeck 1930, pp. 150–1, Wadsworth and Mann 1931, p. 403, Bentley 1780, p. 31). These figures indicate that labour productivity rose by a factor of two to three.

Appendix 2 How profitable was an Arkwright mill?

We can use a similar formula to the one used with the jenny to compare profitability in Britain and France:

$$P_B \Delta K = \Sigma\, w_B\, \Delta L/(1 + i_B)^t \text{ where the summation is from } t = 1, 2 \ldots 10 \quad (3)$$

where ΔK is the additional capital invested in roller spinning to save ΔL labour per year. These are valued at the British prices of P_B for capital and w_B for labour. The rate of return, which is found by solving the equation, is i_B. In Britain in the late 1780s, cotton mills were built at a cost of about £3 per spindle. The water frames in the Papplewick mill had a rated capacity of 0.125 lbs per 12-hour shift or 37.5 lbs per year assuming they were operated six days per week and fifty weeks per year. According to Table 8.1, the saving in operating costs, principally labour costs but also material costs, was about 8d (or £0.0333) per lb of cotton. Assuming a ten-year life for a cotton mill, the rate of return is found by solving the equation:

$$3 = \Sigma\, 37.5 \times 0.0333/(1 + i)^t \text{ where the summation is from } t = 1, 2 \ldots 10 \quad (4)$$

The rate of return was a very satisfactory 40 per cent per year. It is no wonder the British rushed to build Arkwright mills.

How about France? If we had French wage and capital costs, we could compute the rate of return immediately, as with the jenny, using the French counterpart to equation (3):

$$P_F \Delta K = \Sigma\, w_F\, \Delta L/(1 + i_F)^t \text{ where the summation is from } t = 1, 2 \ldots 10 \quad (5)$$

Unfortunately, the parameters cannot be obtained from business records from the 1780s since so little capacity was constructed in pre-Revolutionary France. Therefore, we proceed from other premises. In France, the rate of return was far lower since wages were lower relative to the price of capital. That ratio is measured by:

$$(w_F/P_F)/(w_B/P_B) = R \tag{6}$$

Measuring R as the ratio of a labourer's daily wage to the cost of iron, copper and timber implies that wages in France were only 38 per cent of the wages in England. This is about the same as the French ratio of a spinner's wage to the price of a jenny divided by the corresponding British ratio. We can use this ratio to adapt the English rate-of-return formula to French conditions. If we multiply equation (5) by equation (6), we get:

$$P_B\Delta K = R\,\Sigma\, w_B\, \Delta L/(1 + i_F)^t \text{ where the summation is from } t = 1, 2 \ldots 10 \tag{7}$$

We can convert from British prices and wages to their French counterparts by multiplying the right-hand side of equation (3) by 0.38, i.e. the value of the labour saved relative to the investment, which was only 38 per cent as great in France as it was in Britain. With this figure, the rate of return to building an Arkwright mill in France in the 1780s drops to 9 per cent. Given that fixed capital invested in businesses could earn 15 per cent, this was an unsatisfactory return.

9 Coke smelting

> About 26 years ago my Husband conceived this happy thought – that it might be possible to make bar iron from pit coal pigs . . . Edward Knight Esq. a capitol Iron Master urged my Husband to get a patent, that he might reap the benefit for years of this happy discovery: but he said he would not deprive the public of Such an Acquisition which he was Satisfyed it would be; and so it has proved, for it soon spread and many Furnaces both in this Neighbourhood and Several other places have been erected for this purpose.
>
> Abiah Darby, widow of Abraham Darby II, 1775[1]

Coke smelting is one of the famous inventions of the Industrial Revolution and had an enormous long-run impact, for it was essential for the production of cheap iron, which, in turn, was required for the railroad, steamships and the mechanization of industry. Abraham Darby's success in 1709 was a macro-invention that radically changed factor proportions as coke displaced charcoal in the blast furnace. The macro-invention was followed by a century and a half of improvements in which productivity rose substantially. Technical change was far more neutral than the original invention: between 1709 and 1850, all of the inputs were saved with the greatest economies occurring in coal and labour. Many of these advances were due to local learning. By reducing the coal required for mineral fuel iron, this train of improvements made it profitable for foreign iron producers to replace charcoal with mineral fuel in the middle of the nineteenth century. When the tipping point was reached, the French, Germans and Americans moved directly to the most advanced technology and did not recapitulate the twisting path of development followed by the British.

[1] Quoted by Raistrick (1989, pp. 68–9).

Coke smelting does differ in revealing ways from the inventions of Newcomen, Hargreaves and Arkwright. In the first place, the inventor did not really invent it: Abraham Darby invented ancillary processes and a market niche that made coke smelting commercially viable, but not coke smelting itself. Secondly, the process that Darby perfected had limited applicability. In 1709, coke iron was both too expensive and inferior in quality to compete against charcoal pig in the production of wrought iron (or bar iron as it was called in the trade). This was the main product of the iron industry. It was not until the mid-eighteenth century that coke smelting was perfected sufficiently to turn Britain's cheap coal into a competitive advantage for the iron industry. This history raises the question of the real macro-invention. Was it the constellation of changes made by Abraham Darby I that resulted in the commercial production of coke iron for castings, albeit on a very modest scale? Or was it the whole series of innovations between 1709 and 1755 that made coke pig iron the least-cost technique for smelting forge pig iron? Since wrought iron was a far more important product, the second reading has more economic bite.

From 1709 to 1755, the history of coke iron production in Britain was the history of the Coalbrookdale Iron Company, for little coke iron was produced by anyone else. The firm was led by three generations of Abraham Darbys, but they had short lives (39, 52 and 39 years), so other men also made important contributions to management. Another reason non-Darbys were important was that the first Abraham Darby sold most of the company to raise capital, and the other owners were actively involved in the firm (Raistrick 1989, pp. 6, 40, 45, 50–1). After 1760, when coke iron became competitive with charcoal in the production of bar iron, new firms were founded across Britain to take advantage of the process: John Wilkinson built a coke blast furnace in Staffordshire in 1758, the Carron Works were founded in Scotland in 1760, the Walkers erected a coke furnace in Rotherham in 1766, and four large iron works were established in South Wales between 1758 and 1769. Production had started in the major producing regions that dominated the British trade until the mid-nineteenth century.

To relate the engineering history to economics, the input requirements to produce one ton of pig iron were compiled for key years between 1709 and 1850. Costs of production in current and constant prices were also computed, and some results are shown in Table 9.1. It is based on the history of Coalbrookdale through to 1800. While other

Table 9.1 *Inputs per ton of pig iron, 1709–1850*

	Ore	Coal	Capital	Labour	Real ATC	Tons/ Week
1709	5	17.5	3.76	1.5	9.97	1.55
1719	5	12.3	1.74	1.5	7.06	4.4
1729	4.9	15.4	1.70	1.5	7.45	4.5
1737	3.3	9.1	1.26	1.5	5.44	7.5
1755	4.08	8.52	1.09	0.5	4.40	15.4
1770	3.6	7.68	0.93	0.5	3.71	25.3
1803	3.0	6.72	1.18	0.29	3.95	44.6
1850	2.6	3.56	1.01	0.10	2.62	92.6

Notes: The columns Ore and Coal report tons of the raw material used per ton of pig iron. Capital and labour indicate capital using cost and labour expense per ton of iron valuing the capital and labour in 1755 prices. Real ATC is average total cost valued in 1755 prices. Tons/week is the average production rate.

Sources: The figures for 1709–1803 apply to the Coalbrookdale Iron Company and are derived from Mott (1957, 1957–9a, pp. 68–74, 1957–9b, pp. 280–5, 1959–60, pp. 45–7), Hyde (1977) and Raistrick (1989, pp. 33, 35–6, 112, 114, 305). The details of the furnace crew for 1709 given by Mott (1957, p. 12) in conjunction with the wage rates reported by Raistrick (1989, p. 33) imply considerably lower labour costs than assumed by Hyde (1977, p. 35) for Darby's first blast.
The figures for 1850 are a weighted average of district costs from the mid-nineteenth century. The districts represented are Cleveland, Scotland, Staffordshire (cold blast), Derby and South Wales. The first two statements of costs are from Gruner and Lan (1862, pp. 251, 314, 318, 390) and the rest from Wilkie (1857). Output weighted by 1848 production as given by Porter (1912, p. 240).
Capital costs were derived from Davies and Pollard (1988, pp. 95–101).

firms were important at the end of the eighteenth century, the costs of the Horsehay furnaces in Coalbrookdale were in line with those of other British districts.[2] The information for the 1850s is based on all major British producing regions.

Figure 9.1 plots the average total cost of pig iron. It declined by 63 per cent from 1709 to 1850. This drop might have been due to rising productivity or cheaper inputs. To eliminate the effect of input price changes, average total cost was recomputed valuing inputs at

[2] South Wales is a possible exception, for costs there may have been somewhat lower, perhaps due to cheaper inputs. See Hyde (1977, p. 139).

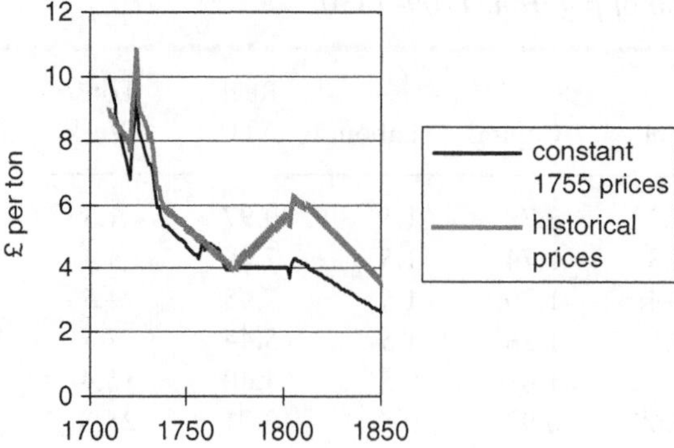

Figure 9.1 Average total cost per ton of pig iron

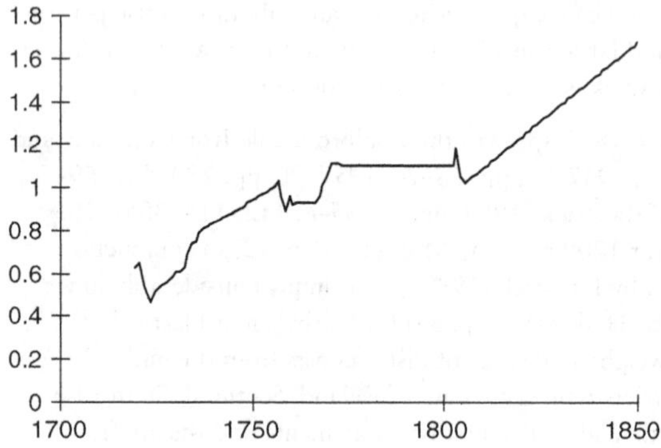

Figure 9.2 Total factor productivity in pig iron production

1755 prices in every year. This 'real cost' per ton of pig iron dropped by three-quarters, and the cost inflation of the Napoleonic Wars is eliminated. Except for the early nineteenth century, productivity growth was driving pig iron costs over the whole period.

When real costs go down, total factor productivity (TFP) is going up. Figure 9.2 shows its evolution. Productivity growth passed through three phases. During the first phase, from 1709 to 1755, productivity improved substantially, and coke iron became a competitive product. For the rest of the eighteenth century, productivity growth was modest. Productivity growth accelerated again during the first half of the nineteenth century.

Table 9.1 shows the evolution of the input requirements in pig iron

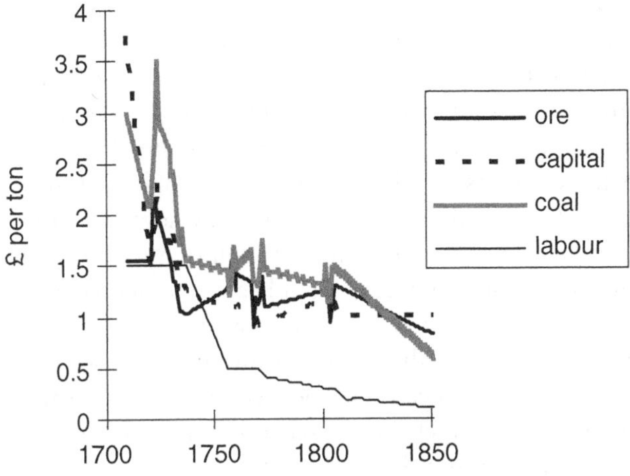

Figure 9.3 Components of cost valued in 1755 prices

production. Figure 9.3 highlights the contributions to real cost saving by valuing the inputs at 1755 prices. The pattern of productivity growth was broadly neutral with savings being made across the board. Coal, which was abundant in Britain, was saved as much as labour, which was scarce. Even iron ore was saved. By the middle of the nineteenth century, the ore requirement depended on its composition, for all the iron in the ore passed into the pigs. That was not true in the early eighteenth century, when iron was lost in the slag (Mott 1957–9a, p. 70). In the century and half after Darby's macro-invention, the history of productivity in iron-making looks like the neutral process described in Chapter 6.

Macro-invention (first phase): Abraham Darby I's achievement

Coke smelting did not depend on any scientific discovery nor did it require an act of genius. In fact, it required almost no thought at all. Coal was a much cheaper source of energy than wood, and attempts were made to substitute the cheaper fuel in most applications during the seventeenth century. If coal was being burnt to heat the house, why not chuck it in the blast furnace instead of expensive charcoal? And, indeed, there were many examples of people doing just that. Dud Dudley was an early pioneer who claimed in his book *Metallum Martis*

(1665) to have successfully smelted iron with coal, and he had the iron goods around his house to prove it.[3] Others followed, and there is no reason to believe that they failed. The problem was that the process was not economic. Most iron in the seventeenth century was refined into wrought iron, and pig iron smelted with coal contained too much sulphur for this to be successful. This was a typical problem in substituting coal for wood: the coal introduced impurities, so new technology had to be invented to eliminate them. One solution was to purify the coal by coking it. The first commercial application of this technique was in Derbyshire where the coke was burnt to heat malt kilns.

Abraham Darby I is usually credited with the invention of coke smelting, but, as noted, he did not conceive the idea. Darby probably learned about coke smelting from Shadrach Fox, who had a contract to supply the Board of Ordnance with cast iron shot in the 1690s. This iron was probably smelted with coke, and Fox's furnace was the one at Coalbrookdale that Darby later leased. The furnace blew up in 1701, and Fox smelted some more iron with coal or coke at the Wombridge Furnace. Darby leased the Coalbrookdale furnace from Fox in 1708, rebuilt it, and set off on his career smelting coke iron (King 2003, p. 52).

The link from Fox to Darby solves several puzzles – why Darby never patented coke smelting (although he patented his casting process) and how he had the confidence to use coke from the very inception of his business. He acted as though he knew the process would work technically, for he did no experimenting with coke nor does he seem to have had a back-up plan to use charcoal if coke smelting failed. Also, Shadrach Fox's experience showed that coke iron was suitable for castings, which was the application Darby had in mind.

Indeed, Darby's contribution to 'inventing' coke smelting was in finding a commercially viable application for the material. In about 1702, Darby and other Quakers established the Baptist Mills Brass Works near Bristol. Most brass was then fabricated by drawing it into wire or by hammering sheets into pots, kettles and such like. Casting was traditionally limited to church bells and cannon. However, by the late seventeenth century, the Dutch were casting many other products using sand moulds and reusable patterns (Hamilton 1926, pp. 344–6). In 1703, Darby set up his own foundry and tried to cast iron

[3] There is some dispute as to what Dudley achieved, but all agree that he probably made pig iron and castings using coal (some think coke) as fuel. See Mott (1934–5) including discussion.

pots with sand moulds, but he was unsuccessful. In 1704, he went to the Netherlands to study sand casting. He brought back some Dutch workers and got them to try casting iron, but they were also unsuccessful. However, an English apprentice, John Thomas, believed he could do it, and Darby paid him until he was successful in 1707. This was Darby's principal R&D project, and it resulted in a patent in 1707 for casting iron with sand moulds. The great virtue of Darby's innovation was that the castings were thin-walled and light. Darby's one-gallon cooking pot, for instance, weighed 6.5 pounds, which was half the weight of a conventional iron pot, and sold at a premium (Mott 1957–9a, p. 78, Hyde 1977, p. 40, Raistrick 1989, pp. 18–23).

Darby can also be credited with a second invention related to casting. The thin-walled castings were not made with molten pig iron as it flowed from the blast furnace. Instead, pig iron was remelted. Darby was the first to use a reverberatory furnace to accomplish this. Reverberatory furnaces had been used since the middle ages to melt the brass for bell founding, and Dud Dudley may have used such a furnace to cast iron. In the 1670s and 1680s, the reverberatory furnace was used to smelt lead and copper by two chartered companies associated with Sir Clement Clark, who may also have experimented with melting iron. Darby, however, was the first to make a commercial success of the reverberatory furnace in the iron foundry (Mott 1957–9a, p. 76, King 2003, p. 51). It remained the standard apparatus for remelting pig iron until John Wilkinson's invention of the cupola furnace.

The preparation of the coke involved another bit of technological borrowing. The first commercial use of coke was in Derby in the seventeenth century where it warmed the sprouting barley in malt mills. Abraham Darby had apprenticed there as a malt mill maker where he learned the technique. Indeed, coke was made at Coalbrookdale in the same manner in which it was made in Derby (Mott 1957, p. 9, Raistrick 1989, pp. 23, 25). Darby's achievements depended on copying and combining several recent developments in the iron, copper and brewing industries.

Abraham Darby's furnace was a conventional charcoal blast furnace. Aside from the use of coke, the main deviation from standard practice was in its rate of drive. A charcoal furnace made about 300 tons of iron per year. In the first nine months of coke operation, Darby operated at the rate of only 44 tons per year. In the last quarter of the year, the annual rate was increased to 150 tons. Coke was a less reactive fuel than charcoal, and neither Darby nor his successors managed to achieve a production rate of 300 tons per year until a reversing engine was introduced in 1735. The use of coke, however, did realize a higher internal temperature than charcoal, with the result that the silica in the ore was reduced to silicon. The high silicon content of the coke pig iron rendered it more fluid than charcoal pig iron, and that fluidity contributed to the success of the thin-walled castings. On the other hand, the silicon made it more expensive to refine into wrought iron. Furthermore, the lower production rate pushed capital costs above those achievable with charcoal as a fuel.

Between 1709 and 1732, the average total cost per ton of pig iron fluctuated between £7.66 and £10.81, with a mean of £8.75. It is probably no coincidence that pig iron was valued at £8.50 in the inventory of the ironworks drawn up in July 1718 (Raistrick 1989, pp. 304–5). In the 1720s, the rate of production was generally higher than in 1709, which reduced capital costs. The consumption of ore and coal fluctuated widely, but, as Table 9.1 suggests, Darby and his successors learned to control the smelting process, and often realized superior results to those of 1709. With pig iron at £8.75 per ton, Darby could make money selling his castings at £14 per ton.[4] Between 1719 and 1737, 70 per cent of the pig iron made at Coalbrookdale was cast on the premises (Hyde 1977, p. 41).

Abraham Darby was not a wealthy man, and his business activities required him to raise external capital to finance expansion as well as his R&D. Darby's partners in Baptist Mills did not want to pay for his research on iron castings, but he found a new financial backer in Thomas Foudney. When he leased the Coalbrookdale ironworks, he sold James Peters and Griffin Prankard three-sixteenths of the business to raise money. By 1711, he had sold another one-sixteenth to Richard Champion, although he repurchased it in 1712. In the next few years, he sold more shares to Thomas Goldney, and borrowed money from his brother-in-law, Thomas Baylies, by mortgaging property. These funds were used to buy interests in the Vale Royal and Dolgyn furnaces and to erect the New Furnace at Coalbrookdale in 1715. In 1717, Darby died intestate at the age of thirty-nine. At that time, all of the

[4] £14 per ton is the value placed on 'Potts & Kettles' in the Ware-house and in the New Warehouse at the New Blast Furnace in the July 1718 inventory of the firm. Some other products are listed at other prices but pots and kettles comprised the greatest share of value by far (Raistrick 1989, pp. 301, 305).

equity of the enterprise belonged to Goldney, Baylies and his widow's son-in-law, Richard Ford. Darby's children would have had no interest in the business had it not been for Joshua Sergeant, who acted as their trustee, and purchased three shares for them from Goldney (Raistrick 1989, pp. 6, 40, 50–1).

Macro-invention (second phase): making coke iron competitive, 1720–1755

The cost of pig iron that allowed a profit in the casting business was one benchmark for assessing the progress of coke pig iron. Another was the price of charcoal pig iron. It sold for £5–6 per ton between 1720 and 1750 (Hyde 1977, p. 44). Coke iron was never going to find a wide market unless it could beat that price. Indeed, it had to do a bit better since the high silicon content of coke pig raised refining costs, and bar iron made from coke pig iron was of inferior quality to bar iron made from charcoal pig. Since coke pig iron cost £8.75 per ton in the 1720s, there was a long way to go. As a result, coke smelting was limited to only a few furnaces making foundry pig during the first half of the eighteenth century. During this period, however, costs were cut and quality raised by 'local learning', that is, by experimental variations in existing practice. Sometimes, the experiments were aimed at solving the problem that was, in the end, solved; at other times, some other goal was the object and technical insight was a complete accident.

There were three major steps in improving coke smelting between the 1720s and 1755. The first occurred in the 1730s. The impetus for the change was to increase output. Abraham Darby I had developed the business to produce products like pots. After his death in 1717, Richard Ford ran the firm. In the early 1730s, he proposed to expand the business by producing cast iron parts for steam engines, which he anticipated would be a growing business after the expiration of the Savery–Newcomen patent in 1733 (Raistrick 1989, p. 148). Attempts to expand were hamstrung by drought in 1733 and 1734. Water wheels provided the power for the blast, and low water in the reservoir meant that production was slowed. To overcome this problem, a horse gig was used to drive a pump that returned water from the tail race to Upper Furnace Pool to be reused. In 1742, the horse gig was replaced with a Newcomen steam engine – the first returning engine to be installed.

The impact of returning the water was dramatic. The furnaces could be operated continuously at top speed. Seasonal irregularity was eliminated. Output rose from 4.5 tons per week to 7.5 tons per week. More dramatically – and unexpectedly – input requirements fell. Ore consumption dropped from about 5 tons to 3.3 tons, which was maximum efficiency for ore with an iron content of one-third. With less ore to smelt, coal and limestone use was also cut. Real unit cost dropped by one-quarter from the level of the 1720s. The average total cost of smelting coke iron was now the same as the price of charcoal iron. Coke was becoming competitive.

The second major improvement was an extension of these principles. The Horsehay blast furnaces were built in the early 1750s, and the first came into operations in 1755. These were not taller than the Coalbrookdale furnaces, but they were wider: interior volume increased from about 350 to 500 cubic feet. They were blown with the 'wooden bellows' invented at Coalbrookdale, and those were driven by a steam engine pumping water directly onto a wheel. Production doubled again – to 15.4 tons per week – and furnaces were operated for longer 'blasts'. In the 1720s, the furnaces were shut down for six or eight weeks each year for relining. The Horsehay furnaces were run three or four years before being relined. Input use also declined, most notably for coal and labour. Real average unit cost dropped another pound to £4.40 per ton. At this point, the average total cost of coke iron was below the variable cost of producing charcoal pig iron and its price. It was cheaper to build a coke furnace than to make pig iron with an existing charcoal furnace. From this point on, no new charcoal furnaces were built in Britain – only coke furnaces.

The third major improvement in coke pig iron was an improvement in its quality. The issue was that bar iron made from coke pig iron was 'cold short', that is, that it unexpectedly shattered or fractured during use. Mott (1957–9a, pp. 80–1) has pointed out that 'cold shortness' was the result of excessive phosphorous in the bar iron and was not intrinsically related to the smelting technology. Phosphorous was a constituent of ore (not of either charcoal or coke) and passed into the pig iron. No one, of course, understood this in the eighteenth century. As it happens, the ore used to make charcoal pig iron in the Forest of Dean had very little phosphorous, and that accounts for the excellent reputation of the charcoal bar iron made there. The ores available in the Coalbrookdale area varied widely in their phosphorous content. Much of the early coke pig iron contained considerable phosphorous. During the 1730s and 1740s, Abraham Darby II experimented with different ore mixtures, and eventually stumbled on a mix (Ball, Black and Penny) that produced a low phosphorous pig iron. This was local learning with a vengeance. The Horsehay furnace was using this mixture, and its output was mainly sold to forges for refining into bar iron (Mott 1957–9a, p. 84, 1957–9b, p. 281). By 1755, a process had finally been developed so that a country like Britain with cheap coal could successfully compete in the manufacture of iron.

Further improvements to the macro-invention, 1755–1850

Table 9.1 and Figure 9.2 show that the century after 1755 can be divided into two segments. The first lasted until the early nineteenth century. Total factor productivity growth was modest. There were further economies in the consumption of coal, and a large proportional saving in labour, although this was more than offset by a rise in capital costs. Indeed, the engineering history of the period emphasizes mechanization. In 1774, a Boulton–Watt engine was installed at Coalbrookdale to replace the water wheels and a cylinder blowing engine replaced the wooden bellows. In 1805, that engine was replaced with yet a newer design. The rate of production tripled from 15 tons per day to 45. Such high output required the movement of a large volume of materials. As early as the 1740s, wooden rails were being laid to move them around the Coalbrookdale site. In 1757, Coalbrookdale had a sixteen-mile rail network (Hyde 1977, p. 120). In 1767, the first rails were cast, and, in the next decade, wooden rails were replaced with iron rails – the world's first iron railway (Raistrick 1989, pp. 177–81). Hoist systems were also introduced to charge the furnaces with materials. Capital intensity rose and labour productivity with it, but the rise in capital costs kept pace with the savings in wages, so overall efficiency gains were modest.

The rate of technical progress accelerated in the first half of the nineteenth century. Coalbrookdale was no longer at the forefront of progress since investment gravitated to districts with cheaper coal and ore. These new production centres pioneered new technology, and, indeed, innovation was needed to use their resources effectively.

The most dramatic development was Neilson's invention of the hot blast, which was patented in 1828. The discovery was the result of scientific research to solve another problem in iron-making – how to increase the air delivered to a blast furnace from a blowing engine half a mile distant. Neilsen considered heating the air to increase its pressure and flow. He found through experimenting on a smith's fire that a heated blast also increased the intensity of burning. Neilson had difficulty organizing a trial of his idea because iron masters thought cold air produced better pig iron, but he finally tested the hot blast at the Clyde Ironworks with great success. To finance his efforts, Neilson sold 40 per cent of his rights to investors, including Charles Macintosh, the inventor of waterproof fabric, and a patent was secured. Further experimentation followed with higher and higher blast temperatures. The fuel savings, particularly in Scotland, were impressive, and costs there were further reduced because the hot blast made it possible to smelt the very cheap black band ore. As a result, Scotland became the cheapest iron-producing region in Britain. The savings in other districts were not as great, but the hot blast was eventually adopted everywhere (*Dictionary of National Biography*, Hyde 1973). Table 9.1 shows that substantial fuel savings were made in the first half of the nineteenth century, and the hot blast was responsible for much of this gain.

The hot blast was not the only improvement of the period, however. The size of furnaces was increased as well as the rate of drive. This is manifest as the doubling of weekly production from 44.6 tons in 1803 to 92.6 in 1850. The Coalbrookdale furnace made 81 tons in 1709, and by 1850 the average blast furnace smelted 4,632 tons per year. This increase brought with it a further rise in labour productivity, this time not swamped by greater capital costs. When the hot blast was used in conjunction with taller and more vigorously blown furnaces, the economies were even greater than when the innovations were used separately. The burning gases vented from the top of the furnaces were used to pre-heat the blast. This recycling of heating reduced fuel consumption yet further.

The result of these improvements was a 40 per cent reduction in real costs between 1755 and 1850. Some of the changes were responses to developments outside the iron industry such as the improvements in steam engines. Many, however, were modifications prompted by existing practice. This local learning led to savings of inputs that were scarce (labour) as well as inputs that were abundant (coal).

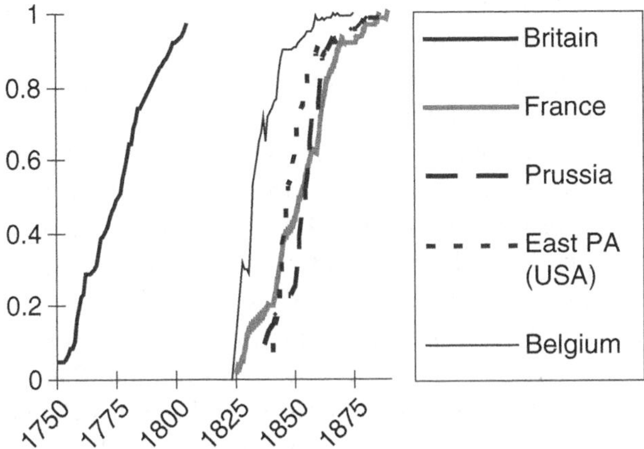

Figure 9.4 Proportion of iron smelted with coal or coke

Source: Britain: Davies and Pollard (1988, pp. 80–1).

Belgium, France and Prussia: Landes (1969, p. 217). Pre-1845 Belgian figures from Fremdling (1986, pp. 75, 78).

Eastern Pennsylvania: Convention of Ironmasters (1849), Johnson (1841, pp. 28–31), American Iron Association, *Bulletin*, 1854–6, Daddow and Bannan (1866, pp. 681–2), manuscript schedules to the 1860 and 1870 US Census, Manufactures, for Pennsylvania. Some of the proportions are based on output and some on the capacity of the furnaces.

The adoption of coke smelting on the continent

Coke smelting replaced charcoal in Britain in the second half of the eighteenth century. In 1750, only three furnaces smelted with coke in England, but, once the problem of making cheap forge pig iron had been solved, output expanded rapidly. No new charcoal furnaces were built, and all increases in capacity were in the coke sector. Charcoal furnaces were under constant competitive pressure. As they aged, costs rose, and the furnaces were shut down once average variable cost exceeded price. By 1800, most iron smelted in Britain was smelted with coke. This is shown graphically in Figure 9.4, where the proportion of iron made with coke is plotted.

Adoption occurred much later on the continent and in North America. Belgium led the way, but, even there, where conditions were most similar to those in Britain, the first furnace built expressly for coke was only erected in 1824 at the Seraing works established by John and Charles Cockerill seven years before (Landes 1969, p. 176). In France and Germany, the switch to coke was delayed even further. In 1850, charcoal iron still predominated.

Why was adoption of coke smelting delayed on the continent? France is the most interesting comparison with Britain, for they were the two countries in western Europe with large and rapidly expanding iron industries in the eighteenth century. British output grew from about 17,000 tons at the beginning of the eighteenth century to 125,000 in the early 1790s. French output increased from 25,000 in the early eighteenth century to 140,000 tons towards the end (Pounds and Parker 1957, p. 27). In contrast, output grew little in Belgium or Germany and reached only 22,000 tons and perhaps 50,000 tons, respectively, at the end.

The British increased their output by using coke, the French by using charcoal, and the difference reflected natural resources. In Britain, there was an abundance of coal and a lack of trees; in France, the situation was reversed. Resource endowments were reflected in prices. Figure 9.5 plots the average price of coal at the pit head in Britain and France.[5] Throughout the period, coal at the mine was three-quarters dearer in France than in England.

The reverse was true for charcoal, at least during the first half of the eighteenth century. Figure 9.6 shows the price in Strasbourg,[6] and it was less than half the price at English furnaces and forges before 1750. Coke pig iron was uncompetitive in England in this period, and the prospects were even less promising south of the channel where charcoal was cheaper and coal dearer.

The competitive position of coke iron did improve after the middle of the eighteenth century, since the price of charcoal was rising. Indeed, the increase in charcoal prices shown in Figure 9.6 occurred across France. National inquiries in 1783 and 1811 both showed large rises in the preceding decades. 'Within a generation of entrepreneurs', between

[5] Before 1780, so little coal was mined in France that we lack prices for it. Since coal at this time was produced in shallow workings at constant cost (Clark and Jacks 2007), the supply price of coal pre-1780 has been extrapolated using the wage rate.

[6] The French mineral statistics in the nineteenth century record the quantity and value of charcoal charged in blast furnaces, so the price in Strasbourg can be compared to the average price at the furnace for that time period. The agreement was close.

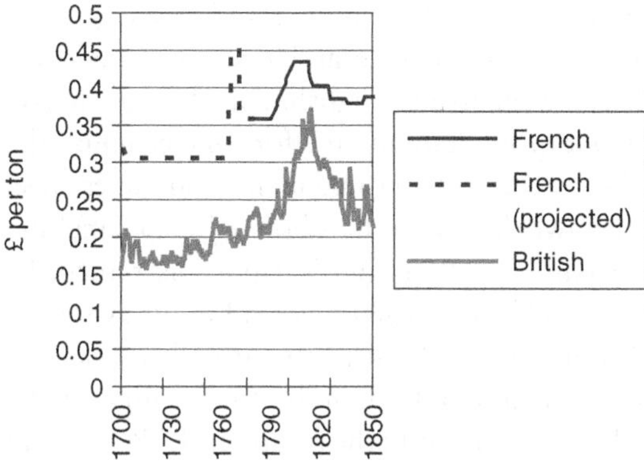

Figure 9.5 Average pit head price of coal

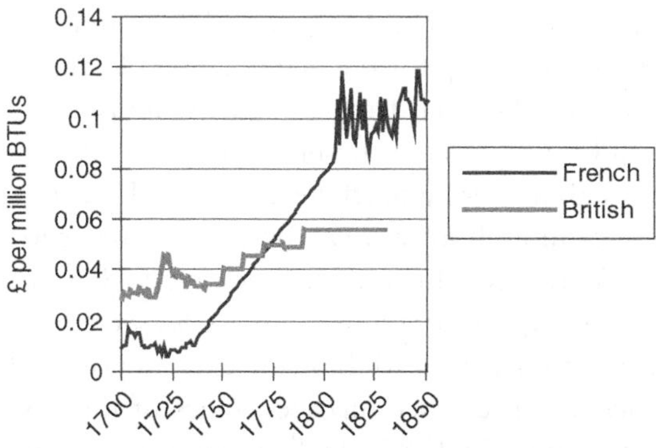

Figure 9.6 Price of charcoal

Source: France: Hanauer (1878). Britain: 1710–1800 from Hyde (1977, pp. 44, 79) and extended to 1820 with Beveridge (1939, pp. 143 *et seq.*).

1773 and 1811, 'the price of charcoal quadrupled' (Woronoff 1984, p. 245). Possibly, the expansion of charcoal iron production had hit a timber constraint. In any event, with charcoal prices only reaching British levels and with French coal still much more expensive, there were few grounds for optimism about a mineral fuel iron industry in France before the Revolution.

Despite this, a very serious attempt was made by the French government to introduce coke smelting in France. Gabriel Jars, son of the owner of a copper mine, was sent on a mission of industrial espionage to Britain in 1764 to learn about British mining and smelting techniques as well as industrial processes in general. He received advice on contacts from John Holker, the expatriate Englishman who was shortly to spirit a spinning jenny out of England in an effort to mechanize the French cotton industry. Jars successfully visited many coal mines, steel works, and the Carron ironworks where he observed coke smelting first hand (*Dictionary of National Biography*). Upon his return, he promoted English methods, and he proposed a site in Burgundy for the establishment of coke blast furnaces. The site was carefully chosen for the quality of its raw materials, and, indeed, in the nineteenth century, production did succeed. But that was far in the future. In 1776, a group of investors began acquiring land on which the Le Creusot works were established (Pounds and Parker 1957, p. 43). In 1775, the artillery officer and metallurgist, De la Houlière, was sent to England where he visited John and William Wilkinson and engaged William to come to France and introduce coke smelting for the manufacture of cannon (Harris 1988b, p. 35). It would be hard to fault the Wilkinsons as technical advisers since John had erected the first coke blast furnace in Staffordshire and invented the boring machine used to make Watt's steam cylinders as well as cannon. Both were accomplished engineers. William was advised by his brother John and received over £7,000 for his services. The state was a major shareholder. The works were built in 1781–4 and had four blast furnaces with blowing engines powered by steam, coking facilities, reverberatory furnaces, miles of railway, and boring machines for cannon. In 1785, the first iron was smelted with coke.

The Le Creusot works were state-of-the-art, yet the endeavour ended in failure. Woronoff (1984, p. 338) thought the iron was too phosphoric – hence cold short.[7] It was never approved for cannon. The iron was also too expensive. One reason was that the works never produced at capacity, so fixed costs per ton smelted were very high. In

[7] The British Iron and Steel Institute's 'The Excursion to Creusot' (1878, pp. 512–3) reports that local ore was smelted (except to make acid Bessemer pig iron for which foreign ore was used). 'The native ores . . . being oolitic, resemble those of Luxembourg and Cleveland; they contain about 30 per cent of metallic iron and as much as 0.5 per cent of phosphorous, but no sulphur'. Cleveland ore produced excellent foundry pig iron, so the local ore resources were intrinsically fit for purpose. The problem was figuring out how to work them. Very large quantities of pig iron made from native ore were successfully refined into wrought iron at Le Creusot in 1878.

addition, Harris (1992) has emphasized that metallurgical technology cannot be easily transferred because raw materials differ, and production procedures must be adapted to them. It is worth remembering how many decades it took the Darbys to fine tune the operation of the Coalbrookdale furnaces and find the right ore mixture to make forge pig iron at a reasonable price. A similar learning process was required at Le Creusot, and success was only achieved when the Schneiders re-established the works after 1836. In the 1780s, coke smelting, even at the technical standard that the Wilkinsons introduced at Le Creusot, was barely more cost-effective than charcoal iron at British factor prices. With French prices, coke iron was probably more expensive than charcoal iron even when everything worked right. And, at the outset, it did not. In a final humiliation, a charcoal blast furnace was erected in An VIII (1799–1800). Looking back on the optimism of 1787, one mining official asked: 'Was it thus possible that the high hopes of fortune and success were simply illusions?' (Harris 1988b, p. 36).

It was another half a century before coke iron became profitable in France. After the Revolution, the fuel price configuration became more favourable for coke. In the 1830s and 1840s, coal was still 75 per cent more expensive in Britain than in France, but charcoal prices had risen substantially with respect to coke and were higher than English prices had been in the eighteenth century. The increase in the price of charcoal was partly due to a rise in wages, which reflected the evolution of the labour market as a whole, and partly to declining supplies of wood. Several dozen furnaces were erected after 1820, but the coke sector only grew slowly, and the charcoal sector continued to expand. Investment in coke iron only accelerated in the 1850s. The number of (exclusively) mineral furnaces in blast rose from 28 in 1841 to 143 in 1870. What had changed? The answer is suggested by the growth in output per furnace which leaped from 2,231 tons per year to 6,922. The expansion of the coke iron sector was effected by building furnaces of the capacity of leading British furnaces. As we have seen, the improvements in furnace design between 1803 and 1850 cut real cost per ton by 30 per cent. It was this cost saving that provided the margin that allowed coke furnaces to be commercially successful even as their managers and workers learned how to adapt the technology to French coals and ores. The state-of-the-art technology of 1780 was not enough to vanquish charcoal smelting: the French iron industry shifted from charcoal to coke only when British technology had reached mid-nineteenth-century levels of efficiency. Then the French skipped all of the intermediate steps that the British had trod in improving their blast furnaces through local learning. The tipping point had been reached.

We can see this in the later history of Le Creusot. The works languished until they were purchased by Aaron Manby and Daniel Wilson in 1826. These English engineers had established a leading engineering works at Charenton near Paris and hoped to expand their enterprise by backward integration into smelting and refining. New puddling furnaces and rolling mills were built at Le Creusot. Manby and Wilson were overstretched financially and the firm failed after the commercial crisis of 1830 when they were refused a state loan (Henderson 1954, pp. 49–58). However, the works were acquired by Adolphe and Eugène Schneider in 1836. The latter built new blast furnaces and puddling furnaces. Production of pig iron rose greatly. In 1835, there were four coke blast furnaces in the département of Saône-et-Loire. These were the furnaces that William Wilkinson had built. Three of them were in blast and produced almost 5,500 tons of pig iron. The production rate of 1,828 tons per year (about 37 tons per week) was typical of furnaces of the 1780s. The works were modernized and extended after the Schneider brothers acquired them. In 1838, the furnaces were fitted with the hot blast, and in 1846 steam-powered mechanical charging equipment was added. 'There was also the realistic recognition of the English lead and the initial modesty of the student who sits at the feet of the English teacher before claiming to overtake the master (exhibiting the same spirit that later succeeded so well for the Japanese)' (Beaud 1995, p. 206). In 1870, eleven coke furnaces were in blast in the same département producing 109,000 tons – almost 10,000 tons per year each or 200 tons per week.[8] This equalled good British practice for the time. The furnaces were 66 feet tall. The ovens for heating the blast were state-of-the-art (Cowper and Whitwell), the blowing engines were the latest design, and the hoists for charging the

[8] Since there were twelve blast furnaces at Le Creusot, it probably accounted for all of the output in the département (Beaud 1995, pp. 212–13). Pounds and Parker (1957, p. 169) report that the pig iron production of Le Creusot 'rose from 5,000 tons in 1837 to 18,000 tons ten years later, to 35,000 tons in 1855 and 133,000 tons in 1867'. See also Villain (1901, pp. 256–87).

furnaces were 'a capital system'.[9] The Schneiders succeeded where the Wilkinsons had failed because of the more favourable configuration of coal and charcoal prices and because of the superior efficiency of the blast furnaces they erected in the middle of the nineteenth century.

The adoption of coke smelting is an example of a 'tipping point', as discussed in Chapter 6. Coke smelting was a biased technical change that shifted input demand from charcoal to coal. The earliest forms of the technology were only viable in Britain because coal was so cheap (and even then the first decades depended on the development of a niche business!). The British then improved the technology, reducing the consumption of all inputs including, in particular, coal on which their competitive advantage had depended. In this period, which lasted until the middle of the nineteenth century, the French tried out the technology, but it was never a success. Failure to jump on the technological bandwagon raises questions about the competence of the managers and engineers (Landes 1969, p. 216). Their performance can be assessed through a detailed analysis of business behaviour, and Fremdling (2000) has made a convincing case that the French were shrewd judges of technology. They did, indeed, adopt English methods on a selective basis that reflected profitability. It was only in the mid-nineteenth century that British engineers invented 'appropriate technology' for France.

The adoption of coke smelting in America

The American iron industry also shifted from charcoal to mineral fuel in the middle of the nineteenth century, and that transition also depended on nineteenth-century technology, but the details were different. The bulk of American economic activity still lay on the eastern seaboard, and it had a large charcoal-based iron industry. Most of the coal found east of the Appalachian Mountains was anthracite. It had a higher carbon content than the bituminous coal that predominated in Europe and in the United States further west. Anthracite contains little volatile organic matter and was charged directly into the blast furnace without being coked. In the 1820s, the Leigh Coal and Navigation Company erected an experimental furnace at Maunch Creek near its coal mines.

9 According to the report on 'The Excursion to Creusot' (1878) of the British Iron and Steel Institute.

The attempts to smelt with anthracite were unsuccessful. At the same time, the French government ran similar experiments at Vizille, and they were equally unsuccessful. Both R&D programmes used furnaces with a cold blast, and both failed because anthracite is a denser fuel than coke and can only be ignited with the hot blast. Consequently, America's shift to mineral fuel awaited Neilson's discovery.

The American reaction was swift, and showed a portentous engineering response reminiscent of Evan's invention of the high-pressure steam engine and Lowell and Moody's re-engineering of the power loom. The parallel in the iron industry was Dr Frederick Geisenheimer's 1833 American patent for using the hot blast to smelt iron with anthracite. This discovery did not, however, lead to immediate application. That depended on developments in South Wales, where a small deposit of anthracite was found. David Thomas was the manager of the Yniscedwyn Ironworks, which were located on that deposit. During the 1820s, he also tried to smelt iron with anthracite but could not make the process work and had to bring in coke for fuel. When Thomas heard of Neilson's invention, he rushed to Scotland, bought a licence, and then installed the hot blast in Wales. In 1837, he succeeded, and a patent was obtained by George Crane, who was a major owner of the Yniscedwyn Ironworks. Thomas' success was reported in 1838 in the *London Mining Journal*, which was read in Pennsylvania. One of the directors of the Leigh Coal and Navigation Company quickly went to Yniscedwyn and offered David Thomas a five-year contract to come to Pennsylvania and oversee the smelting of iron with anthracite. Crane also obtained an American patent and bought Geisenheimer's patent. David Thomas was again successful, and the Leigh Crane Iron Company was the first of many anthracite iron works in Pennsylvania.[10] The hot blast precipitated America's shift to mineral fuel (Temin 1964, pp. 51–80).

Why coke smelting was invented in Britain

The coke smelting technology that finally displaced charcoal in France, Germany and the United States was the highly efficient technology of the mid-nineteenth century. The coke technology of the eighteenth

[10] Johnson (1841, pp. 1–38) and 'David Thomas: The Father of the Anthracite Iron Trade', *New York Times*, 3 June 1874.

century was not economically viable outside of Britain. The sorry story of Le Creusot dramatically proves the point that even a state-of-the-art British ironworks c. 1780 could not make money abroad. It had taken years of work and great expense to develop that technology. Indeed, it was marginal at the outset. There would have been no point incurring those costs to realize a fiasco like Le Creusot. It was not the impracticality of French engineering culture that explains the lack of attention to coke smelting. Inventing the process would not have paid. And, had the first step not eked out a profit in England, the technology might never have been developed, and we might still be smelting with charcoal.

10 *Inventors, Enlightenment and human capital*

> I saw the field was spacious, and the soil so good, as to promise an ample recompence to any one who should labour diligently in its cultivation.
>
> Josiah Wedgwood

The rate of invention is determined by the supply of inventors as well as by the demand for new products and processes. Britain's unique structure of wages and prices led to a demand in the eighteenth century for techniques that substituted energy and capital for labour, and that was an important cause of the technological breakthroughs of the Industrial Revolution. But why was there a supply response? Why did inventors come forward to meet the challenges? These questions require attention, for eighteenth-century Britain was not unique in being a high wage economy. Europe after the Black Death is an important case in point, for wages were extremely high (Figures 2.2, 2.3 and 2.5) and yet there was no Industrial Revolution. While the lack of a coal industry was an important difference, another was a more limited supply of potential inventors. The 'aspirational' theory of Sir James Steuart discussed in Chapter 1 implies that the absence of consumer goods in the late middle ages reduced work effort. The situation was reversed in the seventeenth century when the greater variety of British and imported consumer goods triggered an 'industrious revolution' that was manifest in more active inventing. In addition, we will argue in this chapter, eighteenth-century Britain was much more abundantly endowed with human capital, and that is an important reason for the technological breakthroughs of the period.

The supply of inventors can be approached from two points of view. The first is cultural: British culture developed in a distinctive way that increased the propensity to invent and led to the Industrial Revolution. The second emphasizes human capital accumulation: Britain had more inventors because the population became more literate, numerate and skilled. These views need not be contradictory, but they point to different causes. The first is widely held, and I begin with it.

The Industrial Enlightenment

There were two ways by which the Scientific Revolution might have paved the way for the Industrial. The most direct was through scientific advances that led to new technology. Discoveries made by natural philosophers relating to atmospheric pressure and time-keeping did play that role, as described in Chapters 7 and 8. The other way in which the Scientific Revolution could have led to the Industrial was by changing the culture at large. Mokyr (1993, 1999, 2002, 2009) has developed a powerful theory that attributes the ongoing inventiveness of the Industrial Revolution to the Scientific Revolution and the Enlightenment. The connection was the Industrial Enlightenment, namely, 'that part of the Enlightenment that believed that material progress and economic growth could be achieved through increasing human knowledge of natural phenomena and making this knowledge accessible to those who could make use of it in production'.[1] New knowledge was the key to technical progress, and knowledge came from science and from the study of technology through scientific methods. 'The Industrial Enlightenment was the logical continuation of the Scientific Revolution by other means.'

The theory of the Industrial Enlightenment has four important aspects. The first relates to inventions and inventors. Mokyr distinguishes macro- from micro-inventions. The people who create macro-inventions are the critical actors in unleashing economic growth. During the Industrial Revolution, they were the ten most famous names: Newcomen, Watt, Arkwright, Hargreaves, Crompton, Cartwright, Darby, Cort, Wedgwood and Smeaton.[2] They made the key technological breakthroughs in steam, cotton, iron, porcelain and civil engineering that were the basis for British progress. Mokyr insists on the crucial role played by this 'vital few'. 'Unrepresentativeness is the heart of the process of technological change . . . *averages* are . . .

[1] This and other unsourced quotations in this section are from the manuscript version of Mokyr's *The Enlightened Economy: An Economic History of Britain, 1700–1850* (2009) that he generously made available to me in 2008.

[2] This list reflects my view of which inventions were crucial for economic growth. Mokyr has produced alternative lists of macro-inventions.

not very important: a few critical individuals drive the process' (Mokyr 2002, pp. 52–3). However, the macro-inventors were not alone: the Industrial Revolution would have come to naught if the vital few had not been supported by second- and third-tier inventors, who made the micro-inventions that improved the efficiency and extended the scope of the macro-inventions.

The second aspect of the Industrial Enlightenment relates to the social networks in which the inventors operated. 'The Industrial Enlightenment . . . created a set of bridges between intellectuals and producers, between the *savants* and the *fabricants*.' The bridges consisted of formal and informal meetings. At the apex, information was exchanged at the Royal Society. More people were involved in provincial 'scientific societies' – Birmingham's Lunar Society is a famous example – 'academies, Masonic lodges, coffee house lectures' and similar venues (Mokyr 2002, p. 66). Individual contacts were important. 'But what counted especially were informal relationships and correspondences in which producers sought access to the best knowledge available at their time.' The relationship between James Watt and Joseph Black is the archetype.[3] As a young man, Black made important contributions to basic science. He also befriended Watt, and they became business partners. At the age of 38, Black was appointed Professor of Medicine and Chemistry at the University of Edinburgh. From then on, he concentrated on teaching and industrial consultancy aimed at the economic development of Scotland. Among many initiatives, he offered advice to Archibald Cochrane for his coal tar recovery scheme, discovered the process of extracting alkali from kelp, and conceived of making soda by reacting lime with common salt, a proposal that was (unsuccessfully) put into practice by James Watt and John Roebuck. At this level, the Industrial Enlightenment meant that scientists offered the leading industrialists useful knowledge. Aside from the emphasis on communications networks, there is not a great difference between this proposition and the discussion in the last chapters about the importance of knowledge discovered by scientists for the development of technology.

[3] In this chapter, quotations and most biographical details not otherwise referenced are from the *Oxford Dictionary of National Biography*, online edition, 2008. Other sources for biographical details included Beeson (1989), Halfpenny (2000), Roden (1977, pp. 1–6), Setchell (1970), Shorter (1971, pp. 40–91), Watts (1990), Weedon (1990) and White (1989, pp. 2–5).

The Industrial Enlightenment spread beyond this elite circle, however. 'The Industrial Enlightenment was successful because beneath the giants operated a much larger contingent of scientific writers, tinkerers, engineers, lecturers, and experimental philosophers, who may not have been in the class of a Joseph Priestley, a John Dalton, or a Michael Faraday, but who could stand on those giants' shoulders.' Scientific lectures were popular in eighteenth-century England, as were books explaining the discoveries of Newton and other natural philosophers. The hoi polloi became familiar with the discoveries of science and with the scientific worldview in which knowledge is acquired through the systematic study of empirical phenomena and ordered through a mathematical representation. This worldview was conducive to the improvement of technology.

The third aspect of the Industrial Enlightenment is the application of the scientific method to the study of technology through experimentation. 'The legitimization of systematic experiment as a scientific method carried over to the realm of technology.' Josiah Wedgwood, for instance, performed thousands of controlled experiments to improve his ceramic mixtures and glazes. In the case of machine builders, experimentation was less formal and meant trying out alternative designs until an effective configuration was achieved. 'Engineers from Smeaton and Trevithick to the hundreds of anonymous craftsmen in Britain's mines, mills, and forges, performed experiments trying to see what worked and what did not, and then told the world about it.'

The fourth aspect of the Industrial Enlightenment is its class dimension. Mokyr does not think that the Industrial Revolution came from below, from the cultivators and the artisans. 'The Industrial Enlightenment was not . . . a mass-phenomenon that included the working class. It was a minority affair confined to a fairly thin sliver of highly trained and literate men.' The social exclusiveness of the Enlightenment stands out when the model is applied to agriculture. Mokyr's heroes are not the copyholders of Spelsbury, who ran experimental plots to evaluate sainfoin, clover and turnips, as we saw in Chapter 3. Rather, they are the improving landlords, who dominate the traditional historiography. Mokyr believes these landlords were important because they were the members of rural society who participated actively in Enlightenment culture and who could, therefore, avail themselves of the technical knowledge being dispensed.

The class dimension of the Industrial Enlightenment is clear in Mokyr's choice of exemplars. John Smeaton, 'perhaps more than any other figure in the eighteenth century, personified what the Industrial Enlightenment was all about'. He was a member of the Royal Society and a founder of the Society of Civil Engineers. Smeaton was also one of the first to study technology with controlled experiments. He built small-scale, model water wheels and tested them to improve efficiency. 'He was one of the first to realize that improvements in technological systems can be tested only by varying components one at a time holding all others constant.' He did not learn these skills or acquire this outlook by apprenticing as a millwright, which would have been the working-class route to engineering. His father was an attorney, and Smeaton was educated at Leeds Grammar School until he was sixteen when he entered his father's office to study law. He moved to London at eighteen to continue his legal studies but gave them up when he was twenty. He returned to Austhorpe Lodge, the family home, where he set up a machine shop and taught himself to make scientific instruments. Four years later, he moved back to London and established an engineering business that employed three craftsmen. He quickly became involved with the Royal Society. John Smeaton was no working-class mechanic, and his privileged background smoothed the way into Enlightenment circles.

Statistical analysis of the important inventors

Mokyr's examples of macro-inventors are useful in defining an ideal type, but they cannot establish how representative that type was. We need statistical samples for that. With samples, we can see whether Smeaton was typical of all of the macro-inventors and, indeed, of inventors in general. Did they bear the mark of the Enlightenment? Were they communicating with leading scientists and other members of the Industrial Enlightenment? Were they avid experimenters? What was their social background?

To explore these issues, I have put together a database of seventy-nine important inventors in the seventeenth and eighteenth centuries.[4]

[4] The inspiration is the 'Great Inventors' project of Khan and Sokoloff (1993), who compiled such a database for their study of American patenting. I have called my sample an 'important inventors' database rather than a 'great inventors' database to avoid the confusion that would arise if 'great inventors' were

Concentration on this time period – rather than, say, the first half of the nineteenth century – reflects my view of technological development as a path-dependent process in which the first inventions were the critical inventions. From this perspective, the key test for the Industrial Enlightenment model is whether it can explain the macro-inventions of the eighteenth century whose elaboration drove the British economy forward through much of the nineteenth century.

The database includes all of the inventors mentioned in Singer's great *History of Technology* (1954–84) who were active in Britain between the founding of the Royal Society in 1660 and 1800. This list was cross-checked against the individuals discussed by Mokyr in his *Lever of Riches* and by Mantoux's *Industrial Revolution in the Eighteenth Century.* Biographical information was added from the new *Dictionary of National Biography* and other sources. Enough has been discovered about seventy-nine inventors to include them in the analysis. The sample includes all of the macro-inventors who made the key technological breakthroughs. Of course, one can debate the membership of that group, but I take it to be ten: Josiah Wedgwood, John Smeaton, Thomas Newcomen, James Watt, Abraham Darby I, Henry Cort, James Hargreaves, Richard Arkwright, Samuel Crompton and Edmund Cartwright. In addition, there were sixty-nine second- and third-tier inventors who made less far-reaching inventions. While all members of the Vital Few are included in the database, it contains only a sample of lesser inventors.

Table 10.1 summarizes the distribution of the important inventors by the industries in which they operated. The most famous revolutionized industries – steam, textiles (spinning, weaving and knitting silk, cotton, flax and wool) and metals (smelting and refining ferrous and non-ferrous metals and tin plate) – are well represented, but so are industries like ceramics (pottery and porcelain), machines (millwork, machine tools and factory construction) and chemicals (sulphuric acid, dyes, alkalis, chlorine bleach and glass) that figure less prominently in general histories. There is also a considerable representation of 'high-tech' industries like horology, instrumentation and navigation.

understood to refer to the ten macro-inventors instead of the full sample of seventy-nine inventors. There is probably considerable overlap with Crouzet's (1985b) list of industrialists. Crouzet's study of their social origins is not unrelated to the questions addressed here. See also Honeyman (1982). The inventors in my database are listed in the appendix to this chapter.

Table 10.1 *Characteristics of the important inventors*

	Macro-inventors	Lower tiers	Total
Ceramics	1	11	12
Chemicals	0	10	10
Horology	0	8	8
Instruments	0	3	3
Machines	1	12	13
Metals	2	8	10
Navigation	0	2	2
Steam	2	6	8
Textiles	4	9	13
Total	10	69	79

The inventors in the sample were active over a long time frame. Nine were born before 1650, eighteen in the second half of the seventeenth century, thirty-eight in the first half of the eighteenth, and fourteen after 1750. The inventive activity was evenly distributed over the late seventeenth and eighteenth centuries. The time path lacks the sharp acceleration in invention after 1750 that appears in patent statistics – probably because the inventors tended to live earlier.

Did the important inventors exemplify the Industrial Enlightenment model? The first test is to look for indications of involvement with Enlightenment science through either social intercourse, schooling or private instruction. If there was any involvement, we would like to know whether scientists were passing useful bits of knowledge on to the inventors. The second test is to see whether the inventors themselves were experimenters. The final test is whether they came from upper-class backgrounds.

I begin with connections to the Enlightenment. In this regard, the macro-inventors present a mixed record. Certainly, Watt, Smeaton and Wedgwood worked closely with leading scientists. Smeaton and Wedgwood were Fellows of the Royal Society, and Watt and Wedgwood were members of the Lunar Society. Watt was a close associate and business partner of Joseph Black throughout his adult life, and they discussed technical issues with each other. Wedgwood and Smeaton read papers to the Royal Society and perhaps received useful feedback from scientists.

Edmund Cartwright was also involved in Enlightenment institutions but not such prestigious ones. Cartwright was a member of the Society of Arts and the Board of Agriculture later in life. He was a cleric and accepted Newtonian theology according to which God was seen as a retired engineer no longer involved in the management of the world having set it in motion according to Newton's laws. This theology may have induced him to search for mechanical solutions to technical problems. He does not seem to have received help from any natural philosopher.

Thomas Newcomen had the least substantial links to Enlightenment science. Indeed, there is no direct evidence of any contact. However, it is inconceivable that he could have designed his engine without awareness of atmospheric pressure and the fact that the condensation of steam produced a vacuum. These were important discoveries of seventeenth-century physics. Furthermore, Savery regularly visited Dartmouth between 1705 and 1712 when Newcomen was developing his engine there, and they had at least one acquaintance (Caleb Rockett, the mayor) in common. Since Savery was trying to sell his steam pump to tin mines, and Newcomen supplied the same with iron goods, it would be easy for them to have met. Such a meeting is the presumptive transmission channel by which the inventor was influenced by the scientists and perhaps learned about Papin's proto-steam engine.[5]

The other macro-inventors appear to have had no significant contact with the scientific Enlightenment. Darby's friends and associates were Bristol Quakers and Crompton's activities were centred on the New Jerusalem Church Society, a Swedenborg congregation founded in 1787. Hargreaves lived in Lancashire and Nottingham and associated with artisans. Cort and Newcomen may have travelled more widely. Arkwright is probably the exception who proves the rule. If one simply counted 'links', he would look like he was part of the Enlightenment, for he knew James Watt, Joseph Banks and Erasmus Darwin. However, he met all of these people after he was successful and rich. He had no contacts with Enlightenment figures when he was an active inventor and establishing his business.

Indeed, rather than supportive social relations between these macro-inventors and the scientific community, there was a cool distance.

[5] The issue is controversial. I follow Rolt and Allen (1977, pp. 37–8). This account revises Rolt (1963, pp. 49–57) which claimed that Newcomen conceived the engine without any knowledge of the physics.

Henry Cort is a case in point. Mokyr cites him as an example of manufacturers communicating with leading scientists since he consulted Joseph Black. The correspondence, however, occurred after Cort had patented puddling and rolling. Cort probably met Black for the first time when he visited Edinburgh in May 1784 to apply for a Scottish patent for his inventions. On the trip, he gave several demonstrations, and Black attended one. He was impressed by the chemical reaction. Three years later, Cort sent Black the letter to which Mokyr refers. Cort was considering getting a steam engine from Boulton and Watt and was asking Black, one of their associates, for information about the engine – not about puddling. Black's assessment of Cort was that 'he is a plain Englishman without science but by dint of natural ingenuity and a turn for experiment has made such a discovery as will undoubtedly give to this Island the monopoly of that business' (quoted by Robinson and McKie 1970, p. 140). This was a backhanded compliment, for, as D. C. Coleman (1971, p. 300) observed, '"natural ingenuity and a turn for experiment" were recognizably not enough as passwords to Black's world'. Watt was less restrained in his assessment of Cort: 'a simple good natured man but not very knowing.'[6]

This attitude was not new. Newcomen had been similarly patronized by the scientific establishment of his day. Desaguliers commented of Newcomen and his assistant, John Calley: 'after a great many laborious attempts, they did make the engine work; but not being either philosophers to understand the reason, or mathematicians enough to calculate the powers and to proportion the parts, [they] very luckily by accident found what they sought for.' Relationships between the scientists and inventors were not always easy.

The lack of communication between so many of the macro-inventors and the scientific establishment probably represents differences in social background. Three of the four macro-inventors who had important contacts with scientists – Watt, Smeaton and Cartwright – attended grammar schools and Cartwright also studied at Magdalen College, Oxford. Their fathers were a successful merchant, a lawyer and a landed gentleman. In contrast, neither Arkwright, Hargreaves, Crompton, Darby, Cort nor Newcomen had much schooling. All of them were trained as craftsmen or artisans, and their parents came

[6] In a letter to Matthew Boulton, 14 December 1782, as quoted on www.henrycort.net.

from humble backgrounds. Wedgwood is the only macro-inventor from an artisanal background who developed contacts with leading scientists. He was, indeed, a remarkable man. He was already keeping an experiment book when he was 24, and his acceptance by the scientific establishment occurred late in life (he was 52 when he read his first paper to the Royal Society and 53 when he was elected a Fellow) in recognition of the accomplishments achieved on his own. Mokyr is right that many macro-inventors came from well-off families, and that was important in easing their way into institutions like the Royal Society. But many inventors came from working-class families as well, although craftsmen from those backgrounds did not mix easily in Enlightenment circles.

When they are considered comprehensively, the macro-inventors provide only partial support for the Industrial Enlightenment model. What about inventors in general? In most cases, I have found either evidence of an Enlightenment link or a full enough biography that does not indicate any link to be reasonably confident that there was none. At first blush, the Industrial Enlightenment model does reasonably well since half of the inventors showed some connection. John Dwight (1633–1703), who discovered how to make salt glazed stoneware with English materials, is an excellent example. His father was a yeoman, but he showed such academic promise that he attended Oxford University in the 1650s where he studied law and chemistry. He worked in Boyle's laboratory. After university, he worked as the legal adviser to several bishops. 'Dwight was a serious amateur chemist and numbered many of the foremost scientific thinkers among his circle of friends. In contrast to Wedgwood, he had no training in the potting business, but rather set up his pottery as a speculative venture which would put his successful experiments to practical and lucrative use.' In 1698, he wrote to Sir John Lowther, 'having tryed many experiments he concluded he had the secret of making China Ware. Thereupon he sold his [clerical] Office, came to London, was encouraged therein by Mr Boyl and Dr Hook.'

William Cookworthy (1705–1780), who discovered how to make hard paste porcelain with English minerals, is another good example. He was the son of a serge-maker, attended a school at Kingsbridge followed by a boarding school in Exeter until the age of 13. Then he was apprenticed to the Quaker apothecaries, Timothy and Sylvanus Bevan, whose business was in London. Cookworthy learned the trade so well, that he was taken into the business. They opened a branch in Plymouth where he went to live. After his wife died in 1745, Cookworthy withdrew from active management and devoted his efforts to religious work and experiments on ceramics. He discovered the principal deposits of China clay and China stone in Cornwall and successfully produced porcelain. 'A linguist, he was fluent in Latin and French, and his circle of acquaintances was wide and extended well beyond fellow Quaker intellectuals such as John Fothergill to include such figures as John Smeaton, who lodged with him during the building of the Eddystone lighthouse [1756–9], and Captain James Cook, who, with Joseph Banks and Daniel Solander, dined with him before sailing from Plymouth in 1768.' These visits occurred when he was developing the porcelain manufacturing process, and so he possibly received some useful advice. Despite his proficiency in chemistry, Cookworthy was an enthusiast for divining rods.

Not all of the links between the inventors and the scientific Enlightenment were as substantial as these, however. John Wilkinson is credited with a link because he was a friend of Joseph Priestley, who had married his sister – but how important a connection was that? John Harrison is linked to the Industrial Enlightenment because of his dealings with the Board of Longitude and because, when he was young, a clergyman lent him a copy of Nicholas Saunderson's lectures on natural philosophy and Newtonianism. Harrison copied the entire book so he could study it. Did that encounter influence the invention of his chronometers?

There is clearly a danger here of confusing inconsequential 'links' with historically important influences. John Smeaton wrote an enthusiastic memoir about Henry Hindley, who invented gear-cutting machinery and other tools for watch-making – thus linking Hindley to the Industrial Enlightenment. When they met, however, Hindley was 41 and already an accomplished inventor, while Smeaton was only 17 and starting his career. Their encounter, therefore, was the artisan defining engineering proficiency for the future paragon of the Industrial Enlightenment rather than the other way around. I have, therefore, not coded Hindley as being influenced by the Enlightenment.

While many of the links between the Enlightenment and the inventors may not have been very substantial – and certainly they do not prove the flow of useful knowledge from *savants* to *fabricants* that Mokyr emphasized – the number is still impressive. Its significance,

Table 10.2 *Inventors and enlightenment connections*

	Link	No link	Unknown
Horology	6	2	0
Instruments	2	1	0
Machines	9	3	1
Navigation	2	0	0
Steam	7	1	0
Ceramics	4	5	3
Chemicals	4	4	2
Metals	0	9	1
Textiles	3	10	0
Total	37	35	7

however, is called into question when the data are broken down by industry, for the number of links varied significantly from industry to industry (Table 10.2).

In Table 10.2, the industries have been reordered into three groups reflecting the proportion of inventors linked to the Enlightenment. The group with the most links included the areas where natural philosophers made direct contributions to industrial technology. Steam power, as we have seen, was an application of seventeenth-century physics, and many of the tabulated inventors – e.g. Denis Papin, Thomas Savery and Henry Beighton – reflect that involvement. Later steam engineers like Watt, Boulton and Trevethick maintained contacts with the Royal Society and with establishment scientists. Machinery was not easily separable from steam. Six of the nine machinery inventors with links to the Industrial Enlightenment were Fellows of the Royal Society. Horology was another area in which leading scientists were active, and Hooke himself is one of the inventors tabulated. Continuing interest in the longitude problem maintained contacts between establishment science and clock-makers and also accounts for the links to inventors of navigational aids. Links existed between members of the Royal Society and instrument-makers since they manufactured the telescopes used by astronomers. The links between the Enlightenment and these industries reflected the enthusiasms and priorities of establishment science rather than a general commitment to technological innovation.

Chemicals and ceramics occupy an intermediate position in the table as well as including most of the inventors whose links are 'unknown'. The latter come from such humble backgrounds that it is likely they had no connection to Enlightenment figures. In the case of chemicals, all of the links involve Scots – John Roebuck, Charles Macintosh, Archibald Cochrane and Francis Home – and Joseph Black, Professor of Chemistry and Medicine at the University of Edinburgh, was central. John Roebuck, who invented the lead chamber method of making sulphuric acid, was English, but he studied at the University of Edinburgh (before Black's time), and established many industrial activities there. He was a close associate of James Watt and Joseph Black. Francis Home was a renowned physician and pillar of the Scottish Enlightenment, and a colleague of Black. Home also wrote a book on the use of sulphuric acid to bleach linen, thus broadening the market for John Roebuck's product. Charles Macintosh attended the chemistry lectures of William Irvine in Glasgow and Joseph Black in Edinburgh. Archibald Cochrane, ninth Earl of Dundonald, was an important Scottish chemist and entrepreneur and a close friend of Joseph Black. Much of the invention in Scotland was influenced by this scientific figure. The rest of the inventors, who were English, did not benefit from any comparable connection.

Ceramics presents a mixed picture. Some of the most important inventors – Dwight, Wedgwood and Cookworthy – had Enlightenment connections. Other figures who also made important contributions had purely trade backgrounds, however. Enoch Booth, who invented creamware in the 1740s and the double firing of pottery in the 1750s, grew up in the Potteries and was apprenticed there. John Sadler and John Brooks independently invented transfer printing, and John Wall and Josiah Spode perfected ways of using transfer printing under glaze. Josiah Spode's son, also named Josiah, perfected the formula for bone china. These men had backgrounds in either engraving or pottery and exhibited no personal connection to Enlightenment figures.

Textiles and metals were striking for the absence of much connection to the Enlightenment. West Country Quakers were responsible for many of the inventions in metal smelting – the Darbys' work on iron is notable, and members of the Champion family developed techniques to smelt brass and extract zinc. At the end of the seventeenth century, Sir Clement Clerke and various Quaker companies adapted the reverberatory furnace to smelt copper, tin and lead. John Hanbury, a Pontypool landowner and iron master, invented what became the standard method of making tin plate in the early eighteenth century, and Benjamin Huntsman invented crucible steel in the 1740s. None of these people had Enlightenment connections.

It was the same story in textiles. Three inventors – the macro-inventor Edmund Cartwright, John Kennedy, who invented double speed, which allowed the mule to spin fine yarn, and Matthew Murray, who made many improvements to spinning machinery and applied it to flax – had Enlightenment links. Cartwright, as we have seen, was a member of the Board of Agriculture and the Society of Arts. Murray received a gold medal from the Society of Arts, and Kennedy was an active member of the Manchester Literary and Philosophical Society. These links were established after most of the inventions were made, however, and did not convey useful tips from scientists. The rest were devoid of Enlightenment links. The Lombe brothers, who made the first silk mill, did not associate with scientists, nor did artisans like John Kay and James Hargreaves. Jedediah Strutt, who developed a device to knit ribbed stockings on the frame and who bankrolled Arkwright as well as making some contribution to roller spinning, associated with midlands entrepreneurs. He spent considerable sums on the education of his children, and his son William was elected a Fellow of the Royal Society. William was a friend of Enlightenment figures like Erasmus Darwin and Jeremy Bentham, but this lifestyle led to a falling out with his father who did not approve of it.

These negative findings would not have surprised at least one contemporary, Bernard Mandeville. In *The Fable of the Bees* (1724), he remarked:

> They are very seldom the same Sort of People, those that invent Arts, and Improvements in them, and those that enquire into the Reason of Things: this latter is most commonly practis'd by such, as are idle and indolent, that are fond of Retirement, hate Business, and take delight in Speculation: whereas none succeed oftener in the first, than active, stirring, and laborious Men, such as will put their Hand to the Plough, try Experiments, and give all their Attention to what they are about.

In the cases of metals and textiles, Mandeville looks right. Science and technology were separate spheres with little interaction.

More suspicion that the Industrial Enlightenment was mainly an upper-class cultural phenomenon with little relation to production comes from the study of its twin – the Agrarian Enlightenment. This involved many of the same themes as the Industrial Enlightenment – except applied to farming rather than manufacturing – and, indeed, many of the same people, once returned to their country houses at the close of the London season. These were the celebrated improving landlords of England, who enclosed their estates, turned their home farms into experimental stations, patronized Arthur Young (a great collector of farming data), published reports of new crops and cultivation methods, and promoted improved farming among their tenants. This was the Enlightenment project applied to agriculture, but, unfortunately for the cultural theory, it had little effect on agricultural productivity (Beckett 1986, pp. 158–64, Wilmot 1990). The impact of the Agrarian Enlightenment was inherently limited because it was a movement among the gentry and aristocracy, not among the farmers who actually tilled the land. The books were written by landlords, for landlords. The King could play at being Farmer George, but there was little connection with real production. Was the Industrial Enlightenment as ineffective?

The biographies of the seventy-nine important inventors show that there were links between the Enlightenment and the inventors, but the connections were sometimes tenuous. Moreover, they were industry specific. Links were strongest in the industries where scientists were or had been most active – instrumentation, clocks, watches, steam power, and chemistry in Scotland. Otherwise, links were rare. The importance, therefore, of Enlightenment links depends on which industries one thinks were central to the Industrial Revolution. Steam, of course, was important in the long run, and in that context Enlightenment links mattered. In the late eighteenth and early nineteenth centuries, however, textiles and metals had much greater economic impact. Using that yardstick, the Industrial Enlightenment did not matter much.

The Industrial Enlightenment and experimentation

The second plank of the Industrial Enlightenment model is experimentation. In this regard, the model is much more in accord with the historical record. The *Dictionary of National Biography* and other materials have been searched for descriptions of how inventions were made and whether that involved experimenting. The results are shown in Table 10.3. In forty-nine of the seventy-nine cases, there was reference to

Table 10.3 *Inventors and experimentation*

	Experiment	No experiment	Unknown
Horology	2	0	6
Instruments	2	0	1
Machines	9	0	4
Navigation	1	1	0
Steam	7	1	0
Ceramics	5	0	7
Chemicals	7	0	3
Metals	6	0	4
Textiles	10	1	2
Total	49	3	27

experiments (in a few cases, the process was described but the word was not used). In most of the 'unknown' cases, where descriptions are too slight to establish a conclusion positively, the presumption must be that the inventor experimented, for it is impossible to imagine how the invention could have been made without experimenting.

All of the macro-inventors were 'labourious Men, such as . . . try Experiments'. The experimental programmes of Newcomen, the Darbys, Hargreaves and Arkwright have been described elsewhere in this book under the rubric of Research & Development. Wedgwood is famous for his 5,000 experiments on clay mixtures and glazes; Watt conceived the separate condenser when he performed experiments on a small-scale model of a Newcomen engine; Smeaton, likewise, experimented on model water wheels to improve their efficiency; Cartwright repeatedly replanned and built new power looms gradually evolving a more successful design; Cort developed puddling and rolling by experimenting at his mill at Fontley. The macro-inventions of the Industrial Revolution were the result of experiments.

The second- and third-tier inventors also experimented. George Ravenscroft, who pioneered lead crystal glass, financed glass technicians, who introduced lead to the glass mixture and fine-tuned its composition to prevent 'crizzling' (i.e. becoming opaque from minute cracks). 'The process of experimentation and fine adjustment involved should not be underrated. It was much harder to know whether a new chemical technique would provide a stable product than whether a new machine would work' (MacLeod 1987, p. 803). Thomas Fry's epitaph described him as 'the Inventor and first Manufacturer of PORCELAIN in England: To bring which to Perfection He spent fifteen years among Furnaces, Till his Constitution was destroyed' (Young 1999, p. 42). William Champion experimented from 1730 to 1738 to extract zinc from calmine and adapted local glass-making equipment to the problem. 'To avoid the oxidization of zinc vapour at the high temperatures required for metal production, he built a large-scale distillation furnace, based on the Bristol glass cones and heated by coal.' John Sadler, who developed transfer printing, the technique that allowed the mass production of standardized pottery decorations, stated in 'an affidavit' that he and 'his assistant Guy Green . . . on 27 July 1756 . . . printed 1200 earthenware tiles of different patterns in six hours, and that the process had taken upwards of seven years to perfect'. When William Murdoch worked for Boulton and Watt, James Watt complained about his experiments: 'I wish William could be brought to do as we do, to mind the business in hand, and let such as Symington and Sadler throw away their time and money, hunting shadows.'

'Experiment' did not always mean the same thing. In processing materials, experiments were probably like controlled scientific experiments. In mechanical engineering, however, experimenting means improving designs by trial and error. Letters between Lewis Paul and John Wyatt, for instance, record the successive problems they faced in perfecting a carding machine. First, the spinners pieced together short lengths of roving, then an attempt was made to extract a continuous roving, finally variations in the thickness of the roving had to be addressed in order to produce a continuous, uniform length of loosely formed cotton to feed into the spinning machine (Hills 1970, p. 41). Andrew Meikle's first threshing machine was based on five flails driven by water power. He abandoned this, however, for a design that used a rotating drum to beat the grain. Sir Thomas Lombe's silk mill involved his brother's smuggling the designs of machines out of Italy and then adapting them to work in English conditions. His patent application describes the process: 'I declare that, by constant application and endeavours for severall years past, and employing a great many agents and workmen both here and in foreigne parts, I have at very great expense and hazards found out, discovered, and brought into this country the art of making the three capital engines.'

The appendix to this chapter records three inventors who did not experiment, and they are instructive. John Lombe was the industrial spy who snuck the plans for the Italian silk machinery back to England. Henry Beighton invented a safety valve for Newcomen's steam engine. Whether he experimented to do that is not known. His greatest claims to fame, however, were the measurements he and Desaguliers made of Newcomen's engine as well as later publications of meteorological records and calculations of eclipses. Likewise, Edmund Halley is included as an inventor because his charts of trade winds, tides and magnetic variation were used for a century. These men were observers, if not experimenters.

The Industrial Enlightenment in long-term perspective

Only about a half of the important inventors had a link to scientists or Enlightenment institutions; however, virtually all of them performed experiments to perfect their inventions. Experimentation was, therefore, the common feature that characterized eighteenth-century inventors. There was a fundamental reason for this that had nothing to do with the Enlightenment, namely, inventions could not be made without experiments. Even if the science was known, the engineering was not. Joshua Ward, for instance, enlarged the scale of sulphuric acid production from the laboratory to the factory.

> He had two trained assistants, John White and F. J. D'Osterman, with whose help in 1736 he began to make sulphuric acid at Twickenham, in what were known as the 'Great Vitriol Works'. This acid was produced by igniting nitre (or saltpetre) and sulphur in round-bottomed flasks set in sand. While the chemistry of the process was by then tolerably well known, for the first time manufacture was on a large enough scale to permit continuous production, one operative being able successively to attend the large number of flasks in the works. The price of sulphuric acid was consequently reduced to about one-sixteenth of its former cost.

Sorting out the equipment and the procedures required changes and improvements – that is, experimentation. How could it have been otherwise?

Since experimenting was part of inventing, experiments preceded the Scientific Revolution and the Industrial Enlightenment. Agriculture furnishes examples. In the fifteenth century, beans and peas replaced barley or oats as the spring crop in many midlands villages (Hoskins 1950, 1951). Many new crops and grasses were introduced from abroad: coleseed, hops, woad, tobacco, saffron, clover and sainfoin, for instance. It was necessary to determine where and how they could be successfully grown. This could only be done by experiment. Sir Richard Weston visited the Low Countries in 1644 after his estate was sequestered, and wrote *A Discours of Husbandrie Used in Brabant and Flanders* that promoted clover, turnips and industrial crops, and later he experimented with the crops to perfect their culture. In *Adam out of Eden, or, an Abstract of divers excellent Experiments touching the advancement of Husbandry*, Adam Speed (1658, pp. 34–6) described how Weston planted eight acres with his own clover seed and eight acres with Flemish seed to see which gave the greater yield. He also experimented to determine how to plant the seed. 'For the manner of sowing of it he having experimented divers ways finds the best peece that ever had to be sowed alone without any other grain for the time, the beginning of the mid-April is the best' (Speed 1658, p. 36). He also discovered that clover boosted the yield of subsequent wheat crops. 'He findeth that the grass improves the ground, for he hath this year exceeding great buck Wheat upon a piece of heathy ground, not one shilling the acre before, which hath been Clove grass three years.' He also discovered 'that flax . . . requires a dry Soyl', and 'St Foyn . . . is exceeding profitable, and may be cut seven or eight times in a year, but . . . it requires a very rich Land, and must not be fed at all'. This final conclusion was revised by the copyholders of Spelsbury in their sainfoin experimental field – but that is the nature of experiments.

Joan Thirsk (1985) believed that Weston's experiments were just the tip of the iceberg. She described the circle of correspondents, centred on Samuel Hartlib, who exchanged the details of their trials with new practices. Not everyone was convinced by Hartlib's enthusiasms. Moses Wall, for instance, wrote: 'I have tried divers of your experiments about bees and they signify nothing' (Thirsk 1985, pp. 556–7). Nevertheless, a collective process of agricultural improvement was underway based on the exchange of individual experiences and experiments. Thirsk believed that Hartlib's 'bookish circle of improving farmers was only the smallest of innumerable concentric rings of lively, enthusiastic improvers with a zest for experiment' (Thirsk 1985, p. 557).

Experimentalism before the founding of the Royal Society was not confined to agriculture. In Chapter 4, we saw how the coal-burning house was developed in the late sixteenth century through collective invention. The full-rigged sailing ship, one of the grand inventions of the Renaissance, was developed in a similar process of trial and error (Unger 1980, 1997).

Eighteenth-century experimentalism was, therefore, not novel. It had precedents running back centuries. The difference between the eighteenth century and early periods was quantitative – an increase in the volume of experimenting – rather than qualitative. The increase in experimenting cannot be explained by personal contact with scientists or Enlightenment institutions since, as we have seen, invention in metals and textiles was largely independent of such contacts. If the Scientific Revolution or the Industrial Enlightenment boosted the rate of invention, it did so by changing the culture at large. If this occurred, it would be an example of Weber's 'disenchantment of the world'. English upper class culture evolved in this direction during the Enlightenment. The question is whether this change 'trickled down' to the lower orders. Many historians believe it did. Burke (2006, pp. 244–70), for instance, argues for two reorientations in popular culture. The first is a redefinition of life objectives in worldly rather than religious terms. Related to this is a decline in belief in magic and, conversely, greater credence for naturalistic explanations. The second is a greater interest in politics. This was closely related to the spread of newspaper reading. Historians of science have claimed that artisans picked up Newtonianism from almanacs, science lecturers and latitudinarian preaching (Jacob 1997, pp. 99–115, Stewart 1992, Sharpe 2007, p. 329). The counterpart to the rise of the mechanical worldview was a decline in belief in witchcraft and magic. However, there is no consensus among historians of popular culture that such a decline occurred or what might have caused it (Thomas 1971, pp. 767–800, Briggs 2002, pp. 327–30, Burke 2006, pp. 274–5, Sharpe 2007, p. 330). Consequently, the case for a widespread adoption of the Newtonian worldview must remain conjectural. We must consider other explanations of the rise in experimentalism.

Level of economic and social development

It is fruitful to approach the problem from a different direction. Another cause of the greater supply of inventors in eighteenth-century Britain was the higher level of social and economic development that had been achieved. This was manifest in the growth of the non-agricultural economy and increases in literacy, numeracy and skills generally. A commercial, educated population provided a basis for industrial innovation that an agrarian economy (even an enterprising one) could not match, a view Mokyr (2009) also shares. 'The key to British technological success was that its rich endowment of competent skilled artisans gave it a comparative advantage in microinventions.'

The development of the English economy mattered because inventors were not drawn randomly from the population. They came from a limited range of social strata and had particular characteristics. In the first place, they were children of the commercial manufacturing economy. It almost goes without saying that the industrial inventors themselves worked outside of agriculture. What is more surprising is that their fathers were also mainly non-agricultural. This is clear from the inventors database for which the occupations of the fathers of sixty-seven of the seventy-nine major inventors have been ascertained. These are shown in Table 10.4 along with the corresponding breakdown of the English population according to our revised version of Gregory King's social table for 1688.

Comparing the two sets of figures shows that the likelihood of someone's becoming an inventor increased according to his father's income and status. The least represented group was labourers and cottagers. According to King, they made up 52.9 per cent of the population, but only 3 per cent of the important inventors had fathers from that group. Seventy-two per cent of the labourers and cottagers were agricultural, so the lack of inventors from this group reflected sectoral as well as class issues.

Class was probably more important than sector, but the issue is complicated because many people were in two sectors. Farmers and yeomen made up 18 per cent of the population but only 9.0 per cent of the important inventors had fathers with this background. However, 7.5 per cent of the important inventors had mixed backgrounds. Abraham Darby I's father, for instance, was a farmer and a nailer, and Jedediah Strutt's was a small-scale farmer and a maltster. If we arbitrarily assign half of the people with mixed backgrounds to agriculture, then farmers and yeomen accounted for 13 per cent of the inventors – still less than their share of the population.

Table 10.4 *Important inventors: father's occupation*

	Number	Percentage in England	Percentage overall
Aristocracy, gentry, clergy	8	11.9%	3.5%
Merchants, lawyers, capitalists	22	32.8%	4.6%
Shopkeepers, manufacturers, artisans	24	35.8%	20.9%
Mixed farming and craft	5	7.5%	
Farmers, yeomen	6	9.0%	18.0%
Labourers, cottagers, husbandmen	2	3.0%	54.9%
Total	67		

Note: The percentages for England refer to fractions of the population as indicated by Gregory King's social table of 1688 as revised by Lindert and Williamson (1982) and further modified by removing an estimate of domestic servants from the households of the well-off and entering them in the category 'Labourers, cottagers, husbandmen'.

Higher income, non-agricultural groups were more likely to produce important inventors.[7] Shopkeepers, proto-industrialists and artisans were the most prolific. Almost two-fifths of the important inventors had fathers from that background, while they comprised only one-fifth of the English population. The landed classes and clergy, who comprised 3.5 per cent of the population, produced 12 per cent of the inventors. The most prolific group, by far, were merchants, lawyers and capitalists. They made up 4.6 per cent of the population but accounted for 32.8 per cent of the inventors. Mokyr's Industrial Enlightenment model is certainly correct in emphasizing the upper-class background of many inventors, but the importance of inventors whose fathers were artisans shows that the story was more complex.

Relating inventors to economic sectors highlights one way in which the transformation of the English economy increased the supply

[7] Khan (2008) has her own sample of great inventors for the Industrial Revolution. Their comparison with the corresponding American sample shows that a much greater fraction of British inventors came from upper-class groups than in the United States. The same phenomenon is highlighted here.

of inventors. Between 1500 and 1800, the share of the population working outside of agriculture increased from about 26 per cent to 65 per cent. In itself, that change increased the average propensity to invent in England.

That is only part of the story, however. Another distinctive feature of inventors was their great endowment of human capital. They were well educated and well trained – much more so than the population at large. Literacy was important,[8] and the inventors were highly literate. We are most fully informed about the macro-inventors. Nine out of the ten were certainly literate. Hargreaves is the possible exception. According to Baines (1835, p. 156), he was illiterate, but this judgment is supported only by recollections many years after his death (not by documents) and so is open to question. It is probable that most of the second- and third-tier inventors were also literate. This has been verified for sixty-nine of the seventy-nine on the basis of schooling, surviving correspondence or similar indicators. Based on their backgrounds and activities, most of the remaining ten were probably also literate.

It is not surprising that the inventors were literate given the nature of their work. Most of them ran businesses. That meant that they had to correspond with suppliers and with clients. They also had to lease property, make contracts, draw up inventories, engage apprentices and, in many cases, apply for patents. Participating in the Industrial Enlightenment was also a literary activity.

An illiterate man was not well suited to inventing, so high literacy promoted invention. One reason that invention rose in the eighteenth

[8] In Allen (2003), which is the basis of Chapter 5, literacy was tested as a variable explaining economic success between 1350 and 1800. The estimated effect of literacy was small and statistically insignificant, so it was ignored in the simulations in Chapter 5. The irrelevance of literacy in that context is not inconsistent with its great importance later for two reasons. First, the Industrial Revolution was qualitatively different from the early modern expansion precisely because of the greater importance of invention. Secondly, the statistical tests of literacy were measuring its marginal value rather than its average value. Thus, the nationwide adult literacy rate reached 50 per cent when labourers learned to read. Their ability probably had no economic pay-off, and Reis (2005) has argued that they acquired literacy to study religious tracts and enjoy pulp fiction rather than as an investment. The finding of a negligible economic return on the margin is consistent with literacy's having a high value to merchants, shopkeepers, farmers and inventors but to few others. This view is consistent with Mitch's (1993) argument that schooling had little pay-off during the Industrial Revolution, and Sandberg's (1979) observation that literacy was widespread in backward parts of northern Europe like Sweden.

Table 10.5 *Trends in literacy in English occupations, 1560–1700*

	Percentage of the group that was literate	
	1560	1700
Men		
Aristocracy, gentry, clergy	100	100
Merchants, lawyers, officials	100	100
Shopkeepers, manufacturers, London	60	90
Shopkeepers, manufacturers, rural	30	60
Farmers (yeomen)	50	75
Labourers and servants in husbandry	15	15
Cottagers (husbandmen)	20	20
All men	20	45
Women		
All women	5	25

Source: Cressy (1980, pp. 118–74, 177) reports the percentage who could not sign their names. Literacy in this table is defined to be 100 minus that percentage.

century was because literacy increased dramatically in early modern England, as was documented in Chapter 2. An important feature of the spread of literacy is that it proceeded unevenly across society. Table 10.5 shows the proportion of men and women who could sign their names for different social strata in England in 1560 and 1700. The landed classes, the clergy, rich merchants, lawyers and government officials were fully literate throughout the period. Conversely, labourers, cottagers, small-scale farmers (husbandmen) and agricultural servants were largely illiterate throughout. This is one reason they were not inventors. The expansion of literacy occurred in the middle ranks of society – shopkeepers, tradesmen, artisans and proto-industrial workers – and many inventors came from this group.

Literacy expanded in the sixteenth and seventeenth centuries for three reasons. First, the ability to read and write was always valuable to merchants, traders and shopkeepers who had to communicate by letter and keep records and accounts. Consequently, the growth of cities and manufacturing in itself made England more literate.

The second reason was technological: the invention of the printing press and movable type eventually cut the real price of a book by

90 per cent. Much devotional material was printed, but there were also cheap editions of literature, scurrilous political commentaries, instructional manuals, almanacs and, finally, newspapers. The spread of reading had a snowball effect. Just as with the Internet or e-mail, one could ignore it at the outset, but, as more and more people learned to read and write, the value of the skills rose since there was a larger conversation to join.

Thirdly, the high wage economy caused by commercial expansion meant that many English could afford more education. For the highest strata, this was private tuition, perhaps capped off with time at a university. For everyone else, education meant schooling, and the sixteenth and seventeenth centuries saw a proliferation of new schools. The most basic were village schools. Often, they signified no more than a teacher supported by pupils' fees. Obviously, a community was better placed to finance a school in this way if wages and incomes were high rather than if they were low. Grammar schools also increased in number. They were permanent institutions with endowments. As with fees, endowments could be raised more easily when the economy was doing well rather than when it was doing badly. A third kind of educational institution that undoubtedly expanded in the sixteenth and seventeenth centuries was apprenticeship. This was the standard way of conveying craft skills. Typically, parents had to make a lump-sum payment to a master when their child was taken on, and the ability to save this sum was eased when incomes were high. A common educational trajectory began in a village school or grammar school, where the student learned to read and write, and was followed by an apprenticeship, in which specific job skills were acquired. Britain's high wage economy made it easier for the English to follow this trajectory than for people in poorer countries (Humphries 2009).

The inventors were also a numerate group, although it is difficult to be precise in the matter. Many were engaged in technical activities and experimentation that were intrinsically quantitative. Many were also running businesses, and they had to keep accounts and calculate revenues, costs, interest charges, valuations and so forth.

Since inventing required minimal numeracy, the pool of potential inventors expanded as the population at large became more and more numerate. There were both qualitative and quantitative improvements. Qualitative improvements include the replacement of latin numerals with arabic numbers. They made arithmetic easier and faster and meant that it was done with a pen and paper rather than an abacus, a substitution that facilitated problem-solving. The transition from latin to arabic occurred between the mid-sixteenth and the mid-seventeenth centuries. Quantitatively, the fraction of the population with satisfactory competence increased considerably. The growth of commerce and manufacturing was the driving force. While many people aspired to literacy for non-commercial reasons, very few people studied arithmetic for pleasure – they did it because it helped them in business. This is clear from arithmetic texts, which sold widely, for their examples involved buying and selling, computing interest, foreign exchange dealings, and dividing business income into ownership shares. The mathematician John Wallis remarked that, in the early seventeenth century, mathematics 'were scarce looked upon as academical studies, but rather mechanical; as in the business of traders, merchants, seamen, carpenters, surveyors of land, or the like, and perhaps some almanack-makers in London'. Arithmetic was not part of the grammar school curriculum in this period, but it was taught more widely by the eighteenth century in view of its commercial importance. Science and technology piggybacked on business for mathematics instruction. John Graunt, for instance, explained that his demographic investigations were based on 'the Mathematicks of my Shop-Arithmetik'.[9]

As the commercial sector expanded in early modern England, the level of mathematical competence rose. One indicator is the way people reported their age. If the exact age did not matter greatly (as was the case with adults), then people with little competence in arithmetic often reported an age ending in zero or six (half a dozen). People with more competence reported their age more precisely. At the end of the middle ages, lists of people and their ages show considerable 'heaping'. 'There can be little doubt that numerical skills were more widely dispersed in 1700 than they had been two centuries earlier. The change . . . is reflected in the spread of written account-keeping down the social scale and in a slight, but discernible, improvement in the accuracy of age-reporting' (Thomas 1987, p. 128). Improvement was rapid in the eighteenth century. Baten and Crayen (n.d.) have studied age heaping in many countries in the early nineteenth century.

[9] This paragraph and the next are based on Thomas (1987), which is the source of all quotations.

They report minimal heaping for England and for the other parts of northwestern Europe where literacy was also high. The numeracy revolution probably occurred later than the literacy revolution, but it was as profound.

The important inventors also accumulated an impressive volume of 'vocational skills', to use modern terminology. No one in the sample was 'unskilled' in these terms, and no one had an agricultural formation. What the inventor learned, however, and how he acquired his training, depended on his social background. It has been possible to cross-classify sixty of the important inventors in terms of their education or training, and those data delineate the main channels of skill acquisition.

Inventors whose fathers were landed gentlemen were either privately educated or attended elite institutions. John Hadley, who invented an improved quadrant called the octant, came from a landed family in Hertfordshire. Presumably, he was privately educated, for 'nothing is known of Hadley's education, but he evidently became proficient in mathematics, mechanics, and optics'. On the other hand, Edmund Cartwright attended Wakefield Grammar School and then Magdalen College, Oxford.

Nine of the inventors had fathers who were classed as 'capitalists', that is, they owned large-scale manufacturing establishments. Some attended schools, but many were privately educated like the landed elite. Abraham Darby II and Matthew Boulton went to academies, and John Hanbury, who developed the standard tin plate process and whose family also owned land, attended Pembroke College, Oxford, and then the Middle Temple. 'I read Coke upon Littleton, as far as tenant in dower; but on the suggestion of a friend that I should gain more advantage from the iron works at Pontypool than from the profits of the bar, I laid aside tenant and dower, and turned my attention to mines and forges.' The rest must have been educated privately, for references to schools they attended are uniformly lacking. Most began working in the family business in their teens. William Strutt was 14 when he started with the family business, although he continued to study. Abraham Darby II began to work at the Coalbrookdale Iron Company when he was 17, and Josiah Spode II entered the family firm at about the same age. William and John Champion were unusual for starting their own businesses, although they were in the same industry (brass) as their father.

The sons of merchants, if they were wealthy, and of lawyers were more likely to have attended formal schools than the sons of landowners or the capitalists. Among those whose fathers were merchants was Charles Macintosh, who first attended a Glasgow grammar school and then a school in Yorkshire. 'Although placed for training in a Glasgow counting house, his spare hours were devoted to science. Initially interested in botany, he subsequently turned to chemistry, and he often attended the lectures of William Irvine in Glasgow, and later those of Joseph Black in Edinburgh.' By the age of 20, he had established a chemical manufacturing business and went on to invent waterproof fabric around 1820. John Roebuck first attended Sheffield Grammar School and then the nonconformist academy in Northampton. Next, he studied medicine at the University of Edinburgh and the University of Leiden. George Ravenscroft, who was a Roman Catholic, attended the English College in Douai and then the University of Padua.

The sons of lawyers also attended schools. John Smeaton attended Leeds Grammar School and then was educated in the law in his father's office. However, he had a workshop at home where he pursued his mechanical interests, and he befriended Henry Hindley, the clockmaker, when he was 17 who inspired him in that direction. At the age of 20, he gave up the law to teach himself to be an instrument-maker. Denis Papin went to the protestant academy at Saumur and then to the University of Angers where he studied medicine. Francis Home was taught by a classicist and then apprenticed to a surgeon and studied medicine at the University of Edinburgh.

The largest category was inventors whose fathers were artisans. None of them attended a university. Most of them attended a village school or a grammar school and then learned a trade. If they continued in the same trade as their father or other close relatives, they were taught the trade by family members. Richard Trevithick was the son of a miner and mine manager in Cornwall. He attended the local school in Camborne, and then learned mining from his father. Josiah Wedgwood was the son of a potter. He attended school in Newcastle-under-Lyme and was then apprenticed to his brother for five years to learn the pottery trade. William Murdoch was the son of a miller and millwright. He described his schooling as 'little, though good' and was brought up in his father's trade.

On the other hand, if the boy took up a trade other than his father's, he had a formal apprenticeship. Richard Arkwright, son of a tailor, received his basic education in a night school and from his family, and was then apprenticed to a barber. William Cookworthy, son of a serge-maker, attended school in Kingsbridge and then Exeter until he was thirteen when his father died. After that, he was apprenticed to a London apothecary, and reportedly walked from Devon to London to save money. James Short's father was a wright. His parents died when he was young, and at the age of ten he studied at George Heriot's Hospital 'and then at the age of twelve transferred to the Royal High School, Edinburgh, where he showed considerable ability in the classics. After matriculating in 1726 at Edinburgh University, he followed the arts courses but did not graduate. A pious grandmother had prevailed on him to enter the church, so he studied divinity and is said to have passed his trials for the ministry in 1731. However, he was inspired by the lectures of Colin MacLaurin, professor of mathematics at the university, to abandon divinity for mathematics and astronomy.' With MacLaurin's help, he learned to make telescopes. He discovered how to grind parabolic mirrors and thereby turned the reflecting telescope from a scientific curiosity into a commercial product.

Other lower status trades gave rise to similar career patterns. Sons of less prosperous merchants had educational trajectories like those of artisans. Isaac Wilkinson, for instance, was brought up by his brother who was a wool merchant. 'His education is unknown; he had a rough literacy and could keep accounts, sometimes creatively. He was apprenticed to the iron trade.' Thomas Newcomen was probably educated by John Flavel, a nonconformist scholar who occasionally ran a school in Dartmouth, and then apprenticed as an engineer.

The sons of farmers had similar formations, for they were embarking on a new occupation. Among them were Charles Tennant, who attended Ochiltree parish school and was then apprenticed to a hand loom weaver. John Kennedy grew up in a remote area without a school and received tutoring from itinerant teachers. He was then apprenticed to William Cannan, who made textile machinery. Joseph Bramah went to Silkstone town school and was apprenticed to a carpenter. Benjamin Huntsman was apprenticed to a clock-maker. This kind of formation was also followed by all of the inventors whose fathers were farmers and tradesmen. Samuel Crompton, whose father combined farming with weaving, attended a local school and excelled in arithmetic, algebra and geometry. He was taught to spin and weave at home, and the experience prompted the invention of the mule. The very few labourers and husbandmen who became important inventors also had similar trajectories. Apprenticeship in a trade was a good way for a son to leave agriculture.

While boys from artisan and shopkeeping backgrounds typically attended local schools and were apprenticed to trades, occasionally very clever boys had stellar academic experiences. John Wall, who invented transfer printing in blue under glaze, was the son of a grocer. He attended King's School, Worcester, and then won the Cookes Scholarship to Worcester College, Oxford. John Rennie, whose father was a farmer and a brewer, attended the parish school at Prestonkirk, then Dunbar High School and finally the University of Edinburgh where he studied with Joseph Black. This educational progression was interrupted for several years when Rennie worked with Andrew Meikle, the inventor, and learned machine-building as a practical art. Later, Rennie became famous for building the Albion Mill.

Culture as a cause of the Industrial Revolution

British culture changed in important ways between the late middle ages and the Industrial Revolution. Medieval catholicism was replaced by protestantism, which was itself divided and redefined several times. After the Restoration, the upper classes adopted a mechanical world-view inspired by Newton and the Scientific Revolution. The lower classes may have done likewise, but the matter is hard to pin down. The culture of all social strata above rural cottagers and farm labourers was transformed by the spread of literacy and numeracy and by an expansion of schooling and training through formal and informal apprenticeships. Expanded literacy and numeracy may have facilitated the spread of Newtonianism down the social scale. Causation, indeed, may have gone the other way as well. The transition from a world in which people prayed to improve their lot to one in which they calculated may have made it easier for intellectuals to imagine the world as governed by mathematical laws rather than by a personal god.

How important were these changes in explaining the inventions of the Industrial Revolution? This is a hard question to answer, since there was another cause in play, namely, the emergence of the high wage, cheap energy economy. It increased the demand for inventions at the same time the spread of science and literacy may have also increased the supply.

To decide whether the increase in invention was due to a growth in demand for new technology or to an increase in the supply of inventors, we must find a way to hold one of the potential causes constant, so that the effect of the other can be observed. This can only be done imperfectly. International comparisons are one approach. Mokyr, for instance, notes that the Industrial Enlightenment was a Europe-wide phenomenon. In that case, it may help explain why the Industrial Revolution occurred in Europe rather than Asia, but it will not explain why it happened in Britain rather than the Netherlands. Indeed, as the evidence on signatures and age heaping indicates, there was not much difference between Britain and the rest of northwestern Europe in terms of literacy or numeracy. With the potential supply of inventors the same across northwestern Europe, the greater inventiveness of the British comes down to demand. This conclusion is plausible in view of the industries involved. Much British inventing involved coal – iron, non-ferrous metals, pottery kilns, the steam engine and so forth. There were strong incentives for the British to invent in this area given the great supply of cheap coal, as we have seen. Much other British invention related to cotton textiles and, again, there were industry-specific reasons for the British to invent, including their hand cotton industry and the large watch-making industry, which provided the engineering components and craftsmen to build the water frame and other machinery. The Dutch lacked all of these advantages, which meant they had no incentive to invent the Industrial Revolution. These international comparisons highlight the importance of the demand for technology and emphasize the limitations of cultural and human capital explanations of the Industrial Revolution.

But demand was surely not the whole story. This chapter was prompted by the observation that medieval England was a high wage economy and yet did not invent labour-saving machinery on the scale of the Industrial Revolution. As our discussion of the Netherlands suggests, the fifteenth century is an imperfect analogue to the eighteenth because medieval England did not have a large coal industry, so the incentives to use that resource were lacking. There was also no cotton industry. Nonetheless, the high wage itself was an important similarity and suggests that factors touching on the supply of inventors may explain why the Industrial Revolution happened in 1800 rather than in 1400. The cultural revolution of the early modern period played a role – hard work in pursuit of novel consumer goods, the build-up of literacy, numeracy and craft skills like watch-making, the decline of superstition and the rise of a scientific worldview. These developments were partly the result of economic developments and certainly contributed to them. The cultural changes between 1400 and 1800 were immense and in the direction of promoting invention.

Appendix A list of the great inventors

Surname	First name	Industry
Macro-inventors		
Arkwright	Richard	textiles
Cartwright	Edmund	textiles
Cort	Henry	metals
Crompton	Samuel	textiles
Darby	Abraham I	metals
Hargreaves	James	textiles
Newcomen	Thomas	steam
Smeaton	John	machines
Watt	James	steam
Wedgwood	Josiah	ceramics
Other inventors		
Astbury	John	ceramics
Barlow	Edward	horology
Beighton	Henry	steam
Bell	Thomas	textiles
Bentham	Sir Samuel	machines
Booth	Enoch	ceramics
Boulton	Matthew	steam
Bramah	Joseph	machines
Brooks	John	ceramics
Champion	John	metals
Champion	Nehemiah	metals
Champion	William	metals
Clerke	Sir Clement	metals
Cochrane	Archibald	chemicals
Cookworthy	William	ceramics
Darby	Abraham II	metals

Surname	First name	Industry
Desaguliers	John Theophilus	machines
Dollond	John	instruments
Dwight	John	ceramics
Faccio de Duillier	Nicholas	horology
Fry	Thomas	ceramics
Gordon	Cuthbert	chemicals
Graham	George	horology
Hadley	John	navigation
Hall	Chester Moor	instruments
Halley	Edmund	navigation
Hanbury	John	metals
Harrison	John	horology
Hindley	Henry	machines
Home	Francis	chemicals
Hooke	Robert	machines
Hornblower	Jonathan	steam
Huntsman	Benjamin	metals
Kay	John	textiles
Kennedy	John	textiles
Knibb	Joseph	horology
Littler	William	ceramics
Lombe	John	textiles
Lombe	Sir Thomas	textiles
Macintosh	Charles	chemicals
Maudslay	Henry	machines
Meikle	Andrew	machines
Mudge	Thomas	horology
Murdoch	William	machines
Murray	Matthew	textiles
Oppenheim	Mayer	chemicals
Papin	Denis	steam
Paul	Lewis	textiles
Quare	Daniel	horology
Ramsden	Jesse	machines
Ravenscroft	George	chemicals
Rennie	John	machines
Roebuck	John	chemicals
Sadler	John	ceramics
Savery	Thomas	steam
Short	James	instruments

Surname	First name	Industry
Spode	Josiah I	ceramics
Spode	Josiah II	ceramics
Strutt	Jedediah	textiles
Strutt	William	machines
Taylor	Clement	chemicals
Tennant	Charles	chemicals
Tompion	Thomas	horology
Trevithick	Richard	steam
Wall	John	ceramics
Ward	Joshua	chemicals
Wilkinson	Isaac	metals
Wilkinson	John	machines
Wyatt	John	textiles

11 *From Industrial Revolution to modern economic growth*

The industrially more developed country presents to the less developed country a picture of the latter's future.

Karl Marx, *Capital*, vol. I, preface

I have argued that the famous inventions of the British Industrial Revolution were responses to Britain's unique economic environment and would not have been developed anywhere else. This is one reason that the Industrial Revolution was *British*. But why did those inventions matter? The French were certainly active inventors, and the Scientific Revolution was a pan-European phenomenon. Wouldn't the French, or the Germans, or the Italians, have produced an industrial revolution by another route? Weren't there alternative paths to the twentieth century?

These questions are closely related to another important question asked by Mokyr: why didn't the Industrial Revolution peter out after 1815? He is right that there were previous occasions when important inventions were made. The result, however, was a one-shot rise in productivity that did not translate into sustained economic growth. The nineteenth century was different – the First Industrial Revolution turned into Modern Economic Growth. Why? Mokyr's answer is that scientific knowledge increased enough to allow continuous invention. Technological improvement was certainly at the heart of the matter, but it was not due to discoveries in science – at least not before 1900. The reason that incomes continued to grow in the hundred years after Waterloo was because Britain's pre-1815 inventions were particularly transformative, much more so than continental inventions. That is a second reason that the Industrial Revolution was *British* and also the reason that growth continued throughout the nineteenth century.

Cotton was the wonder industry of the Industrial Revolution – so much so that Gerschenkron (1962), for instance, claimed that economic growth in advanced countries was based on the expansion of consumer goods, while growth in backward countries was based on producer goods. This is an unfortunate conclusion, however, for the great achievement of the British Industrial Revolution was, in fact, the creation of the first large engineering industry that could mass-produce productivity-raising machinery.[1] Machinery production was the basis of three developments that were the immediate explanations of the continuation of economic growth until the First World War. Those developments were: (1) the general mechanization of industry; (2) the railroad; and (3) steam-powered iron ships. The first raised productivity in the British economy itself; the second and third created the global economy and the international division of labour that were responsible for significant rises in living standards across Europe (O'Rourke and Williamson 1999). Steam technology accounted for close to half of the growth in labour productivity in Britain in the second half of the nineteenth century (Crafts 2004).

The nineteenth-century engineering industry was a spin-off from the coal industry. All three of the developments that raised productivity in the nineteenth century depended on two things – the steam engine and cheap iron. Both of these, as we have seen, were closely related to coal. The steam engine was invented to drain coal mines, and it burnt coal. Cheap iron required the substitution of coke for charcoal and was prompted by cheap coal. (A further tie-in with coal was geological – Britain's iron deposits were often found in proximity to coal deposits.) There were more connections: the railroad, in particular, was a spin-off from the coal industry. Railways were invented in the seventeenth century to haul coal in mines and from mines to canals or rivers. Once established, railways invited continuous experimentation to improve road beds and rails. Iron rails were developed in the eighteenth century as a result, and alternative dimensions and profiles were explored. Furthermore, the need for traction provided the first market for locomotives. There was no market for steam-powered land vehicles because roads were unpaved and too uneven to support a steam vehicle (as Cugnot and Trevithick discovered). Railways, however, provided a controlled surface on which steam vehicles could function, and colliery railways were the first purchasers of steam locomotives. When George Stephenson developed the Rocket for the Rainhill trials, he tested his

[1] Hoffman (1955, pp. 72–4) calculated that producer goods industries as a whole grew more rapidly than consumer goods industries in industrializing Britain.

design ideas by incorporating them in locomotives he was building for coal railways. In this way, the commercialization of primitive versions of technology promoted further development as R&D expenses were absorbed as normal business costs.

Cotton played a supporting role in the growth of the engineering industry for two reasons. The first is that it grew to immense size. This was a consequence of global competition. In the early eighteenth century, Britain produced only a tiny fraction of the world's cotton. The main producers were in Asia. As a result, the price elasticity of demand for English cotton was extremely large. If Britain could become competitive, it could expand production enormously by replacing Indian and Chinese producers. Mechanization led to that outcome (Broadberry and Gupta 2006). The result was a huge industry, widespread urbanization (with such external benefits as that conveyed), and a boost to the high wage economy. Mechanization in other activities did not have the same potential. The Jacquard loom, a renowned French invention of the period, cut production costs in lace and knitwear and, thereby, induced some increase in output. But knitting was not a global industry, and the price elasticity of demand was only modest, so output expansion was limited. One reason that British cotton technology was so transformative was that cotton was a global industry with more price-responsive demand than other textiles.

The growth and size of the cotton industry in conjunction with its dependence on machinery sustained the engineering industry by providing it with a large and growing market for equipment. The history of the cotton industry was one of relentlessly improving machine design – first with carding and spinning and later with weaving. Improved machines translated into high investment and demand for equipment. By the 1840s, the initial dependence of cotton manufacturers on water power gave way to steam-powered mills (von Tunzelmann 1978, pp. 175–225). By the middle of the nineteenth century, Britain had a lopsided industrial structure. Cotton was produced in highly mechanized factories, while much of the rest of manufacturing was relatively untransformed. In the mid-nineteenth century, machines spread across the whole of British manufacturing (one of the causes of the continuing rise in income).

There was a great paradox in the history of technology during the Industrial Revolution. As we have emphasized, the macro-inventions of the eighteenth century were biased improvements that increased the demand for capital and energy relative to labour. Since capital and energy were relatively cheap in Britain, it was worth developing the macro-inventions there and worth using them in their early, primitive forms. These forms were not cost-effective elsewhere where labour was cheaper and energy dearer. However, British engineers improved this technology. They studied it, modified it, and made it more efficient. This local learning often saved the input that was used excessively in the early years of the invention's life and which restricted its use to Britain. As the coal consumption of rotary steam power declined from 35 pounds per horsepower-hour to 5 pounds, it paid to apply steam power in more and more uses. This was why mechanization spread beyond the cotton textile industry in the middle of the nineteenth century. But the decline in coal consumption meant a geographical spread as well as an industrial spread. Old-fashioned, thermally inefficient steam engines were not 'appropriate' technology for countries where coal was expensive. These countries did not have to invent an 'appropriate' technology for their conditions, however. The irony is that the British did it for them. As the steam engine became more fuel-efficient, it was taken up in more countries – even those where coal was expensive. In that way, the Industrial Revolution spread around the globe. The genius of British engineering undid Britain's comparative advantage.

It is important that the British inventions of the eighteenth century – cheap iron and the steam engine, in particular – were so transformative, because the technologies invented in France – in paper production, glass and knitting – were not. The French innovations did not lead to general mechanization or globalization. One of the social benefits of an invention is the door it opens to further improvements. British technology in the eighteenth century had much greater possibilities in this regard than French inventions or those made anywhere else. The British were not more rational or prescient than the French in developing coal-based technologies: The British were simply luckier in their geology. The knock-on effect was large, however: there is no reason to believe that French technology would have led to the engineering industry, the general mechanization of industrial processes, the railway, the steamship or the global economy. In other words, there was only one route to the twentieth century – and it traversed northern Britain.

References

Abel, Wilhelm (1980). *Agricultural Fluctuations in Europe from the Thirteenth to the Twentieth Centuries*, trans. by Olive Ordish, London, Methuen.

Acemoglu, Daron (2002). 'Directed Technical Change', *Review of Economic Studies*, vol. 69, pp. 781–809.

(2003). 'Factor Prices and Technical Change: From Induced Innovations to Recent Debates', in Philippe Aghion *et al.* (eds.), *Knowledge, Information and Expectations in Modern Macroeconomics: In Honor of Edmund Phelps*, Princeton, NJ, Princeton University Press.

(2007). 'Equilibrium Bias of Technology', *Econometrica*, vol. 75, pp. 1371–409.

Acemoglu, Daron, Johnson, Simon, and Robinson, James (2005). 'The Rise of Europe: Atlantic Trade, Institutional Change and Economic Growth', *American Economic Review*, vol. 95, pp. 546–79.

A'Hearn, Brian (2003). 'Anthropometric Evidence on Living Standards in Northern Italy, 1730–1860', *Journal of Economic History*, vol. 63, pp. 351–81.

Allen, Robert C. (1983). 'Collective Invention', *Journal of Economic Behavior and Organization*, vol. 4, pp. 1–24.

(1988). 'The Growth of Labor Productivity in Early Modern English Agriculture', *Explorations in Economic History*, vol. 25, pp. 117–46.

(1992). *Enclosure and the Yeoman*, Oxford, Clarendon Press.

(1994). 'Agriculture During the Industrial Revolution', in Roderick Floud and D. N. McCloskey (eds.), *The Economic History of Britain Since 1700*, vol. I, *1700–1860*, Cambridge, Cambridge University Press, second edition, pp. 96–122.

(1999). 'Tracking the Agricultural Revolution', *Economic History Review*, 2nd series, vol. 52, pp. 209–35.

(2000). 'Economic Structure and Agricultural Productivity in Europe, 1300–1800', *European Review of Economic History*, vol. 3, pp. 1–25.

(2001). 'The Great Divergence in European Wages and Prices from the Middle Ages to the First World War', *Explorations in Economic History*, vol. 38, October 2001, pp. 411–47.

(2003a). 'Poverty and Progress in Early Modern Europe', *Economic History Review*, vol. 56, pp. 403–43.

(2003b). 'Was There a Timber Crisis in Early Modern Europe?', *Economia e energia secc. XIII–XVIII*, Serie 'II–Atti delle 'Settimane di Studi' e altri Convegni, 34, Instituto Internazionale di Storia Economica 'F. Datini', Prato, pp. 469–82.

(2005). 'English and Welsh Agriculture, 1300–1850: Output, Inputs, and Income' (unpublished).

(2007a). 'India in the Great Divergence', in Timothy J. Hatton, Kevin H. O'Rourke and Alan M. Taylor (eds.), *The New Comparative Economic History: Essays in Honor of Jeffrey G. Williamson*, Cambridge, MA, MIT Press, pp. 9–32.

(2007b). 'Pessimism Preserved: Real Wages in the British Industrial Revolution', Oxford University, Department of Economics, Working Paper 314.

(2007c). 'Engel's Pause: A Pessimist's Guide to the British Industrial Revolution', Oxford University, Department of Economics, Working Paper 315.

(2007d). 'The Industrial Revolution in Miniature: The Spinning Jenny in Britain, France, and India', Oxford University, Department of Economics, Working Paper 375.

(2008). 'The Nitrogen Hypothesis and the English Agriculture Revolution: A Biological Analysis', *Journal of Economic History*, vol. 68, pp. 182–210.

Allen, Robert C., and O'Grada, Cormac (1988). 'On the Road Again with Arthur Young: English, Irish, and French Agriculture During the Industrial Revolution', *Journal of Economic History*, vol. 38, pp. 93–116.

Allen, Robert C., Bassino, Jean-Paul, Ma, Debin, Moll-Murata, Christine, and van Zanden, Jan Luiten (2007). 'Wages, Prices, and Living Standards in China, 1738–1925: In Comparison with Europe, Japan, and India', Oxford University, Department of Economics, Working Paper 316.

Allen, Robert C., Bengtsson, Tommy, and Dribe, Martin (2005). *Living Standards in the Past: New Perspectives on Well-Being in Asia and Europe*, Oxford, Oxford University Press.

American Iron Association (1854–6), *Bulletin*.

Angerstein, R. R. (1753–5). *R. R. Angerstein's Illustrated Travel Diary, 1753–1755*, trans. by Torsten Berg and Peter Berg, London, Science Museum, 2001.

Arrighi, Giovanni (1994). *The Long Twentieth Century: Money, Power, and the Origins of Our Time*, London, Verso.

Arthur, W. Brian (1994). *Increasing Returns and Path Dependence in the Economy*, Ann Arbor, MI, University of Michigan Press.

Ashton, T. S. (1955). *The Industrial Revolution, 1760–1830*, London, Oxford University Press.

Aspin, C., and Chapman, S. D. (1964). *James Hargreaves and the Spinning Jenny*, Preston, Helmshore Local History Society.

Aston, T. H., and Philpin, C. H. E. (eds.) (1985). *The Brenner Debate*, Cambridge, Cambridge University Press.

Baines, Edward (1835). *History of the Cotton Manufacture in Great Britain*, London, H. Fisher, R. Fisher and P. Jackson.

Bairoch, Paul (1988). *La Population des villes européennes, 800 1850: banque de données et analyse sommaire des résultats*, Geneva, Droz.

Ballot, Charles (1923). *L'introduction du machanisme dans l'industrie française*, Geneva, Slatkine, 1978.

Barro, Robert J. (1997). *Determinants of Economic Growth: A Cross-Country Empirical Study*, Cambridge, MA, MIT Press.

Barton, D. B. (1966). *The Cornish Beam Engine*, Truro, D. Bradford Barton Ltd, new edition.

Bateman, Victoria (2007). 'The Evolution of Markets in Early Modern Europe: 1350–1800: A Study of Grain Prices' (unpublished).

Baten, Joerg, and Crayen, Dorothee (n.d.). 'Global Trends in Numeracy, 1820–1949, and Its Implications for Long Run Growth' (unpublished).

Beaud, Claud (1995). 'L'innovation dans les Etablissements Schneider (1837–1960)', in *Les Schneiders, Le Creusot*, Paris, Libraire Athème Fayard, pp. 204–33.

Beckett, J. V. (1986). *The Aristocracy in England, 1660–1914*, Oxford, Basil Blackwell Ltd.

Beeson, C. F. C. (1989). *Clockmaking in Oxfordshire*, Oxford, Museum of the History of Science, third edition.

Bengtsson, T. (1989). 'Real Wage Variation and Adult Mortality: Life Events in Västanfors, 1750–1859', paper presented at the IUSSP General Conference, New Delhi.

(1993). 'Combined Time-Series and Life Event Analysis: The Impact of Economic Fluctuations and Air Temperature on Adult Mortality by Sex and Occupation in a Swedish Mining Parish, 1757–1850', in David Reher and Roger Schofield (eds.), *Old and New Methods in Historical Demography*. Oxford, Clarendon Press.

(2004). 'Living Standards and Economic Stress', in T. Bengtsson, C. Campbell, J. Z. Lee, *et al.*, *Life under Pressure: Mortality and Living Standards in Europe and Asia, 1700–1900*, Cambridge, MA, MIT Press, chapter 2.

Bengtsson, T., Campbell, C., Lee, J., *et al.* (2004). *Life under Pressure: Mortality and Living Standards in Europe and Asia, 1700–1900*, Cambridge, MA, MIT Press.

Bengtsson, T., and Reher, D. (1998). 'Short and Medium Term Relations Between Population and Economy', in C.-E. Nuñez (ed.), *Debates and Controversies in Economic History: Proceedings of the Twelfth International Economic History Congress*, Madrid, Fundación Ramón Areces.

Bentley, Thomas (1780). *Letters on the Utility and Policy of Employing Machines to Shorten Labour*, London, T. Becket.

Berg, Maxine (1998). 'Product Innovation in Core Consumer Industries in Eighteenth-Century Britain', in Maxine Berg and Kristina Bruland (eds.), *Technological Revolutions in Europe: Historical Perspectives*, Cheltenham, Edward Elgar, pp. 138–60.

(2002). 'From Imitation to Invention: Creating Commodities in Eighteenth-Century Britain', *Economic History Review*, vol. 45, pp. 1–30.

(2004). 'In Pursuit of Luxury: Global History and British Consumer Goods in the Eighteenth Century', *Past and Present*, No. 182, pp. 84–142.

(2005). *Luxury and Pleasure in Eighteenth Century Britain*, Oxford, Oxford University Press.

Berg, Maxine, and Clifford, Helen (1999). *Consumers and Luxury: Consumer Culture in Europe, 1650–1850*, Manchester, Manchester University Press.

Berg, Maxine and Hudson, Pat (1992). 'Rehabilitating the Industrial Revolution', *Economic History Review*, vol. 45, pp. 24–50.

(1994). 'Growth and Change: A Comment on the Crafts–Harley View of the Industrial Revolution', *Economic History Review*, vol. 47, pp. 147–9.

Berry, R. A., and Cline, W. R. (1979). *Agrarian Structure and Productivity in Developing Countries*, Baltimore, MD, Johns Hopkins University Press.

Beveridge, Lord (1939). *Prices and Wages in England from the Twelfth to the Nineteenth Century*, vol. I, *Price Tables: Mercantile Era*, London, Longmans Green & Co. Ltd.

Bhalla, A. S. (1964). 'Investment Allocation and Technological Choice – A Case of Cotton Spinning Techniques', *Economic Journal*, vol. 74, No. 295, pp. 611–22.

Bils, Mark (1984). 'Tariff Protection and Production in the Early US Cotton Textile Industry', *Journal of Economic History*, vol. 44, pp. 1033–45.

Birch, Alan (1967). *The Economic History of the British Iron and Steel Industry, 1784–1879*, London, Frank Cass & Co. Ltd.

Blaut, J. M. (1993). *The Colonizer's Model of the World*, New York, Guildford Press.

Bogart, Dan (2005a). 'Did Turnpike Trusts Increase Transportation Investment in Eighteenth Century England?', *Journal of Economic History*, vol. 65, pp. 439–68.

(2005b). 'Turnpike Trusts and the Transportation Revolution in Eighteenth Century England', *Explorations in Economic History*, vol. 42, pp. 479–508.

Bonney, Richard (1999). *The Rise of the Fiscal State in Europe, c.1200–1815*, Oxford, Oxford University Press.

Booth, A., and Sundrum, R. M. (1985). *Labour Absorption in Agriculture*, Oxford, Oxford University Press.

Boulton, Jeremy (2000). 'London, 1540–1700', in Peter Clark (ed.), *The Cambridge Urban History of Britain*, vol. II, *1540–1840*, Cambridge, Cambridge University Press, pp. 315–46.

Bourne, John (1846). *A Treatise on the Steam Engine: In Its Application to Mines, Mills, Steam Navigation, and Railways*, by the Artizan Club, London, Longman, Brown, Green and Longmans.

Bowden, Peter (1962). *The Wool Trade in Tudor and Stuart England*, London, Macmillan.

Boyden, S. (1987). *Western Civilization in Biological Perspective*, Oxford, Oxford University Press.

Boyle, Robert (1671). *Some Considerations Touching the Usefulnesse of Experimental Naturall Philosophy*, vol. II, Oxford, Hendry Hall, printer to the University.

Braudel, Fernand (1981–4). *Civilization and Capitalism: 15th-18th Century*, London, Collins.

Brenner, Robert (1976). 'Agrarian Class Structure and Economic Development in Pre-Industrial Europe', reprinted in T. H. Aston and C. H. E. Philpin (eds.), *The Brenner Debate*, Cambridge, Cambrdige University Press, 1985, pp. 10–63.

(1993). *Merchants and Revolution: Commercial Change, Political Conflict, and London's Overseas Traders, 1550–1653*, Cambridge, Cambridge University Press.

Brewer, John, and Porter, Roy (1993). *Consumption and the World of Goods*, London, Routledge.

Briggs, Robin (2002). *Witches and Neighbours*, Oxford, Blackwell Publishing, second edition.

Britnell, Richard H. (1993). *The Commercialisation of English Society, 1000–1500*, Cambridge, Cambridge University Press.

Broadberry, Stephen, and Gupta, Bishnupriya (2006). 'Wages, Induced Innovation and the Great Divergence: Lancashire, India and Shifting Competitive Advantage in Cotton Textiles, 1700–1850', revised version CEPR Discussion Paper 5183.

Bruchey, Stuart (1967). *Cotton and the Growth of the American Economy: 1790–1860*, New York, Harcourt, Brace & World Inc.

Bruland, Kristine (2004). 'Industrialisation and Technological Change', in Roderick Floud and Paul Johnson (eds.), *The Cambridge Economic History of Modern Britain*, vol. I, *1700–1860*, Cambridge, Cambridge University Press, pp. 117–46.

Brunt, Liam (1999). 'Estimating English Wheat Yields in the Industrial Revolution', University of Oxford, Discussion Papers in Economic and Social History, No. 29.

(2004). 'Nature or Nurture? Explaining English Wheat Yields in the Industrial Revolution, c.1770', *Journal of Economic History*, vol. 64, pp. 193–225.

(2006). 'Rediscovering Risk: Country Banks as Venture Capital Firms in the First Industrial Revolution', *Journal of Economic History*, vol. 66, pp. 74–102.

Burke, Peter (2006). *Popular Culture in Early Modern Europe*, Aldershot, Ashgate Publishing Ltd, revised reprint.

Burt, R. (1969). *Cornish Mining: Essays on the Organization of Cornish Mines and the Cornish Mining Economy*, Newton Abbot, David & Charles.

Campbell, Bruce M. S. (1983). 'Arable Productivity in Medieval England: Some Evidence from Norfolk', *Journal of Economic History*, vol. 43, pp. 379–404.

(2000). *English Seigneurial Agriculture, 1350–1450*, Cambridge, Cambridge University Press.

Campbell, Bruce M. S., Galloway, J., and Murphy, M. (1993). 'A Medieval City and Its Grain Supply: Agrarian Production and Distribution in the London Region, c.1300', Historical Geography Research Series, No. 30.

Cardwell, D. S. L. (1963). *Steam Power in the Eighteenth Century: A Case Study in the Application of Science*, New York, Sheed and Ward.

Carlos, Ann M., and Neal, Larry (2006). 'The Micro-Foundations of the Early London Capital Market: Bank of England Shareholders During and After the South Sea Bubble, 1720–25', *Economic History Review*, vol. 59, pp. 498–538.

Carus-Wilson, Eleanora (1952). 'The Woollen Industry', in M. M. Postan and E. E. Rich (eds.), *Cambridge Economic History of Europe*, vol. II, *Trade and Industry in the Middle Ages*, Cambridge, Cambridge University Press, pp. 355–428.

Chalklin, Christopher (2001). *The Rise of the English Town, 1650–1850*, Cambridge, Cambridge University Press.

Chandler, Alfred D. (1972). 'Anthracite Coal and the Beginnings of the Industrial Revolution in the United States', *Business History Review*, vol. 46, pp. 141–81.

Chapman, S. D. (1970). 'Fixed Capital Formation in the British Cotton Industry 1770–1815', *Economic History Review*, vol. 23, pp. 235–66.

(1971). 'The Cost of Power in the Industrial Revolution in Britain: The Case of the Textile Industry', *Midland History*, vol. I, No. 2, pp. 1–23.

Chapman, S. D., and Butt, John (1988). 'The Cotton Industry, 1775–1856', in Charles H. Feinstein and Sidney Pollard (eds.), *Studies in Capital Formation in the United Kingdom, 1750–1920*, Oxford, Clarendon Press, pp. 105–25.

Chartier, Roger (1987). *Lectures et lecturers dans la France de l'ancien regime*, Paris, Seuil.

Chassagne, Serge (1991). *Le coton et ses patrons: France, 1780–1840*, Paris, Edition de d'Ecole des hautes études en sciences sociales.

Chaudhury, Sushil (1999). *From Prosperity to Decline: Eighteenth Century Bengal*, New Delhi, Manohar Publishers & Distributors.

Cinnirella, Francesco (2007). 'Optimists or Pessimists? A Reconsideration of Nutritional Status in Britain, 1740–1865', www.econhist.vwl.lmu.de/cinnirella/.

Cipolla, Carlo M. (1969). *Literacy and Development in the West*, Harmondsworth, Penguin.

Clark, Gregory (1993). 'Agriculture and the Industrial Revolution, 1700–1850', in J. Mokyr (ed.), *The British Industrial Revolution: An Economic Perspective*, Boulder, CO, Westview Press, pp. 227–66.

(1996). 'The Political Foundations of Modern Economic Growth: England, 1540–1800', *Journal of Interdisciplinary History*, vol. 26, pp. 563–87.

(1998). 'Commons Sense: Common Property Rights, Efficiency, and Institutional Change', *Journal of Economic History*, vol. 48, pp. 73–102.

(2005). 'The Condition of the Working Class in England, 1209–2004', *Journal of Political Economy*, vol. 113, pp. 1307–40.

(2007). *A Farewell to Alms: A Brief Economic History of the World*, Princeton, NJ, Princeton University Press.

Clark, G., Huberman, M., and Lindert, P. H. (1995). 'A British Food Puzzle, 1770–1850', *Economic History Review*, 2nd series, vol. 48, pp. 215–37.

Clark, Greg, and Jacks, David (2007). 'Coal and the Industrial Revolution, 1700–1860', *European Review of Economic History*, vol. 11, pp. 39–72.

Clow, Archibald, and Clow, Nan (1952). *The Chemical Revolution: A Contribution to Social Technology*, London, Batchworth Press.

Cohen, H. Floris (2004). 'Inside Newcomen's Fire Engine, or the Scientific Revolution and the Rise of the Modern World', *History of Technology*, vol. 25, pp. 111–32.

Cohen, Jon S., and Weitzman, Martin L. (1975). 'A Marxian Model of Enclosures', *Journal of Development Economics*, vol. 1, pp. 287–336.

Coleman, D. C. (1969). 'An Innovation and Its Diffusion: The "New Draperies"', *Economic History Review*, vol. 22, pp. 417–29.

(1971). 'Review of *Partners in Science. Letters of James Watt and Joseph Black*', *Economic History Review*, vol. 24, pp. 299–300.

(1983). 'Protoindustrialization: A Concept Too Many', *Economic History Review*, 2nd series, vol. 36, pp. 435–448.

Convention of Ironmasters (1849). *Documents Relating to the Manufacture of Iron in Pennsylvania*, Philadelphia.

Court, W. (1953). *The Rise of the Midland Industries, 1600–1838*, Oxford, *Oxford* University Press.

Crafts, N. F. R. (1976). 'English Economic Growth in the Eighteenth Century: A Re-examination of Deane and Cole's Estimates', *Economic History Review*, 2nd series, vol. 29, pp. 226–35.

(1977). 'Industrial Revolution in England and France: Some Thoughts on the Question: "Why Was England First?"', *Economic History Review*, vol. 30, pp. 429–41.

(1985). *British Economic Growth During the Industrial Revolution*, Oxford, Clarendon Press.

(1996). 'The Human Development Index: Some Historical Comparisons', Working Papers in Economic History, No. 33/96, London, London School of Economics.

(2004). 'Steam as a General Purpose Technology: A Growth Accounting Perspective', *Economic Journal*, vol. 114 (495), pp. 338–51.

Crafts, N. F. R., and Harley, C. K. (1992). 'Output Growth and the British Industrial Revolution: A Restatement of the Crafts–Harley View', *Economic History Review*, 2nd series, vol. 45, pp. 703–30.

(2000). 'Simulating the Two Views of the Industrial Revolution', *Journal of Economic History*, vol. 60, pp. 819–41.

(2002). 'Precocious British Industrialization: A General Equilibrium Perspective', London School of Economics, Working Papers in Economic History, No. 67/02.

Crafts, N. F. R., and Venables, A. J. (2003). 'Globalization in History: A Geographical Perspective', in Michael Bordo, Alan M. Taylor and Jeffrey G. Williamson (eds.), *Globalization in Historical Perspective*, Chicago, University of Chicago Press, pp. 323–64.

Cressy, David (1980). *Literacy and the Social Order: Reading and Writing in Tudor and Stuart England*, Cambridge, Cambridge University Press.

(1981). 'Levels of Illiteracy in England, 1530–1730', in Harvey J. Graff (ed.), *Literacy and Social Development in the West: A Reader*, Cambridge, Cambridge University Press.

Crouzet, F. (1972). 'Editor's Introduction', in F. Crouzet (ed.), *Capital Formation in the Industrial Revolution*, London, Methuen, pp. 1–69.

(1985a). *Britain Ascendant: Comparative Studies in Franco-British Economic History*, trans. by Martin Thom, Cambridge, Cambridge University Press.

(1985b). *The First Industrialists: The Problem of Origins*, Cambridge, Cambridge University Press.

Curtin, Philip D. (1966). *The Atlantic Slave Trade: A Census*, Madison, WI, University of Wisconsin Press.

Daddow, Samuel Harries, and Bannan, Benjamin (1866). *Coal, Iron, and Oil*, Pottsville, PA, Benjamin Bannan.

Darity, William (1992). 'A Model of "Original Sin": Rise of the West and Lag of the Rest', *American Economic Review*, vol. 82, No. 2, pp. 162–7.

Dasgupta, P., and Weale, M. (1992). 'On Measuring the Quality of Life', *World Development*, vol. 20, pp. 119–31.

David, Paul (1975). *Technical Choice, Innovation, and Economic Growth: Essay on American and British Experience in the Nineteenth Century*, Cambridge, Cambridge University Press.

(1985). 'Clio and the Economics of QWERTY', *American Economic Review*, vol. 75, pp. 332–7.

(1998). 'Common Agency Contracting and the Emergence of "Open Science" Institutions', *American Economic Review*, vol. 88, pp. 15–21.

David, Paul, and Solar, Peter (1977). 'A Bicentenary Contribution to the History of the Cost of Living in America', *Research in Economic History*, vol. 2, pp. 1–80.

Davies, R. S. W., and Pollard, Sidney (1988). 'The Iron Industry, 1750–1850', in Charles H. Feinstein and Sidney Pollard (eds.), *Studies in Capital Formation in the United Kingdom, 1750–1920*, Oxford, Clarendon Press, pp. 73–104.

Davis, Ralph (1954). 'English Foreign Trade, 1660–1700', *Economic History Review*, 2nd series, vol. 7, pp. 150–66.

(1973). *The Rise of the Atlantic Economies*, Ithaca, NY, Cornell University Press.

(1978). *The Rise of the English Shipping Industry in the Seventeenth and Eighteenth Centuries*, London, Macmillan.

(1979). *The Industrial Revolution and British Overseas Trade*, Leicester, Leicester University Press.

Day, Joan, and Tylecote, R. F. (1991). *The Industrial Revolution in Metals*, London, Institute of Metals.

Deane, Phyllis (1957). 'The Output of the British Woollen Industry in the Eighteenth Century', *Journal of Economic History*, vol. 17, pp. 207–23.

Deane, Phyllis, and Cole, W. A. (1969). *British Economic Growth, 1688–1959*, Cambridge, Cambridge University Press, second edition.

Defoe, Daniel (1726). *The Complete English Tradesman*, The Project Gutenberg E-book, 1839 edition, www.gutenberg.org/files/14444/14444-8.txt.

De Long, J. Bradford, and Schleifer, Andrei (1993). 'Princes and Merchants: European City Growth Before the Industrial Revolution', *Journal of Law and Economics*, vol. 36, pp. 671–702.

De Moor, Tina, and van Zanden, Jan Luiten (2005). 'Girl Power: The European Marriage Pattern (EMP) and Labour Markets in the North Sea Region in the Late Medieval and Early Modern Period', www.iisg.nl/hpw/factormarkets.php.

de Tocqueville, Alexis (1833). *Journeys to England and Ireland*, trans. by George Lawrence and K. P. Mayer, ed. by J. P. Mayer, London, Faber and Faber, n.d.

De Vries, Jan (1974). *The Dutch Rural Economy in the Golden Age, 1500–1700*, New Haven, CT, Yale University Press.

(1975). 'Peasant Demand Patterns and Economic Development: Friesland, 1550–1750', in William N. Parker and Eric L. Jones (eds.), *European Peasants and Their Markets: Essay in Agrarian Economic History*, Princeton, NJ, Princeton University Press, pp. 205–65.

(1984). *European Urbanization, 1500–1800*, Cambridge, MA, Harvard University Press; London, Methuen.

(1993). 'Between Purchasing Power and the World of Goods: Understanding the Household Economy in Early Modern Europe', in John Brewer and Roy Porter (eds.), *Consumption and the World of Goods*, London, Routledge, pp. 85–132.

(1994). 'The Industrial Revolution and the Industrious Revolution', *Journal of Economic History*, vol. 54, pp. 249–70.

(2003). 'Luxury in the Dutch Golden Age in Theory and Practice', in Maxine Berg and Elizabeth Eger (eds.), *Luxury in the Eighteenth Century*, Basingstoke, Palgrave Macmillan, pp. 41–56.

(2008). *The Industrious Revolution: Consumer Behavior and the Household Economy, 1650 to the Present*, Cambridge, Cambridge University Press.

De Vries, Jan, and van der Woude, Ad (1997). *The First Modern Economy: Success, Failure and Perseverance of the Dutch Economy, 1500–1815*, Cambridge, Cambridge University Press.

Denison, Edward F. (1962). *The Sources of Economic Growth in the United States and the Alternatives Before Us*, New York, Committee for Economic Development, Supplementary Paper No. 13.

Dermigne, Louis (1964). *Le Commerce à Canton au XVIIIe siècle, 1719–1833*, Paris, SEVPEN.

Desaguliers, J. T. (1734–44). *A Course of Experimental Philosophy*, London, John Senex.

Dickinson, H. W. (1939). *A Short History of the Steam Engine*, Cambridge, Cambridge University Press.

(1958). 'The Steam-Engine to 1830', in Charles Singer, E. J. Holmyard, A. R. Hall, *et al.* (eds.), *A History of Technology*, vol. IV, *The Industrial Revolution, c.1750–c.1850*, Oxford, Clarendon Press, pp. 168–98.

Diewert, W. E. (1976). 'Exact and Superlative Index Numbers', *Journal of Econometrics*, vol. 4, pp. 115–45.

Dosi, Giovanni (1982), 'Technological Paradigms and Technological Trajectories: A Suggested Interpretation of the Determinants and Directions of Technological Change', *Research Policy*, vol. 11, pp. 147–62.

(1988), 'Sources, Procedures and Microeconomic Effects of Innovation', *Journal of Economic Literature*, vol. 26, pp. 1120–71.

Doyon, André (1966). *Jacques Vaucanson: mécanicien de génie*, Paris, Presses Universitaires.

Drelichman, Mauricio (2005). 'The Curse of Montezuma: American Silver and the Dutch Disease, 1501–1650', *Explorations in Economic History*, vol. 42, pp. 349–80.

Dudley, Dud (1665). *Metallum Martis: or Iron Made with Pit-Coale, Sea-Coale, &c.*, London.

Dutton, H. I. (1984). *The Patent System and Inventive Activity During the Industrial Revolution*, Manchester, Manchester University Press.

Dyer, Christopher (1989). *Standards of Living in the Later Middle Ages: Social Change in England, c.1200–1520*, Cambridge, Cambridge University Press.

Eagly, Robert V. (1961). 'Sir James Steuart and the "Aspiration Effect"', *Economica*, new series, vol. 28, No. 109, pp. 53–61.

Eden, Sir Frederick (1797). *The State of the Poor*, London.

Ekelund, Robert B., and Tollinson, Robert D. (1997). *Politicized Economies: Monarchy, Monopoly, and Mercantilism*, College Station, TX, Texas A&M University Press.

Ellis, Joyce (2001). *The Georgian Town, 1680–1840*, Basingstoke, Palgrave.

Ellison, Thomas (1886). *The Cotton Trade of Great Britain*, London, Effingham Willson, Royal Exchange.

Elvin, Mark (1972). 'The High Level Equilibrium Trap: The Causes of the Decline of Invention in the Traditional Chinese Textile Industries', in W. E. Wilmott (ed.), *Economic Organization in Chinese Society*, Stanford, CA, Stanford University Press.

(1973). *The Patterns of the Chinese Past*, Stanford, CA, Stanford University Press.

Engels, Frederich (1845). *The Condition of the Working Class in England*, trans. and ed. by W. O. Henderson and W. H. Chaloner, Oxford, Basil Blackwell, 1958.

Engerman, S. L. (1972). 'The Slave Trade and British Capital Formation in the Eighteenth Century: A Comment on the Williams Thesis', *Business History Review*, vol. 46, pp. 430–3.

(1994). 'Mercantilism and Overseas Trade, 1700–1800', in Roderick Floud and D. N. McCloskey (eds.), *The Economic History of Britain Since 1700*, vol. I, *1700–1860*, Cambridge, Cambridge University Press, second edition, pp. 182–204.

(1998). 'British Imperialism in a Mercantilist Age, 1492–1849', *Revista de Historia Economica*, vol. 1, pp. 195–225.

(2000). 'France, Britain, and the Economic Growth of Colonial North America', in J. J. McCusker and K. Morgan (eds.), *The Early Modern Atlantic Economy*, Cambridge, Cambridge University Press.

Epstein, S. R. (1998). 'Craft Guilds, Apprenticeship, and Technological Change in Pre-industrial Europe', *Journal of Economic History*, vol. 58, pp. 684–713.

(2000). *Freedom and Growth: The Rise of States and Markets in Europe, 1300–1750*, London, Routledge.

(2004). 'Property Rights to Technical Knowledge in Premodern Europe, 1300–1800', *American Economic Review*, vol. 94, pp. 382–7.

Ernle, Lord (1912). *English Farming: Past and Present*, London, Heinemann Educational Books Ltd and Frank Cass & Co. Ltd, 1961.

'Excursion to Creusot', (1878). *Journal of the Iron and Steel Institute*, vol. 20, pp. 512–29.

Fairchilds, Cissie (1993). 'The Production and Marketing of Populuxe Goods in Eighteenth-Century France', in John Brewer and Roy Porter (eds.), *Consumption and the World of Goods*, London, Routledge, pp. 228–48.

Fang, Xing (1996). 'Qingdai Jiangnan shi zhen tanwei (Cities and Towns in Qing Jiangnan)', *Zhongguo jingji shi yanjiu* (Research in Chinese Economic History), vol. 11, No. 3, pp. 91–8.

Farey, John (1827). *A Treatise on the Steam Engine, Historical, Practical, and Descriptive*, London, Longman, Reese, Orme, Brown and Green.

Feinstein, Charles H. (1978). 'Capital Formation in Great Britain', in P. Mathias and M. M. Postan (eds.), *Cambridge Economic History of Europe*, vol. VII, *The Industrial Economies: Capital, Labour, and Enterprise*, Part I, *Britain, France, Germany, and Scandinavia*, Cambridge, Cambridge University Press, pp. 28–96.

(1998). 'Pessimism Perpetuated: Real Wages and the Standard of Living in Britain During and After the Industrial Revolution', *Journal of Economic History*, vol. 58, pp. 625–58.

Ferguson, Niall (2003). *Empire: How Britain Made the Modern World*, London, Allen Lane.

Findlay, Ronald (1990). 'The "Triangular Trade" and the Atlantic Economy of the Eighteenth Century: A Simple General-Equilibrium Model', Essays in International Finance, No. 177, Princeton, NJ, Princeton University.

Findlay, Ronald, and O'Rourke, Kevin H. (2003). 'Commodity Market Integration, 1500–2000', in D. Bordo, A. M. Taylor and J. G. Williamson (eds.), *Globalization in Historical Perspective*, Chicago, University of Chicago Press.

(2007). *Power and Plenty: Trade, War, and the World Economy in the Second Millennium*, Princeton, NJ, Princeton University Press.

Fischer, Ernst (1966). *How to Read Karl Marx*, New York, Monthly Review Press.

Fisher, John (1985). *Commercial Relations Between Spain and Spanish America in the Era of Free Trade, 1778–1796*, Centre for Latin American Studies, University of Liverpool, Monograph Series, 13.

(1997). *The Economic Aspects of Spanish Imperialism in America*, Liverpool, Liverpool University Press.

Fitton, R. S. (1989). *The Arkwrights: Spinners of Fortune*, Manchester, Manchester University Press.

Fitton, R. S., and Wadsworth, A. P. (1958). *The Strutts and the Arkwrights, 1758–1830: A Study of the Early Factory System*, Manchester, Manchester University Press.

Flinn, M. W. (1959). 'Timber and the Advance of Technology', *Annals of Science*, vol. 15, pp. 109–20.

(1984). *The History of the British Coal Industry*, vol. II, *1700–1830: The Industrial Revolution*, Oxford, Clarendon Press.

Floud, Roderick, Wachter, Kenneth, and Gregory, A. (1990). *Height, Health, and History: Nutritional Status in the United Kingdom, 1750–1890*, Cambridge, Cambridge University Press.

Fogel, Robert W. (1991). 'The Conquest of High Mortality and Hunger in Europe and America: Timing and Mechanisms', in Patrice Higonnet, David S. Landes and Henry Rosovsky (eds.), *Favorites of Fortune: Technology, Growth, and Economic Development Since the Industrial Revolution*, Cambridge, MA, Harvard University Press, pp. 33–71.

(2004). *The Escape from Hunger and Premature Death, 1700–2100*, Cambridge, Cambridge University Press.

Fohlen, Claude (1973). 'France, 1700–1914', in *The Fontana Economic History of Europe*, vol. 4(1), *The Emergence of Industrial Societies – 1*, London, Collins.

Forbes, R. J. (1958). 'Power to 1850', in Charles Singer, E. J. Holmyard, A. R. Hall, *et al.* (eds.), *A History of Technology*, vol. IV, *The Industrial Revolution, c.1750–c.1850*, Oxford, Clarendon Press, pp. 148–67.

Fortrey, Samuel (1663). *Englands Interest and Improvement*, Cambridge, John Field.

Foster, Charles F. (2004). *Capital and Innovation: How Britain Became the First Industrial Modern Nation: A Study of the Warrington, Knutsford, Northwich, and Frodsham Area, 1500–1780*, Northwich, Cheshire, Arley Hall Press.

Fraga, Antonio Vinao (1990). 'The History of Literacy in Spain: Evolution, Traits and Questions', *History of Education Quarterly*, vol. 30, pp. 573–99.

Francois, Etienne (1989). 'Lire et écrire en France et en Allemagne au temps de la Révolution', in Helmut Berding, Etienne Francois and Hand-Peter Ullmann (eds.), *La Révolution, la France et l'Allemagne: deux modeles opposés de changement social?*, Paris, Maison des Sciences de l'Homme.

Frank, A. G. (1978). *World Accumulation, 1492–1789*, London, Macmillan Press.

(1998). *ReOrient: Global Economy in the Asian Age*, Berkeley, CA, University of California Press.

Fremdling, Rainer (1986). *Technologischer Wandel und internationaler Handel im 18. und 19. Jahrhundert*, Berlin, Dunker & Humblot.

(2000). 'Transfer Patterns of British Technology to the Continent: The Case of the Iron Industry', *European Review of Economic History*, vol. 4, pp. 195–222.

(2004). 'Continental Responses to British Innovations in the Iron Industry During the Eighteenth and Early Nineteenth Centuries', in Leandro Prados de la Escosura (ed.), *Exceptionalism and Industrialisation: Britain and Its European Rivals, 1688–1815*, Cambridge, Cambridge University Press, pp. 145–69.

Furet, Francois, and Ozouf, Jacques (1977). *Lire et écrire: alphabetisation des Francaises de Calvin à Jules Ferry*, Paris, Editions de Minuit.

Galloway, J., Keene, D., and Murphy, M. (1996). 'Fuelling the City: Production and Distribution of Firewood and Fuel in London's Region, 1290–1400', *Economic History Review*, vol. 39, No. 3, pp. 447–72.

Garcia Fuentes, Lutgardo (1980). *El comercio espanol con America, 1650–1700*, Seville, Escuela de Estudios Hispano-Americanos, CSIS.

Gelabert, J. E. (1987). 'Niveaux d'alphabetisation en Galice (1635–1900)', in *De l'alphabetisation aux circuits du livre en Espagne XVIe XIXe siècles*, Paris, CNRS.

Gerschenkron, Alexander (1962). *Economic Backwardness in Historical Perspective*, Cambridge, MA, Harvard University Press.

Ghai, Dharam P., *et al.* (1977). *The Basic-Needs Approach to Development: Some Issues Regarding Concepts and Methodology*, Geneva, International Labour Office.

Gilboy, Elizabeth W. (1934). *Wages in Eighteenth Century England*, Cambridge, Harvard University Press.

Gill, I. (1998). 'Stature, Consumption, and the Standard of Living in Colonial Korea', in J. Komlos and J. Baten (eds.), *The Biological Standard of Living in Comparative Perspective*, Stuttgart, Franz Steiner Verlag, pp. 122–38.

Goldin, Claudia, and Katz, Lawrence (1998). 'The Origins of Technology-Skill Complementarity', *Quarterly Journal of Economics*, vol. 113, pp. 693–732.

Goldin, Claudia, and Margo, Robert A. (1992). 'Wages, Prices, and Labor Markets Before the Civil War', in Claudia Goldin and Hugh Rockoff (eds.), *Strategic Factors in Nineteenth Century American Economic History*, Chicago, University of Chicago Press, pp. 67–104.

Goldstone, J. A. (2002). 'Efflorescences and Economic Growth in World History: Rethinking the Rise of the West and the British Industrial Revolution', *Journal of World History*, vol. 13, pp. 323–89.

(2003). 'Europe's Peculiar Path: Would the World Be Modern If William III's Invention of England in 1688 Had Failed?', in N. Lebow, G. Parker and P. Tetlock (eds.), *Counterfactual History*, New York.

Goose, Nigel (2005). 'Immigrants and English Economic Development in the Sixteenth and Early Seventeenth Centuries', in Nigel Goose and Lien Luu (eds.), *Immigrants in Tudor and Early Stuart England*, Brighton, Sussex Academic Press, pp. 136–60.

Graff, Harvey J. (1987). *The Legacies of Literacy: Continuities and Contradictions in Western Culture and Society*, Bloomington, IN, Indiana University Press.

Grantham, George (1978). 'The Diffusion of the New Husbandry in Northern France', *Journal of Economic History*, vol. 38, pp. 311–37.

(1989). 'Agricultural Supply During the Industrial Revolution: French Evidence and European Implications', *Journal of Economic History*, vol. 49, pp. 43–72.

Graunt, John (1662). *Natural and Political Observations . . . made upon the Bills of Mortality*, ed. by Walter F. Willcox, Baltimore, MD, Johns Hopkins University Press, 1939.

Greif, Avner (2006). *Institutions and the Path to the Modern Economy: Lessons from Medieval Trade*, Cambridge, Cambridge University Press.

Grendler, Paul F. (1989). *Schooling in Renaissance Italy: Literacy and Learning, 1300–1600*, Baltimore, MD, Johns Hopkins University Press.

Gruner, Louis E., and Lan, Charles (1962). *Etat présent de la métallugie du fer en Angleterre*, Paris.

Guest, Richard (1823). *A Compendious History of the Cotton-Manufacture*, Manchester, J. Pratt.

Gwynn, Robin D. (1985). *Huguenot Heritage: The History and Distribution of the Huguenots in Britain*, London, Routledge & Kegan Paul.

Habakkuk, J. J. (1940). 'English Landownership, 1680–1740', *Economic History Review*, 1st series, vol. 10, pp. 2–17.

(1962). *American and British Technology in the Nineteenth Century*, Cambridge, Cambridge University Press.

Hagen, E. (1962). *The Theory of Social Change: How Economic Growth Begins*, Homewood, IL, Dorsey Press.

Hahn, F. H., and Matthews, F. C. O. (1964). 'The Theory of Economic Growth: A Survey', *Economic Journal*, vol. 74, No. 296, pp. 779–902.

Hajnal, J. (1965). 'European Marriage Patterns in Perspective', in D. V. Glass and D. E. C. Eversley (eds.), *Population in History*, Chicago, Aldine Publishing Co., pp. 101–43.

Halfpenny, Pat (2000). 'Enoch Booth – Pioneer Potter?', *Antique Dealers and Collectors Guide*, June 2000.

Hall, A. Rupert (1974). 'What Did the Industrial Revolution in Britain Owe to Science?', in Neil McKendrick (ed.), *Historical Perspectives: Studies in English Thought and Society*, London, Europa Publications, pp. 129–51.

Hamilton, A. (1744), *A New Account of the East Indies*, London.

Hamilton, Earl J. (1929). 'American Treasure and the Rise of Capitalism', *Economica*, vol. 9, No. 27, pp. 338–57.

(1934). *American Treasure and the Price Revolution in Spain, 1501–1650*, New York, Octagon Books, reissued 1970.

(1936). *Money, Prices, and Wages in Valencia, Aragon, and Navarre, 1351–1500*, Philadelphia, Porcupine Press, reissued 1975.

(1947). *War and Prices in Spain, 1650–1800*, New York, Russell & Russell, reissued 1969.

Hamilton, Henry (1926). *The English Brass and Copper Industries to 1800*, London, Longmans, Green and Co. Ltd.

Hammersley, G. (1957). 'Crown Woods and the Exploitation in the Sixteenth and Seventeenth Centuries', *Bulletin of the Institute of Historical Research*, vol. 30, pp. 136–61.

(1973). 'The Charcoal Iron Industry and Its Fuel, 1540–1750', *Economic History Review*, vol. 26, pp. 593–613.

Hanauer, A. (1878). *Etudes économiques sur l'Alsace, ancienna et moderne*, Strasbourg, Hagemann Librairie.

Hardin, G. J. (1998). *Managing the Commons*, Bloomington, IN, Indiana University Press, second edition.

Harley, C. K. (1971). 'The Shift from Sailing Ships to Steam Ships, 1850–1890: A Study in Technological Change and its Diffusion', in D. N. McCloskey (ed.), *Essays on a Mature Economy: Britain after 1840*, Princeton, NJ, Princeton University Press, pp. 215–34.

(1973). 'On the Persistence of Old Techniques: The Case of North American Wooden Shipbuilding', *Journal of Economic History*, vol. 33, pp. 372–98.

(1992). 'International Competitiveness of the Antebellum American Cotton Textile Industry', *Journal of Economic History*, vol. 52, pp. 559–84.

(1994). 'Foreign Trade: Comparative Advantage and Performance', in Roderick Floud and D. N. McCloskey (eds.), *The Economic History of Britain Since 1700*, vol. I, *1700–1860*, Cambridge, Cambridge University Press, second edition, pp. 300–31.

(1998). 'Cotton Textile Prices and the Industrial Revolution', *Economic History Review*, vol. 51, pp. 49–83.

(1999). 'Reassessing the Industrial Revolution: A Macro View', in J. Mokyr (ed.), *The British Industrial Revolution: An Economic Perspective*, second edition, pp. 160–205.

(2001). 'The Antebellum Tariff: Different Products or Competing Sources? A Comment on Irwin and Temin', *Journal of Economic History*, vol. 61, pp. 799–805.

Harley, C. K., and Crafts, N. F. R. (2000). 'Simulating the Two Views of the Industrial Revolution', *Journal of Economic History*, vol. 60, pp. 819–41.

Harris, J. R. (1975). 'Saint-Gobain and Ravenshead', in Barrie M. Ratcliffe (ed.), *Great Britain and Her World, 1750–1914*, Manchester, Manchester University Press, pp. 27–70.

(1978–9). 'Recent Research on the Newcomen Engine and Historical Studies', *Transactions of the Newcomen Society*, vol. 50, pp. 175–80.

(1988a). *The British Iron Industry, 1700–1850*, Houndmills, Macmillan Education Ltd.

(1988b). 'The Diffusion of English Metallurgical Methods to Eighteenth Century France', *French History*, vol. 2, pp. 22–44.

(1992). *Essays in Industry and Technology in the Eighteenth Century: England and France*, Aldershot, Variorum.

Harte, N. B. (1997). *The New Draperies in the Low Countries and England, 1300–1800*, Oxford, Oxford University Press.

Hartwell, R. M. (1967). *The Causes of the Industrial Revolution*, London, Methuen.

Hatcher, J. (1993). *The History of the British Coal Industry*, vol. I, *Before 1700: Towards the Age of Coal*, Oxford, Oxford University Press.

Haudrère, Phillippe (1989). *La compagnie française des indes au XVIIIe siècle (1719–1795)*, Paris, Libraire de l'Inde Editeur.

Havinden, M. A. (1961). 'Agricultural Progress in Open Field Oxfordshire', *Agricultural History Review*, vol. 9, Part 2, pp. 73–83.

Hayami, Yujiro, and Otsuka, Keijiro (1993). *The Economics of Contract Choice: An Agrarian Perspective*, Oxford, Clarendon Press.

Henderson, W. O. (1954). *Britain and Industrial Europe: 1750–1870*, Liverpool, Liverpool University Press.

Hicks, John (1932). *The Theory of Wages*, London, Macmillan.

Hilaire-Pérez, Liliane (2000). *L'invention technique au siècle des lumières*, Paris, Albin Michel.

Hill, Christopher (1966). *The Century of Revolution, 1603–1714*, New York, Norton.

Hills, Richard L. (1970). *Power in the Industrial Revolution*, Manchester, Manchester University Press.

(1979). 'Hargreaves, Arkwright, and Crompton: Why Three Separate Inventors?', *Textile History*, vol. 10, pp. 114–26.

(1989). *Power from Steam: A History of the Stationary Steam Engine*, Cambridge, Cambridge University Press.

Hoffman, Philip T. (1996). *Growth in a Traditional Society: The French Countryside, 1450–1815*, Princeton, NJ, Princeton University Press.

Hoffman, Philip T., and Norberg, Kathryn (1994). *Fiscal Crises, Liberty, and Representative Government, 1450–1789*, Stanford, CA, Stanford University Press.

(2000). *Priceless Markets: The Political Economy of Credit in Paris, 1660–1870*, Chicago, University of Chicago Press.

Hoffman, Walther G. (1955). *British Industry, 1700–1950*, trans. by W. O. Henderson and W. H. Chaloner, Oxford, Basil Blackwell.

Holderness, B. A. (1997). 'The Reception and Distribution of the New Draperies in England', in N. B. Harte (ed.), *The New Draperies in the Low Countries and England, 1300–1800*, Oxford, Oxford University Press, pp. 217–43.

Hollister-Short, G. J. (1976–7). 'The Introduction of the Newcomen Engine into Europe', *Transactions of the Newcomen Society*, vol. 48.

Homer, Henry (1766). *An Essay on the Nature and Method of Ascertaining the Specifick Shares of Proprietors, upon the Inclosure of Common Fields*, Oxford.

Honeyman, K. (1982). *Origins of Enterprise: Business Leadership in the Industrial Revolution*, Manchester, Manchester University Press.

Hoppit, Julian (1996). 'Patterns of Parliamentary Legislation, 1660–1800', *History Journal*, vol. 39, pp. 109–31.

Hoppit, J., Innes, J., and Styles, J. (1994). 'Towards a History of Parliamentary Legislation, 1660–1800', *Parliamentary History*, vol. 20.

Horrell, Sara, and Humphries, Jane (1992). 'Old Questions, New Data, and Alternative Perspectives: Families' Living Standards in the Industrial Revolution', *Journal of Economic History*, vol. 52, pp. 849–80.

Hoskins, W. G. (1950). 'The Leicestershire Farmer in the Sixteenth Century', in W. G. Hoskins (ed.), *Essays in Leicestershire History*, Liverpool, Liverpool University Press, pp. 123–183.

(1951). 'The Leicestershire Farmer in the Seventeenth Century', in W. G. Hoskins (ed.), *Provincial England*, London, Macmillan & Co. Ltd, 1963, pp. 149–69.

(1953). 'The Rebuilding of Rural England, 1570–1640', *Past and Present*, No. 4, pp. 44–59.

Houston, Robert Allan (1988). *Literacy in Early Modern Europe: Culture and Education, 1500–1800*, London, Longman.

Huberman, M. (1996). *Escape from the Market: Negotiating Work in Lancashire*, Cambridge, Cambridge University Press.

Hudson, P. (1986). *The Genesis of Industrial Capital: A Study of the West Riding Wool Textile Industry, c.1750–1850*, Cambridge, Cambridge University Press.

Hufton, Olwen H. (1974). *The Poor of Eighteenth-Century France, 1750–1789*, Oxford, Clarendon Press.

Humphries, Jane (2009). *Through the Mill: Child Labour During the British Industrial Revolution*, Cambridge, Cambridge University Press.

Hunter, Dard (1930). *Papermaking Through Eighteen Centuries*, New York, William Edwin Rudge.

Hunter, Louis C. (1949). *Steam Boats on the Western Rivers: An Economic and Technological History*, Cambridge, Harvard University Press.

(1985). *A History of Industrial Power in the United States, 1780–1930*, vol. II, *Steam Power*, Charlottesville, VA, University Press of Virginia for Hagley Museum and Library.

Hyde, Charles (1973). 'The Adoption of Coke-Smelting by the British Iron Industry 1709–1790', *Exploration in Economic History*, vol. 10, pp. 397–417.

(1977). *Technological Change and the British Iron Industry, 1700–1870*, Princeton, NJ, Princeton University Press.

Inikori, Joseph E. (2002). *Africans and the Industrial Revolution in England: A Study in International Trade and Economic Development*, Cambridge, Cambridge University Press.

Inkster, Ian (1991). *Science and Technology in History: An Approach to Industrial Development*, New Brunswick, NJ, Rutgers University Press.

Innes, Joanne (1992). 'Politics, Property, and the Middle Class', *Parliamentary History*, vol. 11.

(1998). 'The Local Acts of a National Parliament: Parliament's Role in Sanctioning Local Action in Eighteenth-Century Britain', in D. Dean and C. Jones (eds.), *Parliament and Locality*, Edinburgh, Edinburgh University Press for the Parliamentary History Yearbook Trust, pp. 23–47.

Irwin, Douglas A., and Temin, Peter (2001). *Journal of Economic History*, vol. 61, pp. 777–98.

Jackson, R. V. (1985). 'Growth and Deceleration in English Agriculture, 1660–1790', *Economic History Review*, 2nd series, vol. 38, pp. 333–51.

Jacob, Margaret C. (1988). *The Cultural Meaning of the Scientific Revolution*, Philadelphia, Temple University Press.

(1997). *Scientific Culture and the Making of the Industrial West*, New York, Oxford University Press.

Jacob, Margaret, and Stewart, Larry (2004). *Practical Matter: Newton's Science in the Service of Industry and Empire: 1687–1851*, Cambridge, MA, Harvard University Press.

Jeremy, David J. (1981). *Transatlantic Industrial Revolution: The Diffusion of Textile Technologies Between Britain and America, 1790–1830s*, Oxford, Basil Blackwell Publisher.

Jevons, William Stanley (1865). *The Coal Question: An Inquiry Concerning the Progress of the Nation and the Probable Exhaustion of Our Coal Mines*, London.

Johnson, W. R. (1841). *Notes on the Use of Anthracite in the Manufacture of Iron*, Boston, Charles C. Little and James Brown.

Jones, C. I. (1998). *Introduction of Economic Growth*, New York, W. W. Norton & Co.

Jones, E. L. (1981). *The European Miracle*, Cambridge, Cambridge University Press.

Jörberg, L. (1972). *A History of Prices in Sweden, 1732–1914*, vols. 1–2, Lund, Gleerups.

Kanefsky, John (1979). 'The Diffusion of Power Technology in British Industry', PhD Dissertation, University of Exeter.

Kanefsky, John, and Robey, John (1980). 'Steam Engines in 18th Century Britain: A Quantitative Assessment', *Technology and Culture*, vol. 21, pp. 161–86.

Kerridge, Eric (1972). 'Wool Growing and Wool Textiles in Medieval and Early Modern Times', in J. Geraint Jenkins (ed.), *The Wool Textile Industry in Great Britain*, London, Routledge & Kegan Paul, pp. 19–33.

(1985). *Textile Manufactures in Early Modern England*, Manchester, Manchester University Press.

Khan, Zorina (2005). *The Democratization of Invention: Patents, and Copyrights in American Economic Development: 1790–1920*, Cambridge, Cambridge University Press.

(2008). 'The Evolution of Useful Knowledge: Great Inventors, Science and Technology in British Economic Development, 1750–1930' (unpublished).

Khan, B. Zorina, and Sokoloff, Kenneth L. (1993). '"Schemes of Practical Utility": Entrepreneurship and Innovation Among "Great Inventors" in the United States, 1790–1846', *Journal of Economic History*, vol. 53, pp. 289–307.

(2006). 'Of Patents and Prizes: Great Inventors and the Evolution of Useful Knowledge in Britain and America, 1750–1930', paper presented to the American Economic Association.

King, Peter Wickham (2003). 'The Iron Trade in England and Wales, 1500–1850: The Charcoal Iron Industry and Its Transition to Coke', PhD Dissertation, University of Wolverhampton.

Komlos, John (2003). 'An Anthropometric History of Early Modern France', *European Review of Economic History*, vol. 7, pp. 159–89.

Kowaleski, Maryanne (2006). 'A Consumer Economy', in Rosemary Horrox and W. Mark Ormrod (eds.), *A Social History of England, 1200–1500*, Cambridge, Cambridge University Press, pp. 238–59.

Kuijpers, Erika (1997). 'Lezen en schrijven: Onderzoek naar het Alfabetiseringsniveau in zeventiendeeeuws Amsterdam', *Tijdschrift voor Sociale Geschiedenis*, vol. 23, pp. 490–522.

Kuznets, Simon (1971). *Economic Growth of Nations: Total Output and Production Structure*, Cambridge, MA, Belknap Press.

(1971). *Modern Economic Growth: Rate, Structure, and Spread.* New Haven, CT, and London: Yale University Press.

Landers, J. (1993). *Death and the Metropolis: Studies in the Demographic History of London, 1670–1830*, Cambridge, Cambridge University Press.

Landes, David S. (1969). *The Unbound Prometheus: Technological Change and Industrial Development in Western Europe from 1750 to the Present*, Cambridge, Cambridge University Press.

(1998). *The Wealth and Poverty of Nations: Why Some Are So Rich and Some So Poor*. New York, W. W. Norton & Co.

(2000). *Revolution in Time: Clocks and the Making of the Modern World*, London, Viking, revised edition.

Langer, William (1975). 'American Foods and Europe's Population Growth, 1750–1850', *Journal of Social History*, vol. 8, No. 2, pp. 51–66.

LaPorta, R., Lopez-de-Silanes, F., Schleifer, A., *et al.* (1998). 'Law and Finance', *Journal of Political Economy*, vol. 106, pp. 1113–55.

Larguie, Claude (1987). 'L'Alphabetisation des Madrilenos dans la Seconde Moitie du xviieme siecle: stagnation our evolution?', in *De l'alphabetisation aux circuits du livre en Espagne, XVIe–XIXe siècles*, Paris, CNRS.

Laveley, W., and Wong, R. B. (1998). 'Revising the Malthusian Narrative: The Comparative Study of Population Dynamics in Late Imperial China', *Journal of Asian Studies*, vol. 57, pp. 714–48.

Le Roy Ladurie (1974). *The Peasants of Languedoc*, trans. by John Day, Urbana, IL, University of Illinois Press.

Lean, Thomas (1839). *On the Steam Engines in Cornwall*, Truro, D. Bradford Barton Ltd, 1969.

Lee, J., Campbell, C., and Tan, G. (1992). 'Infanticide and Family Planning in Late Imperial China: The Price and Population History of Rural Liaoning, 1774–1873', in T. G. Rawski and L. Li (eds.), *Chinese History in Economic Perspective*, Berkeley, CA, University of California Press.

Lee, J. Z., and Wang, F. (1999). *One Quarter of Humanity: Malthusian Mythology and Chinese Realities, 1700–2000*. Cambridge, MA, Harvard University Press.

Lefebre, Georges (1962). *Etudes Orléanaises*, Paris, Centre national de la recherche scientifique.

Lehmann, Hartmut, and Roth, Guenther (1995). *Weber's Protestant Ethic: Origins, Evidence, Contexts*, Cambridge, Cambridge University Press.

Lemire, Beverly (1991). *Fashion's Favourite: The Cotton Trade and the Consumer in Britain, 1660–1800*, Oxford, Oxford University Press.

(1997). *Dress, Culture and Commerce: The English Clothing Trade Before the Factory, 1660–1800*, Basingstoke, Macmillan.

Levasseur, E. (1911). *Histoire de la commerce de France*, Paris, Arthur Rousseau, Editeur.

Levere, Trevor, and Turner, Gerard L'E. (eds.) (2002). *Discussing Chemistry and Steam: The Minutes of a Coffee House Philosophical Society, 1780–1787*, Oxford, Oxford University Press.

Lewis, Sir W. A. (1954). 'Economic Development with Unlimited Supplies of Labour', *The Manchester School*, vol. 22, pp. 139–91.

Li, Bozhong (1998). *Agricultural Development in Jiangnan, 1620–1850*, Basingstoke, Macmillan.

Lindert, Peter H., and Williamson, Jeffrey G. (1982). 'Revising England's Social Tables, 1688–1812', *Explorations in Economic History*, vol. 19, pp. 385–408.

Lipsey, Richard G., Carlaw, Kenneth I., and Bekar, Clifford T. (2005). *Economic Transformations: General Purpose Technologies and Long-Term Economic Growth*, Oxford, Oxford University Press.

Livi-Bacci, M. (1991). *Population and Nutrition*, Cambridge, Cambridge University Press.

Lockyer, Charles (1711). *An Account of the Trade in India*, London.

Lucassen, Jan (1987). *Migrant Labour in Europe, 1600–1900*, trans. by Donald A. Bloch, London, Croom Helm.

Luraghi, Raimondo (1978). *The Rise and Fall of the Plantation South*, New York, New Viewpoints.

Luu, Lien Bich (2005). *Immigrants and the Industries of London*, Aldershot, Ashgate.

Lyons, John S. (1987). 'Powerloom Profitability and Steam Power Costs: Britain in the 1830s', *Explorations in Economic History*, vol. 24, pp. 392–408.

Machlup, Fritz (1962). *The Production and Distribution of Knowledge in the United States*, Princeton, NJ, Princeton University Press.

MacLeod, Christine (1986). 'The 1690s Patent Boom: Invention or Stock-jobbing?', *Economic History Review*, vol. 39, pp. 549–71.

(1987). 'Accident or Design? George Ravencroft's Patent and the Invention of Lead-Crystal Glass', *Technology and Culture*, vol. 28, No. 4, pp. 776–803.

(1988). *Inventing the Industrial Revolution: The English Patent System, 1660–1800*, Cambridge, Cambridge University Press.

(2007). *Heroes of Invention: Technology, Liberalism, and British Identity, 1750–1914*, Cambridge, Cambridge University Press.

Maddison, Angus (1995). *Monitoring the World Economy, 1820–1992*, Paris, OECD.

Malanima, Paolo. (2000). 'The Energy Basis for Early Modern Growth, 1650–1820', in M. Prak (ed.), *Early Modern Capitalism: Economic and Social Change in Europe, 1400–1800*, London, Routledge.

(2006). 'Energy Crisis and Growth, 1650–1850: The European Deviation in a Comparative Perspective', *Journal of Global History*, vol. I, pp. 101–21.

Malthus, T. R. (1803). *An Essay on the Principle of Population*, ed. by Patricia James, Cambridge, Cambridge University Press, 1989.

Mandeville, Bernard (1724). *The Fable of the Bees, or Private Vices, Publick Benefits*, ed. by F. B. Kaye, Indianapolis, IN, Liberty Fund, 1988, *The Third Dialogue between Horatio and Cleomenes*, online edition at http://oll.libertyfund.org/Texts/LFBooks/Mandeville0162/FableOfBees/HTMLs/0014-02_Pt02_Part2.html.

Marglin, Stephen (1976). 'What Do Bosses Do?', in André Gorz (ed.), *The Division of Labour: The Labour Process and the Class Struggle in Modern Capitalism*, London, pp. 13–54.

Margo, R. A. (2000). *Wages and Labor Markets in the United States 1820–1860*, Chicago: University of Chicago Press.

Margo, Robert A., and Villaflor, Georgia C. (1987). 'The Growth of Wages in Antebellum America: New Evidence', *Journal of Economic History*, vol. 47, pp. 873–95.

Martin, Luc (1997). 'The Rise of the New Draperies in Norwich', in N. B. Harte (ed.), *The New Draperies in the Low Countries and England, 1300–1800*, Oxford, Oxford University Press, pp. 245–74.

Marx, K. (1853). 'The British Rule in India' and 'The Future Results of British Rule in India', in *The Portable Karl Marx*, ed. by E. Kamenka. New York, Penguin Books USA, 1983, pp. 329–41.

(1867). *Capital*, in *The Portable Karl Marx*, ed. by E. Kamenka, New York, Penguin Books USA, 1983, pp. 432–503.

Mathias, Peter (1972). 'Who Unbound Prometheus? Science and Technical Change, 1600–1800', in A. E. Musson, *Science, Technology and Economic Growth in the Eighteenth Century*, London, Methuen, pp. 69–96.

(1979). 'Leisure and Wages in Theory and Practice', in Peter Mathias (ed.), *The Transformation of England*, London, Methuen, pp. 148–67.

Mathias, P., and O'Brien, P. K. (1976). 'Taxation in England and France, 1715–1810', *Journal of European Economic History*, vol. 5, pp. 601–50.

(1978). 'The Incidence of Taxes and the Burden of Proof', *Journal of European Economic History*, vol. 7, pp. 211–13.

McClelland, D. (1961). *The Achieving Society*, Princeton, NJ, Van Nostrand.

McCloskey, D. N. (1970–1). 'Britain's Loss from Foreign Industrialisation: A Provisional Estimate', *Explorations in Economic History*, vol. 8, pp. 141–52.

McCusker, John J., and Morgan, Kenneth (2000). *The Early Modern Atlantic Economy*, Cambridge, Cambridge University Press.

(1972). 'The Enclosure of Open Fields: Preface to its Impact on the Efficiency of English Agriculture in the Eighteenth Century', *Journal of Economic History*, vol. 32, pp. 15–35.

(1980). 'Magnanimous Albion: Free Trade and British National Income, 1841/1881', *Explorations in Economic History*, vol. 17, pp. 303–20.

(1981). 'The Industrial Revolution 1780–1860: A Survey', in Roderick Floud and D. N. McCloskey (eds.), *The Economic History of Britain Since 1700*, vol. I, *1700–1860*, Cambridge, Cambridge University Press, pp. 103–27.

McEvedy, C., and Jones, R. (1978). *Atlas of World Population History*, London, Penguin Books.

McKendrick, Neil, Brewer, John, and Plumb, J. H. (1982). *The Birth of a Consumer Society: The Commercialization of Eighteenth-Century England*, London, Europa.

Mellor, John H., and Mudahar, Mohinder S. (1992). 'Agriculture in Economic Development: Theories, Findings, and Challenges in an Asian Context', in *A Survey of Agriculture Economics Literature, vol. 4, Agriculture in Economic Development, 1940s to 1990s*, ed. by Lee R. Martin, Minneapolis, University of Minnesota Press, pp. 331–544.

Ménard, Claude, and Shirley, Mary M. (2005). *Handbook of New Institutional Economics*, Dordrecht, Springer.

Mendels, F. F. (1972). 'Proto-Industrialization: The First Phase of the Industrialization Process', *Journal of Economic History*, vol. 32, pp. 241–61.

Minchinton, W. E. (1969). *The Growth of English Overseas Trade in the Seventeenth and Eighteenth Centuries*, London, Methuen.

Mitch, David (1993). *The Role of Human Capital in the First Industrial Revolution*, in J. Mokyr (ed.), *The British Industrial Revolution: An Economic Perspective*, Boulder, CO, Westview Press, pp. 267–307.

(2004). 'Education and Skill of the British Labour Force', in Roderick Floud and Paul Johnson (eds.), *The Cambridge Economic History of Modern Britain*, vol. I, *1700–1860*, Cambridge, Cambridge University Press, pp. 332–56.

Mitchell, Brian R. (1973). 'Statistical Appendix, 1700–1914', in *The Fontana Economic History of Europe: The Emergence of Industrial Societies*, vol. 4, Part 2, ed. by Carlo Cipolla, London, Collins/Fontana Books, pp. 738–820.

Mitchell, Brian R., and Deane, Phyllis (1971). *Abstract of British Historical Statistics*, Cambridge, Cambridge University Press.

Mokyr, Joel (1990). *The Lever of Riches: Technological Creativity and Economic Progress*, New York, Oxford University Press.

(1991). 'Was There a British Industrial Evolution?', in Joel Mokyr, *The Vital One: Essays in Honor of Jonathan R. T. Hughes*, Research in Economic History: Supplement 6.

(1993). 'Editor's Introduction: The New Economic History and the Industrial Revolution', in Joel Mokyr (ed.), *The British Industrial Revolution: An Economic Perspective*, Boulder, CO, Westview Press, pp. 1–131.

(1999). 'Editor's Introduction: The New Economic History and the Industrial Revolution', in J. Mokyr (ed.), *The British Industrial Revolution: An Economic Perspective*, Boulder, CO, Westview Press.

(2002). *The Gifts of Athena: Historical Origins of the Knowledge Economy*, Princeton, NJ, Princeton University Press.

(2009). *The Enlightened Economy: The Economic History of Britain, 1700–1850*, Penguin Press.

Montgomery, James (1836). *The Theory and Practice of Cotton Spinning*, Glasgow, John Niven, Jun.

(1840). *A Practical Guide of the Cotton Manufacture of the United States of America*, Glasgow, John Niven, Jun.

Morgan, Kenneth (2001). *Slavery, Atlantic Trade and the British Economy*, New York, Cambridge University Press.

Morgan, S. L. (1998). 'Biological Indicators of Change in the Standard of Living in China During the 20th Century', in J. Komlos and J. Baten (eds.), *The Biological Standard of Living in Comparative Perspective*, Stuttgart, Franz Steiner Verlag, pp. 7–34.

Morineau, Michel (1985). *Incroyable gazettes et fabuleux métaux*, Paris, Editions de la Maison des Sciences de l'Homme.

Morris, Morris D. (1983). 'The Growth of Large-Scale Industry to 1947', in Dharma Kumar, *The Cambridge Economic History of India*, Vol. 2, *C.1757–c.1970*, Cambridge, Cambridge University Press, pp. 553–676.

Morse, H. B. (1926–9). *The Chronicles of the East India Company Trading to China, 1635–1834*, Oxford, Clarendon Press.

Mott, R. A. (1934–5). 'Dud Dudley and the Early Coal–Iron Industry', *Transactions of the Newcomen Society*, vol. 15, pp. 17–37.

(1957). 'The Earliest Use of Coke for Iron Making', *The Gas World – Coking Section*, Supplement 7, pp. 7–18.

(1957–9a). 'Abraham Darby (I and II) and the Coal–Iron Industry', *Transactions of the Newcomen Society*, vol. 31, pp. 49–93.

(1957–9b). 'The Coalbrookdale Group Horsehay Works, Part I', *Transactions of the Newcomen Society*, vol. 31, pp. 271–87.

(1959–60). 'The Coalbrookdale Group Horsehay Works, Part II', *Transactions of the Newcomen Society*, vol. 32, pp. 43–56.

Muellbauer, J. (1987). 'Professor Sen and the Standard of Living', in G. Hawthorn (ed.), *The Standard of Living*, Cambridge, Cambridge University Press, pp. 39–58.

Muldrew, Craig (1998). *The Economy of Obligation: The Culture of Credit and Social Relations in Early Modern England*, Basingstoke, Macmillan.

(2007). 'The "Ancient Distaff and Whirling Spindle": Measuring the Contribution of Spinning to Household Earnings and the National Economy in England, 1550–1770', paper presented to the Economic History Society Conference, Exeter.

Munro, John H. (1997). 'The Origin of the English "New Draperies": The Resurrection of an Old Flemish Industry, 1270–1570', in N. B. Harte (ed.), *The New Draperies in the Low Countries and England, 1300–1800*, Oxford, Oxford University Press, pp. 35–127.

Musson, A. E., and Robinson, Eric (1969). *Science and Technology in the Industrial Revolution*, Manchester, Manchester University Press.

Myrdal, G. (1933). *The Cost of Living in Sweden, 1830–1930*, London, P. S. King and Sons.

Nalle, Sara T. (1989). 'Literacy and Culture in Early Modern Castille', *Past and Present*, No. 125, pp. 65–96.

Neal, Larry (1990). *The Rise of Financial Capitalism: International Capital Markets in the Age of Reason*, Cambridge, Cambridge University Press.

Needham, Joseph (1954). *Science and Civilisation in China*, vol. I, *Introductory Orientations*, Cambridge, Cambridge University Press.

Nef, J. U. (1932). *The Rise of the British Coal Industry*, London, George Routledge & Sons Ltd.

North, D. C., and Thomas, R. P. (1973). *The Rise of the Western World*, Cambridge, Cambridge University Press.

North, D. C., and Weingast, B. R. (1989). 'Constitutions and Commitment: Evolution of Institutions Governing Public Choice in Seventeenth Century England', *Journal of Economic History*, vol. 49, pp. 803–32.

Nugent, J. B., and Sanchez, N. (1989). 'The Efficiency of the Mesta: A Parable', *Explorations in Economic History*, vol. 26, pp. 261–84.

Nuvolari, Alessandro (2004a). *The Making of Steam Power Technology: A Study of Technical Change During the Industrial Revolution*, Eindhoven, Technische Universiteit Eindhoven.

(2004b). 'Collective Invention During the British Industrial Revolution: The Cast of the Cornish Pumping Engine', *Cambridge Journal of Economics*, vol. 28, pp. 347–63.

Nuvolari, Alessandro, and Verspagen, Bart (2007). '*Lean's Engine Reporter* and the Development of the Cornish Engine: A Reappraisal', *Transactions of the Newcomen Society*, vol. 77, pp. 167–89.

(2008). 'Technical Choice, Innovation and British Steam Engineering, 1800–1850', *Economic History Review*, forthcoming.

O'Brien, Patrick K. (1982). 'European Economic Development: The Contribution of the Periphery', *Economic History Review*, 2nd series, vol. 35, pp. 1–18.

(1996). 'Path Dependency, or Why Britain Became an Industrialized and Urbanized Economy Long Before France', *Economic History Review*, 2nd series, vol. 49, pp. 213–49.

(1999). 'Imperialism and the Rise and Decline of the British Economy, 1688–1989', *New Left Review*, No. 238, pp. 48–80.

(2005). 'Fiscal and Financial Pre-conditions for the Rise of British Naval Hegemony, 1485–1815', London School of Economics, Working Papers in Economic History, No. 91-05.

(2006). 'It's Not the Economy, Silly. It's the Navy'.

O'Brien, Patrick K., and Engerman, Stanley L. (1991). 'Exports and the Growth of the British Economy from the Glorious Revolution to the Peace of Amiens', in Barbara L. Solow (ed.), *Slavery and the Rise of the Atlantic System*, Cambridge, Cambridge University Press, pp. 177–209.

O'Brien, Patrick K., and Keyder, C. (1978). *Economic Growth in Britain and France, 1780–1914: Two Paths to the Twentieth Century*, London, George Allen and Unwin.

O'Brien, Patrick, and Prados de la Escosura, Leandro (1998). 'The Costs and Benefits of European Imperialism from the Conquest of Cueta, 1451, to the Treaty of Lusaka, 1974', in C.-E. Nunez (eds.), *Debates and Controversies in Economic History*, Madrid, pp. 9–69.

O'Grada, Cormac (1994). 'British Agriculture, 1860–1914', in Roderick Floud and Donald N. McCloskey (eds.), *The Economic History of Britain Since 1700*, vol. 2, *1860–1939*, Cambridge, Cambridge University Press, pp. 145–72.

O'Rourke, Kevin H., and Williamson, Jeffrey G. (1999). *Globalization and History: The Evolution of a Nineteenth-Century Atlantic Economy*, Cambridge, MA, MIT Press.

(2002a). 'After Columbus: Explaining the Global Trade Boom, 1500–1800', *Journal of Economic History*, vol. 62, pp. 417–56.

(2002b). 'When Did Globalization Begin?', *European Review of Economic History*, vol. 6, pp. 23–50.

Ormrod, David (2003). *The Rise of Commercial Empires*, Cambridge, Cambridge University Press.

Overton, Mark (1996). *The Agricultural Revolution: The Transformation of the Agrarian Economy: 1500–1850*, Cambridge, Cambridge University Press.

Özmucur, Süleyman, and Pamuk, Sevket (2002). 'Real Wages and Standards of Living in the Ottoman Empire, 1489–1914', *Journal of Economic History*, vol. 62, pp. 293–321.

Park, Geoffrey (1980). 'An Education Revolution? The Growth of Literacy and School in Early Modern Europe', *Tijdschrift voor Geschiendenis*, vol. 93, pp. 210–22.

Parthasarathi, P. (1998). 'Rethinking Wages and Competitiveness in the Eighteenth Century: Britain and South India', *Past and Present*, No. 158, pp. 79–109.

(2001). *The Transition to a Colonial Economy: Weavers, Merchants and Kings in South India, 1720–1800*, Cambridge, Cambridge University Press.

Peaucelle, Jean-Louis (1999). 'La division du travail: Adam Smith et les encyclopédistes observant la fabrication des épingles en Normandie', *Gérer et Comprendre*, No. 57, pp. 36–51.

(2005). 'Raisonner sur les épingles, l'exemple de Adam Smith sur la division du travail', *Revue d'Economie Politique*, pp. 499–519.

(2007). *Adam Smith et la division du travail*, Paris, L'Harmattan.

Penderill-Church, John (1972). *William Cookworthy, 1705–1780*, Truro, Bradford Barton.

Persson, Karl Gunnar (1999). *Grain Markets in Europe, 1500–1900: Integration and Deregulation*, Cambridge, Cambridge University Press.

Petersen, Christian (1995). *Bread and the British Economy, c.1770–1870*, Aldershot, Scolar Press.

Phelps Brown, E. H., and Hopkins, Sheila V. (1955). 'Seven Centuries of Building Wages', *Economica*, new series, vol. 22, pp. 195–206.

Pinchbeck, Ivy (1930). *Women Workers and the Industrial Revolution, 1750–1850*, London, Routledge.

Pollard, Sydney (1965). *The Genesis of Modern Management: A Study of the Industrial Revolution in Great Britain*, London, Edward Arnold.

Pomeranz, K. (2000). *The Great Divergence: China, Europe, and the Making of the Modern World*, Princeton, NJ, Princeton University Press.

Porter, George Richardson (1912). *The Progress of the Nation in Its Various Social and Economic Relations from the Beginning of the Nineteenth Century*, ed. by F. W. Hirst, London, Methuen.

Postan, M. M. (1950). 'Some Agrarian Evidence of Declining Population in the Later Middle Ages', *Economic History Review*, 2nd series, vol. 2, pp. 221–46.

(1975). *The Medieval Economy and Society*, Harmondsworth, Penguin Books.

Pounds, N. J. G. (1990). *An Historical Geography of Europe*, Cambridge, Cambridge University Press.

Pounds, Norman J. G., and Parker, William N. (1957). *Coal and Steel in Western Europe*, London, Faber and Faber.

Prados de la Escosura, Leandro (2000). 'International Comparisons of Real Product, 1820–1990: An Alternative Data Set', *Explorations in Economic History*, vol. 37, pp. 1–41.

Quinn, Stephen (2001). 'The Glorious Revolution's Effect on English Private Finance: A Microhistory, 1680–1705', *Journal of Economic History*, vol. 61, pp. 593–615.

Raistrick, Arthur (1972). *Industrial Archaeology: An Historical Survey*, London, Eyre Methuen.

(1989). *Dynasty of Iron Founders: The Darbys and Coalbrookdale*, Ironbridge Gorge Trust.

Ramsay, G. D. (1982). *The English Woollen Industry, 1500–1750*, London, Macmillan.

Rapp, R. (1975). 'The Unmaking of the Mediterranean Trade Hegemony: International Trade Rivalry and the Commercial Revolution', *Journal of Economic History*, vol. 35, pp. 499–525.

Rappaport, Steve (1989). *Worlds with Worlds: Structures of Life in Sixteenth-Century London*, Cambridge, Cambridge University Press.

Raychaudhuri, Tapan, and Habib, Irfan (1982). *The Cambridge Economic History of India*, vol. I, *C.1200–c.1750*, Cambridge, Cambridge University Press.

Redlich, Fritz (1944). 'The Leaders of the German Steam-Engine Industry During the First Hundred Years', *Journal of Economic History*, vol. 4, pp. 121–48.

Rees, Abraham (1819–20). *Rees's Manufacturing Industry (1819–20)*, ed. by Neil Cossons, David & Charles Reprints.

Reis, Jaime (2005). 'Economic Growth, Human Capital, and Consumption in Western Europe Before 1800', in Robert C. Allen, Tommy Bengtsson and Martin Dribe (eds.), *Living Standards in the Past: New Perspectives on Well-Being in Asia and Europe*, Oxford, Oxford University Press, pp. 195–225.

Ringrose, David R. (1983). *Madrid and the Spanish Economy, 1560–1850*, Berkeley, CA, University of California Press.

Robinson, E., and McKie, D. (1970). *Partners in Science: Letters of James Watt and Joseph Black*, London, Constable.

Roden, Peter F. C. (1977). 'Josiah Spode (1733–1797), His Formative Influences and the Various Potworks Associated with Him', *Northern Ceramic Society Journal*, vol. 14, pp. 1–43.

Rogers, E. (1962). *The Diffusion of Innovations*, New York, Free Press.

Rolt, L. T. C. (1963). *Thomas Newcomen: The Prehistory of the Steam Engine*, Dawlish, David & Charles.

Rolt, L. T. C., and Allen, J. S. (1977). *The Steam Engine of Thomas Newcomen*, Hartington, Moorland Publishing Co.

Rose, Mary (1986). *The Gregs of Quarry Bank: The Rise and Decline of a Family Firm, 1750–1914*, Cambridge, Cambridge University Press.
(1996). *The Lancashire Cotton Industry: A History Since 1750*, Preston, Lancashire County Books.
(2000). *Firms, Networks, and Business Values: The British and American Cotton Industries Since 1750*, Cambridge, Cambridge University Press.
Rosenberg, Nathan (1976). *Perspectives on Technology*, Cambridge, Cambridge University Press.
(1982). *Inside the Black Box*, Cambridge, Cambridge University Press.
Rosenthal, J.-L. (1990). 'The Development of Irrigation in Provence', *Journal of Economic History*, vol. 50, pp. 615–38.
Rowe, D. J. (1983). *Lead Manufacturing in Britain: A History*, London, Croom Helm Ltd.
Russell, P. (1769). *England Displayed. Being a New, Complete, and Accurate Survey and Description of the Kingdom of England, and Principality of Wales . . . by a Society of Gentlemen*, London.
Ruttan, Vernon W. (2001). *Technology, Growth, and Development: An Induced Innovation Perspective*, Oxford, Oxford University Press.
Ruttan, Vernon W., and Thirtle, Colin (2001). *The Role of Demand and Supply in the Generation and Diffusion of Technical Change*, London, Routledge.
Ruwet, J., and Wellemans, Y. (1978). *L'inalphébetisme en Belgique, XVIIIe-XIXe siècle: travaux d'étudiants*, Louvain, Bibliothèque centrale, Université catholique de Louvain.
Salter, W. E. G. (1960). *Productivity and Technical Change*, Cambridge, Cambridge University Press.
Sandberg, L. G. (1979). 'The Case of the Impoverished Sophisticate: Human Capital and Swedish Economic Growth Before World War I', *Journal of Economic History*, vol. 39, pp. 225–41.
Sandberg, L. G., and Steckel, R. H. (1980). 'Soldier, Soldier, What Made You Grow so Tall?', *Economy and History*, vol. 23, pp. 91–105.
Schmitz, Christopher J. (1979). *World Non-Ferrous Metal Production and Prices, 1700–1976*, London, Frank Cass & Co. Ltd.
Scholliers, E. (1960). *De levenstandaard in de XVe en XVIe eeuw te Antwerpen: loonarbeid en honger*, Antwerp, De Sikkel.
Schultz, Theodore W. (1964). *Transforming Traditional Agriculture*, New Haven, CT, Yale University Press.
Schwartz, L. D. (1985). 'The Standard of Living in the Long Run: London, 1700–1860', *Economic History Review*, vol. 38, pp. 24–41.
(1992). *London in the Age of Industrialization: Entrepreneurs, Labour Force and Living Conditions, 1700–1850*, Cambridge, Cambridge University Press.

Sen, A. (1968). *Choice of Techniques: An Aspect of the Theory of Planned Economic Development*, Oxford, Basil Blackwell, third edition.

(1987). 'The Standard of Living', Lectures I and II in G. Hawthorn (ed.), *The Standard of Living*, Cambridge, Cambridge University Press.

(1992). *Inequality Reexamined*. New York: Russell Sage Foundation.

Setchell, J. R. M. (1970). 'The Friendship of John Smeaton, FRS, with Henry Hindley, Instrument and Clockmaker of York and the Development of Equatorial Mounting Telescopes', *Notes and Records of the Royal Society of London*, vol. 25, pp. 79–86.

Shammas, Carole (1990). *The Pre-Industrial Consumer in England and America*, Oxford, Oxford University Press.

Shapiro, Seymour (1967). *Capital and the Cotton Industry in the Industrial Revolution*, Ithaca, NY, Cornell University Press.

Sharpe, J. A. (2007). *Early Modern England: A Social History, 1550–1760*, London, Arnold, second edition.

Shaw-Taylor, L. (2001). 'Parliamentary Enclosure and the Emergence of an English Agricultural Proletariat', *Journal of Economic History*, vol. 61, pp. 640–62.

Shorter, Alfred H. (1971). *Papermaking in the British Isles*, Newton Abbot, David & Charles.

Sieferle, R. (2001). *The Subterranean Forest: Energy Systems and the Industrial Revolution*, Cambridge, White Horse Press.

Simpson, James (1995). *Spanish Agriculture: The Long Siesta, 1765–1965*, Cambridge, Cambridge University Press.

Singer, Charles, Holmyard, E. J., Hall, A. R., *et al.* (1957). *A History of Technology*, vol. III, *From the Renaissance to the Industrial Revolution, c.1500–c.1750*, Oxford, Clarendon Press.

(1958), *A History of Technology*, vol. IV, *The Industrial Revolution, c.1750–c.1850*, Oxford, Clarendon Press.

(1994). *Energy in World History*, Boulder, CO, Westview Press.

Smith, A. (1776). *An Inquiry into the Nature and Causes of the Wealth of Nations*, ed. by E. Cannan, New York, Modern Library, 1937.

Smith, Sir Charles (1766). *Three Tracts on the Corn-Trade and Corn-Laws*, London.

Sokoloff, Kenneth, and Villaflor, Georgia C. (1992). 'The Market for Manufacturing Workers During Early Industrialization: The American Northeast, 1820 to 1860', in Claudia Goldin and Hugh Rockoff (eds.), *Strategic Factors in Nineteenth Century American Economic History*, Chicago, University of Chicago Press, pp. 29–65.

Solar, Peter (1995). 'Poor Relief and English Economic Development Before the Industrial Revolution', *Economic History Review*, vol. 48, pp. 1–22.

Solow, B. (1991). *Slavery and the Rise of the Atlantic System*, Cambridge, Cambridge University Press.

Solow, B., and Engerman, S. L. (1987). *British Capitalism and Caribbean Slavery: The Legacy of Eric Williams*, Cambridge, Cambridge University Press.

Somerville, Alexander (1843). *A Letter to the Farmers on England on the Relationship of Manufactures and Agriculture, by One Who Has Whistled at the Plough*, London, James Ridgeway.

Somogy, S. (1973). 'L'alimentatione dell'Italia', in *Storia d'Italia*, vol. 5, Turin, Einaudi.

Speed, Adam (1658). *Adam out of Eden, or, an Abstract of Divers Excellent Experiments Touching the Advancement of Husbandry*, London, Henry Brome.

Stamp, Dudley (1965). *Land Use Statistics of the Countries of Europe*, The World Land Use Survey, Occasional Papers No. 3, Bude, Cornwall, Geographical Publications Ltd.

Staunton, G. L. (1798). *An Authentic Account of an Embassy from the King of Great Britain to the Emperor of China*, Dublin, P. Wogan.

Steckel, R. H. (1995). 'Stature and the Standard of Living', *Journal of Economic Literature*, vol. 33, pp. 1903–40.

Steuart, Sir James (1767). *An Inquiry into the Principles of Political Economy*, ed. by Andrew F. Skinner with Noboru Kobayashi and Hiroshi Mizuta, London, Pickering & Chatto, 1998.

Stewart, Larry (1992). *The Rise of Public Science: Rhetoric, Technology, and Natural Philosophy in Newtonian Britain, 1660–1750*, Cambridge, Cambridge University Press.

Styles, John (2007). *The Dress of the People: Everyday Fashion in Eighteenth-Century England*, New Haven, CT, Yale University Press.

Sullivan, R. (1990). 'The Revolution of Ideas: Widespread Patenting and Invention During the Industrial Revolution', *Journal of Economic History*, vol. 50, pp. 340–62.

Sweet, Rosemary (1999). *The English Town, 1680–1840*, Harlow, Longman.

Symonds, R. W. (1969). *Thomas Tompion: His Life and Work*, London, Spring Books.

Symons, J. C. (1839). *Artisans at Home and Abroad*, Edinburgh, William Tait.

Tann, Jennifer (1970). *The Development of the Factory*, London, Cornmarket Press.

(1978–9). 'Makers of Improved Newcomen Engines in the Late 18th Century', *Transactions of the Newcomen Society*, vol. 50.

Tawney, R. H. (1938). *Religion and the Rise of Capitalism*, Harmondsworth, Penguin.

Temin, Peter (1964). *Iron and Steel in Nineteenth Century America: An Economic Inquiry*, Cambridge, MA, MIT Press.

(1966). 'Labor Scarcity and the Problem of American Industrial Efficiency in the 1850s', *Journal of Economic History*, vol. 26, pp. 277–98.

(1971). 'Notes on Labor Scarcity in America', *Journal of Interdisciplinary History*, vol. 1, pp. 251–64.

(1988). 'Product Quality and Vertical Integration in the Early Cotton Textile Industry', *Journal of Economic History*, vol. 48, pp. 891–907.

(1997). 'Two Views of the British Industrial Revolution', *Journal of Economic History*, vol. 57, pp. 63–82.

(2000). 'A Response to Harley and Crafts', *Journal of Economic History*, vol. 60, pp. 842–6.

Thirsk, Joan (1961). 'Industries in the Countryside', in F. J. Fisher (ed.), *Essays in the Economic and Social History of Tudor and Stuart England*, Cambridge, Cambridge University Press, pp. 1–112.

(1978). *Economic Policy and Projects: The Development of a Consumer Society in Early Modern England*, Oxford, Clarendon Press.

(1985). 'Agricultural Innovations and Their Diffusion', in Joan Thirsk (ed.), *The Agrarian History of England and Wales, 1640–1750: Agrarian Change*, vol. V, Part II, pp. 533–89.

Thomas, B. (1986). 'Was There an Energy Crisis in Great Britain in the 17th Century?', *Explorations in Economic History*, vol. 23, pp. 124–52.

Thomas, Keith (1971). *Religion and the Decline of Magic*, London, Weidenfeld & Nicolson.

(1987). 'Numeracy in Early Modern England: The Prothero Lecture', *Transactions of the Royal Historical Society*, 5th series, vol. 37, pp. 103–32.

Thomas, R. P., and Bean, R. N. (1974). 'The Fishers of Men: The Profits of the Slave Trade', *Journal of Economic History*, vol. 34, pp. 885–914.

Thompson, James K. J. (2003). 'Transferring the Spinning Jenny to Barcelona: An Apprenticeship in the Technology of the Industrial Revolution', *Textile History*, vol. 34, pp. 21–46.

Thorold-Rogers, J. E. T. (1866–1902). *A History of Agriculture and Prices in England*, Oxford.

Trevor-Roper, Hugh (1967). *The Crisis of the Seventeenth Century*, New York, Harper & Row.

Trow-Smith, R. (1957). *A History of British Livestock Husbandry to 1700*, London, Routledge & Kegan Paul.

Turner, M. E., Beckett, J. V., and Afton, B. (1997). *Agricultural Rent in England, 1690–1914*, Cambridge, Cambridge University Press.

(2001). *Farm Production in England, 1700–1914*, Oxford, Oxford University Press.

Unger, Richard W. (1980). *The Ship in the Medieval Economy, 600–1600*, Montreal, McGill-Queen's University Press.

(1984). 'Energy Sources for the Dutch Golden Age: Peat, Wind, and Coal', *Research in Economic History*, vol. 9, pp. 221–53.

(1997). *Ships and Shipping in the North Sea and Atlantic, 1400–1800*, Aldershot, Ashgate.

van der Woude, Ad, and Schuurman, Anton (1980). *Probate Inventories: A New Source for the Historical Study of Wealth, Material Culture and Agricultural Development*, Wageningen, A. A. G. Bijdragen, No. 23.

Van Zanden, Jan Luiten (1993). *The Rise and Decline of Holland's Economy: Merchant Capitalism and the Labour Market*, Manchester, Manchester University Press.

(2002). 'The "Revolt of the Early Modernists" and the "First Modern Economy": An Assessment', *Economic History Review*, 2nd series, vol. 55, pp. 619–41.

(2004a). 'The Skill Premium and the "Great Divergence"', www.iisg.nl/hpw/papers/vanzanden.pdf.

(2004b). 'Common Workmen, Philosophers and the Birth of the European Knowledge Economy: About the Price and Production of Useful Knowledge in Europe 1300–1850', www.iisg.nl/research/jvz-knowledge_economy.pdf.

Villain, George (1901). *Le fer, la houille et la métallurgie à la fin du XIXe siècle*, Paris.

Villiers, Patrick (1991). 'The Slave and Colonial Trade in France Just Before the Revolution', in Barbara Solow (ed.), *Slavery and the Rise of the Atlantic System*, Cambridge, Cambridge University Press, pp. 210–36.

Von Guericke, Otto (1672). *Experimenta Nova (ut Vocantur) Magdeburgica de Vacuo Spatio*, Amsterdam, Joannem Janssonium à Waesberge.

Von Thünen, J. H. (1826). 'Der isolierte Staat', in *Von Thünen's Isolated State*, ed. by P. Hall, Oxford, Pergamon Press, 1966.

von Tunzelmann, G. N. (1978). *Steam Power and British Industrialization to 1860*, Oxford, Clarendon Press.

Voth, Hans-Joachim (2000). *Time and Work in England, 1750–1830*, Oxford, Oxford University Press.

Wadsworth, Alfred P., and Mann, Julia de Lacy (1931). *The Cotton Trade and Industrial Lancashire, 1600–1780*, Manchester, Manchester University Press.

Wallerstein, I. M. (1974–91). *The Modern World System*, New York, Academic Press.

Warde, Paul (2007). *Energy Consumption in England and Wales*, Rome, Consiglio Nazionale delle Ricerche.

Watts, D. C. (1990). 'Why George Ravenscroft Introduced Lead Oxide into Crystal Glass', *Glass Technology*, vol. 31, pp. 208–12.

Weatherill, Lorna (1996). *Consumer Behaviour and Material Culture in Britain, 1660–1760*, London, Routledge, second edition.

Weber, Max (1904–5). *The Protestant Ethic and the Spirit of Capitalism*, trans. by Talcott Parsons, London, Allen & Unwin, 1930.

(1927). *General Economic History*, New Brunswick, NJ, Transaction Books, 1981.

Weedon, Cyril (1990). 'William Cookworthy and Bristol Blue Glass', *Glass Technology*, vol. 31, pp. 256–65.

Weir, D. (1984). 'Life under Pressure: France and England, 1670–1870', *Journal of Economic History*, vol. 44, pp. 27–47.

Weisdorf, Jacob L. (2006). 'From Domestic Manufacture to Industrial Revolution: Long-Run Growth and Agricultural Development', *Oxford Economic Papers*, vol. 58, pp. 264–87.

Weiss, Leonard (1982). *Watch-Making in England, 1760–1820*, London, Robert Hale.

White, Leonard (1989). *Spode: A History of the Family Factory and Wares from 1733 to 1833*, London, Barrie & Jenkins.

Wiebe, G. (1895). *Zur Geschichte der Preisrevolution des 16. und 17. Jahrhunderts*, Leipzig.

Wilkie, George (1857). *The Manufacture of Iron in Great Britain*, Edinburgh.

Wilkinson, R. (1973). *Poverty and Progress: An Ecological Model of Economic Development*, London, Methuen.

Williams, Eric (1944). *Capitalism and Slavery*, New York, Capricorn Books.

Williamson, Jeffrey G. (1976). 'American Prices and Urban Inequality', *Journal of Economic History*, vol. 36, pp. 303–33.

(1990). 'The Impact of the Corn Laws Just Prior to Repeal', *Explorations in Economic History*, vol. 27, pp. 123–56.

Williamson, Jeffrey G., and Lindert, Peter H. (1980). *American Inequality: A Macroeconomic History*, New York, Academic Press.

Wilmot, Sarah (1990). *'The Business of Improvement': Agriculture and Scientific Culture in Britain, c.1770–c.1870*, Historical Geography Research Series, No. 24.

Wittfogel, K. A. (1957). *Oriental Despotism: A Comparative Study of Total Power*. New Haven, CT, Yale University Press.

Woolf, Stuart (1986). *The Poor in Western Europe in the Eighteenth and Nineteenth Centuries*, London, Methuen.

Wong, R. B. (1997). *China Transformed: Historical Change and the Limits of European Experience*. Ithaca, NY, Cornell University Press.

Wood, G. H. (1910). 'Real Wages and the Standard of Comfort Since 1850', *Journal of the Royal Statistical Society*, vol. 72, pp. 91–103.

Woodward, Donald (1995). *Men at Work: Labourers and Building Craftsmen in the Towns of Northern England, 1450–1750*, Cambridge, Cambridge University Press.

Wordie, J. R. (1983). 'The Chronology of English Enclosure, 1500–1914', *Economic History Review*, 2nd series, vol. 36, pp. 483–505.

Woronoff, Denis (1984). *L'industrie sidérurgique en France pendant la révolution and l'empire*, Paris, Edition de d'Ecole des hautes études en sciences sociales.

Wright, Carroll D. (1885). 'Historical Review of Wages and Prices, 1752–1860', in *Sixteenth Annual Report of the Massachusetts Bureau of the Statistics of Labor*, Boston, Wright & Potter.

Wrigley, E. A. (1985). 'Urban Growth and Agricultural Change: England and the Continent in the Early Modern Period', *Journal of Interdisciplinary History*, vol. 15, pp. 683–728, and in E. A. Wrigley, *People, Cities, and Wealth*, Oxford, Basil Blackwell, 1987, pp. 157–93.

(1987). 'A Simple Model of London's Importance in Changing English Society and Economy, 1650–1750', in E. A. Wrigley (ed.), *People, Cities and Wealth*, Oxford, Basil Blackwell, pp. 133–56.

(1988). *Continuity, Chance and Change*, Cambridge, Cambridge University Press.

Wrigley, E. A., and Schofield, R. S. (1981). *The Population History of England, 1541–1871*, London, Edward Arnold.

Wyczanski, Andrzej (1974). 'Alphabetisation et structure sociale en Pologne au XVIe siècle', *Annales: Economies, Societes, Civilisations*, vol. 29, pp. 705–13.

Youatt, William (1883). *Sheep, Their Breeds, Management, and Diseases*, London, Simpkin, Marshall and Co., new edition.

Young, Arthur (1771a). *A Six Weeks Tour Through the South Counties of England and Wales*, Dublin, J. Milliken.

(1771b). *A Six Month's Tour Through the North of England*, London, W. Strahan, second edition.

(1771c). *A Farmer's Tour Through the East of England*, London, W. Strahan, second edition.

(1774). *Political Arithmetic*, London, W. Nicoll.

(1792). *Travels in France During the Years 1787, 1788, and 1789*, ed. by Constantia Maxwell, Cambridge, Cambridge University Press, 1950.

Young, Hilary (1999). *English Porcelain: 1745–95*, London, V&A Publications.

Index

Note: page numbers in bold refer to Tables and Appendices; those in italics refer to Figures.